SEND IN THE CLOWNS

By Stephen Francis & Rico

JACANA

For our wives, Bronwyn and Danya, for putting up with the daily circus that is the life of a cartoonist.

Published in 2014 in South Africa by
Jacana Media
10 Orange Street, Auckland Park, 2092
PO Box 291784, Melville, 2109
www.jacana.co.za

ISBN 978-1-4314-2031-5
Job number 002304
Printed and bound by Shumani Mills Communications, Parow, Cape Town

OTHER MADAM & EVE BOOKS

Madam & Eve Collection (Rapid Phase, 1993, reprint 1999)
Free At Last (Penguin Books, 1994)
All Aboard for the Gravy Train (Penguin Books, 1995)
Somewhere over the Rainbow Nation (Penguin Books, 1996)
Madam & Eve's Greatest Hits (Penguin Books, 1997)
Madams are from Mars, Maids are from Venus (Penguin Books, 1997)
It's a Jungle Out There (David Philip, 1998)
International Maid of Mystery (David Philip, 1999)
Has anyone seen my Vibrating Cellphone? (interactive.Africa, 2000)
The Madams are Restless (Rapid Phase, 2000)
Crouching Madam, Hidden Maid (Rapid Phase, 2001)
Madam & Eve, 10 Wonderful Years (Rapid Phase, 2002)
The Maidtrix (Rapid Phase, 2003)
Gin & Tonic for the Soul (Rapid Phase, 2004)
Desperate Housemaids (Rapid Phase, 2005)
Madams of the Caribbean (Rapid Phase, 2006)
Bring me my (new) Washing Machine (Rapid Phase, 2007)
Madam & Eve Unplugged (Rapid Phase, 2008)

Strike While The Iron Is Hot (Jacana, 2009)
Twilight of the Vuvuzelas (Jacana, 2010)
Mother Anderson's Secret Book of Wit & Wisdom (Jacana, 2011)
The Pothole at the End of the Rainbow (Jacana, 2011)
Twenty (Jacana, 2012)
Keep Calm and Take Another Tea Break (Jacana, 2013)
Jamen sort kaffe er pa mode nu, Madam! (Gyldendal, Denmark, 1995)
Jeg gyver Mandela Skylden for det her! (Gyldendal, Denmark, 1995)
Alt under kontrol I Sydafrika! (Bogfabrikken, Denmark, 1997)
Men alla dricker kaffet svart nufortiden, Madam! (Bokfabrikken, Sweden, 1998)
Madame & Eve, Enfin Libres! (Vents D'Ouest, France, 1997)
Votez Madame & Eve (Vents D'Ouest, France, 1997)
La coupe est pleine (Vents D'Ouest, France, 1998)
Rennue-Ménage à deux (Vents D'Ouest, France, 1999)
En voient de toutes les couleurs (Vents D'Ouest, France, 2000)
Madame vient de Mars, Eve de Venus (Vents D'Ouest, France, 2000)
Madam & Eve (LIKE, Finland, 2005)

MADAM & EVE APPEARS REGULARLY IN:
Mail & Guardian, The Star, Saturday Star, Herald, Mercury, Witness, Daily Dispatch, Cape Times, Pretoria News, Diamond Fields Advertiser, Die Volksblad, EC Today, Kokstad Advertiser, The Namibian.

TO CONTACT MADAM & EVE:
PO Box 413667, Craighall 2024, Johannesburg, South Africa
ricos@rapidphase.co.za
www.madamandeve.co.za

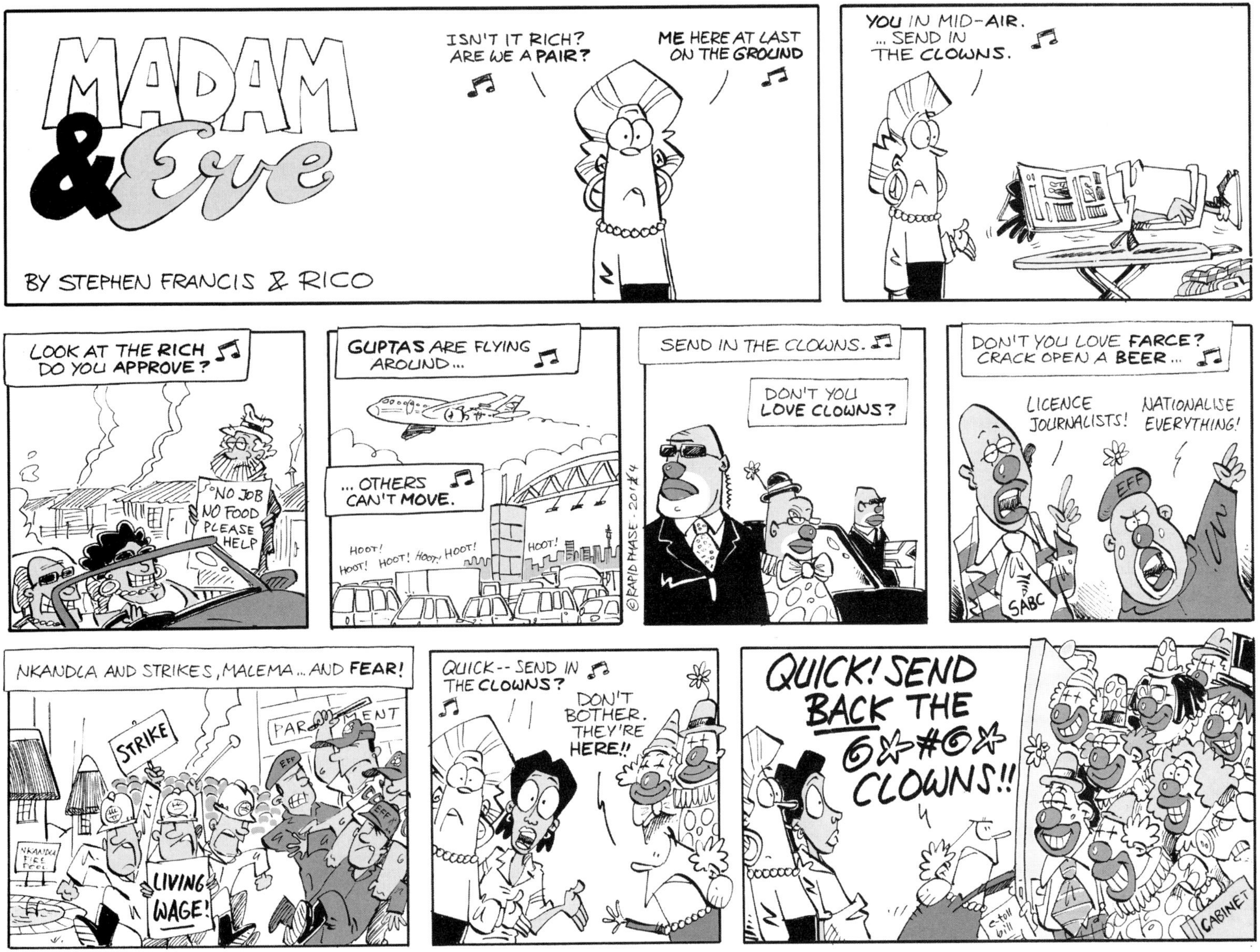
MADAM & Eve
BY STEPHEN FRANCIS & RICO
ISN'T IT RICH? ARE WE A PAIR?
ME HERE AT LAST ON THE GROUND
YOU IN MID-AIR. ... SEND IN THE CLOWNS.
LOOK AT THE RICH DO YOU APPROVE?
NO JOB NO FOOD PLEASE HELP
GUPTAS ARE FLYING AROUND...
... OTHERS CAN'T MOVE.
HOOT! HOOT! HOOT! HOOT! HOOT! HOOT!
©RAPID PHASE · 2014
SEND IN THE CLOWNS.
DON'T YOU LOVE CLOWNS?
DON'T YOU LOVE FARCE? CRACK OPEN A BEER...
LICENCE JOURNALISTS!
NATIONALISE EVERYTHING!
EFF
SABC
NKANDLA AND STRIKES, MALEMA... AND FEAR!
STRIKE
PAR MENT
LIVING WAGE!
QUICK-- SEND IN THE CLOWNS?
DON'T BOTHER. THEY'RE HERE!!
QUICK! SEND BACK THE @*#@* CLOWNS!!
e-toll bill
CABINET

Many thanks to John Curtis and Dr Jack for the original inspiration behind "Send in the Clowns"

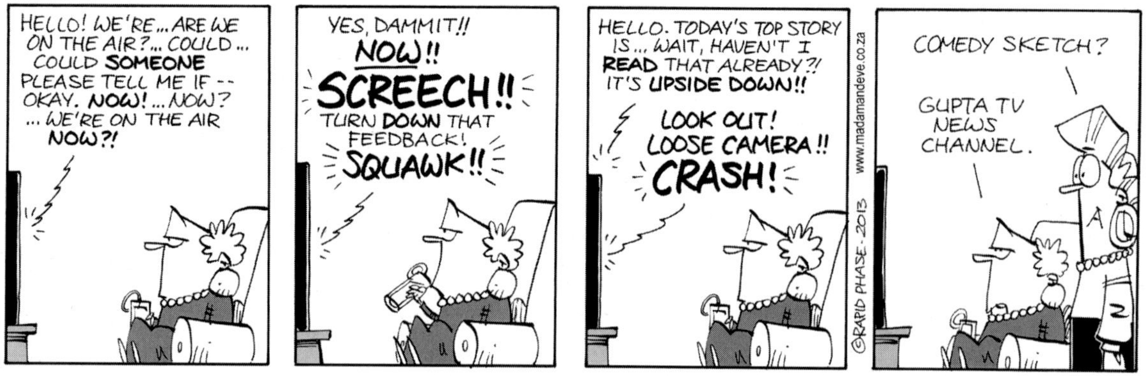
HELLO! WE'RE... ARE WE ON THE AIR?... COULD... COULD SOMEONE PLEASE TELL ME IF -- OKAY. NOW! ... NOW? ... WE'RE ON THE AIR NOW?!
YES, DAMMIT!! NOW!!
SCREECH!!
TURN DOWN THAT FEEDBACK!
SQUAWK!!
HELLO. TODAY'S TOP STORY IS... WAIT, HAVEN'T I READ THAT ALREADY?! IT'S UPSIDE DOWN!!
LOOK OUT! LOOSE CAMERA!!
CRASH!
www.madamandeve.co.za
©RAPID PHASE · 2013
COMEDY SKETCH?
GUPTA TV NEWS CHANNEL.

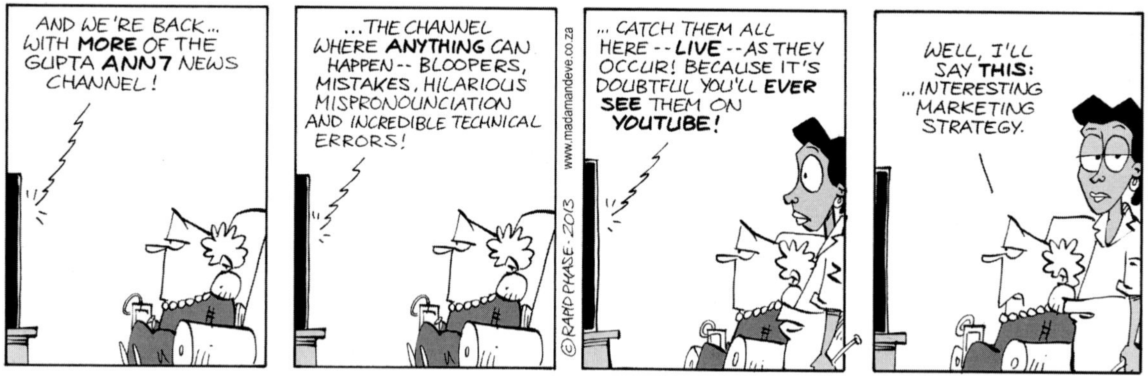
AND WE'RE BACK... WITH MORE OF THE GUPTA ANN7 NEWS CHANNEL!
...THE CHANNEL WHERE ANYTHING CAN HAPPEN -- BLOOPERS, MISTAKES, HILARIOUS MISPRONOUNCIATION AND INCREDIBLE TECHNICAL ERRORS!
www.madamandeve.co.za
©RAPID PHASE · 2013
... CATCH THEM ALL HERE -- LIVE -- AS THEY OCCUR! BECAUSE IT'S DOUBTFUL YOU'LL EVER SEE THEM ON YOUTUBE!
WELL, I'LL SAY THIS: ... INTERESTING MARKETING STRATEGY.

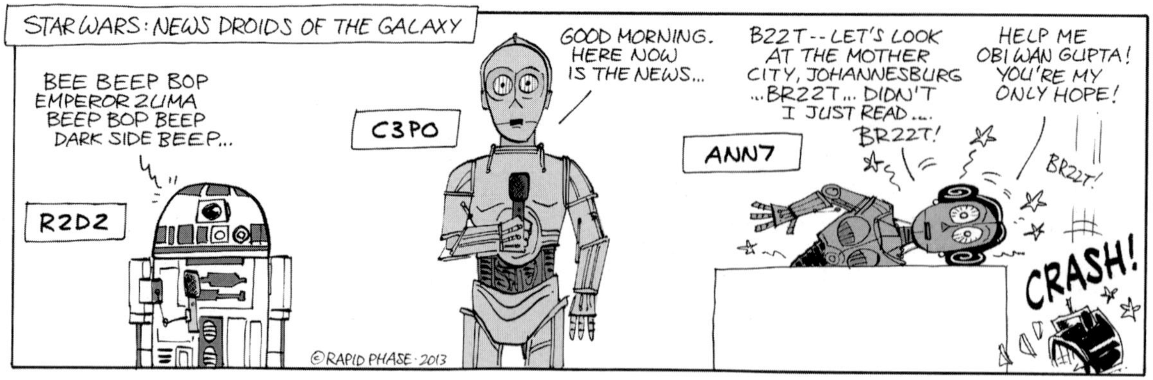
STAR WARS: NEWS DROIDS OF THE GALAXY
BEE BEEP BOP EMPEROR ZUMA BEEP BOP BEEP DARK SIDE BEEP...
R2D2
C3PO
GOOD MORNING. HERE NOW IS THE NEWS...
ANN7
BZZT -- LET'S LOOK AT THE MOTHER CITY, JOHANNESBURG ...BRZZT... DIDN'T I JUST READ....
BRZZT!
HELP ME OBI WAN GUPTA! YOU'RE MY ONLY HOPE!
BRZZT!
CRASH!
©RAPID PHASE · 2013

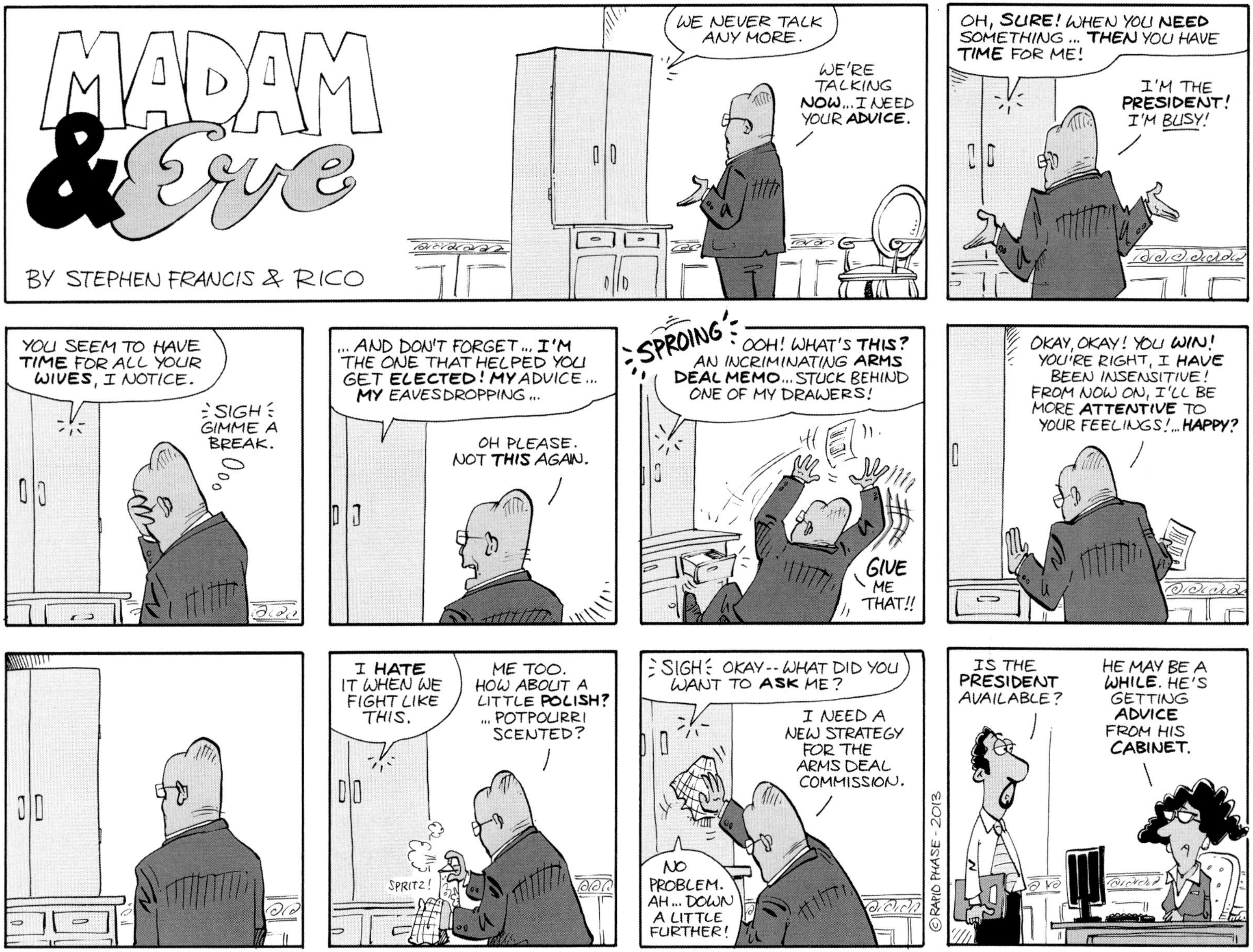
MADAM & Eve
BY STEPHEN FRANCIS & RICO
WE NEVER TALK ANY MORE.
WE'RE TALKING NOW... I NEED YOUR ADVICE.
OH, SURE! WHEN YOU NEED SOMETHING ... THEN YOU HAVE TIME FOR ME!
I'M THE PRESIDENT! I'M BUSY!
YOU SEEM TO HAVE TIME FOR ALL YOUR WIVES, I NOTICE.
SIGH GIMME A BREAK.
... AND DON'T FORGET ... I'M THE ONE THAT HELPED YOU GET ELECTED! MY ADVICE ... MY EAVESDROPPING ...
OH PLEASE. NOT THIS AGAIN.
SPROING
OOH! WHAT'S THIS? AN INCRIMINATING ARMS DEAL MEMO... STUCK BEHIND ONE OF MY DRAWERS!
GIVE ME THAT!!
OKAY, OKAY! YOU WIN! YOU'RE RIGHT, I HAVE BEEN INSENSITIVE! FROM NOW ON, I'LL BE MORE ATTENTIVE TO YOUR FEELINGS! ... HAPPY?
I HATE IT WHEN WE FIGHT LIKE THIS.
ME TOO. HOW ABOUT A LITTLE POLISH? ... POTPOURRI SCENTED?
SPRITZ!
SIGH OKAY -- WHAT DID YOU WANT TO ASK ME?
I NEED A NEW STRATEGY FOR THE ARMS DEAL COMMISSION.
NO PROBLEM. AH ... DOWN A LITTLE FURTHER!
©RAPID PHASE - 2013
IS THE PRESIDENT AVAILABLE?
HE MAY BE A WHILE. HE'S GETTING ADVICE FROM HIS CABINET.

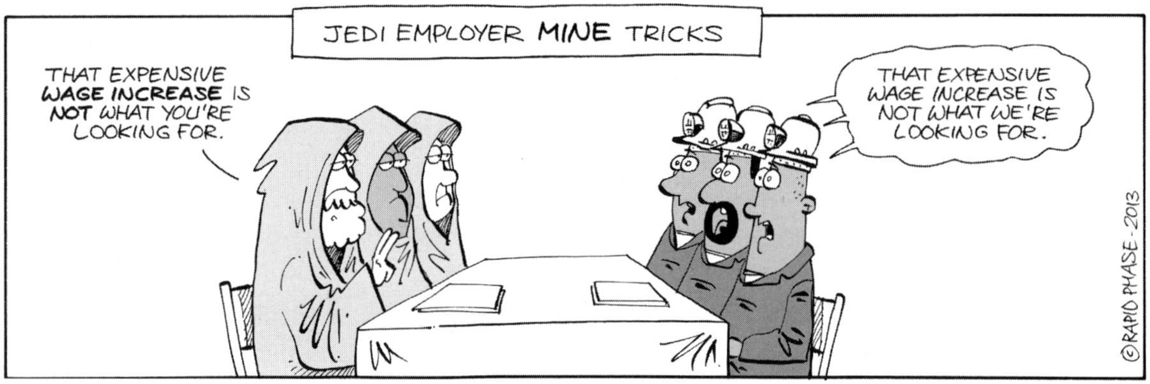
JEDI EMPLOYER **MINE** TRICKS
THAT EXPENSIVE **WAGE INCREASE** IS **NOT** WHAT YOU'RE LOOKING FOR.
THAT EXPENSIVE WAGE INCREASE IS NOT WHAT WE'RE LOOKING FOR.
©RAPID PHASE-2013

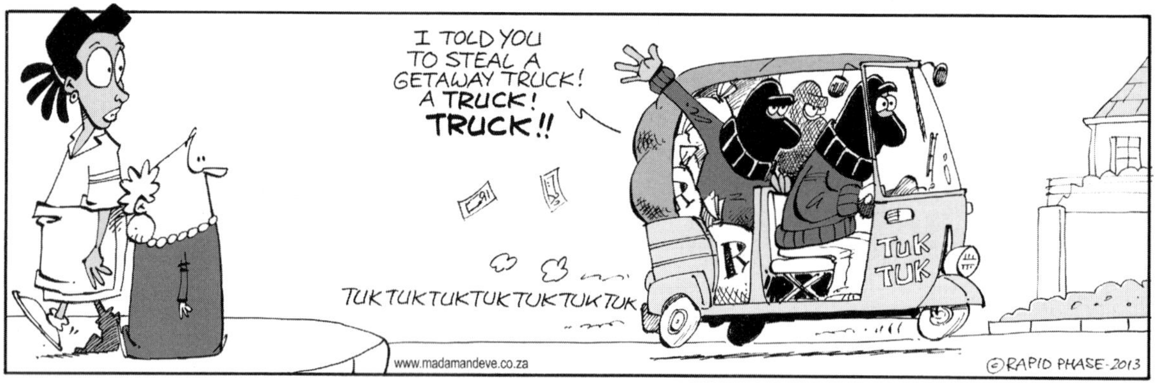
I TOLD YOU TO STEAL A GETAWAY TRUCK! A **TRUCK!** **TRUCK!!**
TUK TUK
TUKTUKTUKTUKTUKTUKTUK
www.madamandeve.co.za
©RAPID PHASE-2013

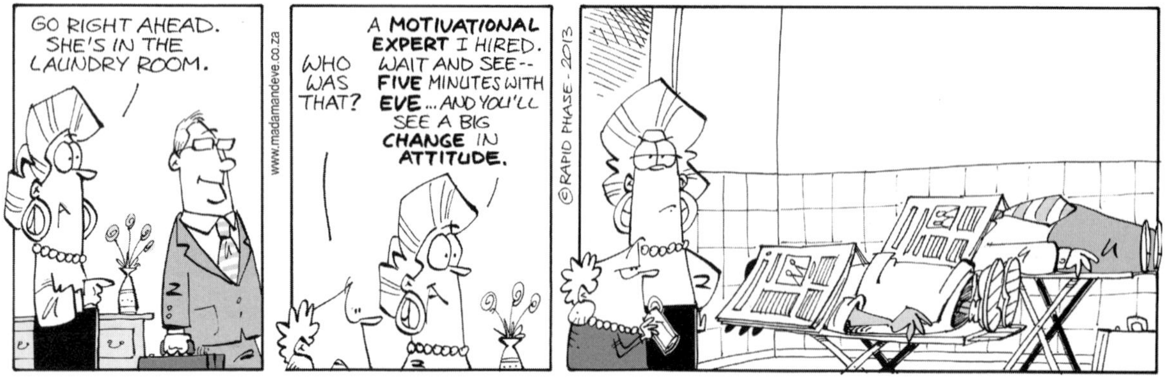
GO RIGHT AHEAD. SHE'S IN THE LAUNDRY ROOM.
www.madamandeve.co.za
WHO WAS THAT?
A **MOTIVATIONAL EXPERT** I HIRED. WAIT AND SEE-- **FIVE** MINUTES WITH **EVE**... AND YOU'LL SEE A BIG **CHANGE** IN **ATTITUDE**.
©RAPID PHASE-2013

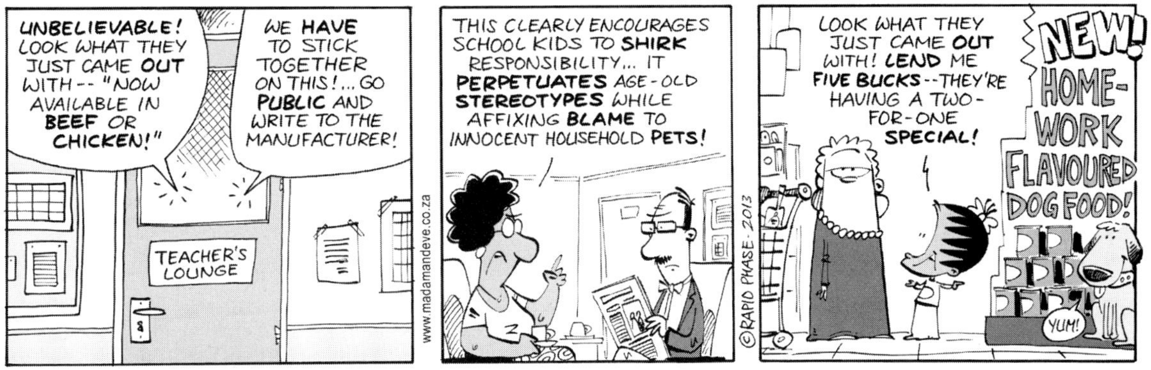
UNBELIEVABLE! LOOK WHAT THEY JUST CAME OUT WITH -- "NOW AVAILABLE IN BEEF OR CHICKEN!"
WE HAVE TO STICK TOGETHER ON THIS! ... GO PUBLIC AND WRITE TO THE MANUFACTURER!
TEACHER'S LOUNGE
www.madamandeve.co.za
THIS CLEARLY ENCOURAGES SCHOOL KIDS TO SHIRK RESPONSIBILITY... IT PERPETUATES AGE-OLD STEREOTYPES WHILE AFFIXING BLAME TO INNOCENT HOUSEHOLD PETS!
©RAPID PHASE-2013
LOOK WHAT THEY JUST CAME OUT WITH! LEND ME FIVE BUCKS--THEY'RE HAVING A TWO-FOR-ONE SPECIAL!
NEW! HOME-WORK FLAVOURED DOG FOOD!
YUM!

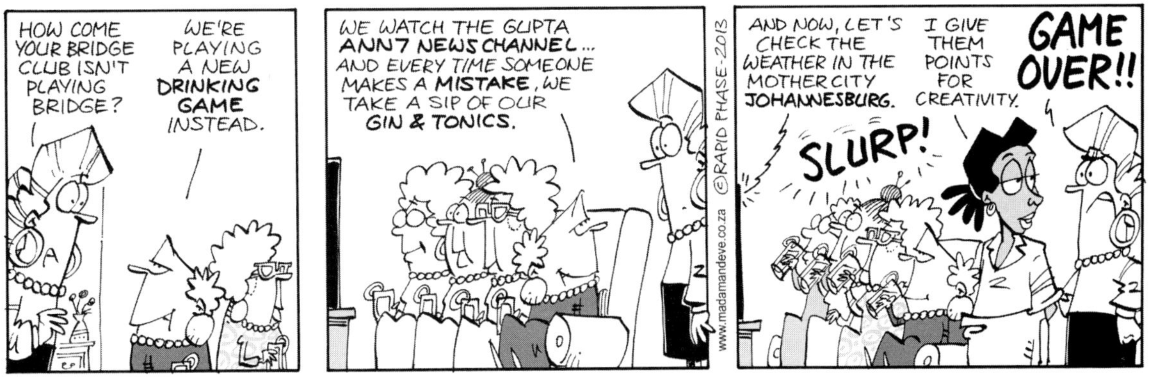
HOW COME YOUR BRIDGE CLUB ISN'T PLAYING BRIDGE?
WE'RE PLAYING A NEW DRINKING GAME INSTEAD.
WE WATCH THE GUPTA ANN7 NEWS CHANNEL... AND EVERY TIME SOMEONE MAKES A MISTAKE, WE TAKE A SIP OF OUR GIN & TONICS.
www.madamandeve.co.za
©RAPID PHASE-2013
AND NOW, LET'S CHECK THE WEATHER IN THE MOTHER CITY JOHANNESBURG.
I GIVE THEM POINTS FOR CREATIVITY.
GAME OVER!!
SLURP!

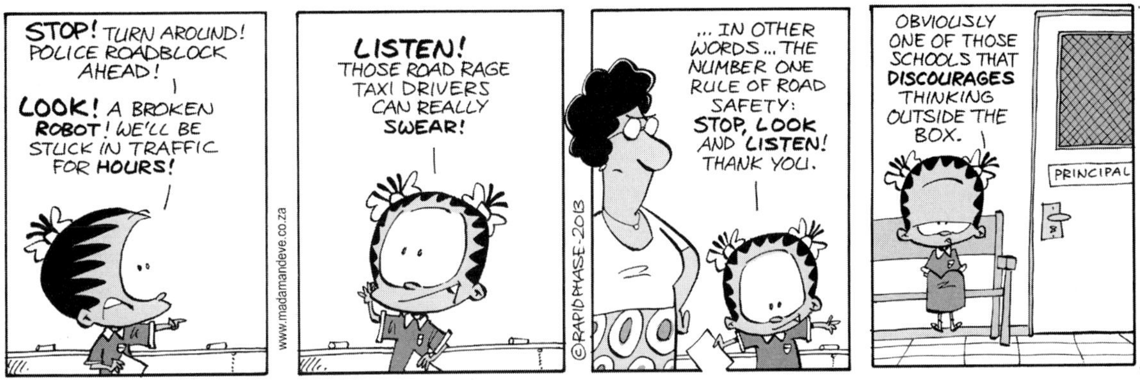
STOP! TURN AROUND! POLICE ROADBLOCK AHEAD!
LOOK! A BROKEN ROBOT! WE'LL BE STUCK IN TRAFFIC FOR HOURS!
www.madamandeve.co.za
LISTEN! THOSE ROAD RAGE TAXI DRIVERS CAN REALLY SWEAR!
©RAPID PHASE-2013
... IN OTHER WORDS... THE NUMBER ONE RULE OF ROAD SAFETY: STOP, LOOK AND LISTEN! THANK YOU.
OBVIOUSLY ONE OF THOSE SCHOOLS THAT DISCOURAGES THINKING OUTSIDE THE BOX.
PRINCIPAL

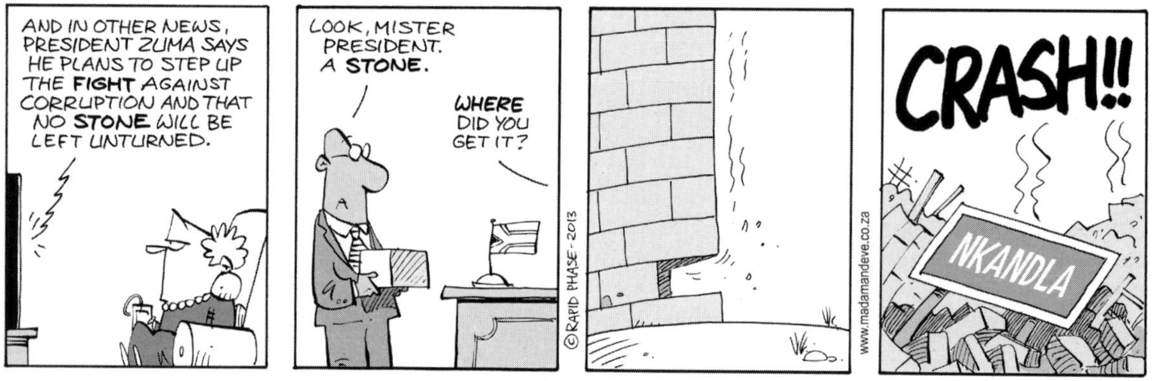
AND IN OTHER NEWS, PRESIDENT ZUMA SAYS HE PLANS TO STEP UP THE FIGHT AGAINST CORRUPTION AND THAT NO STONE WILL BE LEFT UNTURNED.
LOOK, MISTER PRESIDENT. A STONE.
WHERE DID YOU GET IT?
© RAPID PHASE · 2013
www.madamandeve.co.za
CRASH!!
NKANDLA

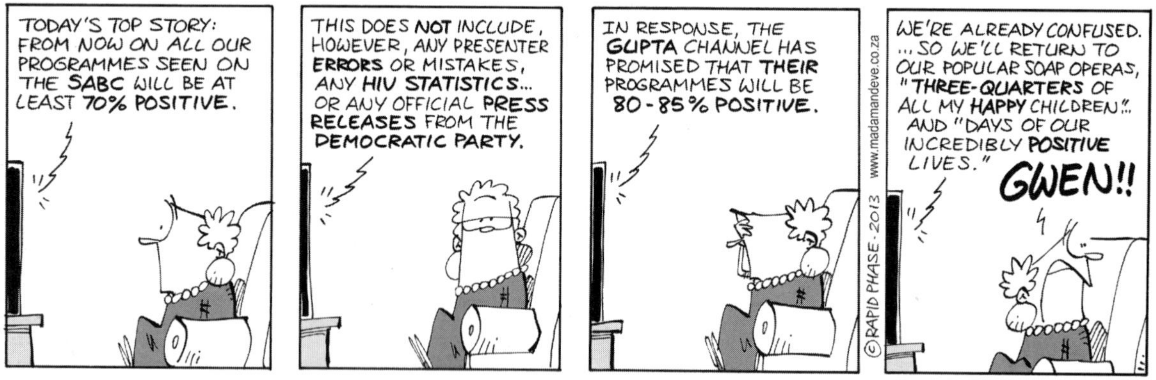
TODAY'S TOP STORY: FROM NOW ON ALL OUR PROGRAMMES SEEN ON THE SABC WILL BE AT LEAST 70% POSITIVE.
THIS DOES NOT INCLUDE, HOWEVER, ANY PRESENTER ERRORS OR MISTAKES, ANY HIV STATISTICS... OR ANY OFFICIAL PRESS RELEASES FROM THE DEMOCRATIC PARTY.
IN RESPONSE, THE GUPTA CHANNEL HAS PROMISED THAT THEIR PROGRAMMES WILL BE 80-85% POSITIVE.
www.madamandeve.co.za
© RAPID PHASE · 2013
WE'RE ALREADY CONFUSED. ...SO WE'LL RETURN TO OUR POPULAR SOAP OPERAS, "THREE-QUARTERS OF ALL MY HAPPY CHILDREN"... AND "DAYS OF OUR INCREDIBLY POSITIVE LIVES."
GWEN!!

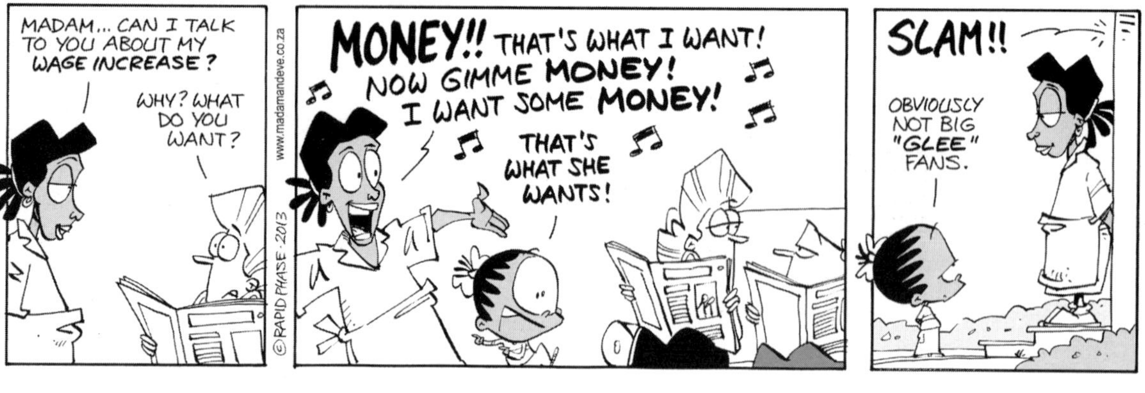
MADAM... CAN I TALK TO YOU ABOUT MY WAGE INCREASE?
WHY? WHAT DO YOU WANT?
www.madamandeve.co.za
© RAPID PHASE · 2013
MONEY!! THAT'S WHAT I WANT! NOW GIMME MONEY! I WANT SOME MONEY!
THAT'S WHAT SHE WANTS!
SLAM!!
OBVIOUSLY NOT BIG "GLEE" FANS.

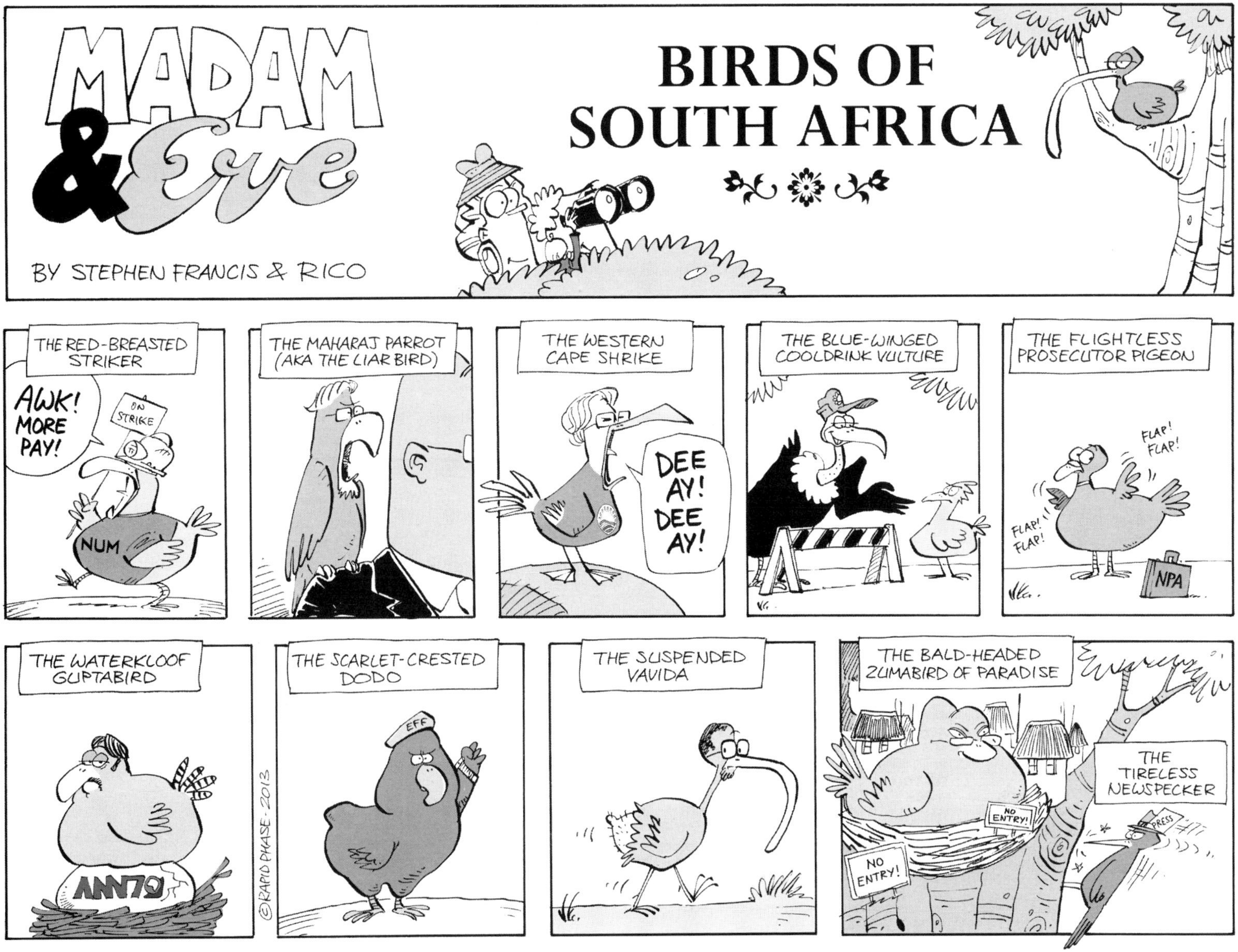
MADAM & Eve
BY STEPHEN FRANCIS & RICO
BIRDS OF SOUTH AFRICA
THE RED-BREASTED STRIKER
AWK! MORE PAY!
ON STRIKE
NUM
THE MAHARAJ PARROT (AKA THE LIAR BIRD)
THE WESTERN CAPE SHRIKE
DEE AY! DEE AY!
THE BLUE-WINGED COOLDRINK VULTURE
THE FLIGHTLESS PROSECUTOR PIGEON
FLAP! FLAP!
FLAP! FLAP!
NPA
THE WATERKLOOF GUPTABIRD
ANN7
©RAPID PHASE - 2013
THE SCARLET-CRESTED DODO
EFF
THE SUSPENDED VAVIDA
THE BALD-HEADED ZUMABIRD OF PARADISE
NO ENTRY!
NO ENTRY!
THE TIRELESS NEWSPECKER
PRESS

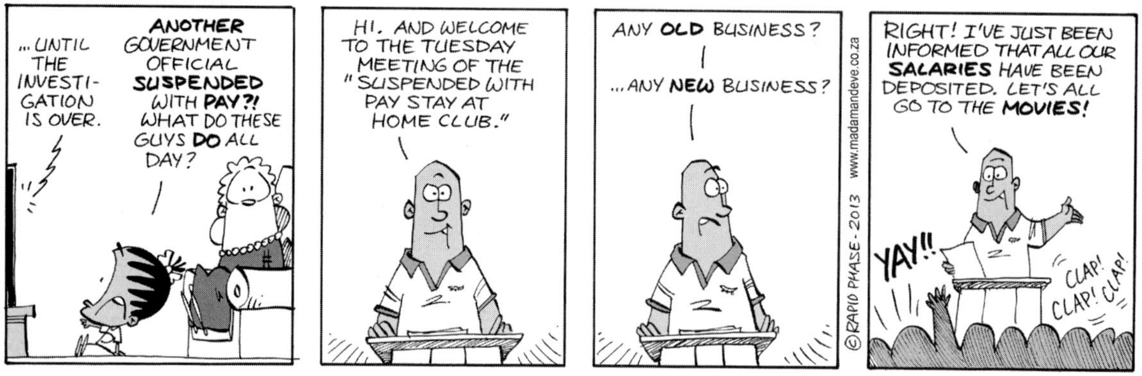
...UNTIL THE INVESTIGATION IS OVER.
ANOTHER GOVERNMENT OFFICIAL SUSPENDED WITH PAY?! WHAT DO THESE GUYS DO ALL DAY?
HI. AND WELCOME TO THE TUESDAY MEETING OF THE "SUSPENDED WITH PAY STAY AT HOME CLUB."
ANY OLD BUSINESS?
...ANY NEW BUSINESS?
RIGHT! I'VE JUST BEEN INFORMED THAT ALL OUR SALARIES HAVE BEEN DEPOSITED. LET'S ALL GO TO THE MOVIES!
YAY!!
CLAP! CLAP! CLAP!
©RAPID PHASE - 2013 www.madamandeve.co.za

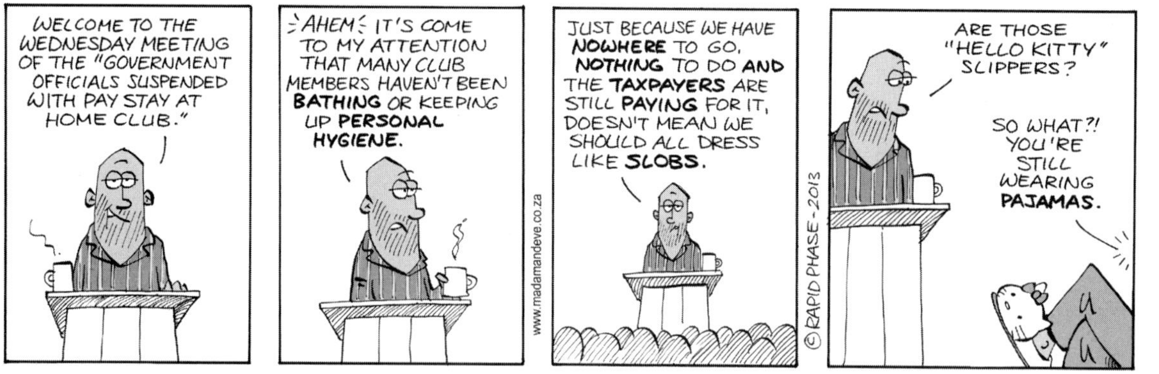
WELCOME TO THE WEDNESDAY MEETING OF THE "GOVERNMENT OFFICIALS SUSPENDED WITH PAY STAY AT HOME CLUB."
AHEM IT'S COME TO MY ATTENTION THAT MANY CLUB MEMBERS HAVEN'T BEEN BATHING OR KEEPING UP PERSONAL HYGIENE.
JUST BECAUSE WE HAVE NOWHERE TO GO, NOTHING TO DO AND THE TAXPAYERS ARE STILL PAYING FOR IT, DOESN'T MEAN WE SHOULD ALL DRESS LIKE SLOBS.
ARE THOSE "HELLO KITTY" SLIPPERS?
SO WHAT?! YOU'RE STILL WEARING PAJAMAS.
www.madamandeve.co.za
©RAPID PHASE - 2013

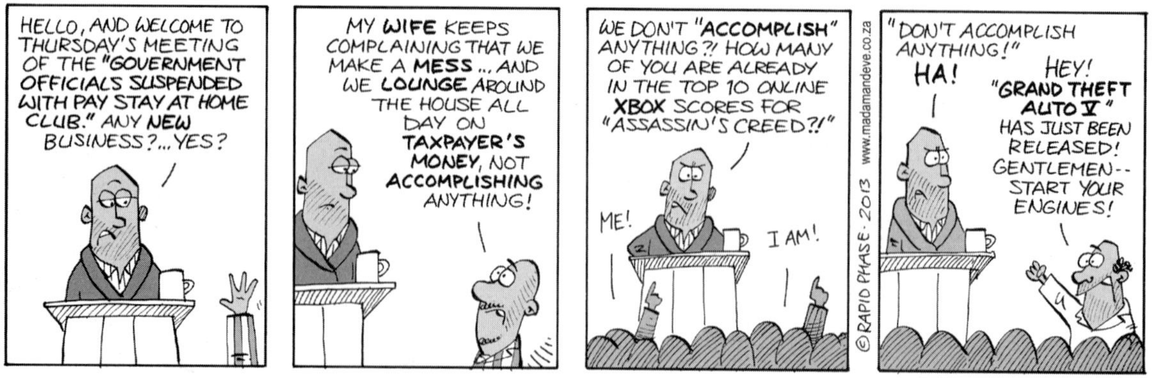
HELLO, AND WELCOME TO THURSDAY'S MEETING OF THE "GOVERNMENT OFFICIALS SUSPENDED WITH PAY STAY AT HOME CLUB." ANY NEW BUSINESS?...YES?
MY WIFE KEEPS COMPLAINING THAT WE MAKE A MESS... AND WE LOUNGE AROUND THE HOUSE ALL DAY ON TAXPAYER'S MONEY, NOT ACCOMPLISHING ANYTHING!
WE DON'T "ACCOMPLISH" ANYTHING?! HOW MANY OF YOU ARE ALREADY IN THE TOP 10 ONLINE XBOX SCORES FOR "ASSASSIN'S CREED?!"
ME!
I AM!
"DON'T ACCOMPLISH ANYTHING!"
HA!
HEY! "GRAND THEFT AUTO V" HAS JUST BEEN RELEASED! GENTLEMEN-- START YOUR ENGINES!
©RAPID PHASE · 2013 www.madamandeve.co.za

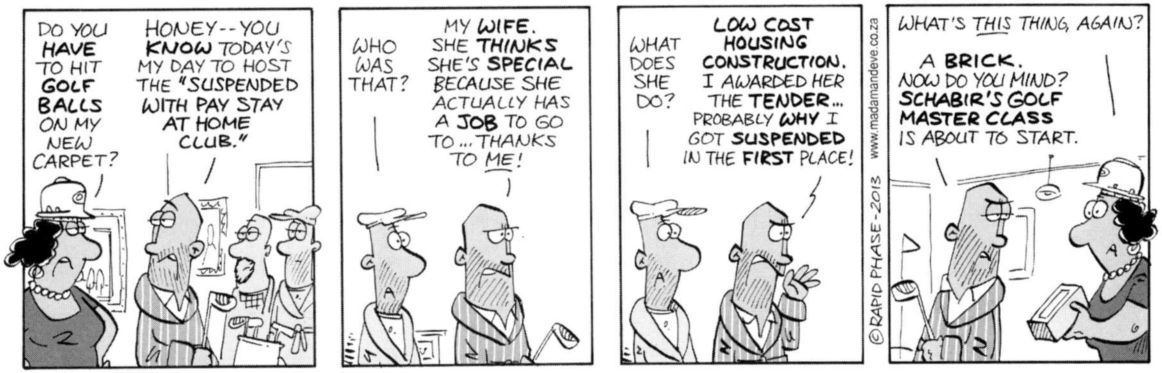
DO YOU HAVE TO HIT GOLF BALLS ON MY NEW CARPET?
HONEY--YOU KNOW TODAY'S MY DAY TO HOST THE "SUSPENDED WITH PAY STAY AT HOME CLUB."
WHO WAS THAT?
MY WIFE. SHE THINKS SHE'S SPECIAL BECAUSE SHE ACTUALLY HAS A JOB TO GO TO... THANKS TO ME!
WHAT DOES SHE DO?
LOW COST HOUSING CONSTRUCTION. I AWARDED HER THE TENDER... PROBABLY WHY I GOT SUSPENDED IN THE FIRST PLACE!
© RAPID PHASE - 2013 www.madamandeve.co.za
WHAT'S THIS THING, AGAIN?
A BRICK. NOW DO YOU MIND? SCHABIR'S GOLF MASTER CLASS IS ABOUT TO START.

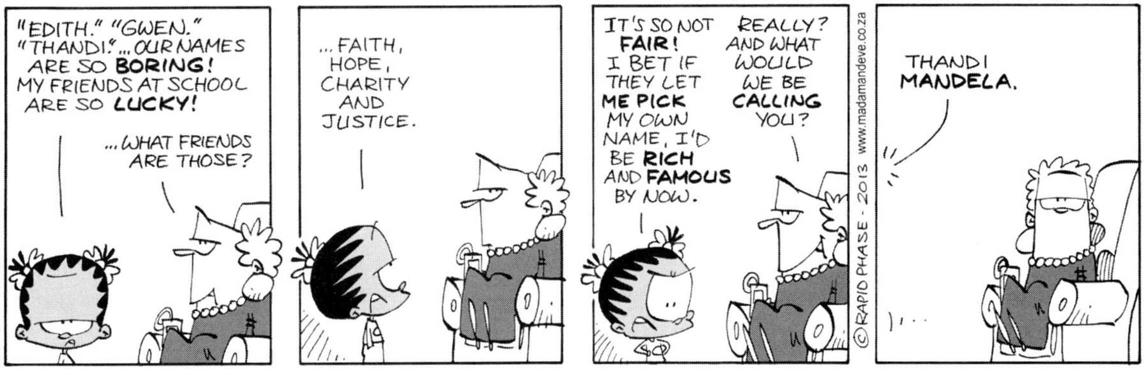
"EDITH." "GWEN." "THANDI."... OUR NAMES ARE SO BORING! MY FRIENDS AT SCHOOL ARE SO LUCKY!
...WHAT FRIENDS ARE THOSE?
...FAITH, HOPE, CHARITY AND JUSTICE.
IT'S SO NOT FAIR! I BET IF THEY LET ME PICK MY OWN NAME, I'D BE RICH AND FAMOUS BY NOW.
REALLY? AND WHAT WOULD WE BE CALLING YOU?
© RAPID PHASE - 2013 www.madamandeve.co.za
THANDI MANDELA.

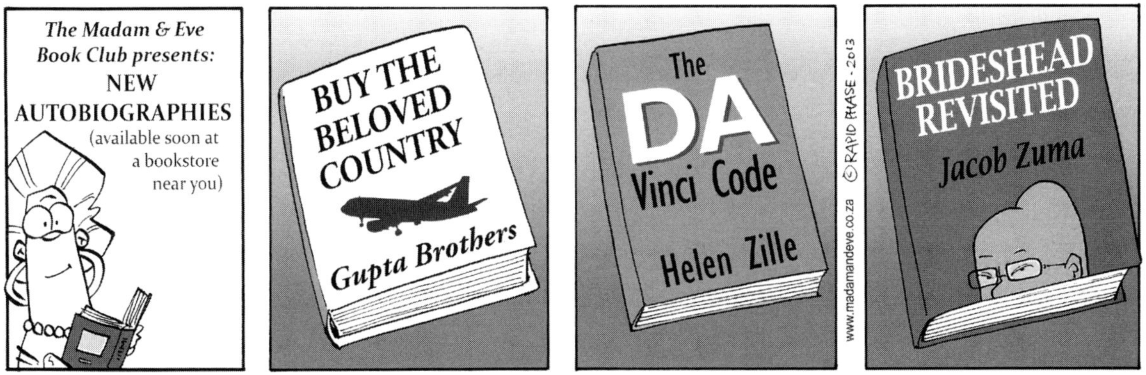
The Madam & Eve Book Club presents:
NEW AUTOBIOGRAPHIES
(available soon at a bookstore near you)
BUY THE BELOVED COUNTRY
Gupta Brothers
The DA Vinci Code
Helen Zille
© RAPID PHASE - 2013 www.madamandeve.co.za
BRIDESHEAD REVISITED
Jacob Zuma

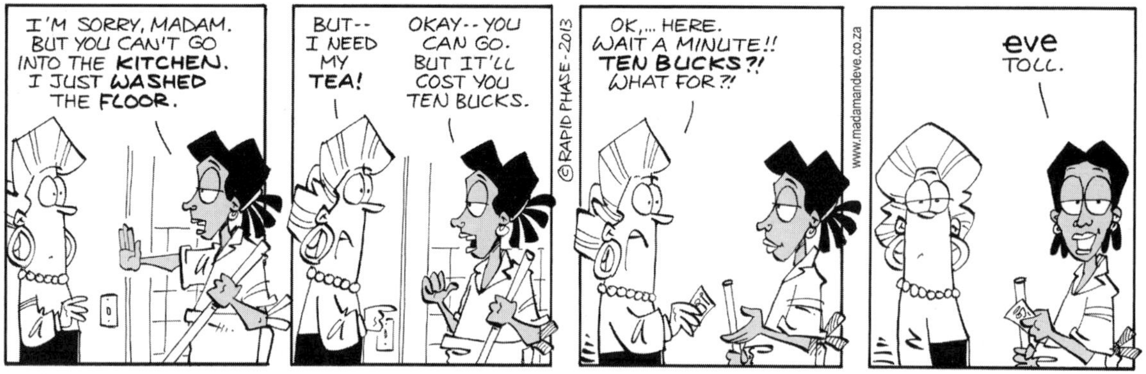
I'M SORRY, MADAM. BUT YOU CAN'T GO INTO THE KITCHEN. I JUST WASHED THE FLOOR.
BUT-- I NEED MY TEA!
OKAY--YOU CAN GO. BUT IT'LL COST YOU TEN BUCKS.
© RAPID PHASE - 2013
OK,... HERE. WAIT A MINUTE!! TEN BUCKS?! WHAT FOR?!
www.madamandeve.co.za
eve TOLL.

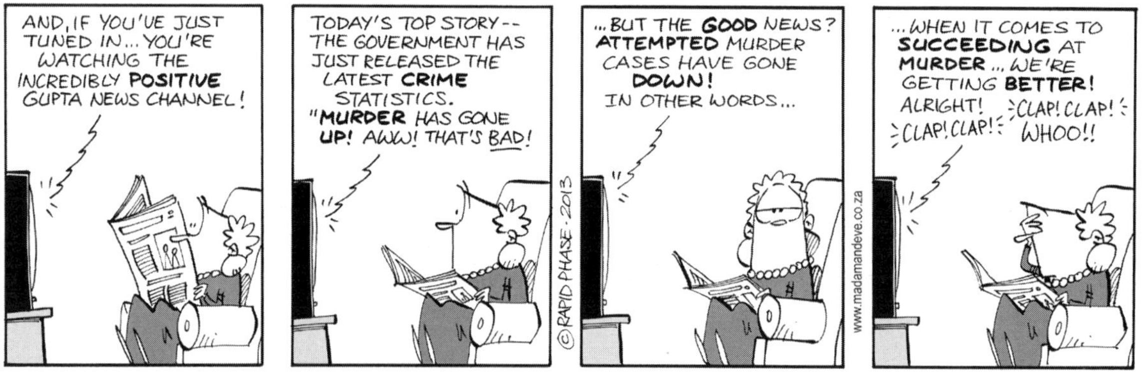
AND, IF YOU'VE JUST TUNED IN... YOU'RE WATCHING THE INCREDIBLY POSITIVE GUPTA NEWS CHANNEL!
TODAY'S TOP STORY-- THE GOVERNMENT HAS JUST RELEASED THE LATEST CRIME STATISTICS. "MURDER HAS GONE UP! AWW! THAT'S BAD!
© RAPID PHASE - 2013
...BUT THE GOOD NEWS? ATTEMPTED MURDER CASES HAVE GONE DOWN! IN OTHER WORDS...
www.madamandeve.co.za
...WHEN IT COMES TO SUCCEEDING AT MURDER... WE'RE GETTING BETTER!
ALRIGHT!
CLAP! CLAP!
CLAP! CLAP!
WHOO!!

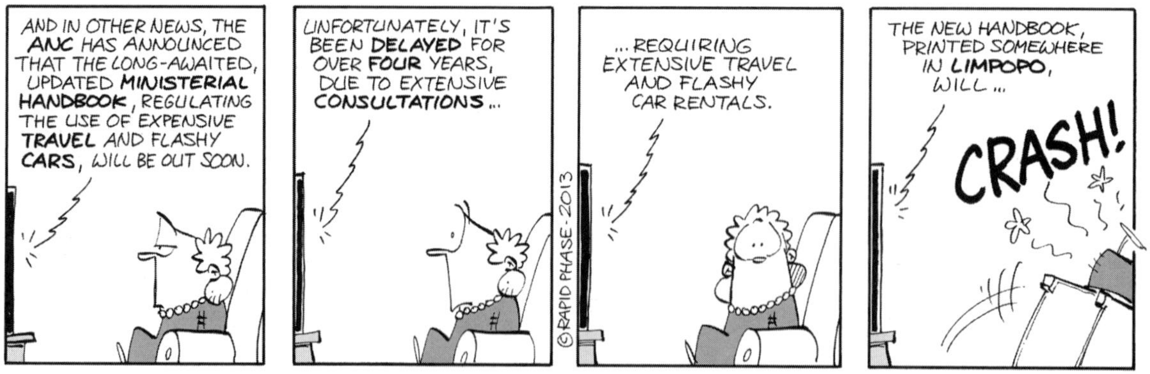
AND IN OTHER NEWS, THE ANC HAS ANNOUNCED THAT THE LONG-AWAITED, UPDATED MINISTERIAL HANDBOOK, REGULATING THE USE OF EXPENSIVE TRAVEL AND FLASHY CARS, WILL BE OUT SOON.
UNFORTUNATELY, IT'S BEEN DELAYED FOR OVER FOUR YEARS, DUE TO EXTENSIVE CONSULTATIONS...
© RAPID PHASE - 2013
...REQUIRING EXTENSIVE TRAVEL AND FLASHY CAR RENTALS.
THE NEW HANDBOOK, PRINTED SOMEWHERE IN LIMPOPO, WILL...
CRASH!

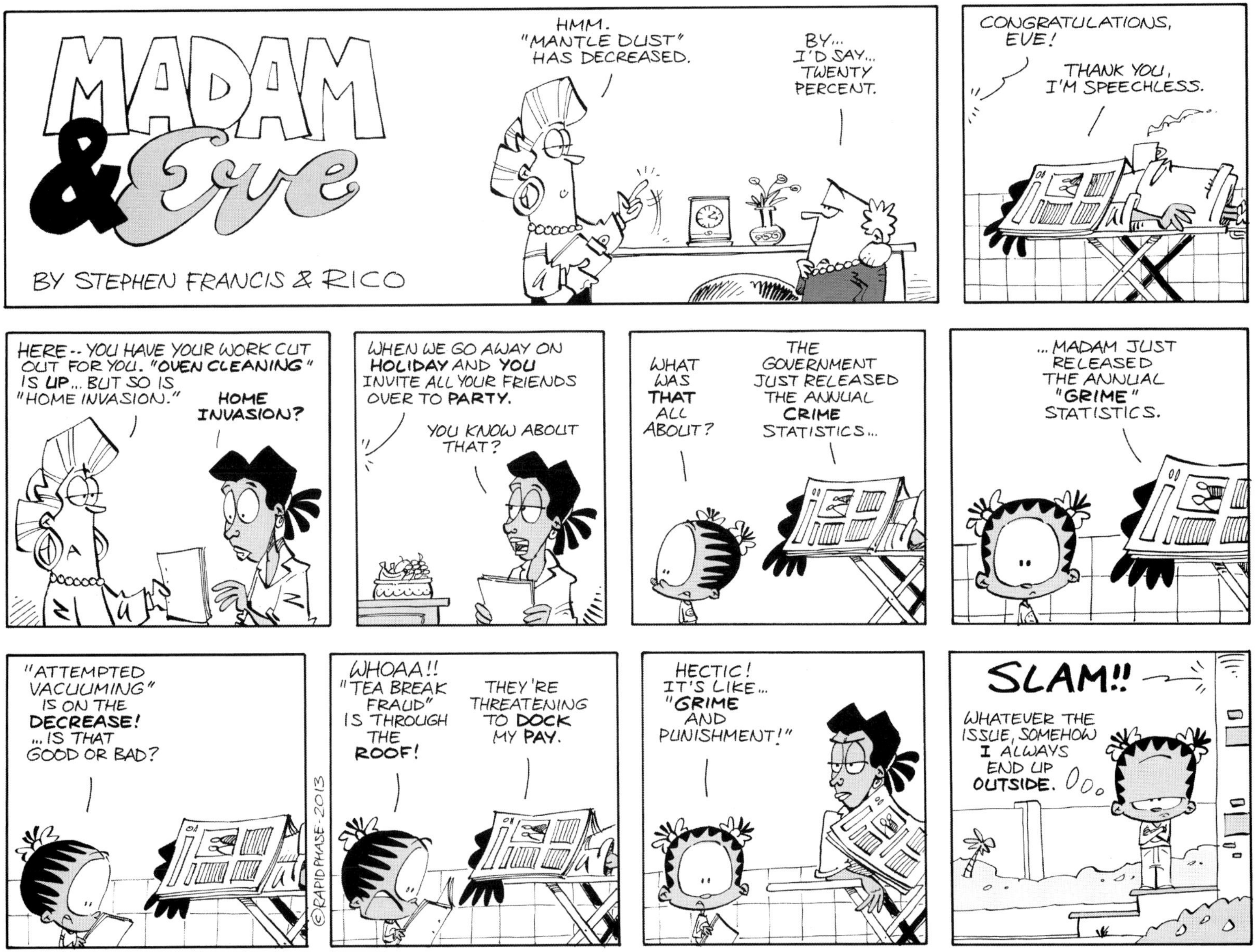
MADAM & Eve
BY STEPHEN FRANCIS & RICO
HMM. "MANTLE DUST" HAS DECREASED.
BY... I'D SAY... TWENTY PERCENT.
CONGRATULATIONS, EVE!
THANK YOU, I'M SPEECHLESS.
HERE -- YOU HAVE YOUR WORK CUT OUT FOR YOU. "OVEN CLEANING" IS UP... BUT SO IS "HOME INVASION."
HOME INVASION?
WHEN WE GO AWAY ON HOLIDAY AND YOU INVITE ALL YOUR FRIENDS OVER TO PARTY.
YOU KNOW ABOUT THAT?
WHAT WAS THAT ALL ABOUT?
THE GOVERNMENT JUST RELEASED THE ANNUAL CRIME STATISTICS...
...MADAM JUST RELEASED THE ANNUAL "GRIME" STATISTICS.
"ATTEMPTED VACUUMING" IS ON THE DECREASE! ...IS THAT GOOD OR BAD?
©RAPIDPHASE 2013
WHOAA!! "TEA BREAK FRAUD" IS THROUGH THE ROOF!
THEY'RE THREATENING TO DOCK MY PAY.
HECTIC! IT'S LIKE... "GRIME AND PUNISHMENT!"
SLAM!!
WHATEVER THE ISSUE, SOMEHOW I ALWAYS END UP OUTSIDE.

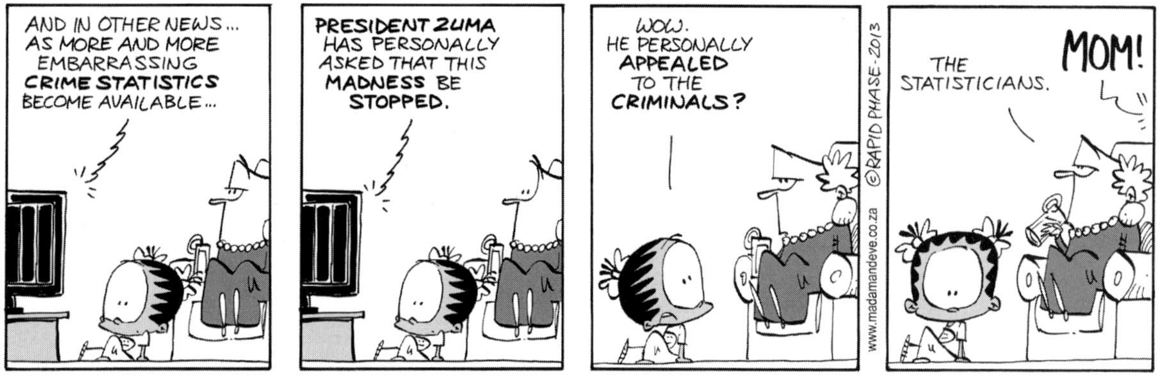
AND IN OTHER NEWS... AS MORE AND MORE EMBARRASSING **CRIME STATISTICS** BECOME AVAILABLE...
PRESIDENT ZUMA HAS PERSONALLY ASKED THAT THIS **MADNESS** BE **STOPPED.**
WOW. HE PERSONALLY **APPEALED** TO THE **CRIMINALS?**
©RAPID PHASE-2013
www.madamandeve.co.za
THE STATISTICIANS.
MOM!

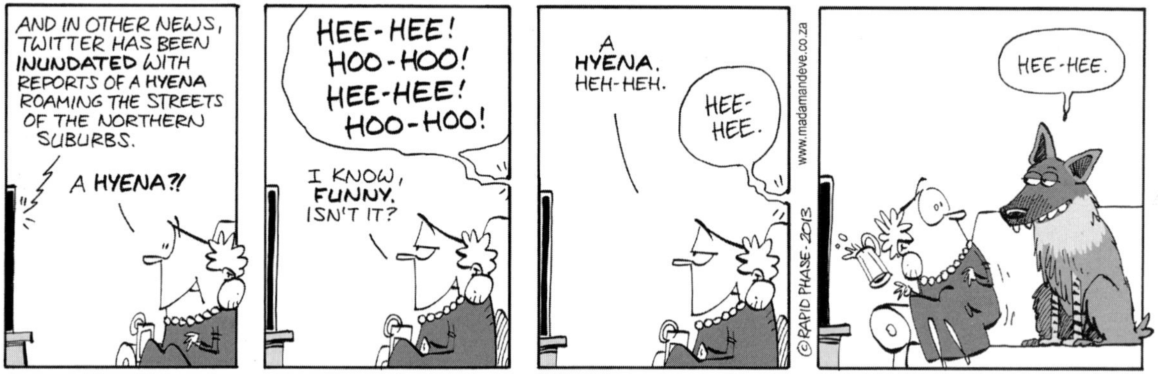
AND IN OTHER NEWS, TWITTER HAS BEEN **INUNDATED** WITH REPORTS OF A **HYENA** ROAMING THE STREETS OF THE NORTHERN SUBURBS.
A **HYENA?!**
HEE-HEE! HOO-HOO! HEE-HEE! HOO-HOO!
I KNOW, **FUNNY.** ISN'T IT?
A **HYENA.** HEH-HEH.
HEE-HEE.
www.madamandeve.co.za
©RAPID PHASE-2013
HEE-HEE.

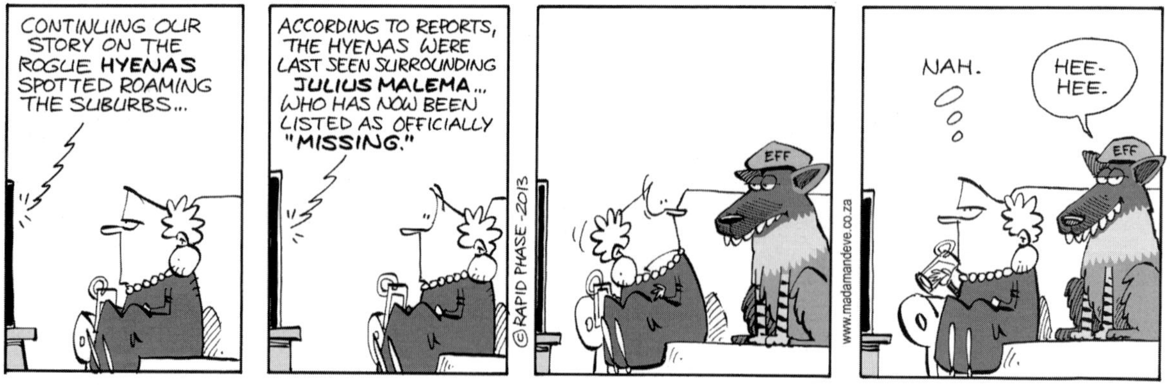
CONTINUING OUR STORY ON THE ROGUE **HYENAS** SPOTTED ROAMING THE SUBURBS...
ACCORDING TO REPORTS, THE HYENAS WERE LAST SEEN SURROUNDING **JULIUS MALEMA**... WHO HAS NOW BEEN LISTED AS OFFICIALLY **"MISSING."**
©RAPID PHASE-2013
EFF
www.madamandeve.co.za
NAH.
HEE-HEE.
EFF

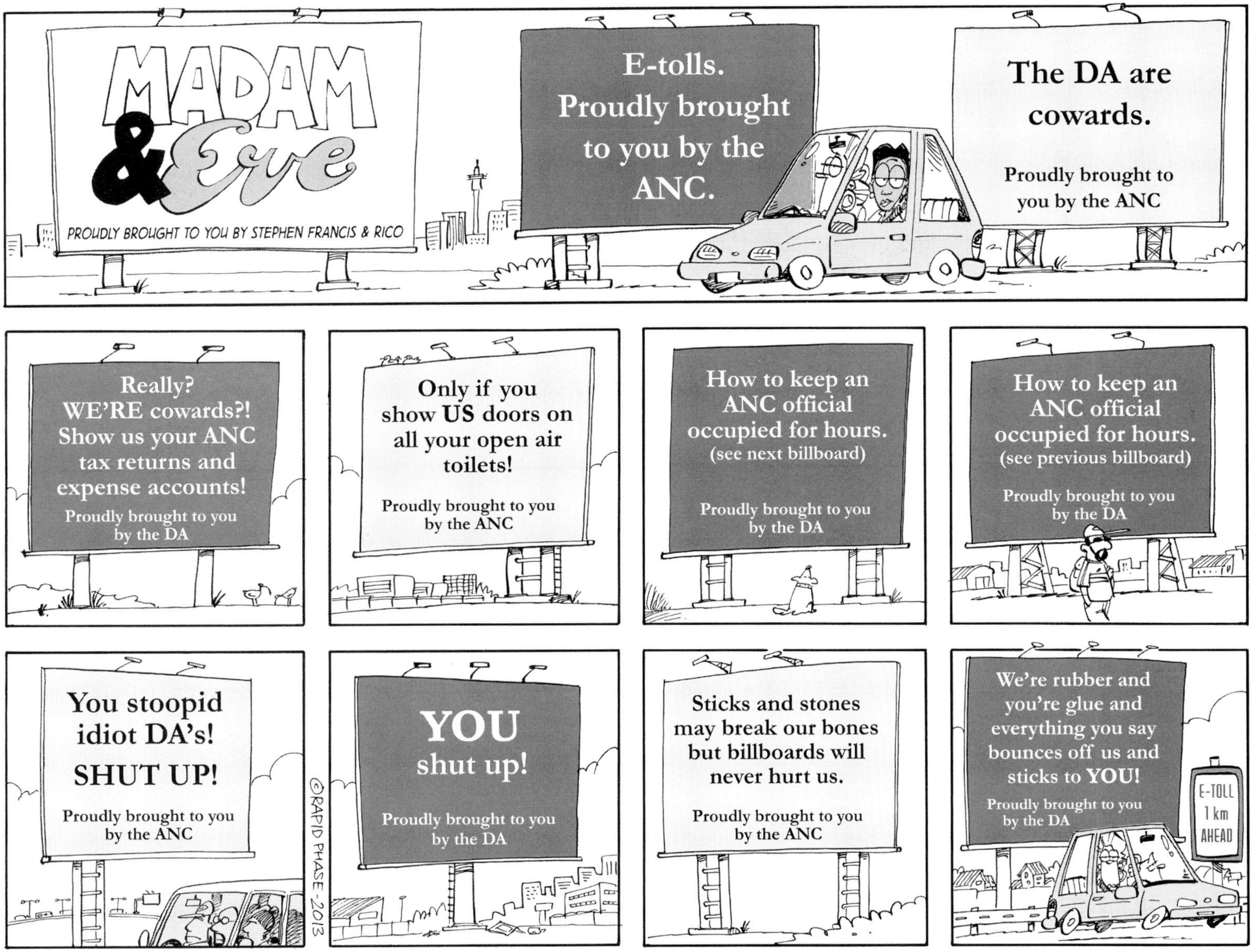
MADAM & Eve
PROUDLY BROUGHT TO YOU BY STEPHEN FRANCIS & RICO
E-tolls. Proudly brought to you by the ANC.
The DA are cowards.
Proudly brought to you by the ANC
Really? WE'RE cowards?! Show us your ANC tax returns and expense accounts!
Proudly brought to you by the DA
Only if you show US doors on all your open air toilets!
Proudly brought to you by the ANC
How to keep an ANC official occupied for hours.
(see next billboard)
Proudly brought to you by the DA
How to keep an ANC official occupied for hours.
(see previous billboard)
Proudly brought to you by the DA
You stoopid idiot DA's!
SHUT UP!
Proudly brought to you by the ANC
©RAPID PHASE-2013
YOU shut up!
Proudly brought to you by the DA
Sticks and stones may break our bones but billboards will never hurt us.
Proudly brought to you by the ANC
We're rubber and you're glue and everything you say bounces off us and sticks to YOU!
Proudly brought to you by the DA
E-TOLL 1 km AHEAD

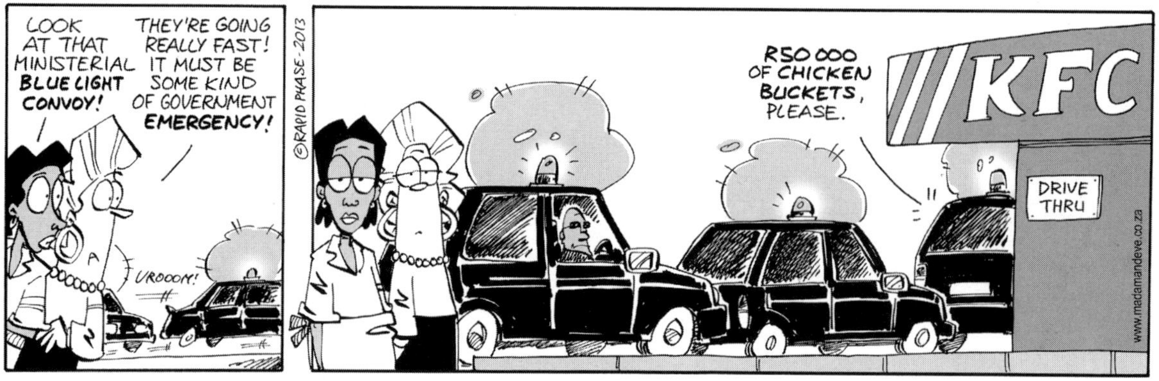
LOOK AT THAT MINISTERIAL BLUE LIGHT CONVOY!
THEY'RE GOING REALLY FAST! IT MUST BE SOME KIND OF GOVERNMENT EMERGENCY!
VROOOM!
©RAPID PHASE · 2013
R50 000 OF CHICKEN BUCKETS, PLEASE.
KFC
DRIVE THRU
www.madamandeve.co.za

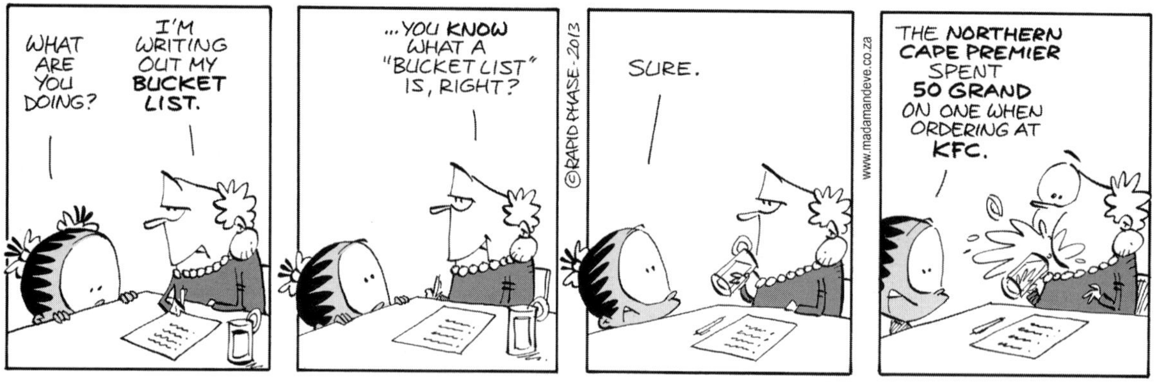
WHAT ARE YOU DOING?
I'M WRITING OUT MY BUCKET LIST.
...YOU KNOW WHAT A "BUCKET LIST" IS, RIGHT?
©RAPID PHASE · 2013
SURE.
www.madamandeve.co.za
THE NORTHERN CAPE PREMIER SPENT 50 GRAND ON ONE WHEN ORDERING AT KFC.

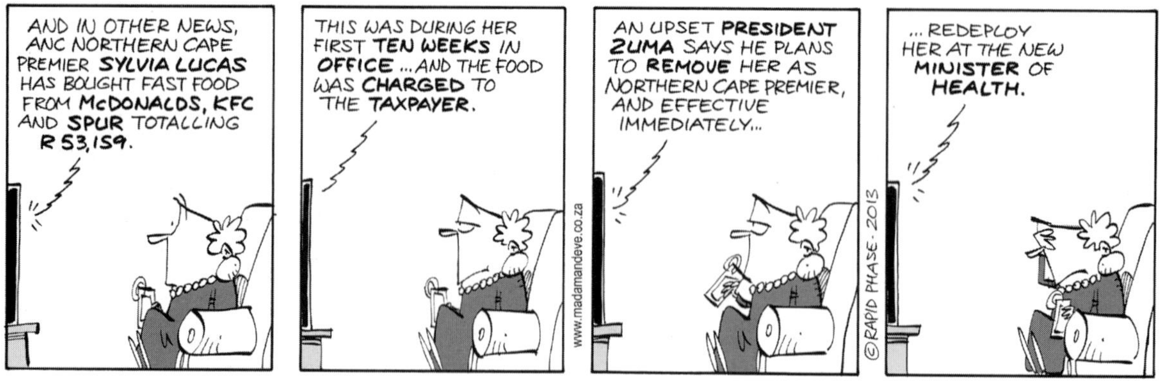
AND IN OTHER NEWS, ANC NORTHERN CAPE PREMIER SYLVIA LUCAS HAS BOUGHT FAST FOOD FROM McDONALDS, KFC AND SPUR TOTALLING R 53,159.
THIS WAS DURING HER FIRST TEN WEEKS IN OFFICE ...AND THE FOOD WAS CHARGED TO THE TAXPAYER.
www.madamandeve.co.za
AN UPSET PRESIDENT ZUMA SAYS HE PLANS TO REMOVE HER AS NORTHERN CAPE PREMIER, AND EFFECTIVE IMMEDIATELY...
©RAPID PHASE · 2013
...REDEPLOY HER AT THE NEW MINISTER OF HEALTH.

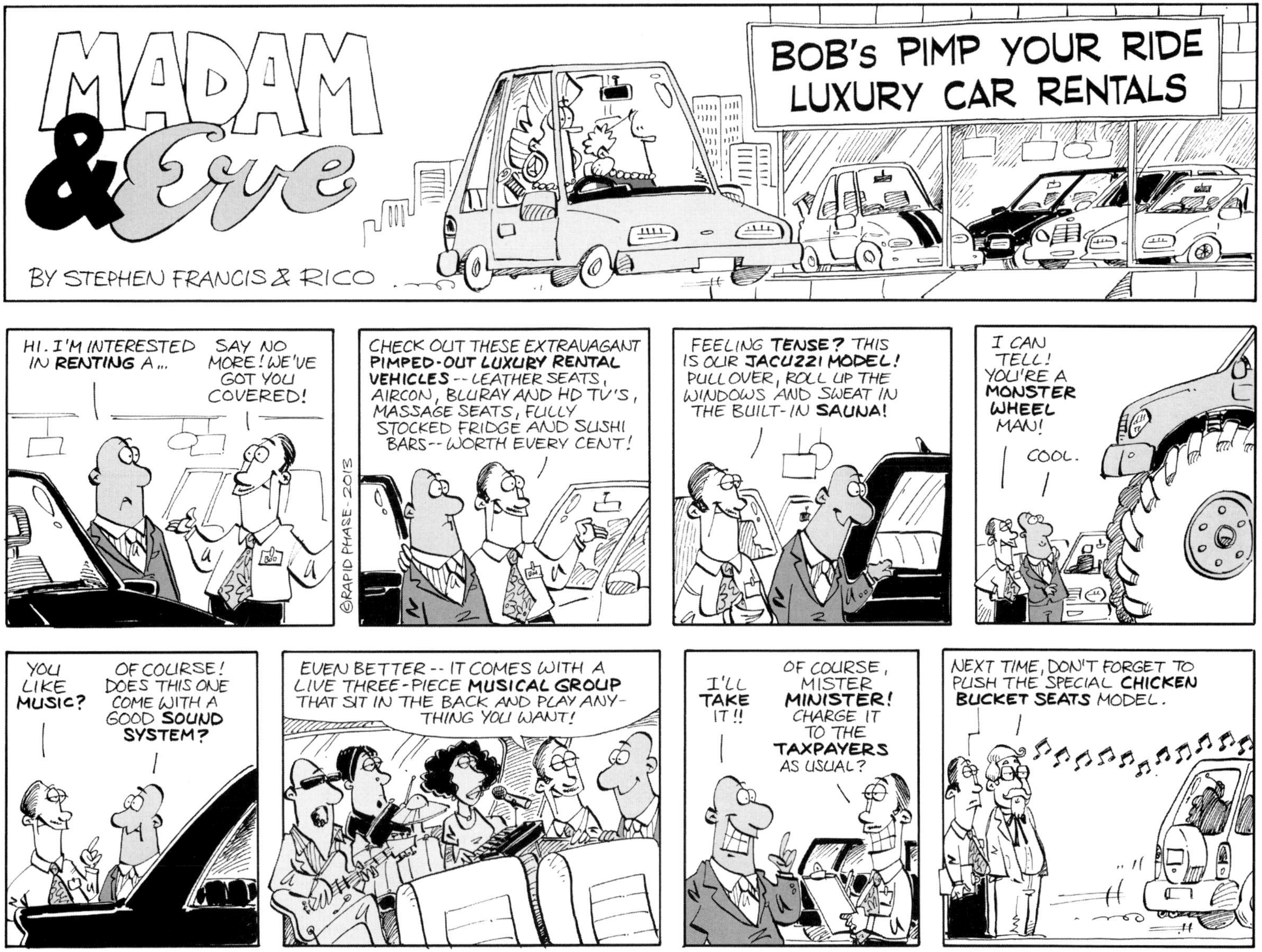
MADAM & Eve
BY STEPHEN FRANCIS & RICO
BOB's PIMP YOUR RIDE LUXURY CAR RENTALS
HI. I'M INTERESTED IN RENTING A...
SAY NO MORE! WE'VE GOT YOU COVERED!
©RAPID PHASE - 2013
CHECK OUT THESE EXTRAVAGANT PIMPED-OUT LUXURY RENTAL VEHICLES -- LEATHER SEATS, AIRCON, BLURAY AND HD TV'S, MASSAGE SEATS, FULLY STOCKED FRIDGE AND SUSHI BARS -- WORTH EVERY CENT!
FEELING TENSE? THIS IS OUR JACUZZI MODEL! PULL OVER, ROLL UP THE WINDOWS AND SWEAT IN THE BUILT-IN SAUNA!
I CAN TELL! YOU'RE A MONSTER WHEEL MAN!
COOL.
YOU LIKE MUSIC?
OF COURSE! DOES THIS ONE COME WITH A GOOD SOUND SYSTEM?
EVEN BETTER -- IT COMES WITH A LIVE THREE-PIECE MUSICAL GROUP THAT SIT IN THE BACK AND PLAY ANYTHING YOU WANT!
I'LL TAKE IT!!
OF COURSE, MISTER MINISTER! CHARGE IT TO THE TAXPAYERS AS USUAL?
NEXT TIME, DON'T FORGET TO PUSH THE SPECIAL CHICKEN BUCKET SEATS MODEL.

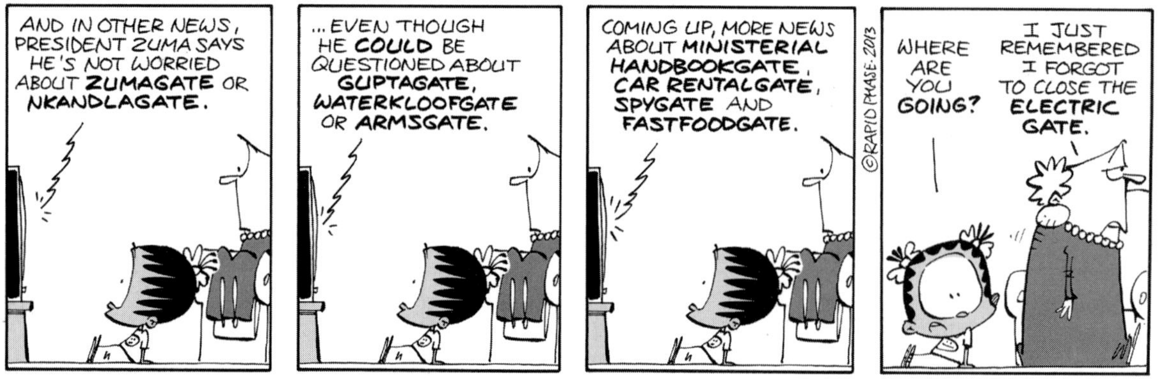
AND IN OTHER NEWS, PRESIDENT ZUMA SAYS HE'S NOT WORRIED ABOUT **ZUMAGATE** OR **NKANDLAGATE**.
... EVEN THOUGH HE **COULD** BE QUESTIONED ABOUT **GUPTAGATE**, **WATERKLOOFGATE** OR **ARMSGATE**.
COMING UP, MORE NEWS ABOUT **MINISTERIAL HANDBOOKGATE**, **CAR RENTALGATE**, **SPYGATE** AND **FASTFOODGATE**.
©RAPID PHASE·2013
WHERE ARE YOU **GOING?**
I JUST REMEMBERED I FORGOT TO CLOSE THE **ELECTRIC GATE**.

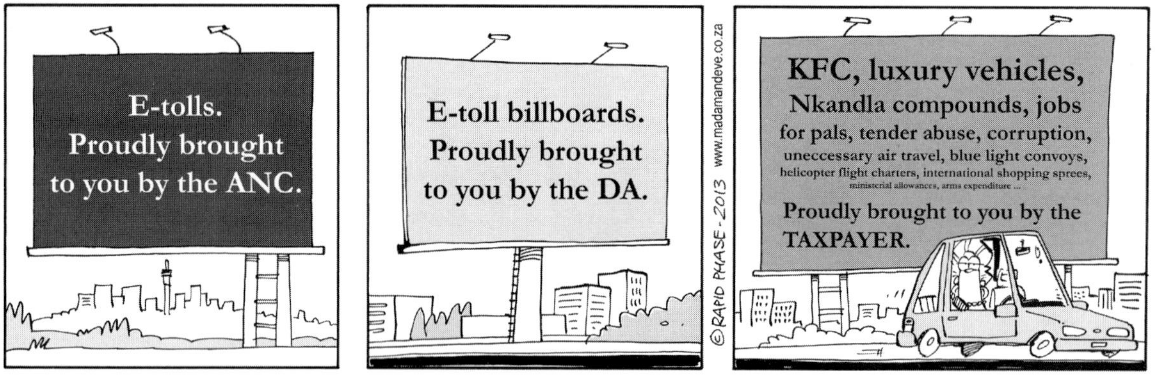
E-tolls.
Proudly brought
to you by the ANC.
E-toll billboards.
Proudly brought
to you by the DA.
©RAPID PHASE·2013 www.madamandeve.co.za
KFC, luxury vehicles,
Nkandla compounds, jobs
for pals, tender abuse, corruption,
uneccessary air travel, blue light convoys,
helicopter flight charters, international shopping sprees,
ministerial allowances, arms expenditure ...
Proudly brought to you by the
TAXPAYER.

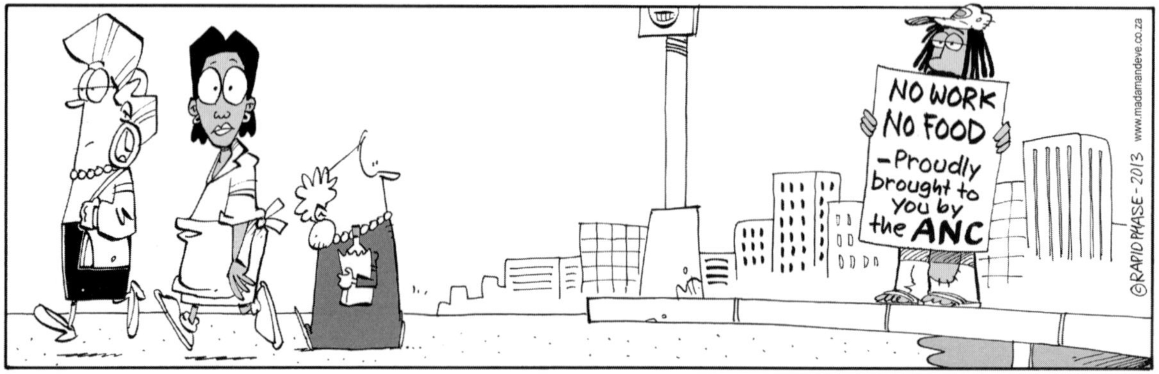
NO WORK NO FOOD
– Proudly brought to you by the ANC
©RAPID PHASE·2013 www.madamandeve.co.za

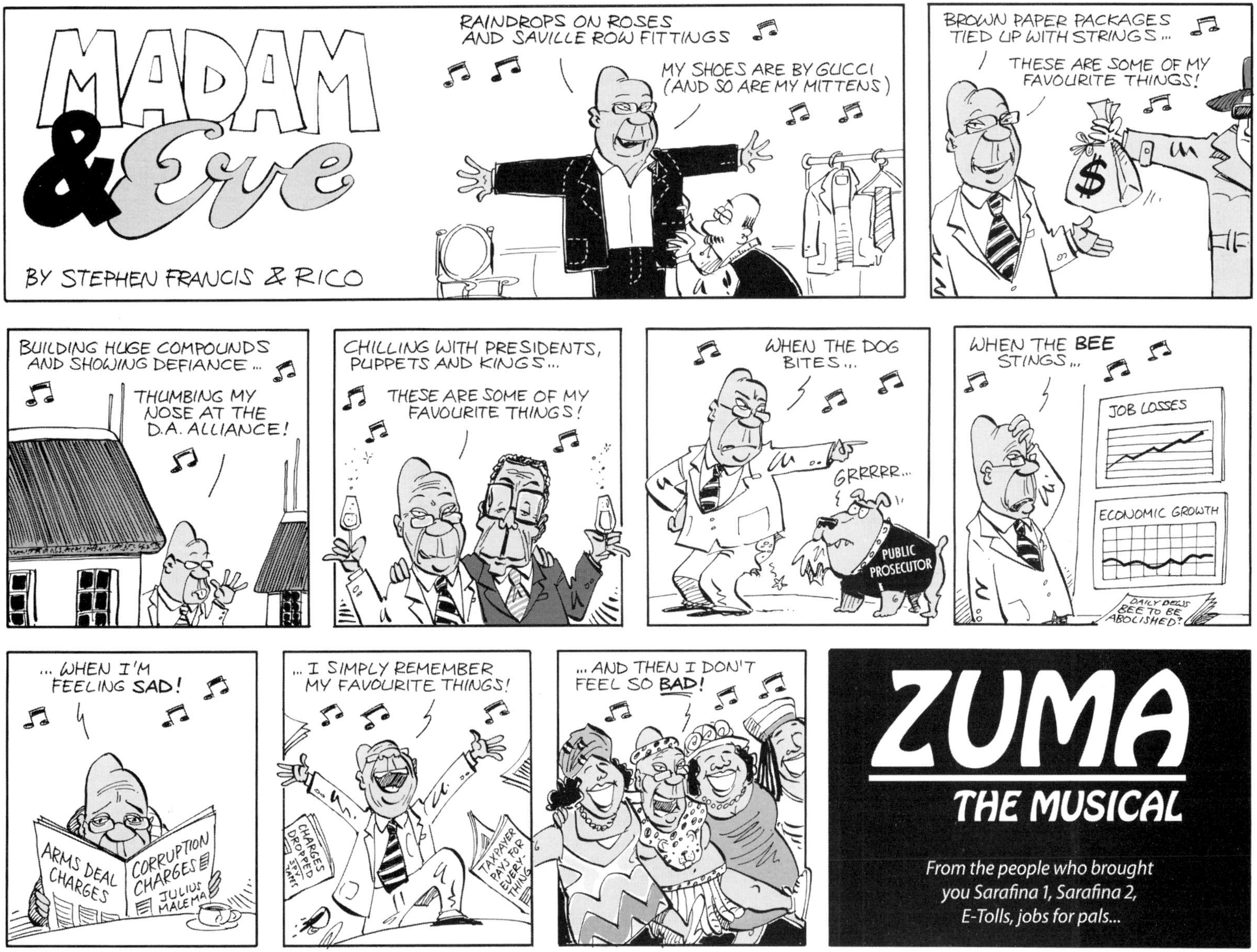
MADAM & Eve
BY STEPHEN FRANCIS & RICO
RAINDROPS ON ROSES AND SAVILLE ROW FITTINGS
MY SHOES ARE BY GUCCI (AND SO ARE MY MITTENS)
BROWN PAPER PACKAGES TIED UP WITH STRINGS...
THESE ARE SOME OF MY FAVOURITE THINGS!
BUILDING HUGE COMPOUNDS AND SHOWING DEFIANCE...
THUMBING MY NOSE AT THE D.A. ALLIANCE!
CHILLING WITH PRESIDENTS, PUPPETS AND KINGS...
THESE ARE SOME OF MY FAVOURITE THINGS!
WHEN THE DOG BITES...
GRRRRR...
PUBLIC PROSECUTOR
WHEN THE BEE STINGS...
JOB LOSSES
ECONOMIC GROWTH
DAILY DEWS BEE TO BE ABOLISHED?
...WHEN I'M FEELING SAD!
ARMS DEAL CHARGES
CORRUPTION CHARGES
JULIUS MALEMA
...I SIMPLY REMEMBER MY FAVOURITE THINGS!
CHARGES DROPPED
SPY TAPES
TAXPAYER PAYS FOR EVERYTHING
...AND THEN I DON'T FEEL SO BAD!
ZUMA
THE MUSICAL
From the people who brought you Sarafina 1, Sarafina 2, E-Tolls, jobs for pals...

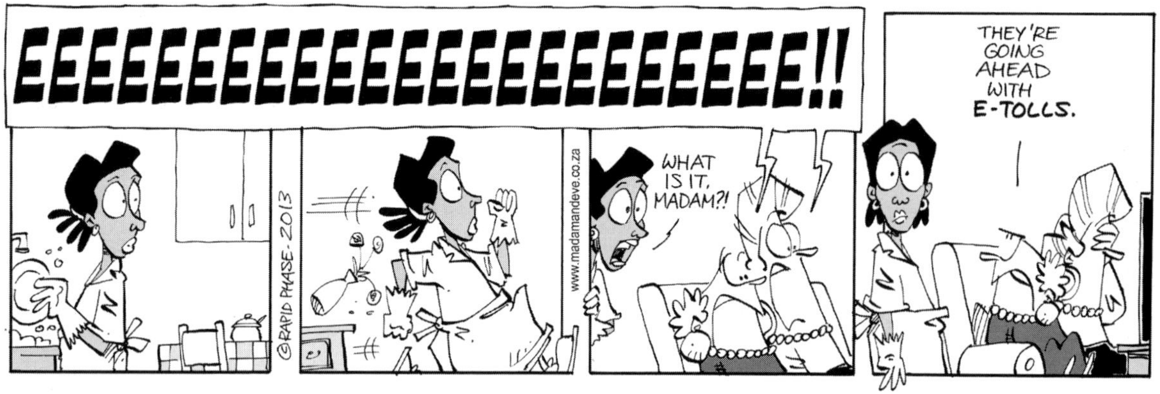
EEEEEEEEEEEEEEEEEEEEEEEE!!
©RAPID PHASE · 2013
www.madamandeve.co.za
WHAT IS IT, MADAM?!
THEY'RE GOING AHEAD WITH **E-TOLLS.**

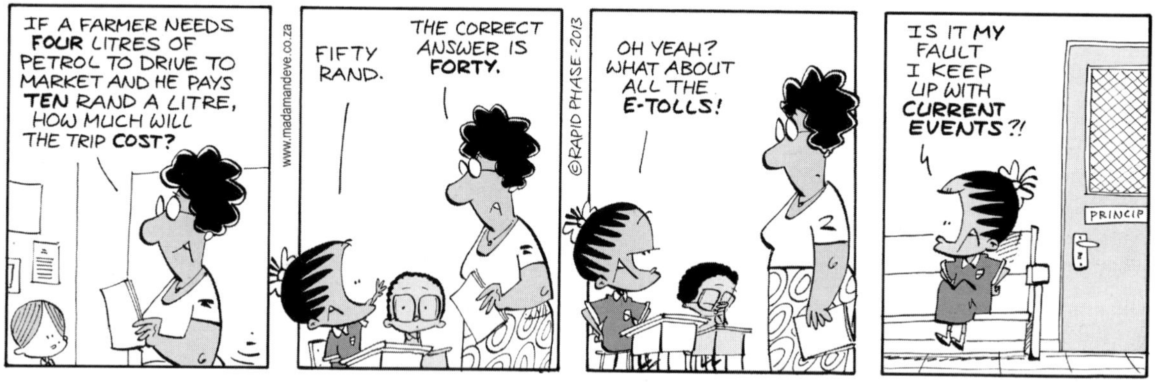
IF A FARMER NEEDS **FOUR** LITRES OF PETROL TO DRIVE TO MARKET AND HE PAYS **TEN** RAND A LITRE, HOW MUCH WILL THE TRIP **COST?**
www.madamandeve.co.za
FIFTY RAND.
THE CORRECT ANSWER IS **FORTY.**
©RAPID PHASE · 2013
OH YEAH? WHAT ABOUT ALL THE **E-TOLLS!**
IS IT **MY** FAULT I KEEP UP WITH **CURRENT EVENTS**?!
PRINCIP

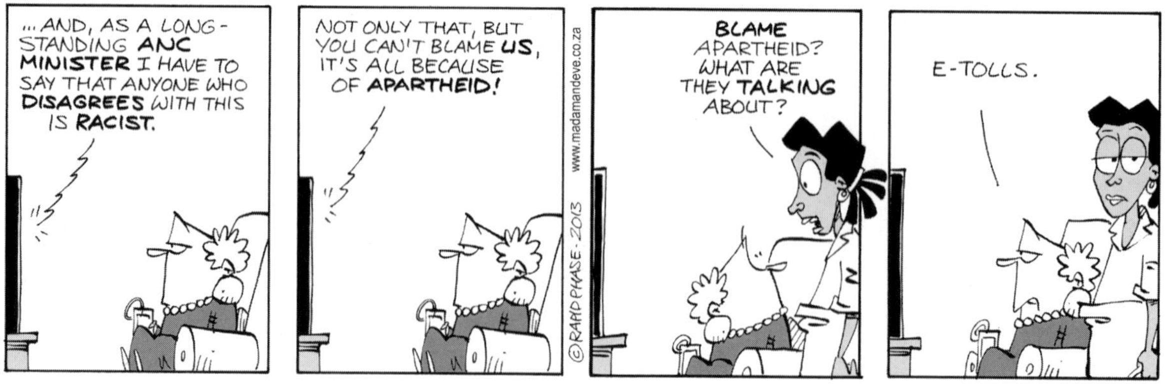
...AND, AS A LONG-STANDING **ANC MINISTER** I HAVE TO SAY THAT ANYONE WHO **DISAGREES** WITH THIS IS **RACIST.**
NOT ONLY THAT, BUT YOU CAN'T BLAME **US**, IT'S ALL BECAUSE OF **APARTHEID!**
www.madamandeve.co.za
©RAPID PHASE · 2013
BLAME APARTHEID? WHAT ARE THEY **TALKING** ABOUT?
E-TOLLS.

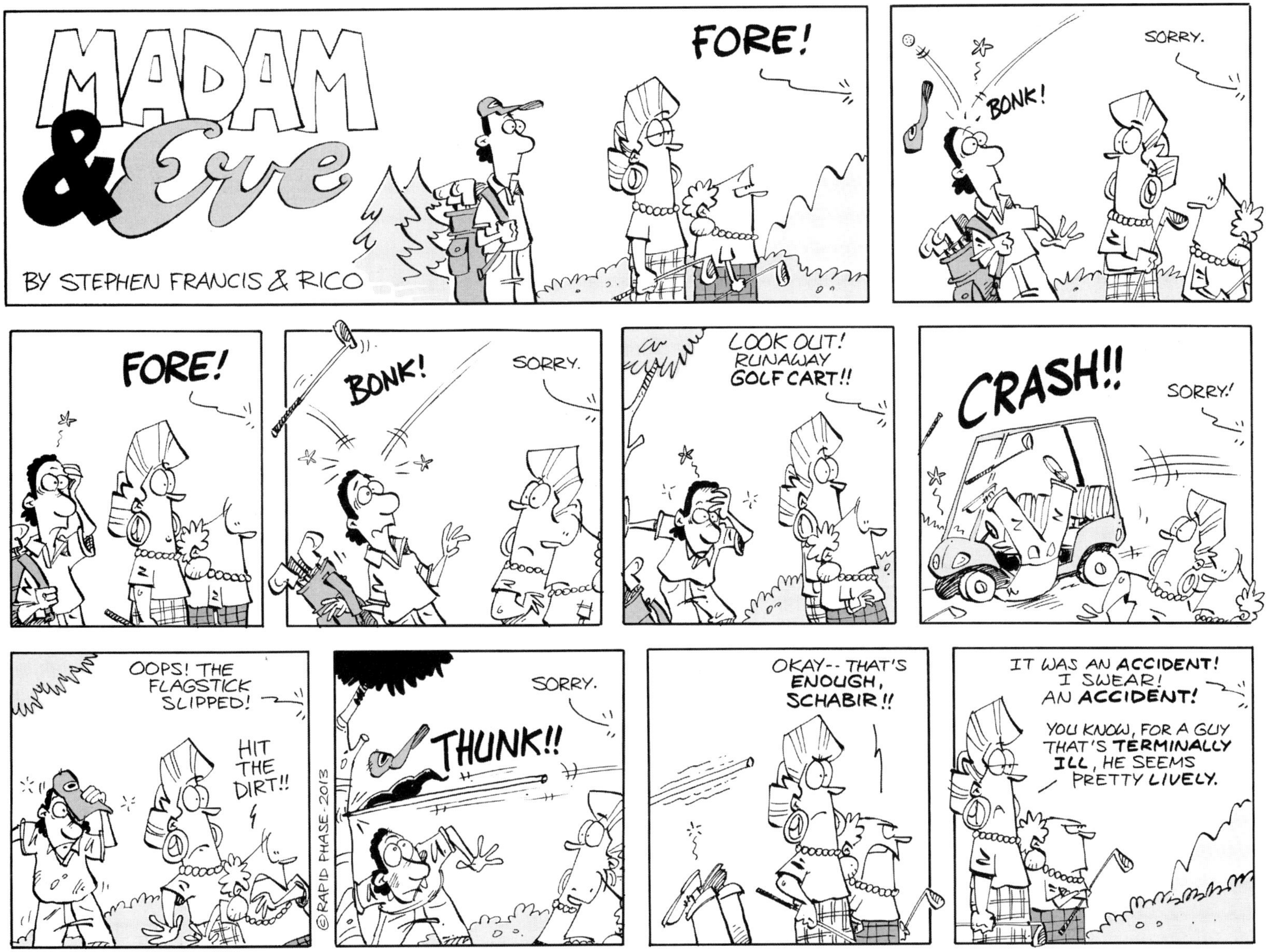
MADAM & Eve
BY STEPHEN FRANCIS & RICO
FORE!
BONK!
SORRY.
FORE!
BONK!
SORRY.
LOOK OUT! RUNAWAY GOLF CART!!
CRASH!!
SORRY!
OOPS! THE FLAGSTICK SLIPPED!
HIT THE DIRT!!
SORRY.
THUNK!!
©RAPID PHASE 2013
OKAY-- THAT'S ENOUGH, SCHABIR!!
IT WAS AN ACCIDENT! I SWEAR! AN ACCIDENT!
YOU KNOW, FOR A GUY THAT'S TERMINALLY ILL, HE SEEMS PRETTY LIVELY.

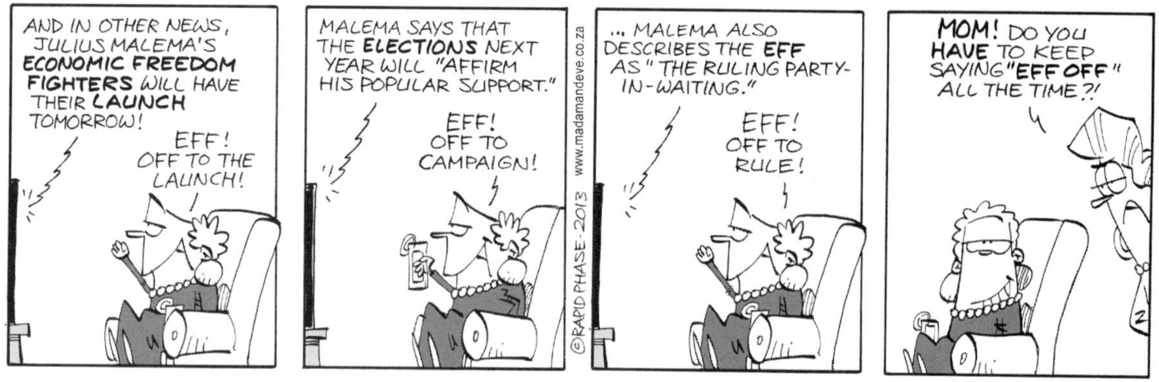
AND IN OTHER NEWS, JULIUS MALEMA'S **ECONOMIC FREEDOM FIGHTERS** WILL HAVE THEIR **LAUNCH** TOMORROW!
EFF! OFF TO THE LAUNCH!
MALEMA SAYS THAT THE **ELECTIONS** NEXT YEAR WILL "AFFIRM HIS POPULAR SUPPORT."
EFF! OFF TO CAMPAIGN!
www.madamandeve.co.za ©RAPID PHASE·2013
... MALEMA ALSO DESCRIBES THE **EFF** AS "THE RULING PARTY-IN-WAITING."
EFF! OFF TO RULE!
MOM! DO YOU **HAVE** TO KEEP SAYING **"EFF OFF"** ALL THE TIME?!

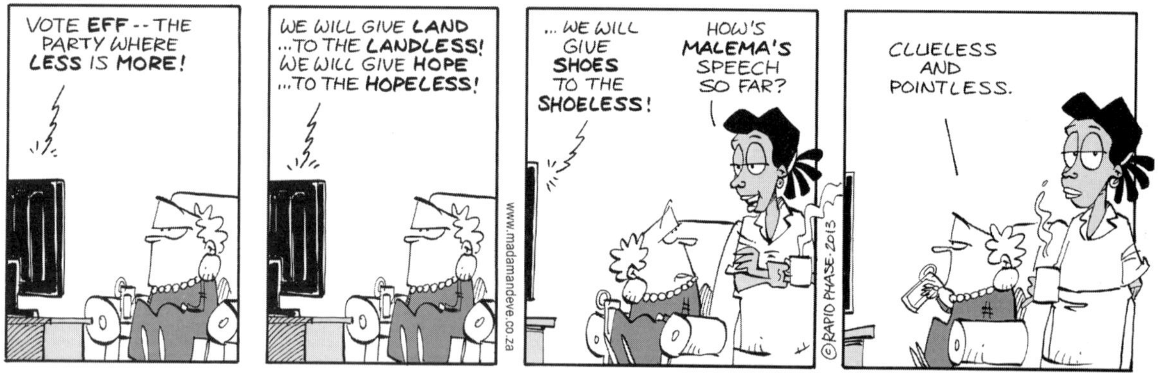
VOTE **EFF** -- THE PARTY WHERE **LESS** IS **MORE**!
WE WILL GIVE **LAND** ...TO THE **LANDLESS**! WE WILL GIVE **HOPE** ...TO THE **HOPELESS**!
www.madamandeve.co.za
... WE WILL GIVE **SHOES** TO THE **SHOELESS**!
HOW'S **MALEMA'S** SPEECH SO FAR?
©RAPID PHASE·2013
CLUELESS AND POINTLESS.

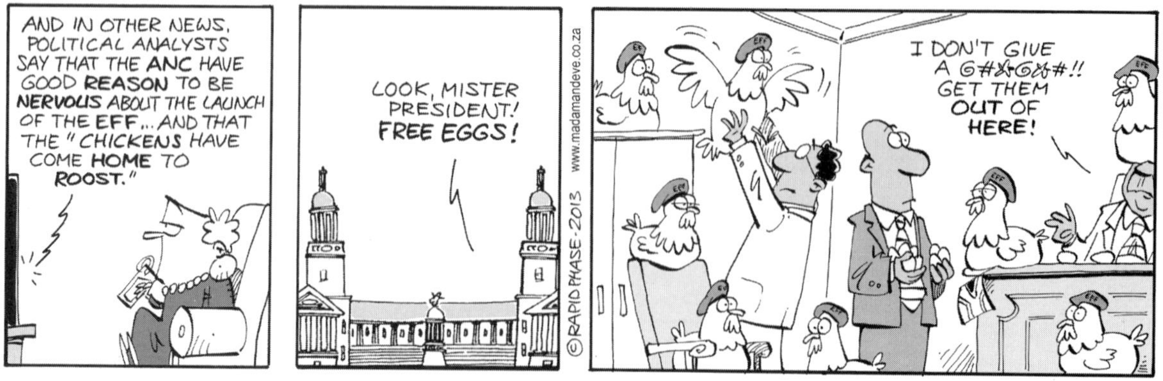
AND IN OTHER NEWS, POLITICAL ANALYSTS SAY THAT THE **ANC** HAVE GOOD **REASON** TO BE **NERVOUS** ABOUT THE LAUNCH OF THE **EFF**... AND THAT THE "**CHICKENS** HAVE COME **HOME** TO **ROOST**."
LOOK, MISTER PRESIDENT! **FREE EGGS!**
www.madamandeve.co.za ©RAPID PHASE·2013
I DON'T GIVE A
GET THEM **OUT** OF **HERE!**

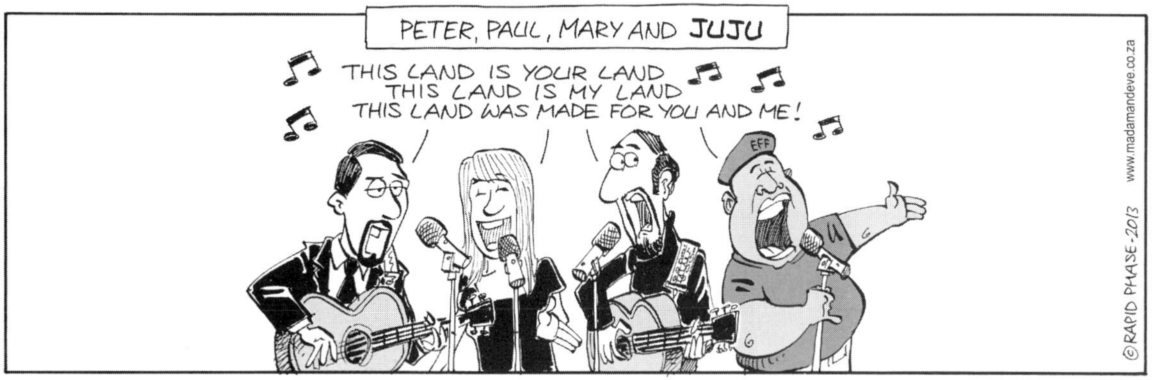
PETER, PAUL, MARY AND JUJU
THIS LAND IS YOUR LAND
THIS LAND IS MY LAND
THIS LAND WAS MADE FOR YOU AND ME!
EFF
©RAPID PHASE-2013
www.madamandeve.co.za

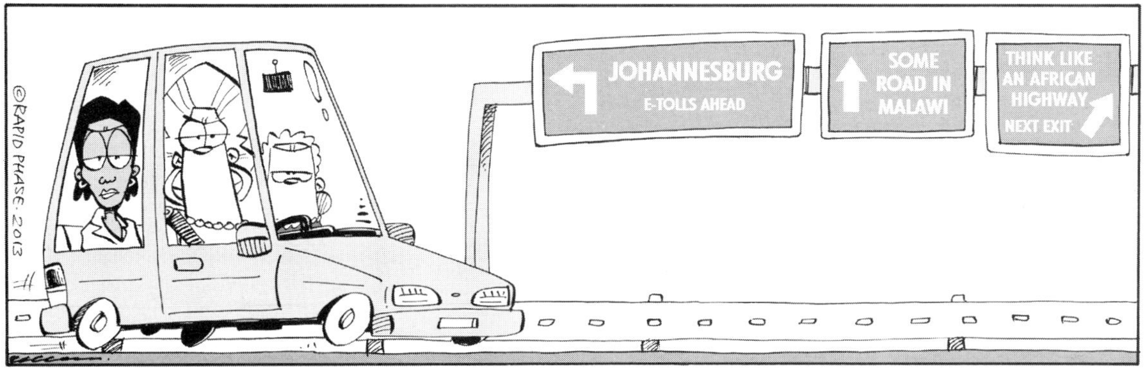
©RAPID PHASE-2013
JOHANNESBURG
E-TOLLS AHEAD
SOME ROAD IN MALAWI
THINK LIKE AN AFRICAN HIGHWAY
NEXT EXIT

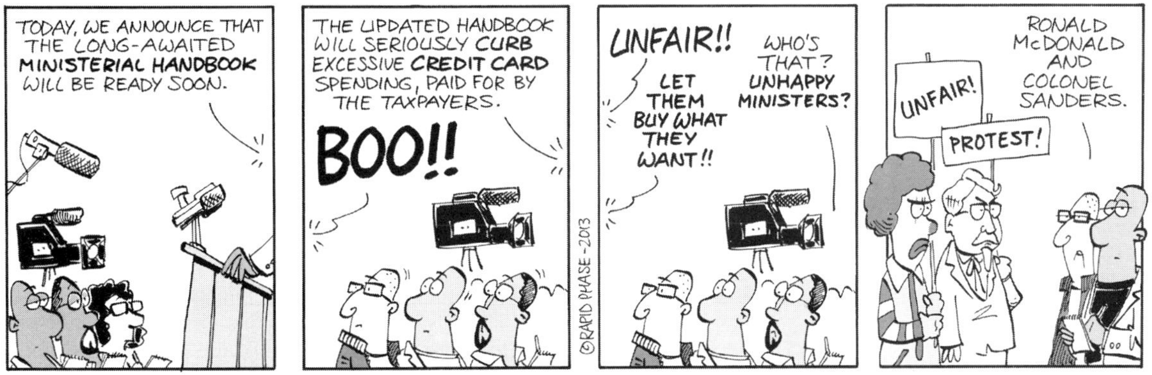
TODAY, WE ANNOUNCE THAT THE LONG-AWAITED MINISTERIAL HANDBOOK WILL BE READY SOON.
THE UPDATED HANDBOOK WILL SERIOUSLY CURB EXCESSIVE CREDIT CARD SPENDING, PAID FOR BY THE TAXPAYERS.
BOO!!
©RAPID PHASE-2013
UNFAIR!!
LET THEM BUY WHAT THEY WANT!!
WHO'S THAT?
UNHAPPY MINISTERS?
UNFAIR!
PROTEST!
RONALD McDONALD AND COLONEL SANDERS.

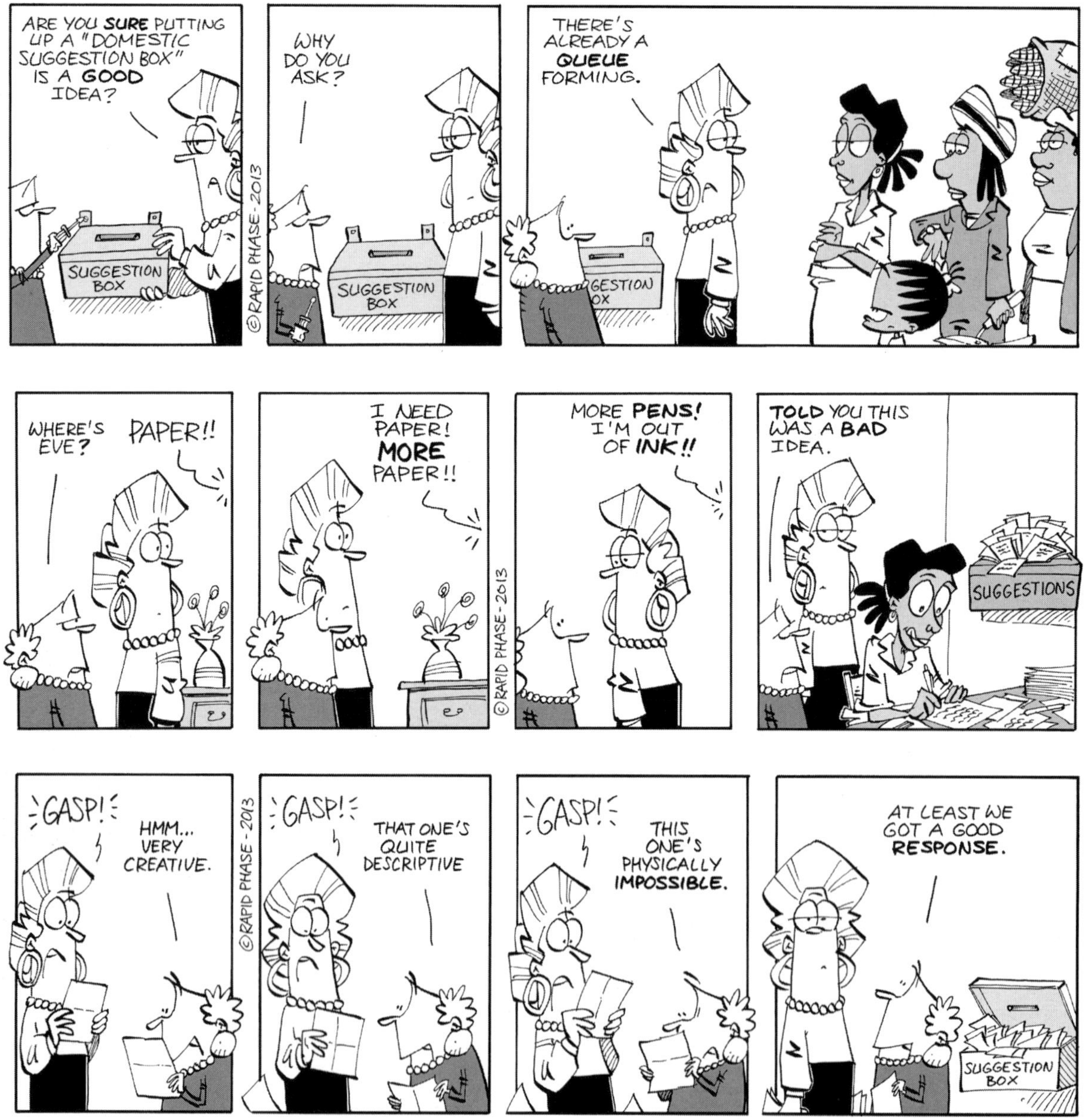
ARE YOU SURE PUTTING UP A "DOMESTIC SUGGESTION BOX" IS A GOOD IDEA?
SUGGESTION BOX
©RAPID PHASE - 2013
WHY DO YOU ASK?
SUGGESTION BOX
THERE'S ALREADY A QUEUE FORMING.
WHERE'S EVE?
PAPER!!
I NEED PAPER! MORE PAPER!!
©RAPID PHASE - 2013
MORE PENS! I'M OUT OF INK!!
TOLD YOU THIS WAS A BAD IDEA.
SUGGESTIONS
GASP!
HMM... VERY CREATIVE.
©RAPID PHASE - 2013
GASP!
THAT ONE'S QUITE DESCRIPTIVE
GASP!
THIS ONE'S PHYSICALLY IMPOSSIBLE.
AT LEAST WE GOT A GOOD RESPONSE.
SUGGESTION BOX

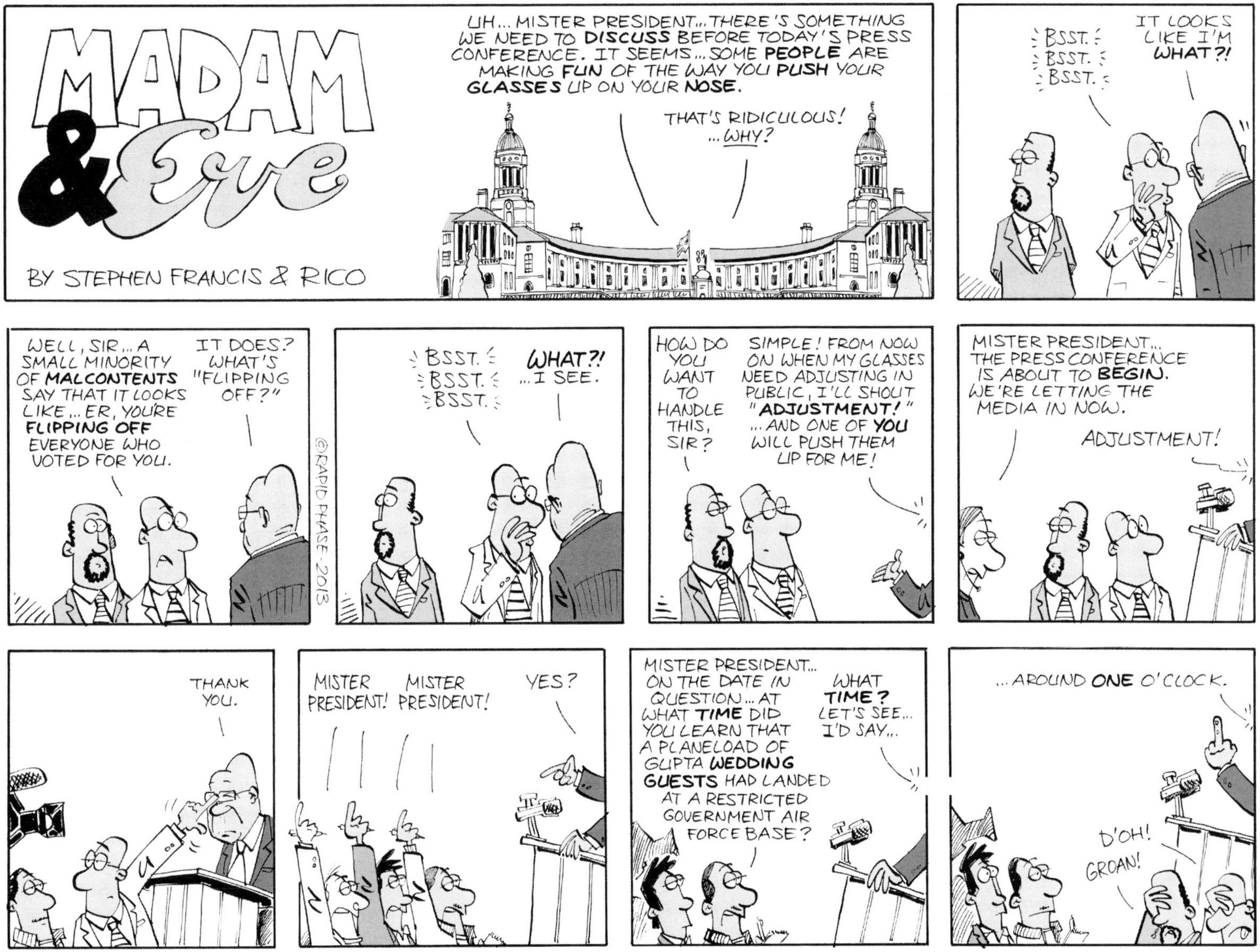
MADAM & Eve
BY STEPHEN FRANCIS & RICO
UH... MISTER PRESIDENT... THERE'S SOMETHING WE NEED TO DISCUSS BEFORE TODAY'S PRESS CONFERENCE. IT SEEMS... SOME PEOPLE ARE MAKING FUN OF THE WAY YOU PUSH YOUR GLASSES UP ON YOUR NOSE.
THAT'S RIDICULOUS! ...WHY?
BSST. BSST. BSST.
IT LOOKS LIKE I'M WHAT?!
WELL, SIR... A SMALL MINORITY OF MALCONTENTS SAY THAT IT LOOKS LIKE... ER, YOU'RE FLIPPING OFF EVERYONE WHO VOTED FOR YOU.
IT DOES? WHAT'S "FLIPPING OFF?"
©RAPID PHASE 2013
BSST. BSST. BSST.
WHAT?! ...I SEE.
HOW DO YOU WANT TO HANDLE THIS, SIR?
SIMPLE! FROM NOW ON WHEN MY GLASSES NEED ADJUSTING IN PUBLIC, I'LL SHOUT "ADJUSTMENT!" ...AND ONE OF YOU WILL PUSH THEM UP FOR ME!
MISTER PRESIDENT... THE PRESS CONFERENCE IS ABOUT TO BEGIN. WE'RE LETTING THE MEDIA IN NOW.
ADJUSTMENT!
THANK YOU.
MISTER PRESIDENT!
MISTER PRESIDENT!
YES?
MISTER PRESIDENT... ON THE DATE IN QUESTION... AT WHAT TIME DID YOU LEARN THAT A PLANELOAD OF GUPTA WEDDING GUESTS HAD LANDED AT A RESTRICTED GOVERNMENT AIR FORCE BASE?
WHAT TIME? LET'S SEE... I'D SAY...
...AROUND ONE O'CLOCK.
D'OH!
GROAN!

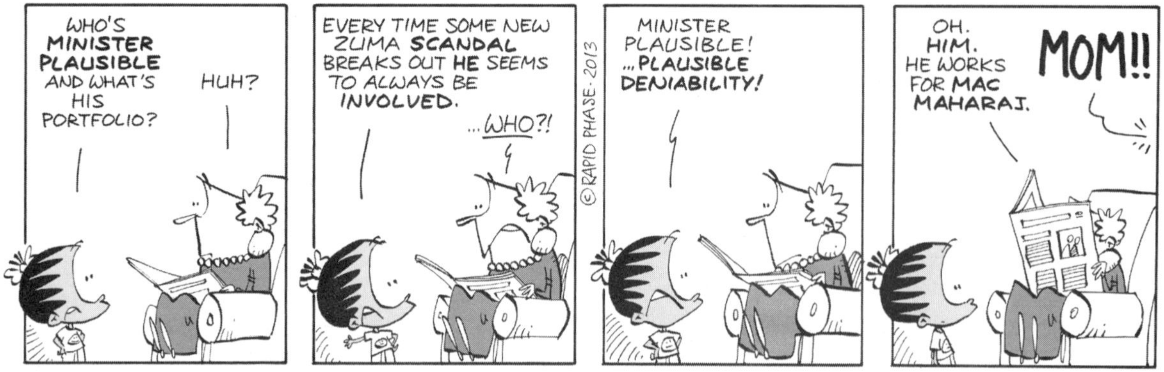
WHO'S MINISTER PLAUSIBLE AND WHAT'S HIS PORTFOLIO?
HUH?
EVERY TIME SOME NEW ZUMA SCANDAL BREAKS OUT HE SEEMS TO ALWAYS BE INVOLVED.
...WHO?!
©RAPID PHASE · 2013
MINISTER PLAUSIBLE! ...PLAUSIBLE DENIABILITY!
OH. HIM. HE WORKS FOR MAC MAHARAJ.
MOM!!

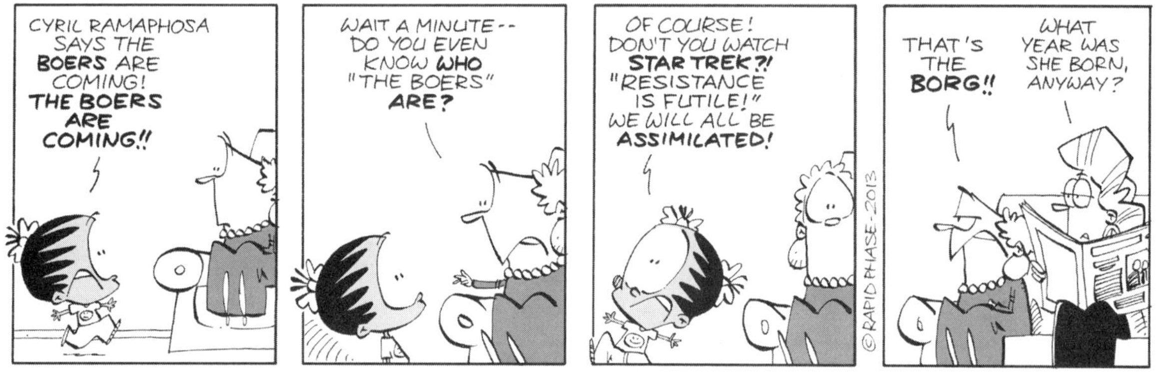
CYRIL RAMAPHOSA SAYS THE BOERS ARE COMING! THE BOERS ARE COMING!!
WAIT A MINUTE-- DO YOU EVEN KNOW WHO "THE BOERS" ARE?
OF COURSE! DON'T YOU WATCH STAR TREK?! "RESISTANCE IS FUTILE!" WE WILL ALL BE ASSIMILATED!
©RAPID PHASE · 2013
THAT'S THE BORG!!
WHAT YEAR WAS SHE BORN, ANYWAY?

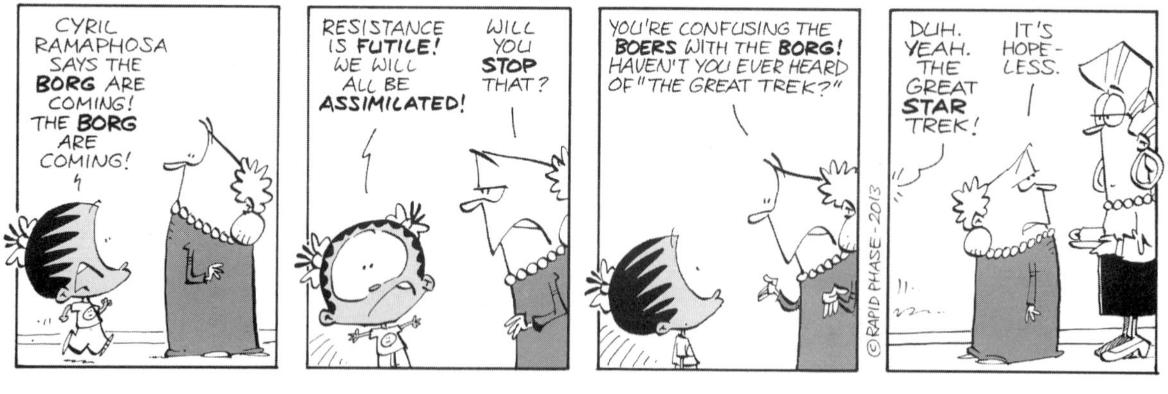
CYRIL RAMAPHOSA SAYS THE BORG ARE COMING! THE BORG ARE COMING!
RESISTANCE IS FUTILE! WE WILL ALL BE ASSIMILATED!
WILL YOU STOP THAT?
YOU'RE CONFUSING THE BOERS WITH THE BORG! HAVEN'T YOU EVER HEARD OF "THE GREAT TREK?"
©RAPID PHASE · 2013
DUH. YEAH. THE GREAT STAR TREK!
IT'S HOPE-LESS.

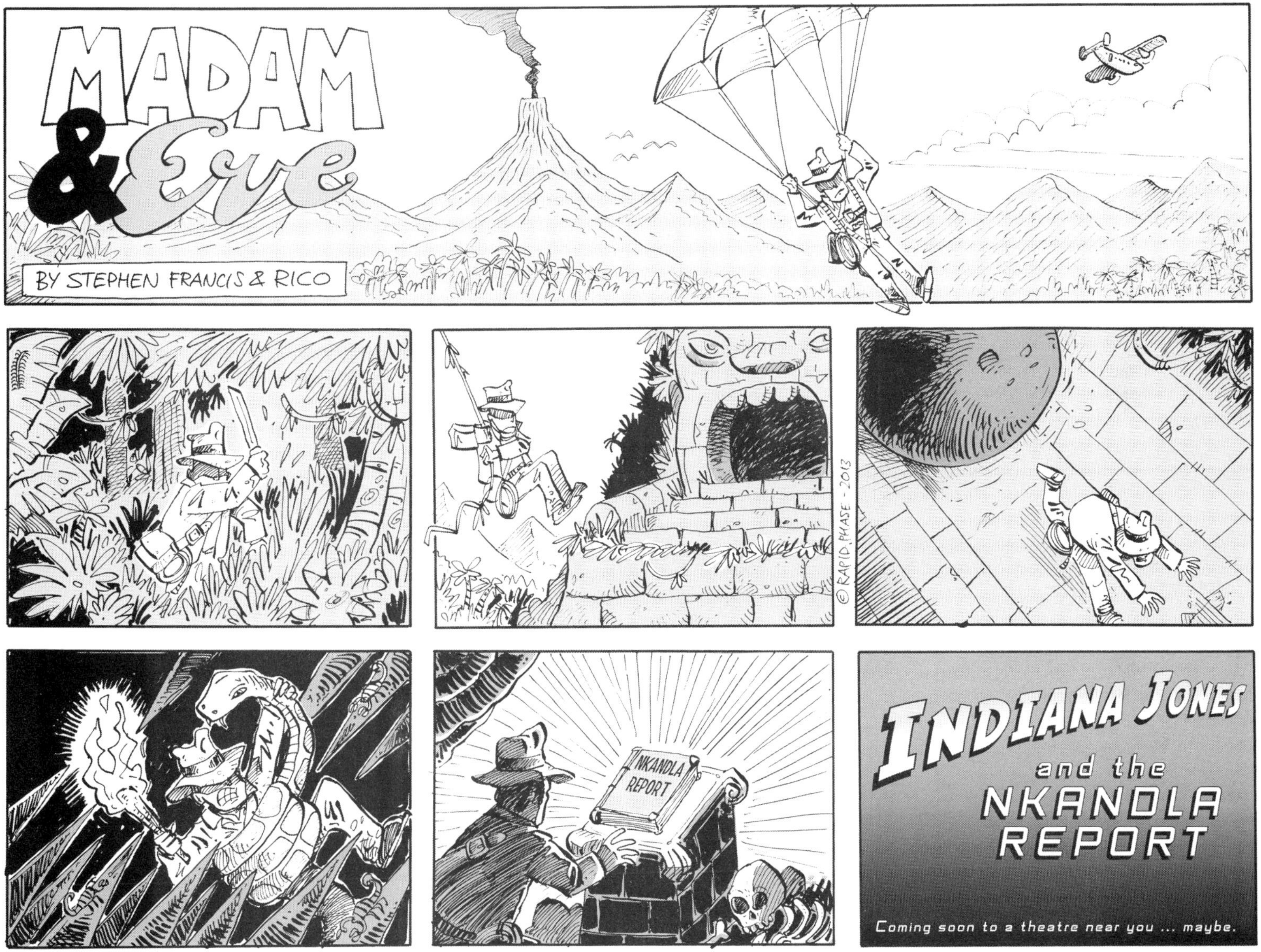
MADAM & Eve
BY STEPHEN FRANCIS & RICO
© RAPID PHASE · 2013
NKANDLA REPORT
INDIANA JONES
and the
NKANDLA
REPORT
Coming soon to a theatre near you ... maybe.

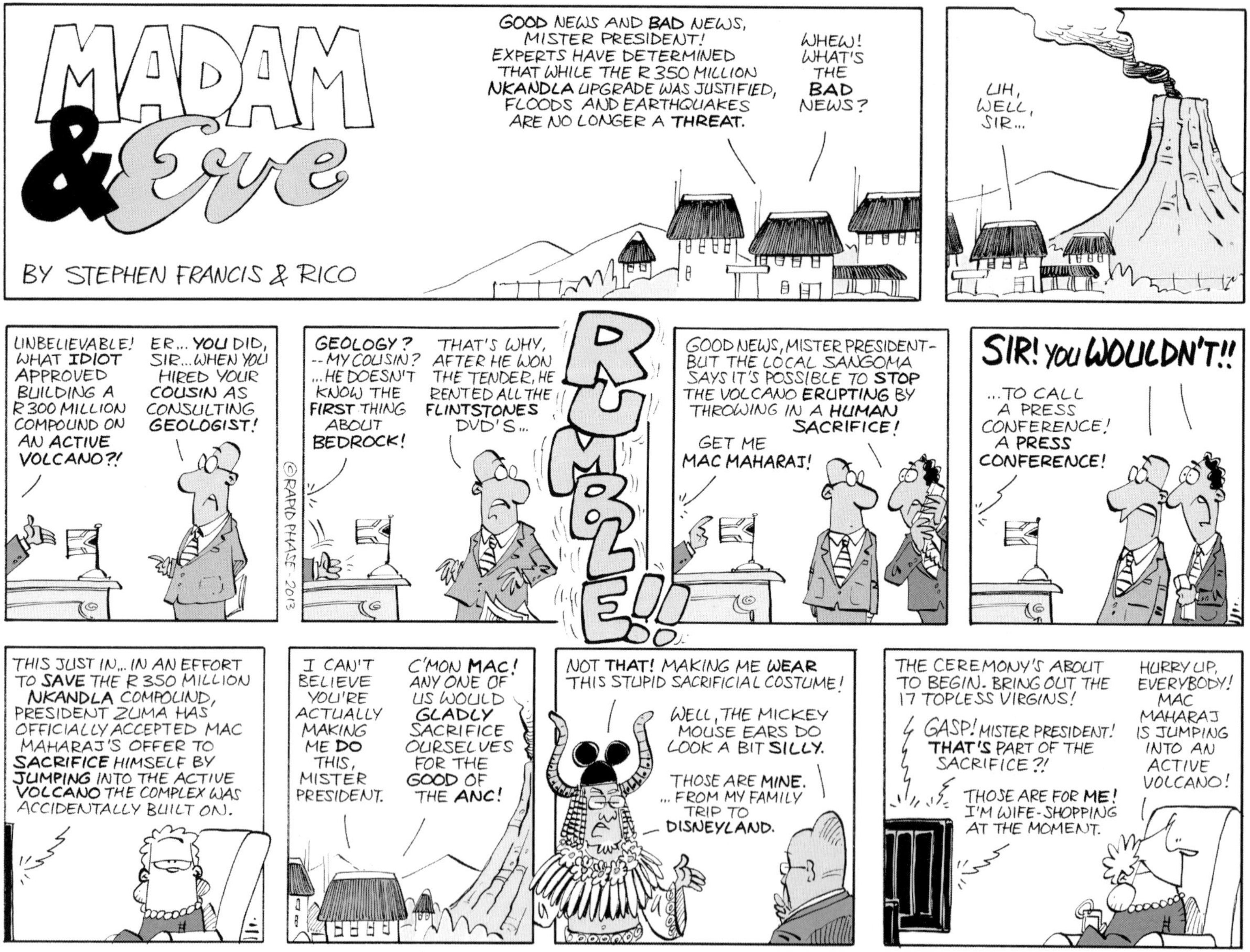
MADAM & Eve
BY STEPHEN FRANCIS & RICO
GOOD NEWS AND BAD NEWS, MISTER PRESIDENT! EXPERTS HAVE DETERMINED THAT WHILE THE R350 MILLION NKANDLA UPGRADE WAS JUSTIFIED, FLOODS AND EARTHQUAKES ARE NO LONGER A THREAT.
WHEW! WHAT'S THE BAD NEWS?
UH, WELL, SIR...
UNBELIEVABLE! WHAT IDIOT APPROVED BUILDING A R300 MILLION COMPOUND ON AN ACTIVE VOLCANO?!
ER... YOU DID, SIR... WHEN YOU HIRED YOUR COUSIN AS CONSULTING GEOLOGIST!
©RAPID PHASE - 2013
GEOLOGY? --MY COUSIN? ...HE DOESN'T KNOW THE FIRST THING ABOUT BEDROCK!
THAT'S WHY, AFTER HE WON THE TENDER, HE RENTED ALL THE FLINTSTONES DVD'S...
RUMBLE!!
GOOD NEWS, MISTER PRESIDENT- BUT THE LOCAL SANGOMA SAYS IT'S POSSIBLE TO STOP THE VOLCANO ERUPTING BY THROWING IN A HUMAN SACRIFICE!
GET ME MAC MAHARAJ!
SIR! YOU WOULDN'T!!
...TO CALL A PRESS CONFERENCE! A PRESS CONFERENCE!
THIS JUST IN... IN AN EFFORT TO SAVE THE R350 MILLION NKANDLA COMPOUND, PRESIDENT ZUMA HAS OFFICIALLY ACCEPTED MAC MAHARAJ'S OFFER TO SACRIFICE HIMSELF BY JUMPING INTO THE ACTIVE VOLCANO THE COMPLEX WAS ACCIDENTALLY BUILT ON.
I CAN'T BELIEVE YOU'RE ACTUALLY MAKING ME DO THIS, MISTER PRESIDENT.
C'MON MAC! ANY ONE OF US WOULD GLADLY SACRIFICE OURSELVES FOR THE GOOD OF THE ANC!
NOT THAT! MAKING ME WEAR THIS STUPID SACRIFICIAL COSTUME!
WELL, THE MICKEY MOUSE EARS DO LOOK A BIT SILLY.
THOSE ARE MINE. ...FROM MY FAMILY TRIP TO DISNEYLAND.
THE CEREMONY'S ABOUT TO BEGIN. BRING OUT THE 17 TOPLESS VIRGINS!
GASP! MISTER PRESIDENT! THAT'S PART OF THE SACRIFICE?!
THOSE ARE FOR ME! I'M WIFE-SHOPPING AT THE MOMENT.
HURRY UP, EVERYBODY! MAC MAHARAJ IS JUMPING INTO AN ACTIVE VOLCANO!

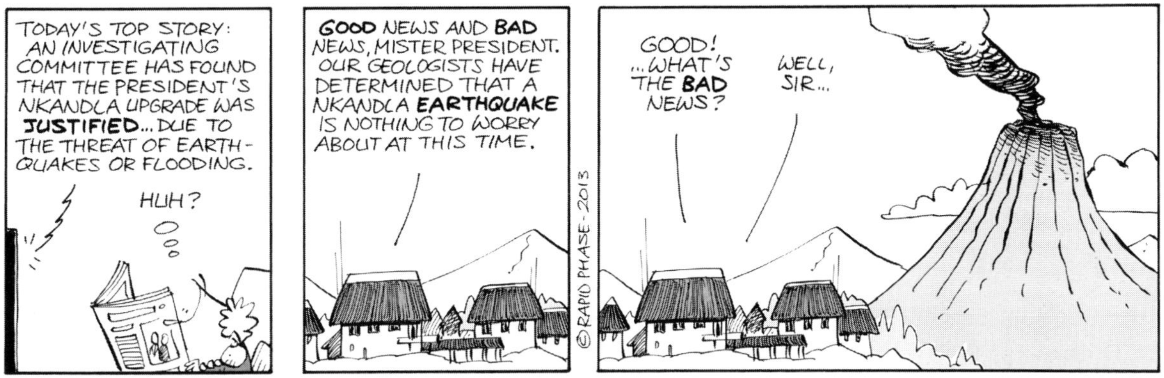
TODAY'S TOP STORY: AN INVESTIGATING COMMITTEE HAS FOUND THAT THE PRESIDENT'S NKANDLA UPGRADE WAS JUSTIFIED... DUE TO THE THREAT OF EARTH-QUAKES OR FLOODING.
HUH?
GOOD NEWS AND BAD NEWS, MISTER PRESIDENT. OUR GEOLOGISTS HAVE DETERMINED THAT A NKANDLA EARTHQUAKE IS NOTHING TO WORRY ABOUT AT THIS TIME.
©RAPID PHASE-2013
GOOD! ...WHAT'S THE BAD NEWS?
WELL, SIR...

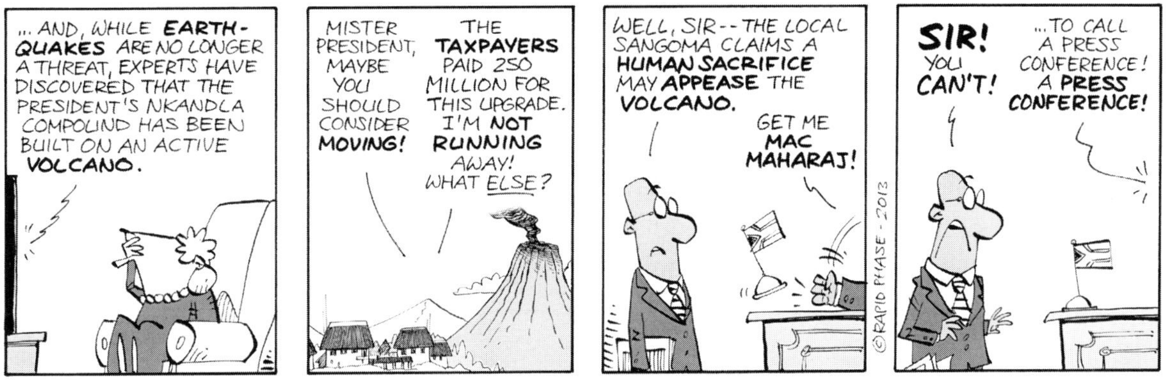
... AND, WHILE EARTH-QUAKES ARE NO LONGER A THREAT, EXPERTS HAVE DISCOVERED THAT THE PRESIDENT'S NKANDLA COMPOUND HAS BEEN BUILT ON AN ACTIVE VOLCANO.
MISTER PRESIDENT, MAYBE YOU SHOULD CONSIDER MOVING!
THE TAXPAYERS PAID 250 MILLION FOR THIS UPGRADE. I'M NOT RUNNING AWAY! WHAT ELSE?
WELL, SIR-- THE LOCAL SANGOMA CLAIMS A HUMAN SACRIFICE MAY APPEASE THE VOLCANO.
GET ME MAC MAHARAJ!
©RAPID PHASE-2013
SIR! YOU CAN'T!
...TO CALL A PRESS CONFERENCE! A PRESS CONFERENCE!

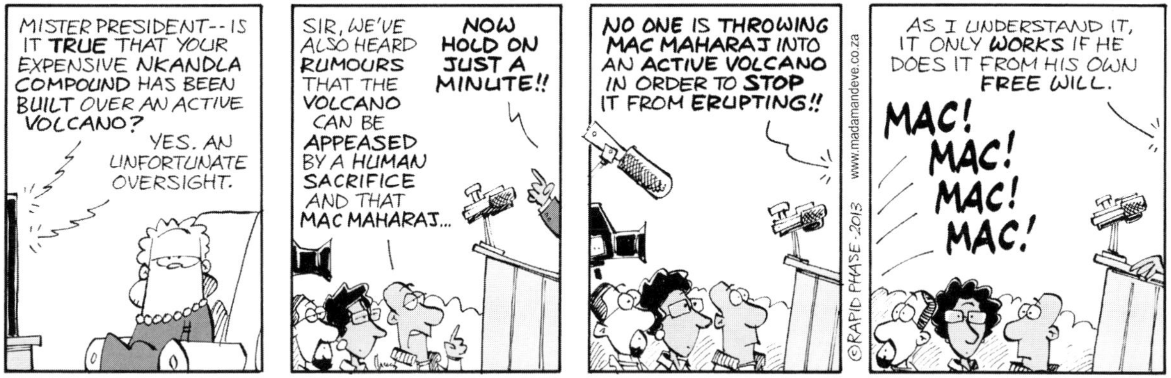
MISTER PRESIDENT-- IS IT TRUE THAT YOUR EXPENSIVE NKANDLA COMPOUND HAS BEEN BUILT OVER AN ACTIVE VOLCANO?
YES. AN UNFORTUNATE OVERSIGHT.
SIR, WE'VE ALSO HEARD RUMOURS THAT THE VOLCANO CAN BE APPEASED BY A HUMAN SACRIFICE AND THAT MAC MAHARAJ...
NOW HOLD ON JUST A MINUTE!!
NO ONE IS THROWING MAC MAHARAJ INTO AN ACTIVE VOLCANO IN ORDER TO STOP IT FROM ERUPTING!!
©RAPID PHASE-2013 www.madamandeve.co.za
AS I UNDERSTAND IT, IT ONLY WORKS IF HE DOES IT FROM HIS OWN FREE WILL.
MAC! MAC! MAC! MAC!

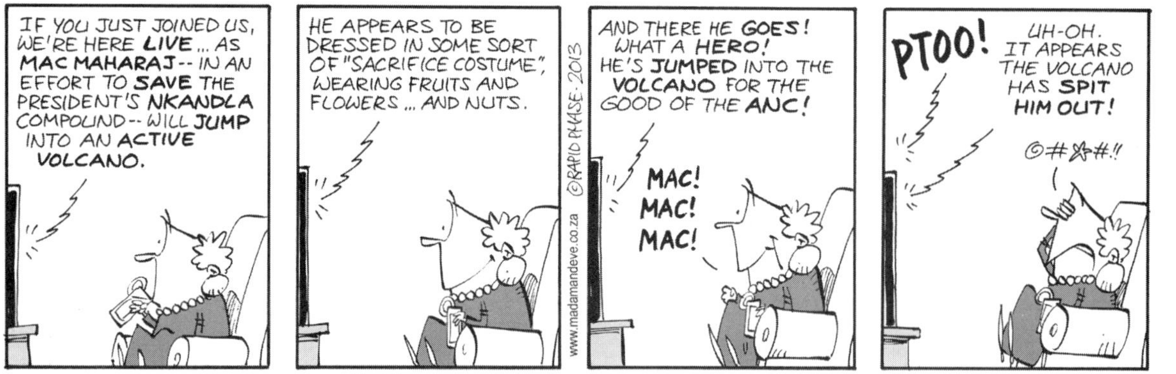
IF YOU JUST JOINED US, WE'RE HERE **LIVE** ... AS **MAC MAHARAJ** -- IN AN EFFORT TO **SAVE** THE PRESIDENT'S **NKANDLA** COMPOUND -- WILL **JUMP** INTO AN **ACTIVE VOLCANO**.
HE APPEARS TO BE DRESSED IN SOME SORT OF "SACRIFICE COSTUME", WEARING FRUITS AND FLOWERS ... AND NUTS.
©RAPID PHASE · 2013
www.madamandeve.co.za
AND THERE HE **GOES**! WHAT A **HERO**! HE'S **JUMPED** INTO THE **VOLCANO** FOR THE GOOD OF THE **ANC**!
MAC! MAC! MAC!
PTOO!
UH-OH. IT APPEARS THE VOLCANO HAS **SPIT HIM OUT**!
©#✲#!!

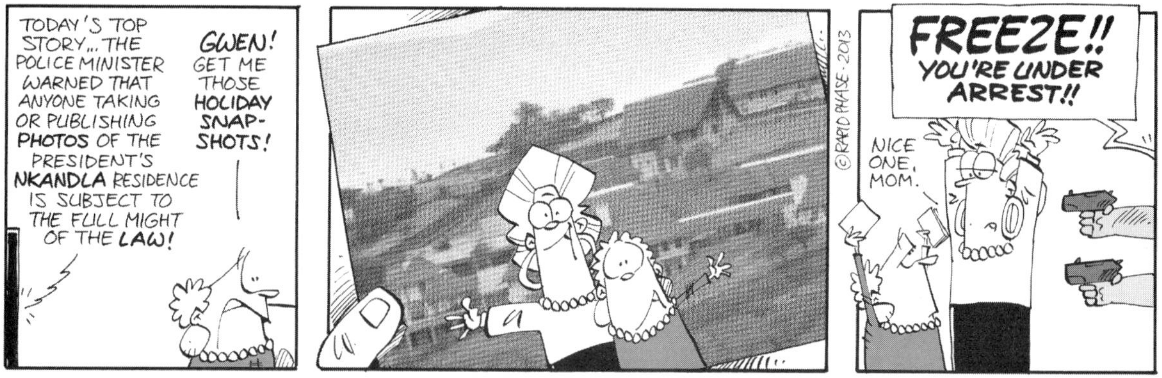
TODAY'S TOP STORY... THE POLICE MINISTER WARNED THAT ANYONE TAKING OR PUBLISHING **PHOTOS** OF THE PRESIDENT'S **NKANDLA** RESIDENCE IS SUBJECT TO THE FULL MIGHT OF THE **LAW**!
GWEN! GET ME THOSE **HOLIDAY SNAP-SHOTS**!
©RAPID PHASE · 2013
FREEZE!! **YOU'RE UNDER ARREST!!**
NICE ONE, MOM.

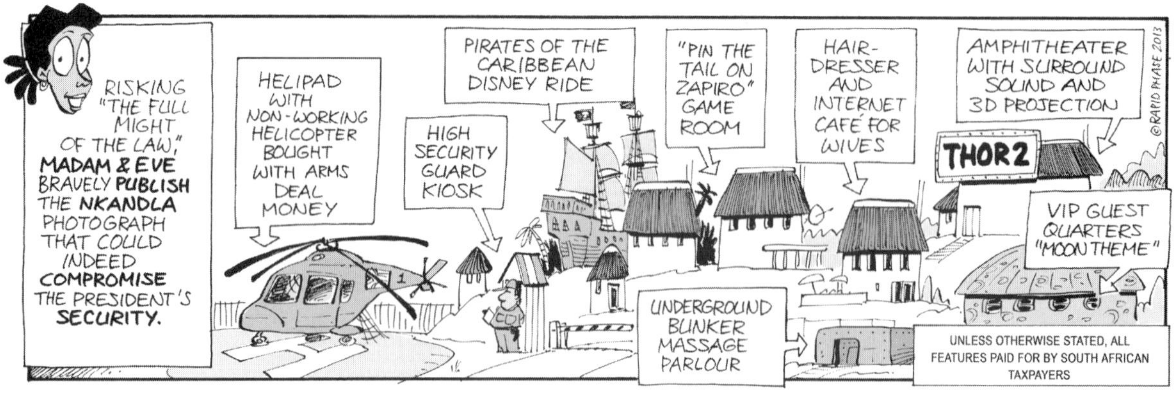
RISKING "THE FULL MIGHT OF THE LAW," **MADAM & EVE** BRAVELY **PUBLISH** THE **NKANDLA** PHOTOGRAPH THAT COULD INDEED **COMPROMISE** THE PRESIDENT'S **SECURITY**.
HELIPAD WITH NON-WORKING HELICOPTER BOUGHT WITH ARMS DEAL MONEY
HIGH SECURITY GUARD KIOSK
PIRATES OF THE CARIBBEAN DISNEY RIDE
"PIN THE TAIL ON ZAPIRO" GAME ROOM
HAIR-DRESSER AND INTERNET CAFÉ FOR WIVES
AMPHITHEATER WITH SURROUND SOUND AND 3D PROJECTION
©RAPID PHASE 2013
THOR 2
VIP GUEST QUARTERS "MOON THEME"
UNDERGROUND BUNKER MASSAGE PARLOUR
UNLESS OTHERWISE STATED, ALL FEATURES PAID FOR BY SOUTH AFRICAN TAXPAYERS

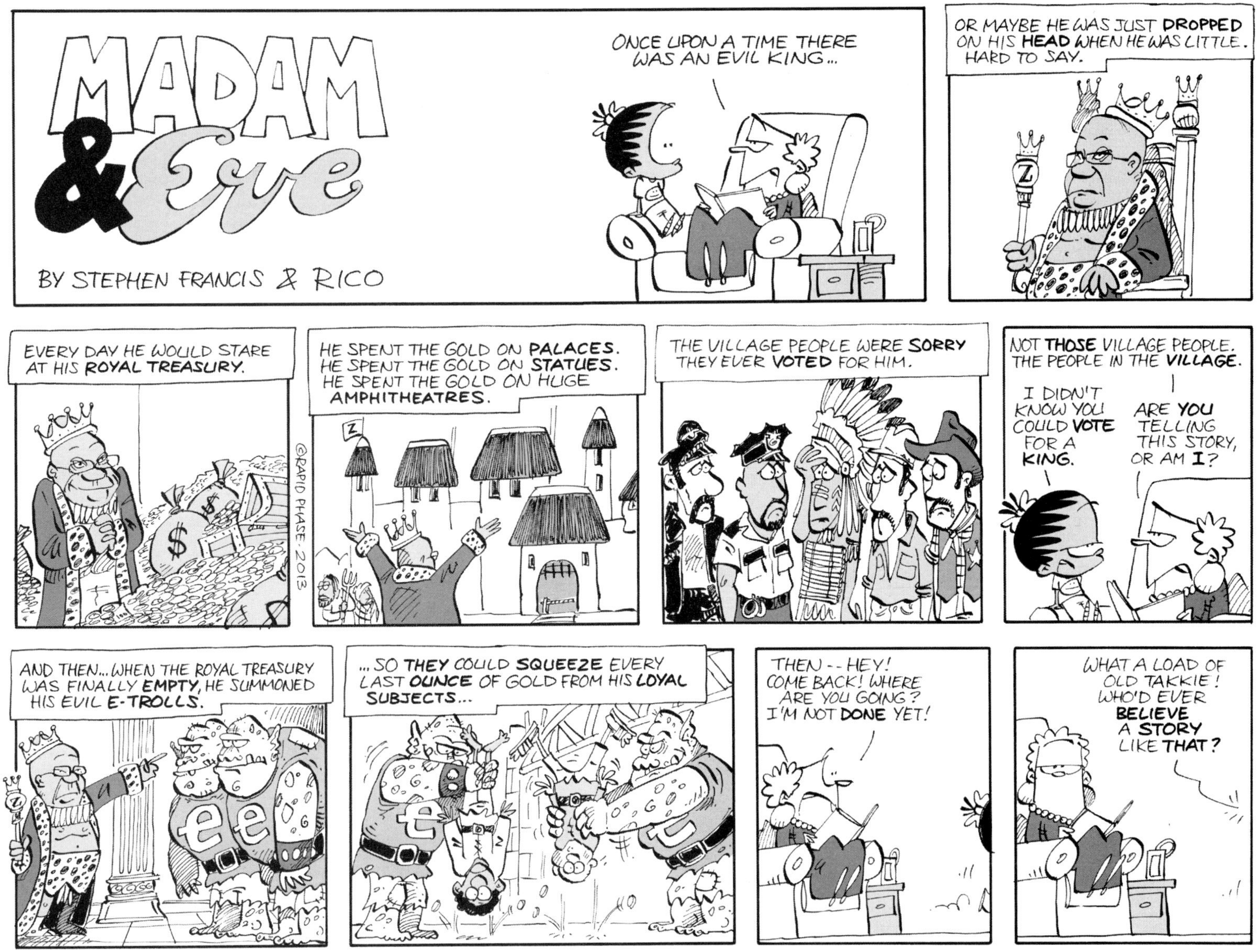
MADAM & Eve
BY STEPHEN FRANCIS & RICO
ONCE UPON A TIME THERE WAS AN EVIL KING...
OR MAYBE HE WAS JUST DROPPED ON HIS HEAD WHEN HE WAS LITTLE. HARD TO SAY.
EVERY DAY HE WOULD STARE AT HIS ROYAL TREASURY.
©RAPID PHASE 2013
HE SPENT THE GOLD ON PALACES. HE SPENT THE GOLD ON STATUES. HE SPENT THE GOLD ON HUGE AMPHITHEATRES.
THE VILLAGE PEOPLE WERE SORRY THEY EVER VOTED FOR HIM.
NOT THOSE VILLAGE PEOPLE. THE PEOPLE IN THE VILLAGE.
I DIDN'T KNOW YOU COULD VOTE FOR A KING.
ARE YOU TELLING THIS STORY, OR AM I?
AND THEN... WHEN THE ROYAL TREASURY WAS FINALLY EMPTY, HE SUMMONED HIS EVIL E-TROLLS.
...SO THEY COULD SQUEEZE EVERY LAST OUNCE OF GOLD FROM HIS LOYAL SUBJECTS...
THEN -- HEY! COME BACK! WHERE ARE YOU GOING? I'M NOT DONE YET!
WHAT A LOAD OF OLD TAKKIE! WHO'D EVER BELIEVE A STORY LIKE THAT?

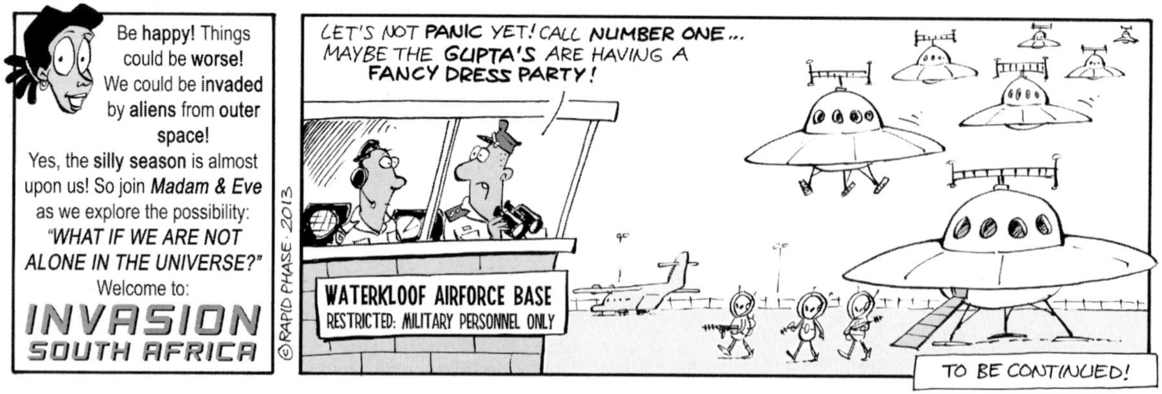
Be happy! Things could be worse! We could be invaded by aliens from outer space!
Yes, the silly season is almost upon us! So join Madam & Eve as we explore the possibility: "WHAT IF WE ARE NOT ALONE IN THE UNIVERSE?" Welcome to:
INVASION SOUTH AFRICA
©RAPID PHASE·2013
LET'S NOT PANIC YET! CALL NUMBER ONE... MAYBE THE GUPTA'S ARE HAVING A FANCY DRESS PARTY!
WATERKLOOF AIRFORCE BASE
RESTRICTED: MILITARY PERSONNEL ONLY
TO BE CONTINUED!

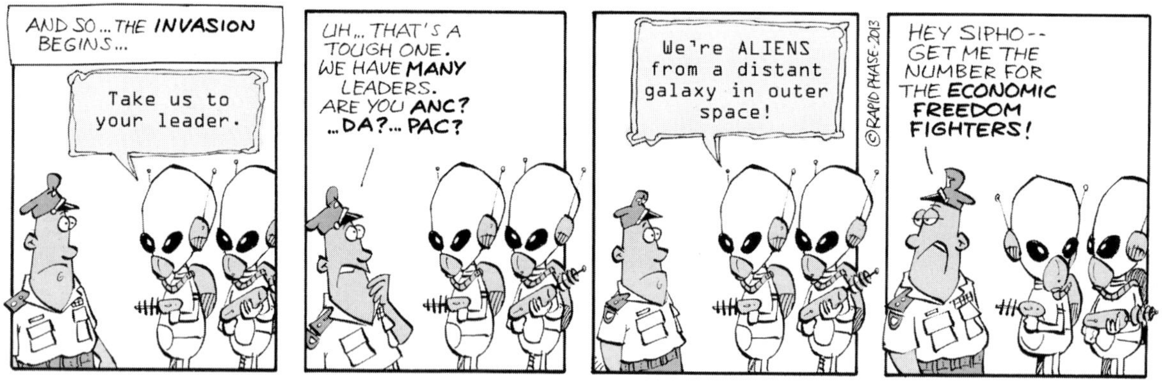
AND SO... THE INVASION BEGINS...
Take us to your leader.
UH... THAT'S A TOUGH ONE. WE HAVE MANY LEADERS. ARE YOU ANC? ...DA?... PAC?
We're ALIENS from a distant galaxy in outer space!
©RAPID PHASE·2013
HEY SIPHO-- GET ME THE NUMBER FOR THE ECONOMIC FREEDOM FIGHTERS!

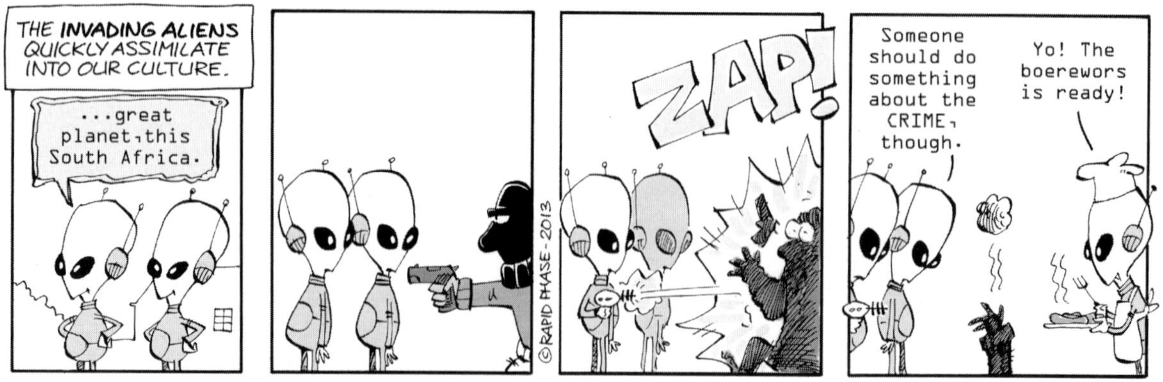
THE INVADING ALIENS QUICKLY ASSIMILATE INTO OUR CULTURE.
...great planet, this South Africa.
©RAPID PHASE·2013
ZAP!
Someone should do something about the CRIME, though.
Yo! The boerewors is ready!

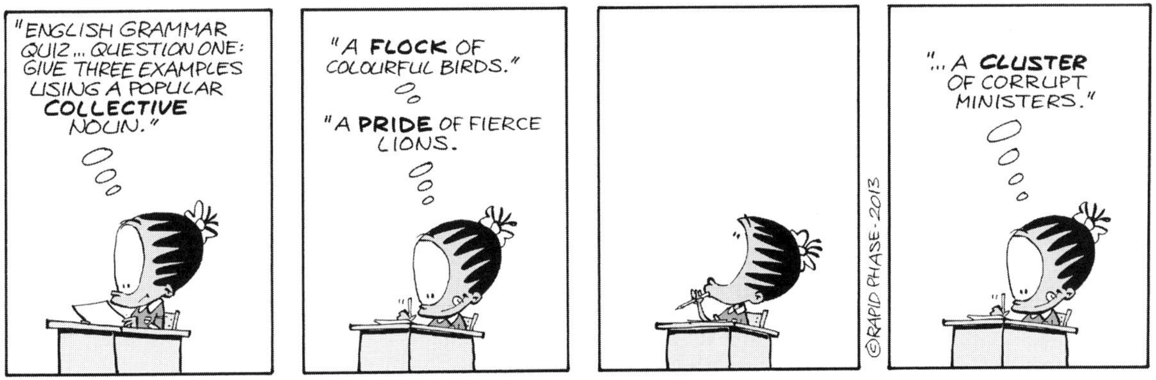
"ENGLISH GRAMMAR QUIZ... QUESTION ONE: GIVE THREE EXAMPLES USING A POPULAR COLLECTIVE NOUN."
"A FLOCK OF COLOURFUL BIRDS."
"A PRIDE OF FIERCE LIONS.
"... A CLUSTER OF CORRUPT MINISTERS."
© RAPID PHASE - 2013

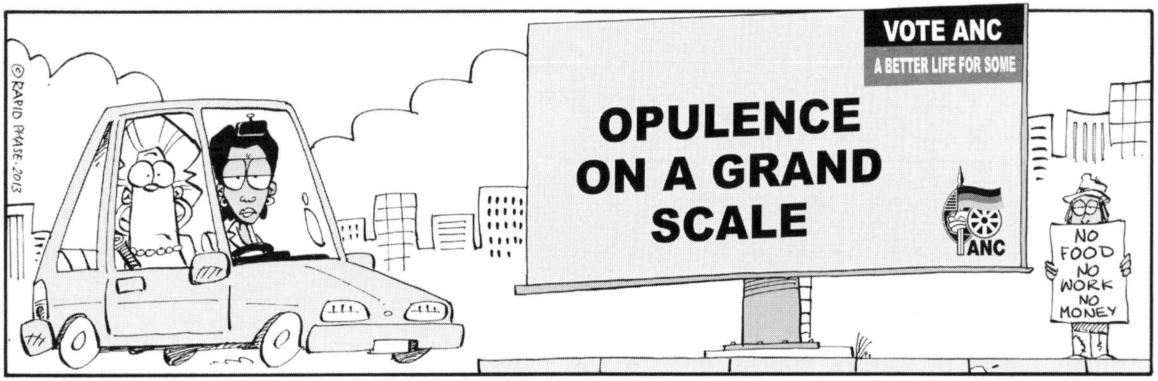
© RAPID PHASE - 2013
VOTE ANC
A BETTER LIFE FOR SOME
OPULENCE ON A GRAND SCALE
ANC
NO FOOD NO WORK NO MONEY

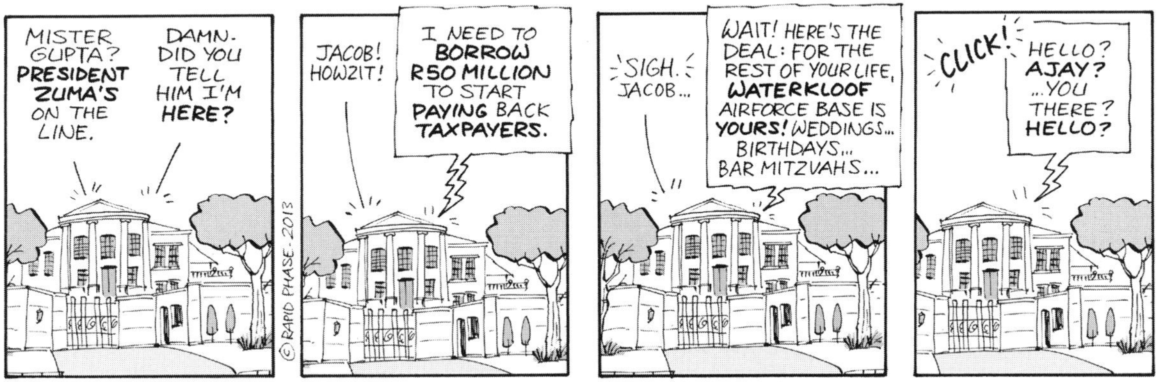
MISTER GUPTA? PRESIDENT ZUMA'S ON THE LINE.
DAMN. DID YOU TELL HIM I'M HERE?
© RAPID PHASE - 2013
JACOB! HOWZIT!
I NEED TO BORROW R50 MILLION TO START PAYING BACK TAXPAYERS.
SIGH. JACOB...
WAIT! HERE'S THE DEAL: FOR THE REST OF YOUR LIFE, WATERKLOOF AIRFORCE BASE IS YOURS! WEDDINGS... BIRTHDAYS... BAR MITZVAHS...
CLICK!
HELLO? AJAY? ...YOU THERE? HELLO?

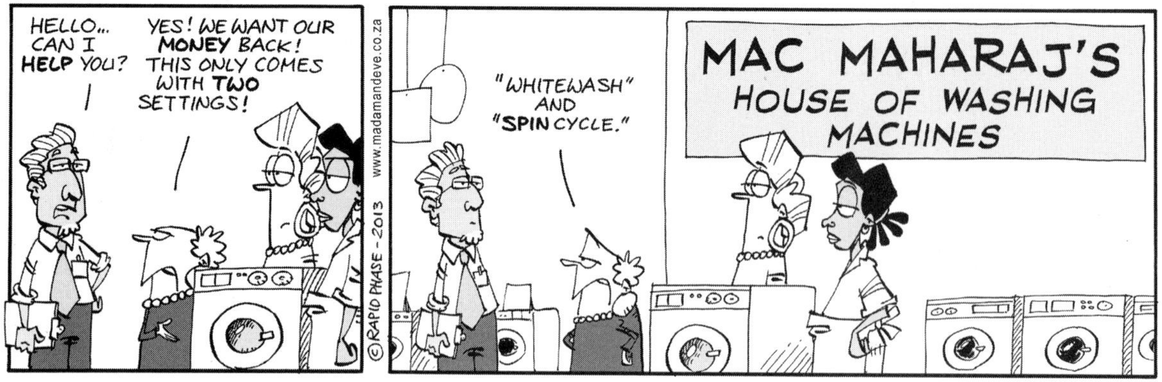
HELLO... CAN I HELP YOU?
YES! WE WANT OUR MONEY BACK! THIS ONLY COMES WITH TWO SETTINGS!
© RAPID PHASE - 2013
www.madamandeve.co.za
MAC MAHARAJ'S HOUSE OF WASHING MACHINES
"WHITEWASH" AND "SPIN CYCLE."

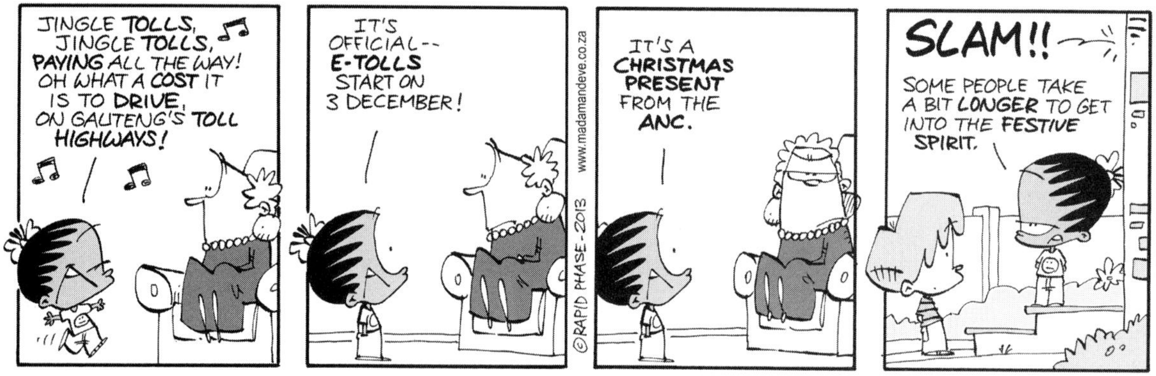
JINGLE TOLLS, JINGLE TOLLS, PAYING ALL THE WAY! OH WHAT A COST IT IS TO DRIVE, ON GAUTENG'S TOLL HIGHWAYS!
IT'S OFFICIAL -- E-TOLLS START ON 3 DECEMBER!
© RAPID PHASE - 2013
www.madamandeve.co.za
IT'S A CHRISTMAS PRESENT FROM THE ANC.
SLAM!!
SOME PEOPLE TAKE A BIT LONGER TO GET INTO THE FESTIVE SPIRIT.

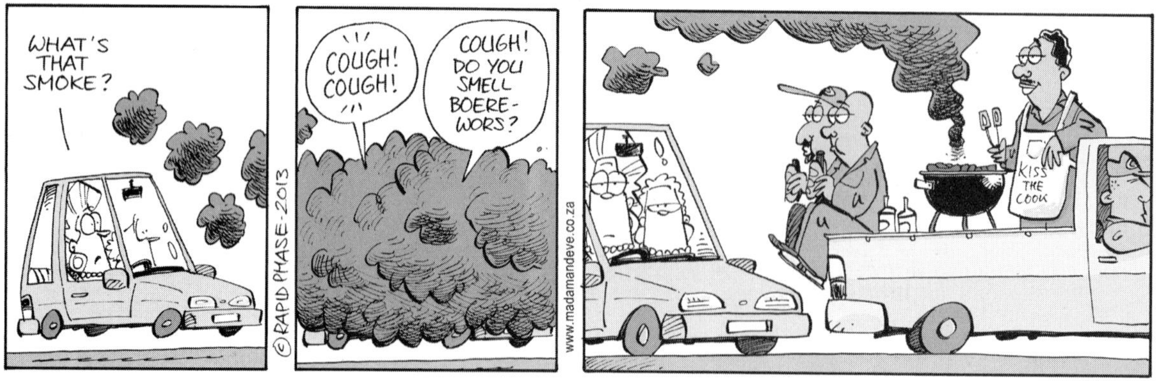
WHAT'S THAT SMOKE?
© RAPID PHASE - 2013
COUGH! COUGH!
COUGH! DO YOU SMELL BOERE-WORS?
www.madamandeve.co.za
KISS THE COOK

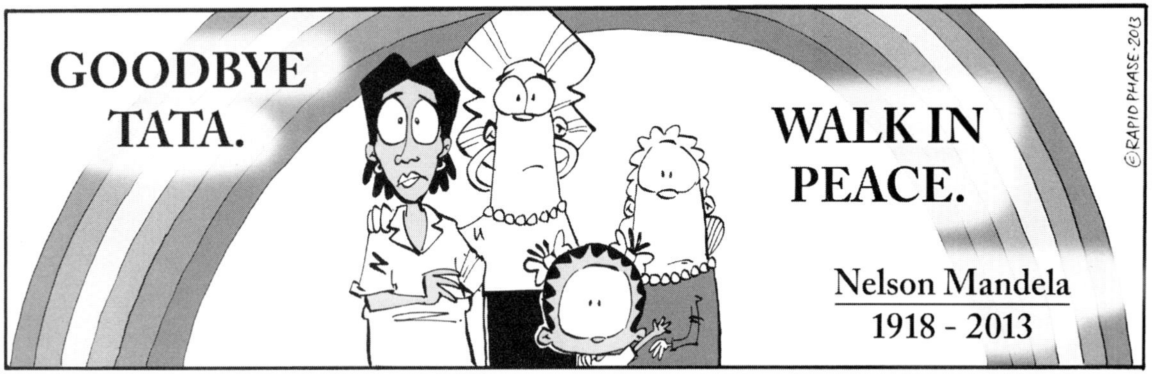
GOODBYE TATA.
WALK IN PEACE.
Nelson Mandela
1918 - 2013
©RAPID PHASE·2013

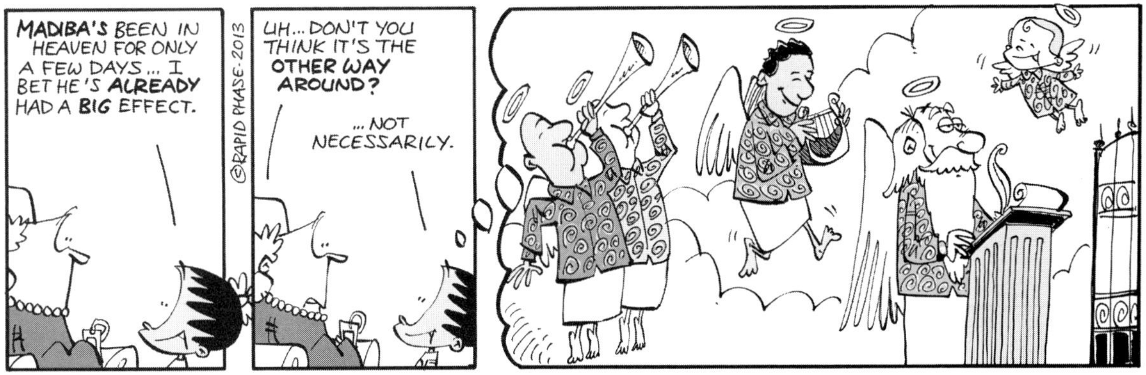
MADIBA'S BEEN IN HEAVEN FOR ONLY A FEW DAYS... I BET HE'S ALREADY HAD A BIG EFFECT.
©RAPID PHASE·2013
UH... DON'T YOU THINK IT'S THE OTHER WAY AROUND?
...NOT NECESSARILY.

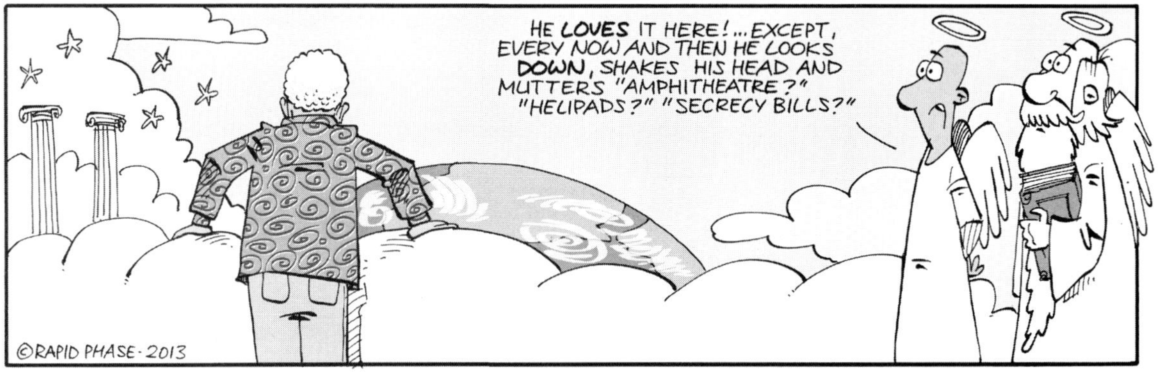
HE LOVES IT HERE! ... EXCEPT, EVERY NOW AND THEN HE LOOKS DOWN, SHAKES HIS HEAD AND MUTTERS "AMPHITHEATRE?" "HELIPADS?" "SECRECY BILLS?"
©RAPID PHASE·2013

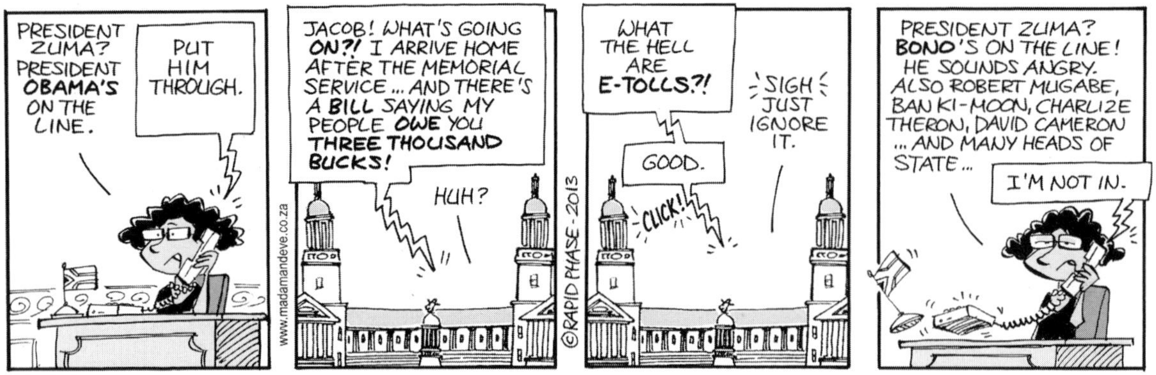
PRESIDENT ZUMA? PRESIDENT OBAMA'S ON THE LINE.
PUT HIM THROUGH.
www.madamandeve.co.za
JACOB! WHAT'S GOING ON?! I ARRIVE HOME AFTER THE MEMORIAL SERVICE ... AND THERE'S A BILL SAYING MY PEOPLE OWE YOU THREE THOUSAND BUCKS!
HUH?
©RAPID PHASE - 2013
WHAT THE HELL ARE E-TOLLS?!
GOOD.
CLICK!
SIGH JUST IGNORE IT.
PRESIDENT ZUMA? BONO'S ON THE LINE! HE SOUNDS ANGRY. ALSO ROBERT MUGABE, BAN KI-MOON, CHARLIZE THERON, DAVID CAMERON ... AND MANY HEADS OF STATE ...
I'M NOT IN.

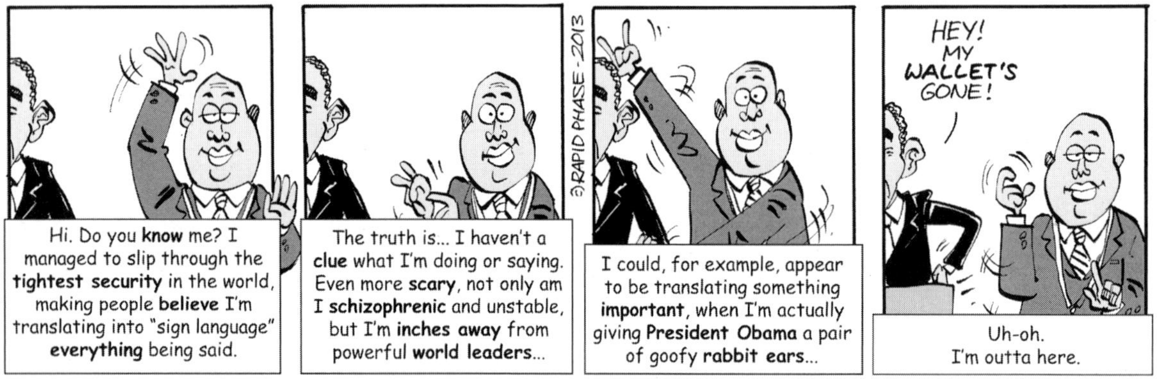
Hi. Do you know me? I managed to slip through the tightest security in the world, making people believe I'm translating into "sign language" everything being said.
The truth is... I haven't a clue what I'm doing or saying. Even more scary, not only am I schizophrenic and unstable, but I'm inches away from powerful world leaders...
©RAPID PHASE - 2013
I could, for example, appear to be translating something important, when I'm actually giving President Obama a pair of goofy rabbit ears...
HEY! MY WALLET'S GONE!
Uh-oh.
I'm outta here.

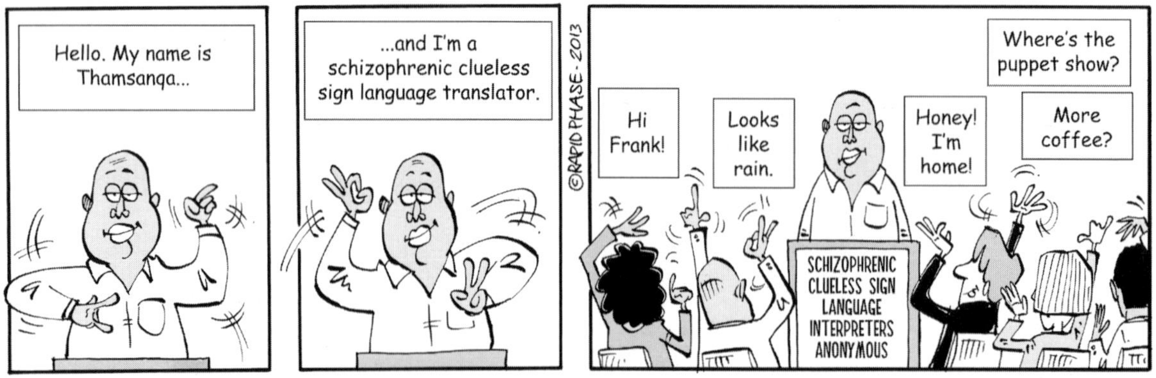
Hello. My name is Thamsanqa...
...and I'm a schizophrenic clueless sign language translator.
©RAPID PHASE - 2013
Where's the puppet show?
Hi Frank!
Looks like rain.
Honey! I'm home!
More coffee?
SCHIZOPHRENIC CLUELESS SIGN LANGUAGE INTERPRETERS ANONYMOUS

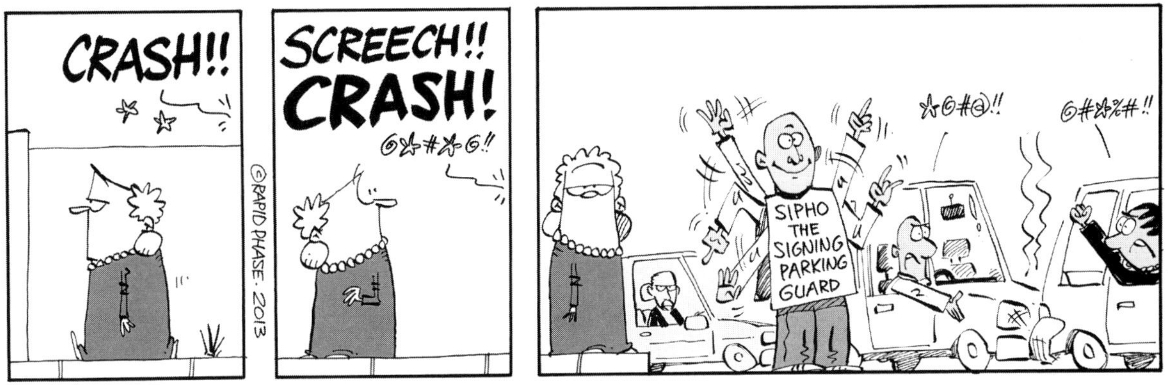
CRASH!!
SCREECH!! CRASH!
©RAPID PHASE · 2013
SIPHO THE SIGNING PARKING GUARD

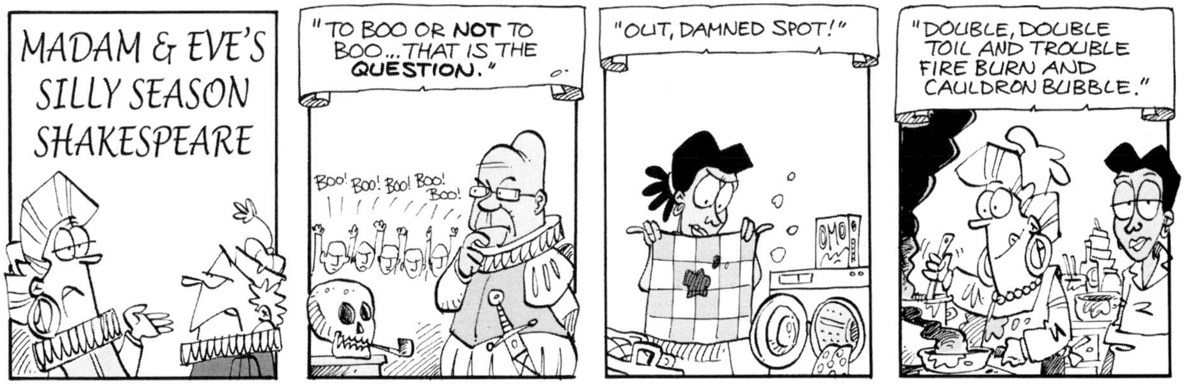
MADAM & EVE'S SILLY SEASON SHAKESPEARE
"TO BOO OR NOT TO BOO... THAT IS THE QUESTION."
BOO! BOO! BOO! BOO! BOO!
"OUT, DAMNED SPOT!"
OMO
"DOUBLE, DOUBLE TOIL AND TROUBLE FIRE BURN AND CAULDRON BUBBLE."

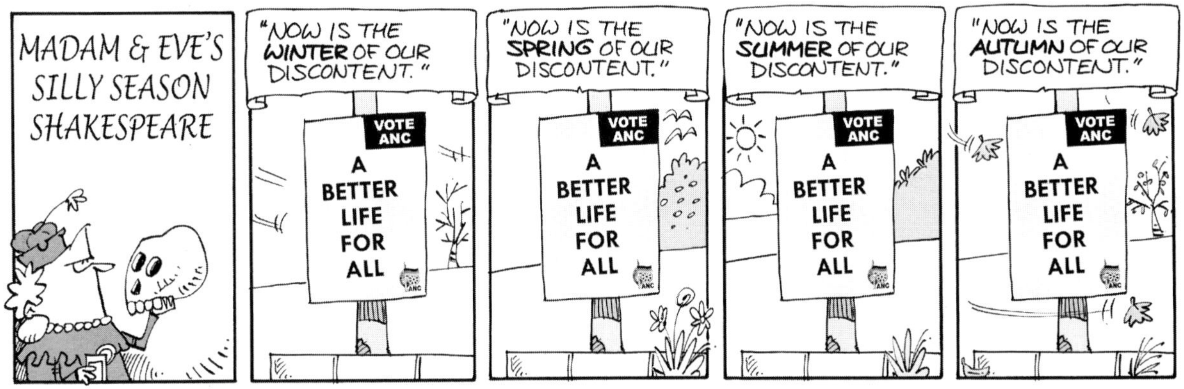
MADAM & EVE'S SILLY SEASON SHAKESPEARE
"NOW IS THE WINTER OF OUR DISCONTENT."
VOTE ANC
A BETTER LIFE FOR ALL
"NOW IS THE SPRING OF OUR DISCONTENT."
VOTE ANC
A BETTER LIFE FOR ALL
"NOW IS THE SUMMER OF OUR DISCONTENT."
VOTE ANC
A BETTER LIFE FOR ALL
"NOW IS THE AUTUMN OF OUR DISCONTENT."
VOTE ANC
A BETTER LIFE FOR ALL

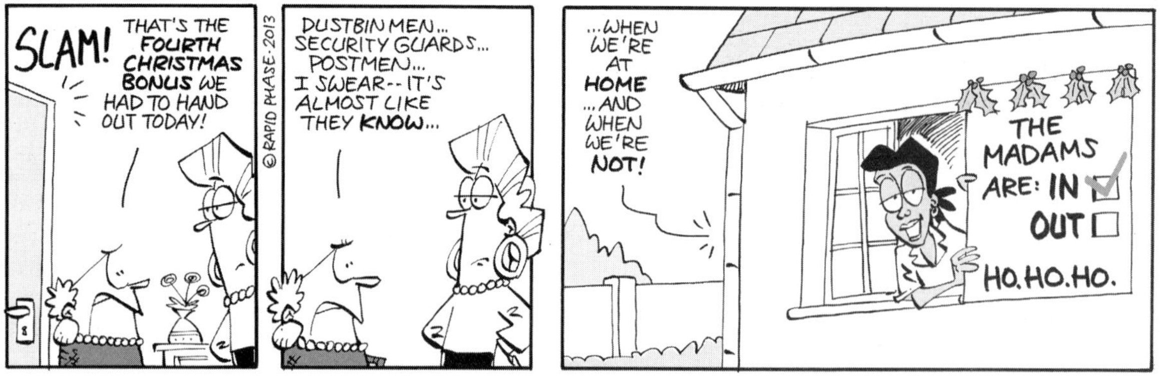
SLAM!
THAT'S THE FOURTH CHRISTMAS BONUS WE HAD TO HAND OUT TODAY!
©RAPID PHASE-2013
DUSTBIN MEN... SECURITY GUARDS... POSTMEN... I SWEAR-- IT'S ALMOST LIKE THEY KNOW...
...WHEN WE'RE AT HOME ...AND WHEN WE'RE NOT!
THE MADAMS ARE: IN
OUT
HO.HO.HO.

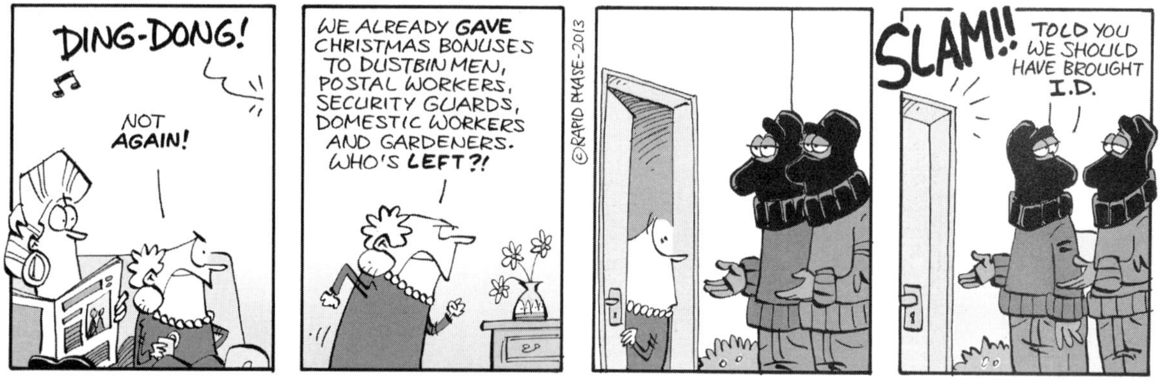
DING-DONG!
NOT AGAIN!
WE ALREADY GAVE CHRISTMAS BONUSES TO DUSTBIN MEN, POSTAL WORKERS, SECURITY GUARDS, DOMESTIC WORKERS AND GARDENERS. WHO'S LEFT?!
©RAPID PHASE-2013
SLAM!!
TOLD YOU WE SHOULD HAVE BROUGHT I.D.

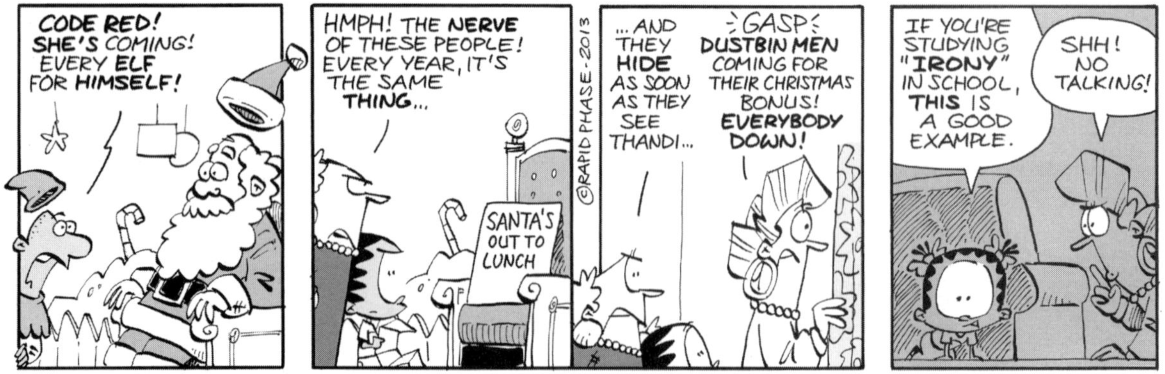
CODE RED! SHE'S COMING! EVERY ELF FOR HIMSELF!
HMPH! THE NERVE OF THESE PEOPLE! EVERY YEAR, IT'S THE SAME THING...
SANTA'S OUT TO LUNCH
©RAPID PHASE-2013
...AND THEY HIDE AS SOON AS THEY SEE THANDI...
GASP
DUSTBIN MEN COMING FOR THEIR CHRISTMAS BONUS! EVERYBODY DOWN!
IF YOU'RE STUDYING "IRONY" IN SCHOOL, THIS IS A GOOD EXAMPLE.
SHH! NO TALKING!

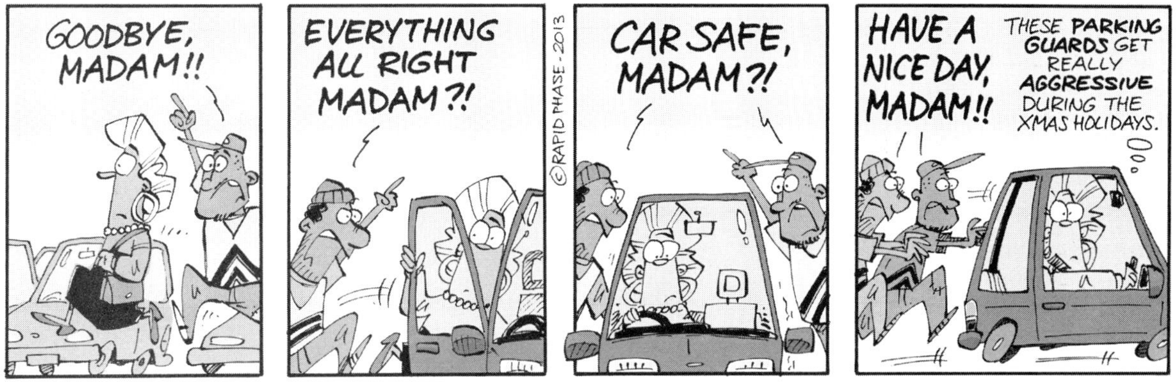
GOODBYE, MADAM!!
EVERYTHING ALL RIGHT MADAM?!
©RAPID PHASE - 2013
CAR SAFE, MADAM?!
HAVE A NICE DAY, MADAM!!
THESE PARKING GUARDS GET REALLY AGGRESSIVE DURING THE XMAS HOLIDAYS.

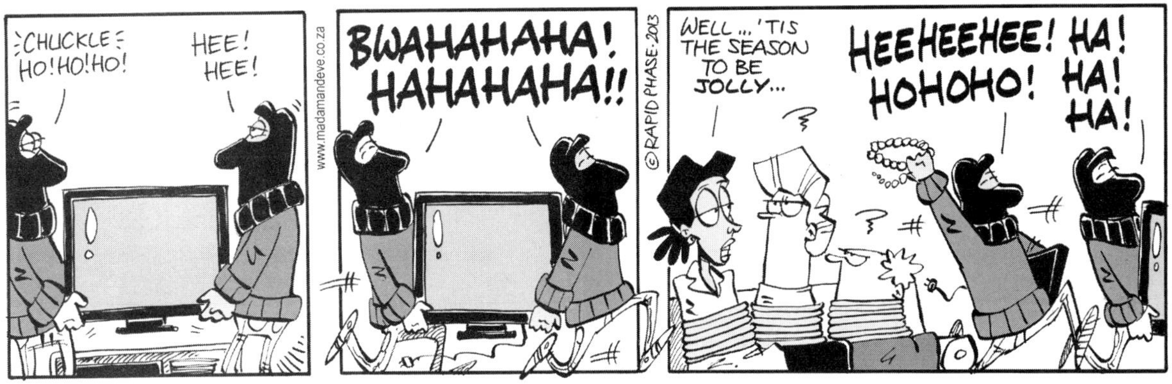
CHUCKLE HO!HO!HO!
HEE! HEE!
www.madamandeve.co.za
BWAHAHAHA! HAHAHAHA!!
©RAPID PHASE. 2013
WELL... 'TIS THE SEASON TO BE JOLLY...
HEEHEEHEE! HOHOHO!
HA! HA! HA!

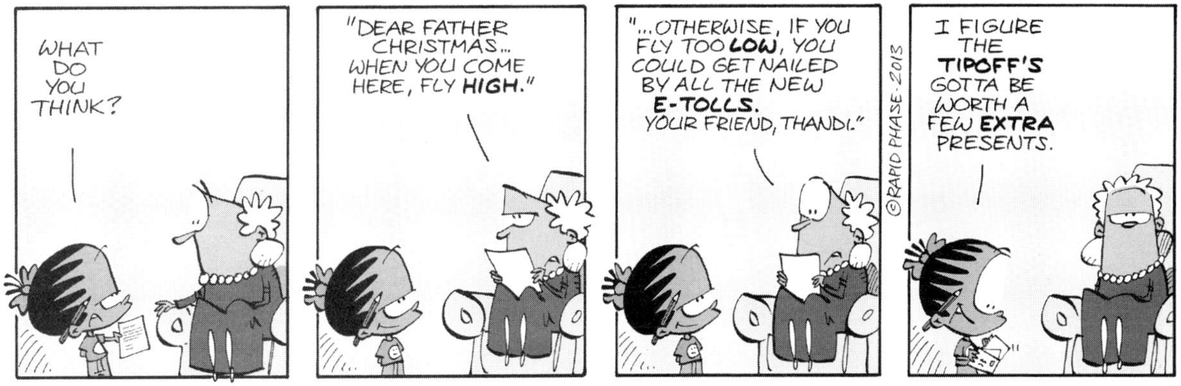
WHAT DO YOU THINK?
"DEAR FATHER CHRISTMAS... WHEN YOU COME HERE, FLY HIGH."
"...OTHERWISE, IF YOU FLY TOO LOW, YOU COULD GET NAILED BY ALL THE NEW E-TOLLS. YOUR FRIEND, THANDI."
©RAPID PHASE · 2013
I FIGURE THE TIPOFF'S GOTTA BE WORTH A FEW EXTRA PRESENTS.

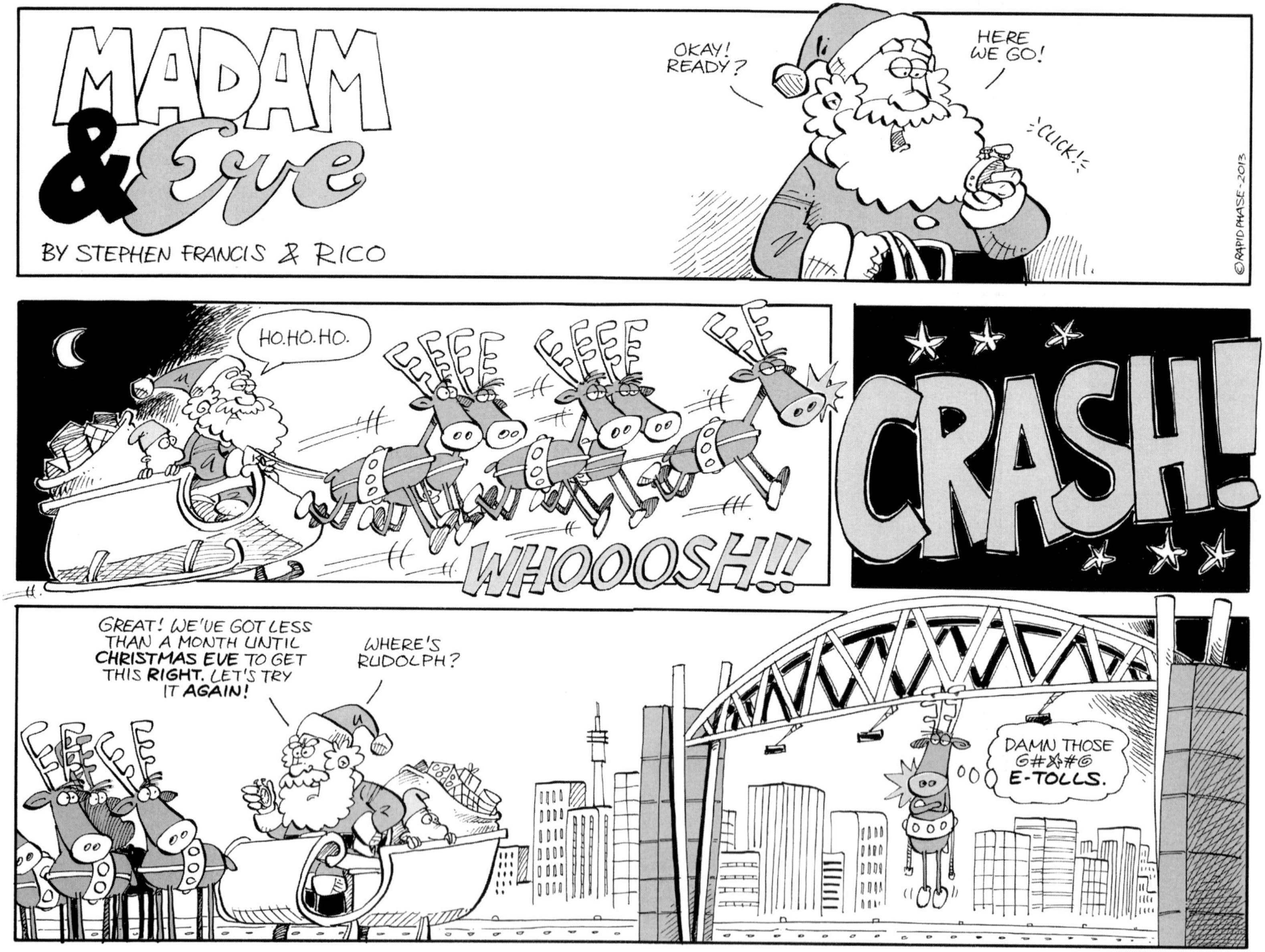
MADAM & Eve
BY STEPHEN FRANCIS & RICO
OKAY! READY?
HERE WE GO!
CLICK!
©RAPID PHASE · 2013
HO.HO.HO.
WHOOOSH!!
CRASH!
GREAT! WE'VE GOT LESS THAN A MONTH UNTIL CHRISTMAS EVE TO GET THIS RIGHT. LET'S TRY IT AGAIN!
WHERE'S RUDOLPH?
DAMN THOSE @#*#@ E-TOLLS.

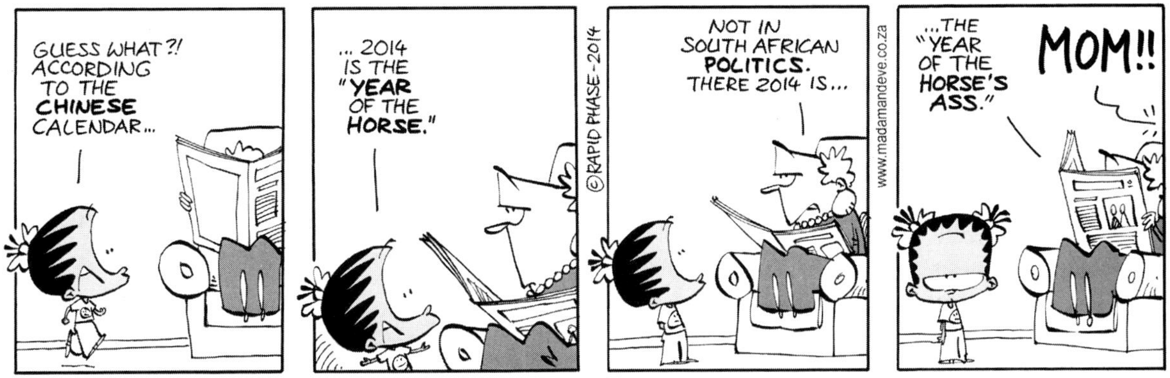
GUESS WHAT?! ACCORDING TO THE CHINESE CALENDAR...
... 2014 IS THE "YEAR OF THE HORSE."
©RAPID PHASE - 2014
NOT IN SOUTH AFRICAN POLITICS. THERE 2014 IS...
www.madamandeve.co.za
...THE "YEAR OF THE HORSE'S ASS."
MOM!!

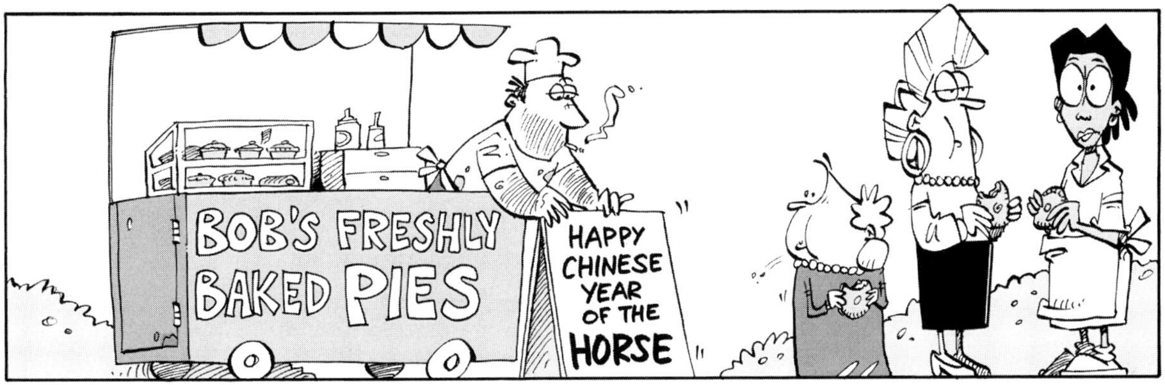
BOB'S FRESHLY BAKED PIES
HAPPY CHINESE YEAR OF THE HORSE

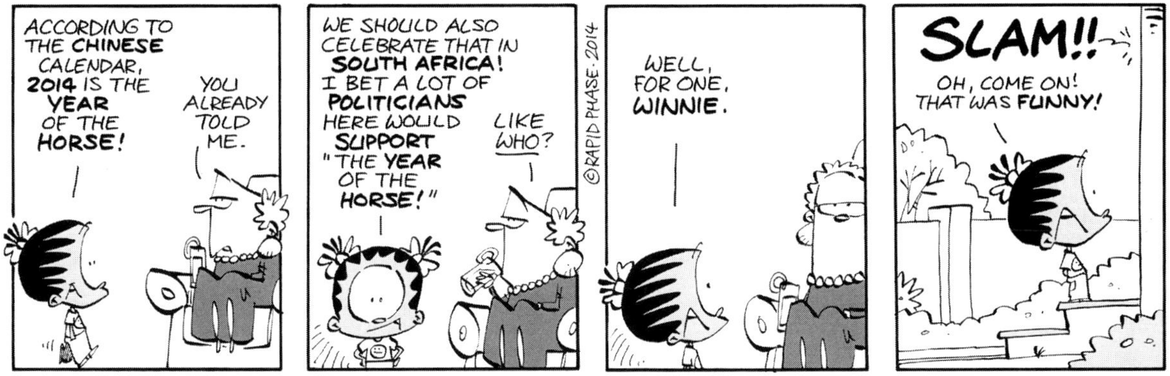
ACCORDING TO THE CHINESE CALENDAR, 2014 IS THE YEAR OF THE HORSE!
YOU ALREADY TOLD ME.
WE SHOULD ALSO CELEBRATE THAT IN SOUTH AFRICA! I BET A LOT OF POLITICIANS HERE WOULD SUPPORT "THE YEAR OF THE HORSE!"
LIKE WHO?
©RAPID PHASE · 2014
WELL, FOR ONE, WINNIE.
SLAM!!
OH, COME ON! THAT WAS FUNNY!

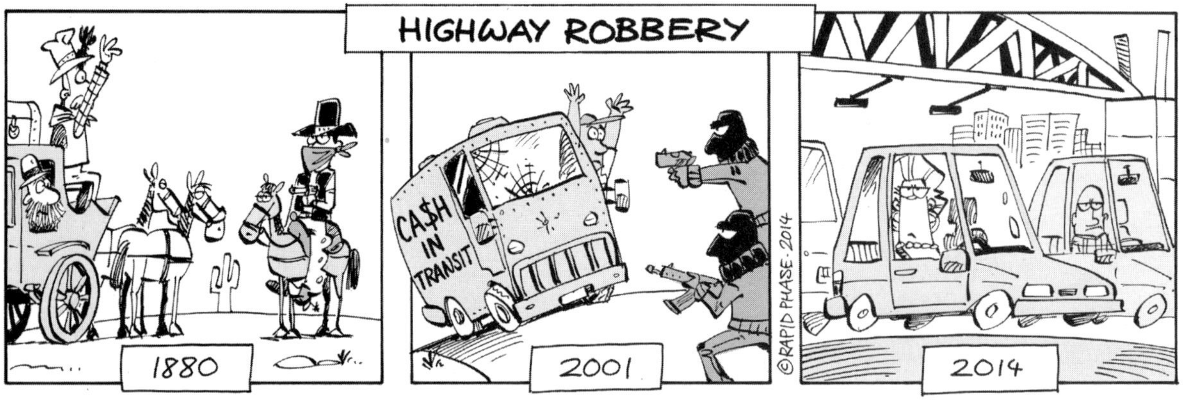
HIGHWAY ROBBERY
1880
CA$H IN TRANSIT
2001
©RAPID PHASE · 2014
2014

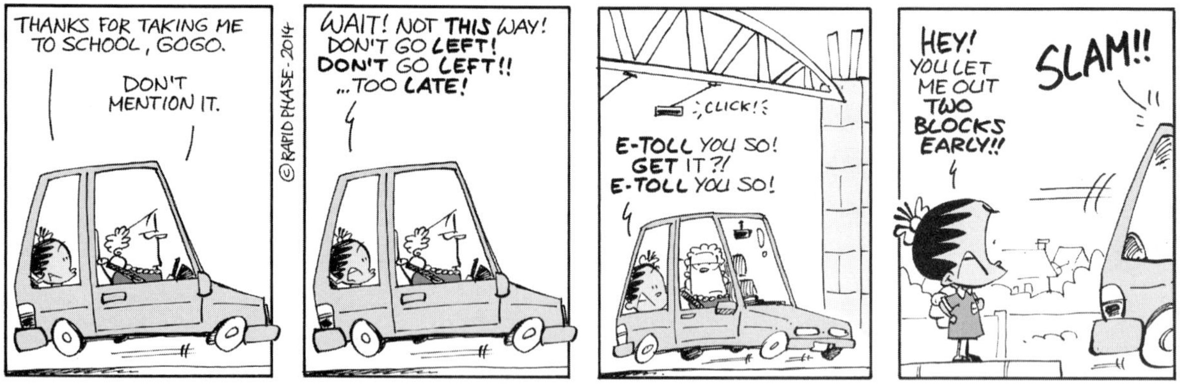
THANKS FOR TAKING ME TO SCHOOL, GOGO.
DON'T MENTION IT.
©RAPID PHASE · 2014
WAIT! NOT THIS WAY! DON'T GO LEFT! DON'T GO LEFT!! ...TOO LATE!
CLICK!
E-TOLL YOU SO! GET IT?! E-TOLL YOU SO!
HEY! YOU LET ME OUT TWO BLOCKS EARLY!!
SLAM!!

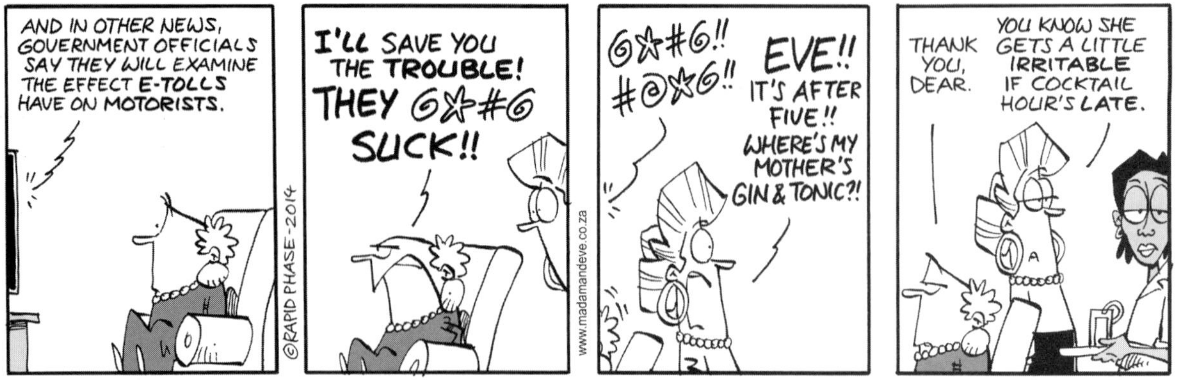
AND IN OTHER NEWS, GOVERNMENT OFFICIALS SAY THEY WILL EXAMINE THE EFFECT E-TOLLS HAVE ON MOTORISTS.
©RAPID PHASE · 2014
I'LL SAVE YOU THE TROUBLE! THEY 6☆#6 SUCK!!
www.madamandeve.co.za
6☆#6!! #@☆6!!
EVE!! IT'S AFTER FIVE!! WHERE'S MY MOTHER'S GIN & TONIC?!
THANK YOU, DEAR.
YOU KNOW SHE GETS A LITTLE IRRITABLE IF COCKTAIL HOUR'S LATE.

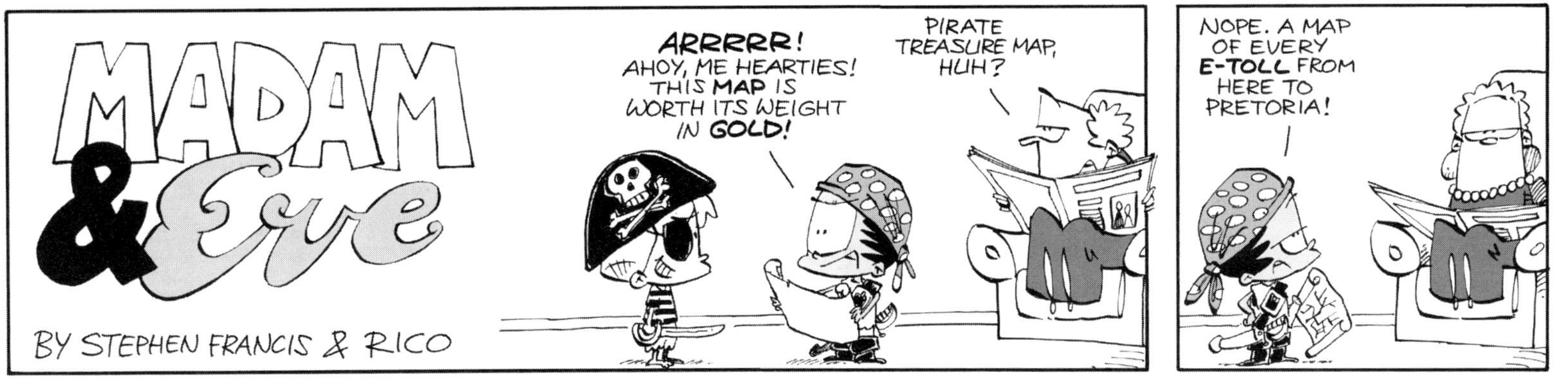
MADAM & Eve
BY STEPHEN FRANCIS & RICO
ARRRRR! AHOY, ME HEARTIES! THIS MAP IS WORTH ITS WEIGHT IN GOLD!
PIRATE TREASURE MAP, HUH?
NOPE. A MAP OF EVERY E-TOLL FROM HERE TO PRETORIA!

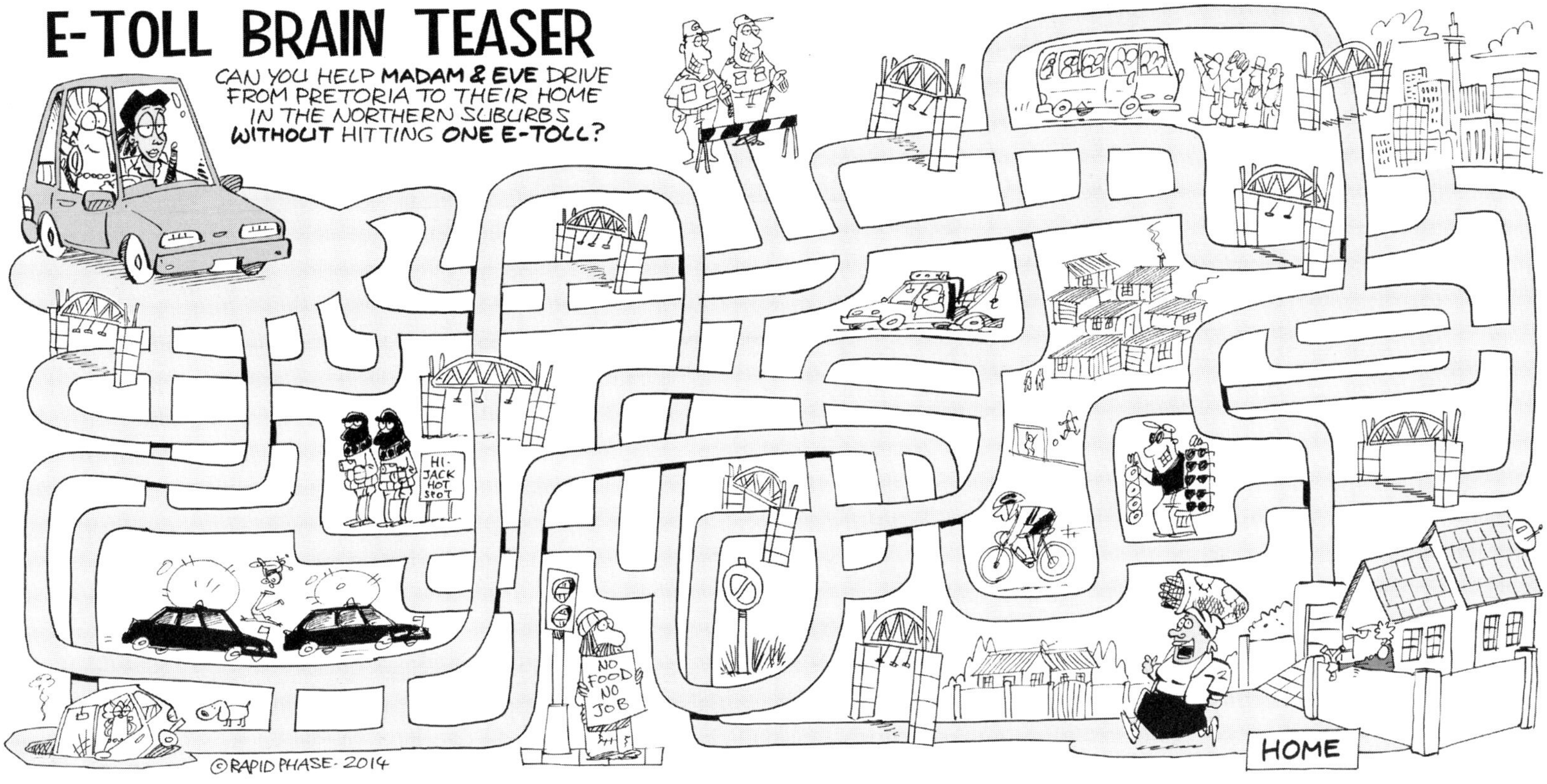
E-TOLL BRAIN TEASER
CAN YOU HELP MADAM & EVE DRIVE FROM PRETORIA TO THEIR HOME IN THE NORTHERN SUBURBS WITHOUT HITTING ONE E-TOLL?
HI-JACK HOT SPOT
NO FOOD NO JOB
HOME
©RAPID PHASE·2014

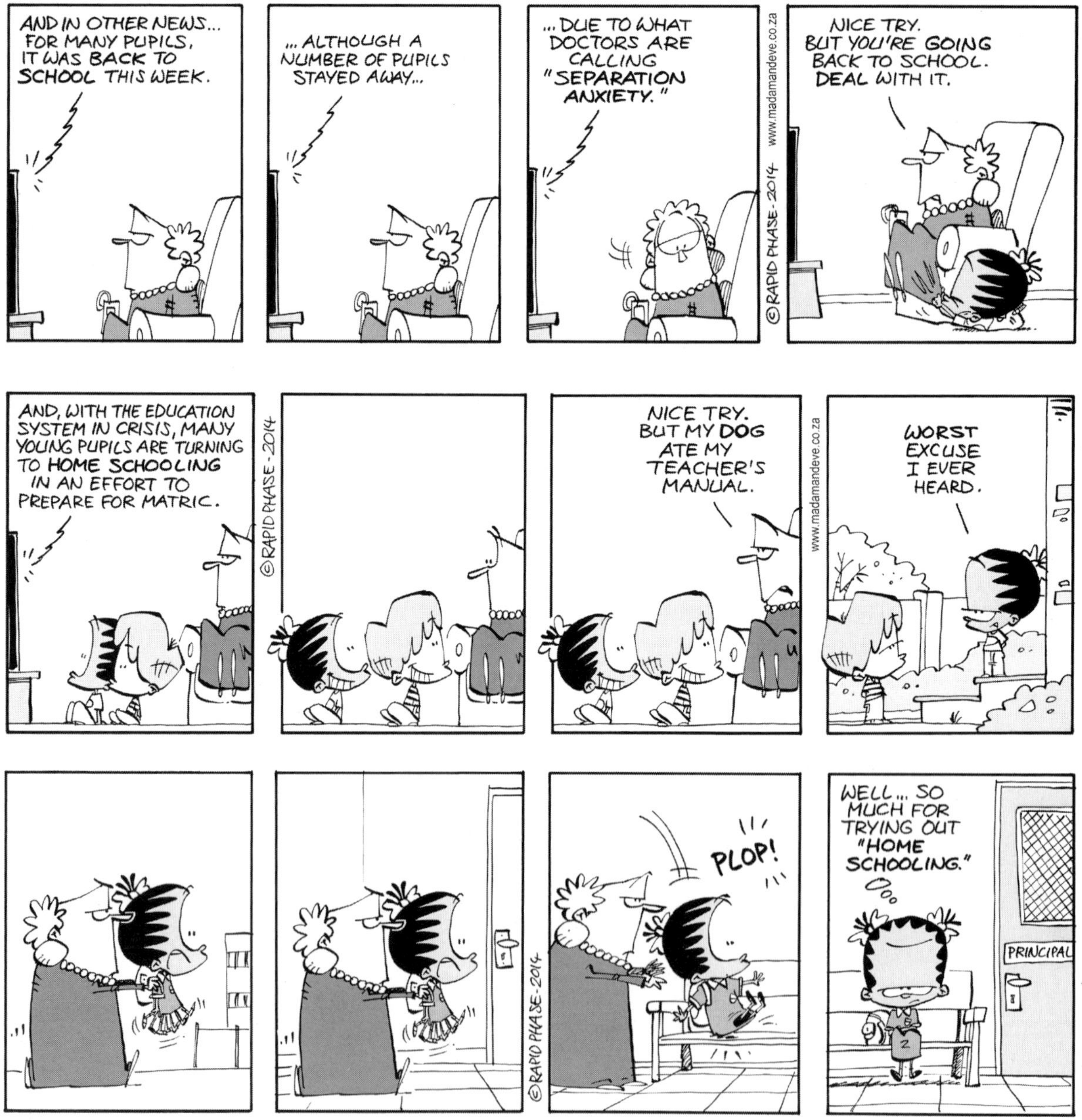
AND IN OTHER NEWS... FOR MANY PUPILS, IT WAS BACK TO SCHOOL THIS WEEK.
...ALTHOUGH A NUMBER OF PUPILS STAYED AWAY...
...DUE TO WHAT DOCTORS ARE CALLING "SEPARATION ANXIETY."
©RAPID PHASE · 2014 www.madamandeve.co.za
NICE TRY. BUT YOU'RE GOING BACK TO SCHOOL. DEAL WITH IT.
AND, WITH THE EDUCATION SYSTEM IN CRISIS, MANY YOUNG PUPILS ARE TURNING TO HOME SCHOOLING IN AN EFFORT TO PREPARE FOR MATRIC.
©RAPID PHASE · 2014
NICE TRY. BUT MY DOG ATE MY TEACHER'S MANUAL.
www.madamandeve.co.za
WORST EXCUSE I EVER HEARD.
©RAPID PHASE · 2014
PLOP!
WELL... SO MUCH FOR TRYING OUT "HOME SCHOOLING."
PRINCIPAL

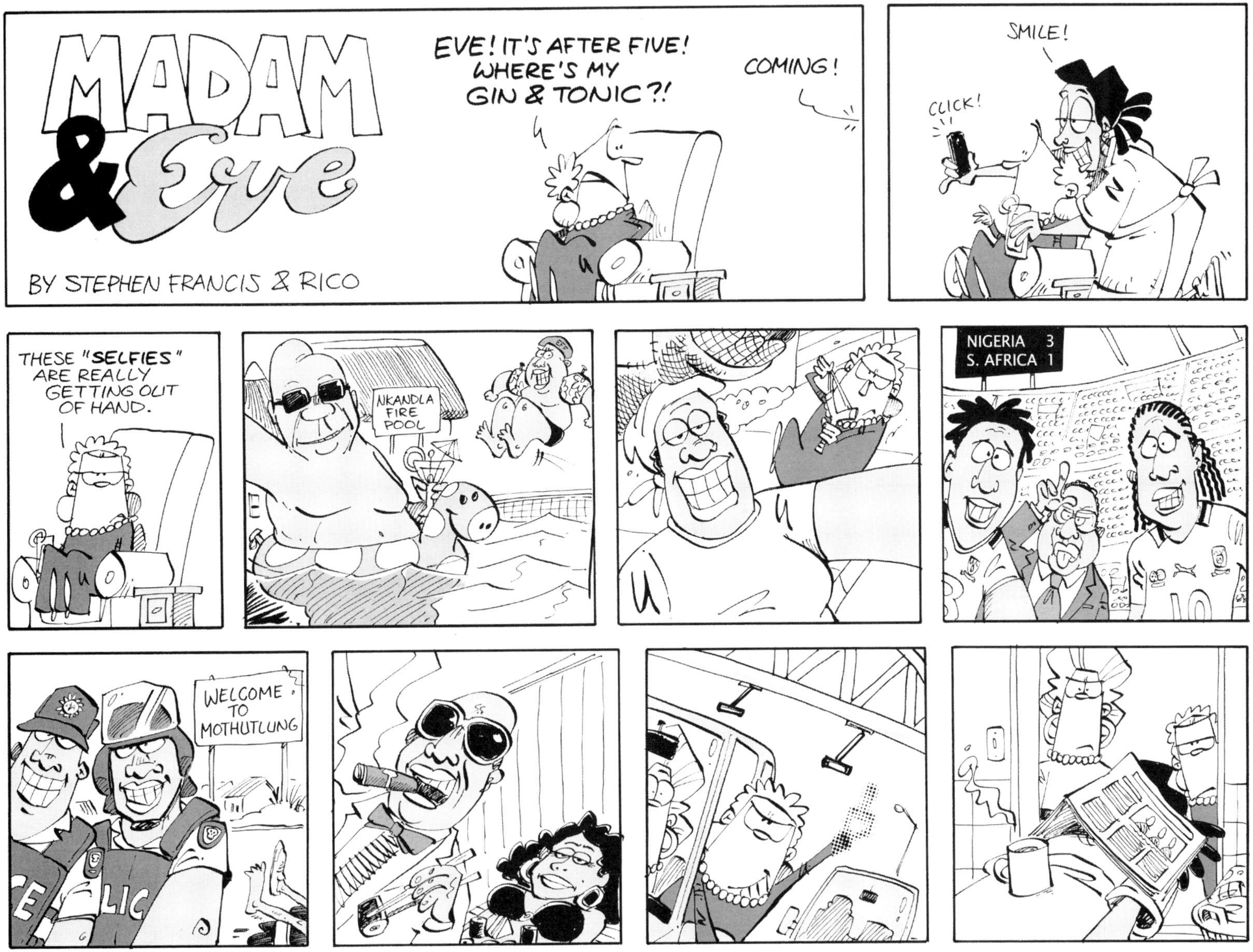
MADAM & Eve
BY STEPHEN FRANCIS & RICO
EVE! IT'S AFTER FIVE! WHERE'S MY GIN & TONIC?!
COMING!
SMILE!
CLICK!
THESE "SELFIES" ARE REALLY GETTING OUT OF HAND.
NKANDLA FIRE POOL
NIGERIA 3
S. AFRICA 1
WELCOME TO MOTHUTLUNG

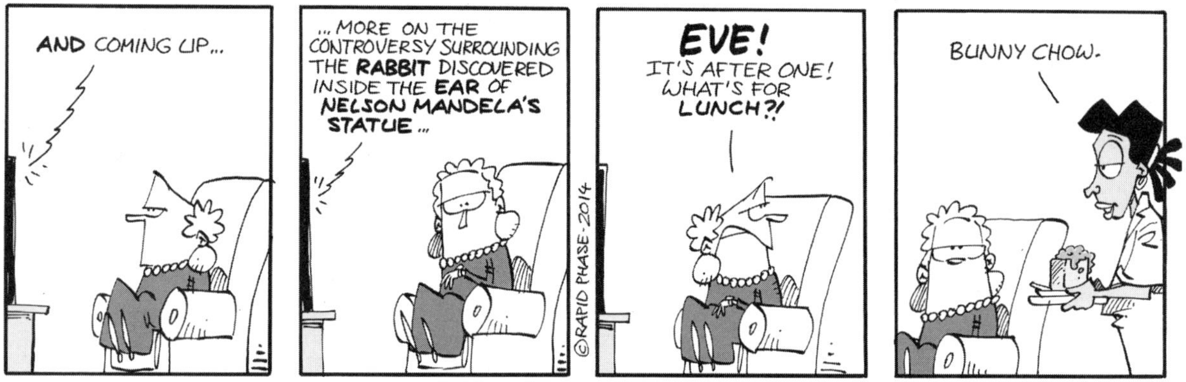
AND COMING UP...
... MORE ON THE CONTROVERSY SURROUNDING THE RABBIT DISCOVERED INSIDE THE EAR OF NELSON MANDELA'S STATUE ...
©RAPID PHASE · 2014
EVE! IT'S AFTER ONE! WHAT'S FOR LUNCH?!
BUNNY CHOW.

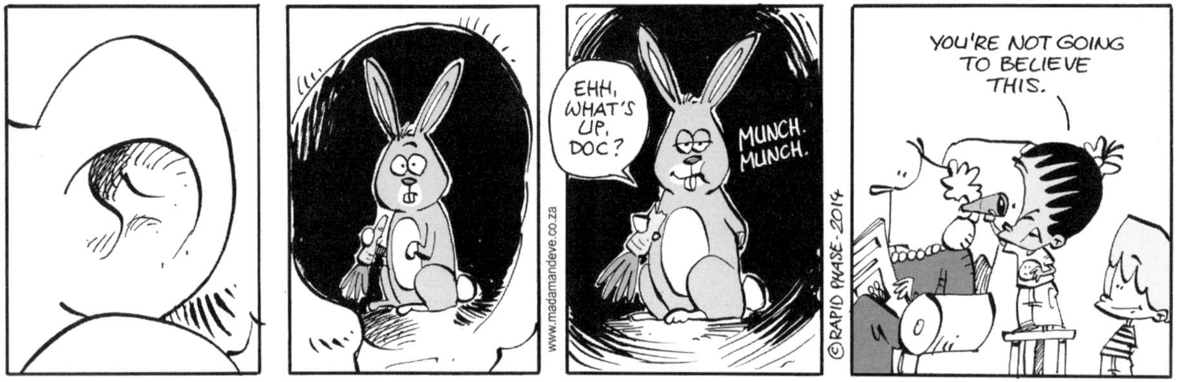
www.madamandeve.co.za
EHH, WHAT'S UP, DOC?
MUNCH. MUNCH.
©RAPID PHASE · 2014
YOU'RE NOT GOING TO BELIEVE THIS.

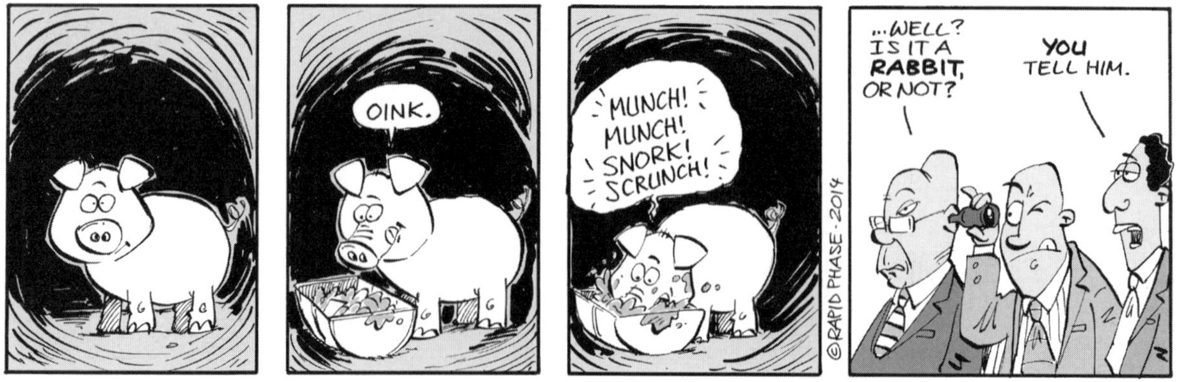
OINK.
MUNCH! MUNCH! SNORK! SCRUNCH!
©RAPID PHASE · 2014
... WELL? IS IT A RABBIT, OR NOT?
YOU TELL HIM.

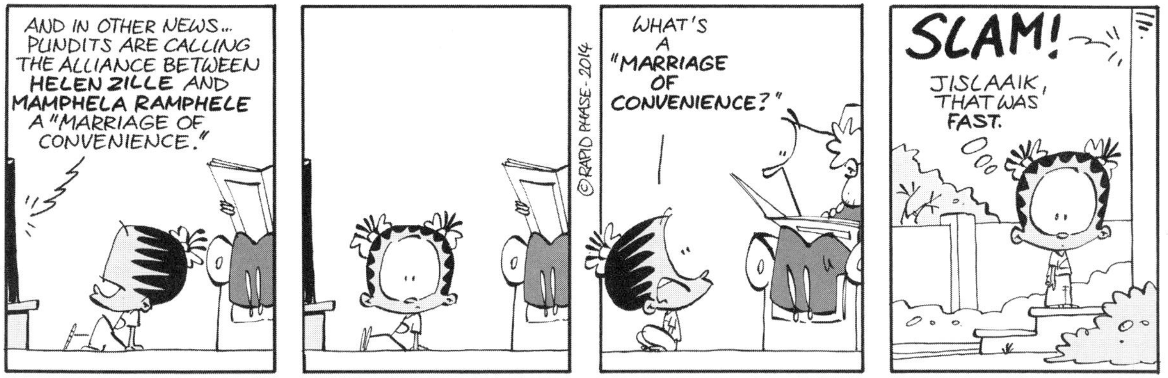
AND IN OTHER NEWS... PUNDITS ARE CALLING THE ALLIANCE BETWEEN **HELEN ZILLE** AND **MAMPHELA RAMPHELE** A "MARRIAGE OF CONVENIENCE."
©RAPID PHASE - 2014
WHAT'S A "**MARRIAGE OF CONVENIENCE?**"
SLAM!
JISLAAIK, THAT WAS **FAST**.

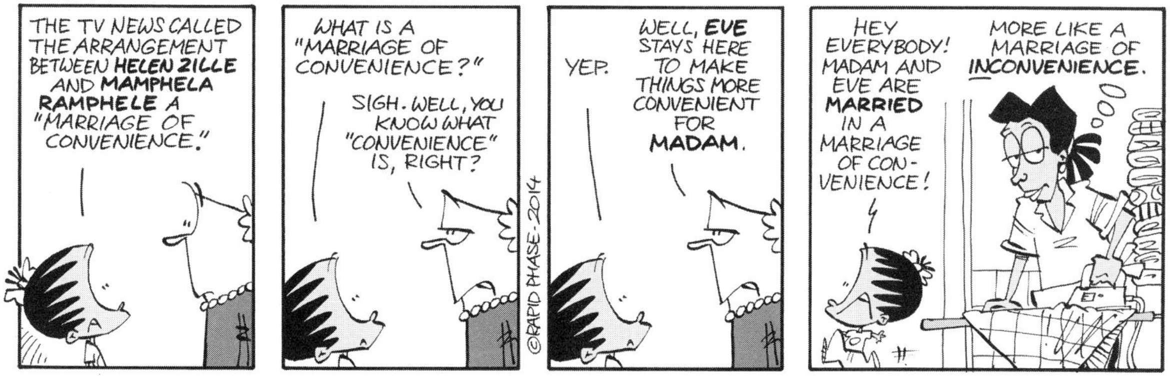
THE TV NEWS CALLED THE ARRANGEMENT BETWEEN **HELEN ZILLE** AND **MAMPHELA RAMPHELE** A "MARRIAGE OF CONVENIENCE."
WHAT IS A "MARRIAGE OF CONVENIENCE?"
SIGH. WELL, YOU KNOW WHAT "CONVENIENCE" IS, RIGHT?
©RAPID PHASE - 2014
YEP.
WELL, **EVE** STAYS HERE TO MAKE THINGS MORE CONVENIENT FOR **MADAM**.
HEY EVERYBODY! MADAM AND EVE ARE **MARRIED** IN A MARRIAGE OF CON-VENIENCE!
MORE LIKE A MARRIAGE OF **INCONVENIENCE**.

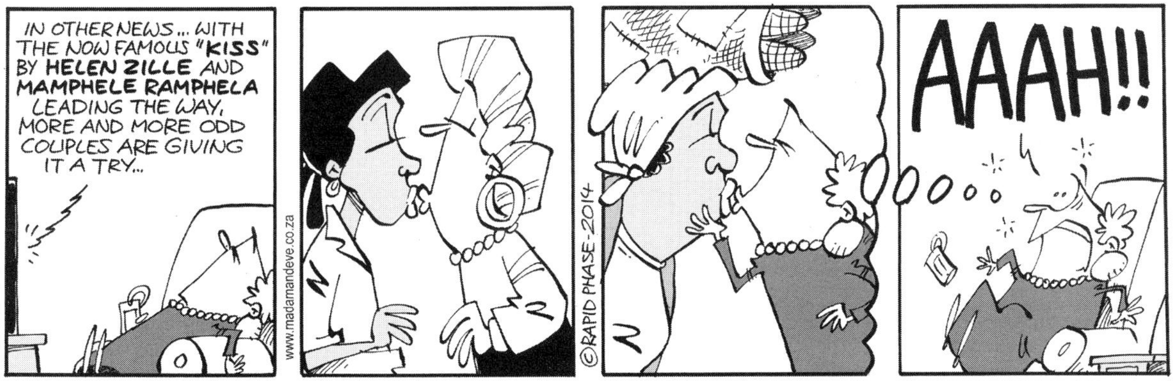
IN OTHER NEWS... WITH THE NOW FAMOUS "**KISS**" BY **HELEN ZILLE** AND **MAMPHELE RAMPHELA** LEADING THE WAY, MORE AND MORE ODD COUPLES ARE GIVING IT A TRY...
www.madamandeve.co.za
©RAPID PHASE - 2014
AAAH!!

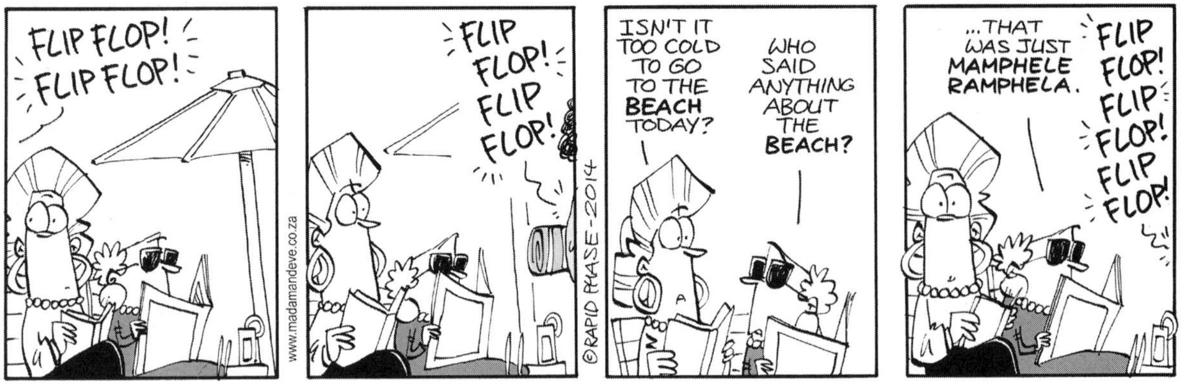
FLIP FLOP! FLIP FLOP!
www.madamandeve.co.za
FLIP FLOP! FLIP FLOP!
©RAPID PHASE-2014
ISN'T IT TOO COLD TO GO TO THE **BEACH** TODAY?
WHO SAID ANYTHING ABOUT THE **BEACH?**
...THAT WAS JUST **MAMPHELE RAMPHELA**.
FLIP FLOP! FLIP FLOP! FLIP FLOP!

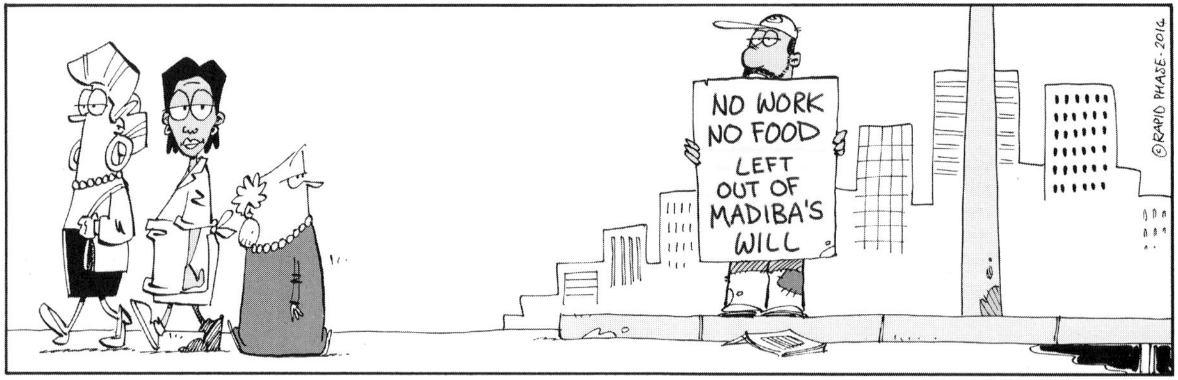
NO WORK
NO FOOD
LEFT OUT OF MADIBA'S WILL
©RAPID PHASE-2014

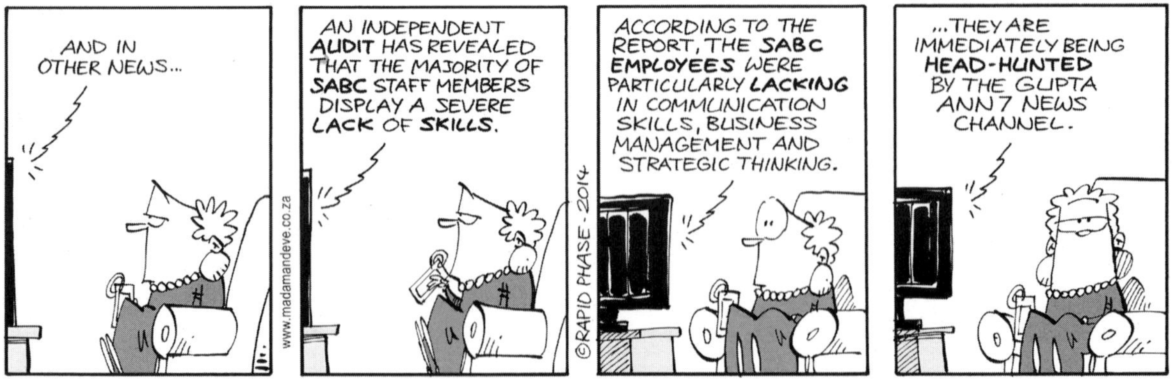
AND IN OTHER NEWS...
www.madamandeve.co.za
AN INDEPENDENT **AUDIT** HAS REVEALED THAT THE MAJORITY OF **SABC** STAFF MEMBERS DISPLAY A SEVERE **LACK** OF **SKILLS**.
©RAPID PHASE-2014
ACCORDING TO THE REPORT, THE **SABC EMPLOYEES** WERE PARTICULARLY **LACKING** IN COMMUNICATION SKILLS, BUSINESS MANAGEMENT AND STRATEGIC THINKING.
...THEY ARE IMMEDIATELY BEING **HEAD-HUNTED** BY THE GUPTA ANN7 NEWS CHANNEL.

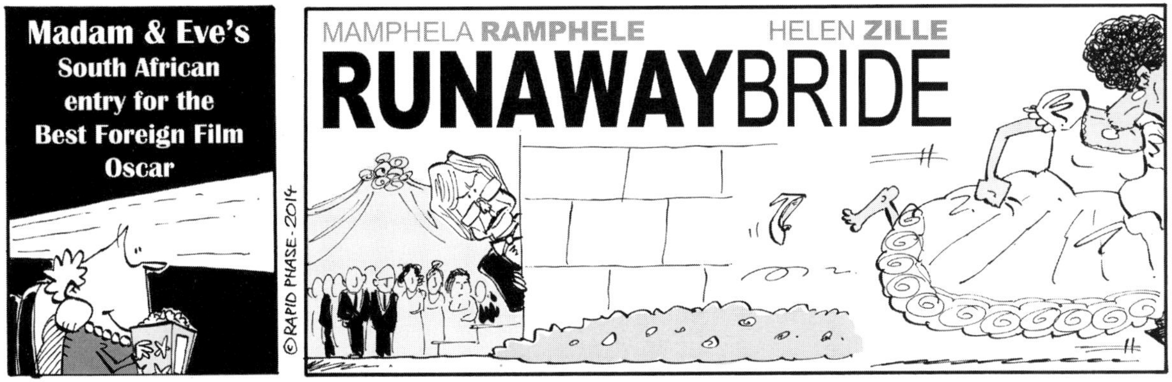
Madam & Eve's South African entry for the Best Foreign Film Oscar
MAMPHELA RAMPHELE
HELEN ZILLE
RUNAWAYBRIDE
©RAPID PHASE-2014

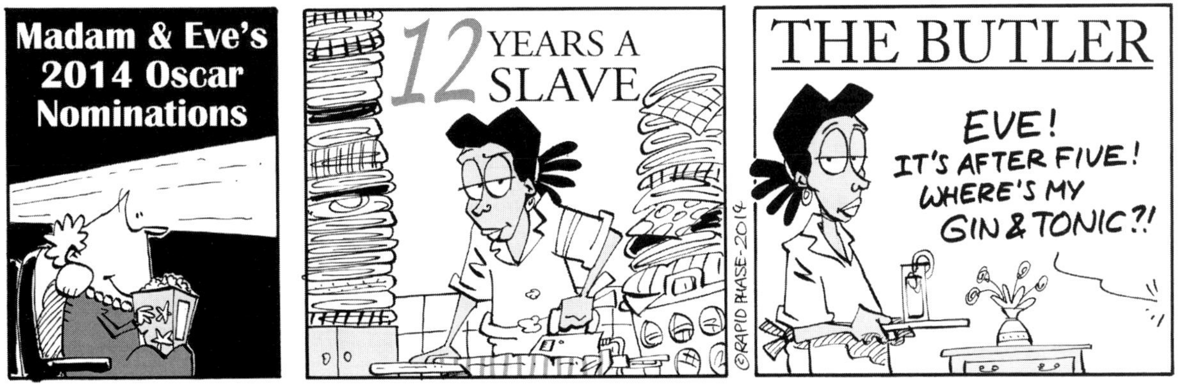
Madam & Eve's 2014 Oscar Nominations
12 YEARS A SLAVE
©RAPID PHASE-2014
THE BUTLER
EVE! IT'S AFTER FIVE! WHERE'S MY GIN & TONIC?!

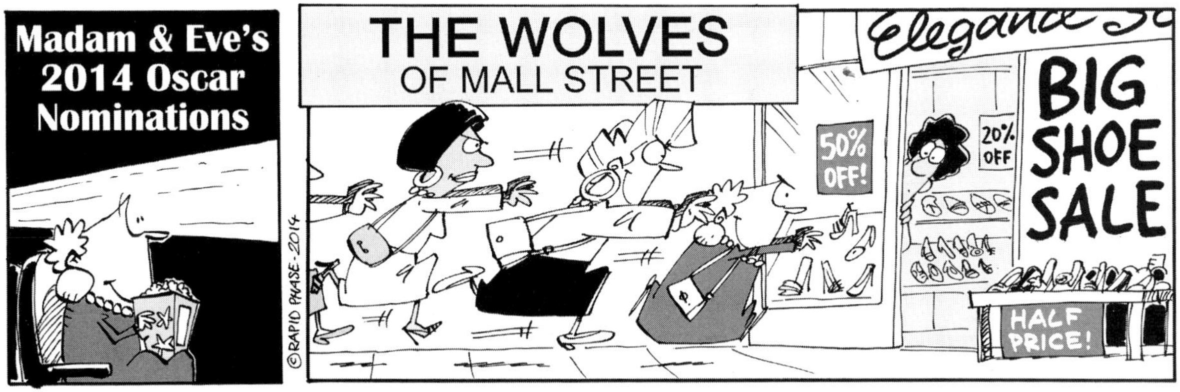
Madam & Eve's 2014 Oscar Nominations
©RAPID PHASE-2014
THE WOLVES OF MALL STREET
50% OFF!
20% OFF
BIG SHOE SALE
HALF PRICE!

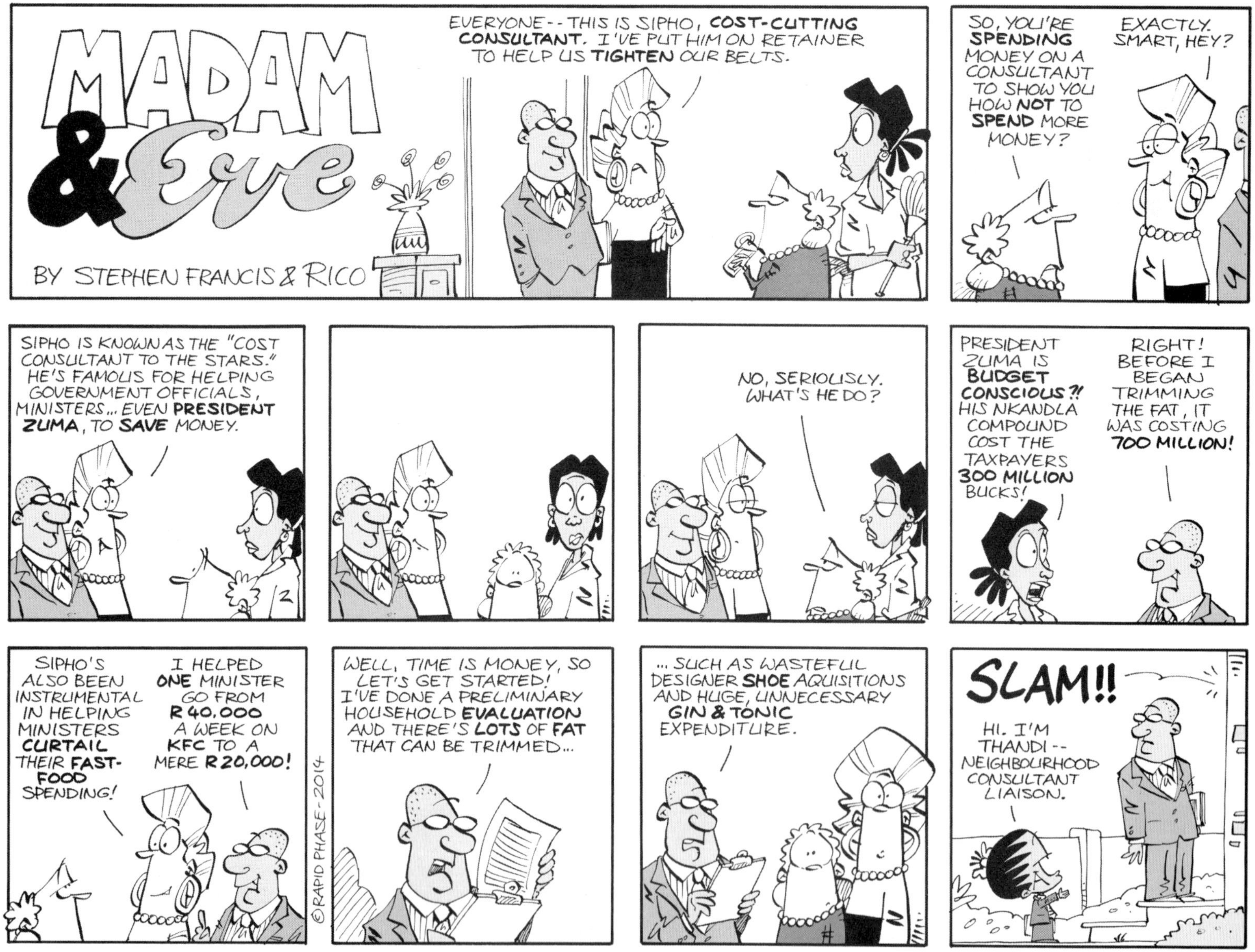

MADAM & Eve
BY STEPHEN FRANCIS & RICO
EVERYONE -- THIS IS SIPHO, COST-CUTTING CONSULTANT. I'VE PUT HIM ON RETAINER TO HELP US TIGHTEN OUR BELTS.
SO, YOU'RE SPENDING MONEY ON A CONSULTANT TO SHOW YOU HOW NOT TO SPEND MORE MONEY?
EXACTLY. SMART, HEY?
SIPHO IS KNOWN AS THE "COST CONSULTANT TO THE STARS." HE'S FAMOUS FOR HELPING GOVERNMENT OFFICIALS, MINISTERS... EVEN PRESIDENT ZUMA, TO SAVE MONEY.
NO, SERIOUSLY. WHAT'S HE DO?
PRESIDENT ZUMA IS BUDGET CONSCIOUS?! HIS NKANDLA COMPOUND COST THE TAXPAYERS 300 MILLION BUCKS!
RIGHT! BEFORE I BEGAN TRIMMING THE FAT, IT WAS COSTING 700 MILLION!
SIPHO'S ALSO BEEN INSTRUMENTAL IN HELPING MINISTERS CURTAIL THEIR FAST-FOOD SPENDING!
I HELPED ONE MINISTER GO FROM R40,000 A WEEK ON KFC TO A MERE R20,000!
©RAPID PHASE - 2014
WELL, TIME IS MONEY, SO LET'S GET STARTED! I'VE DONE A PRELIMINARY HOUSEHOLD EVALUATION AND THERE'S LOTS OF FAT THAT CAN BE TRIMMED...
... SUCH AS WASTEFUL DESIGNER SHOE AQUISITIONS AND HUGE, UNNECESSARY GIN & TONIC EXPENDITURE.
SLAM!!
HI. I'M THANDI -- NEIGHBOURHOOD CONSULTANT LIAISON.

MADAM & Eve

BY STEPHEN FRANCIS & RICO

HELLO! TODAY'S TOP HEADLINES! PRESIDENT ZUMA'S TRUSTED ALLIES HAVE FINALLY "COME OUT." THIS IS THE THANDI SISULU NEWS CHANNEL!

President Zuma

...AND IN THE TIME-HONOURED TRADITION OF THE FOX NEWS CHANNEL AND THE GUPTA NEWS CHANNEL, I'M AVAILABLE FOR SPONSORSHIP.(DEPENDING ON YOUR POLITICAL LEANINGS)

TSN

CONTINUING WITH OUR LEAD STORY...PRESIDENT ZUMA'S TRUSTED ALLIES AND LIEUTENANTS HAVE COME OUT ON TOP AFTER EATING GRUEL THIS WEEKEND.

ANC Election List

...AFTER THE ANC'S GRUELLING NATIONAL LIST CONFERENCE THIS WEEKEND.

ANC Election List

THIS CAME AFTER ZUMA'S LIST WAS LEAKED AT A PARTY BY HIS LEADING SECURITY STRUCTURES.

...WAS ENDORSED BY STRUCTURES TO LEAD THE PARTY...

...STRUCTURES TO LEAD THE PARTY IN THE FOUR UPCOMING GENERAL ELECTIONS.

...IN THE FORTHCOMING GENERAL ELECTIONS.

ANC Election List

IN OUR NEXT STORY... A DISTURBING NEW TREND OF SENIOR MANAGEMENT INTERFERING WITH EDITORIAL NEWS CONTENT.

SIGH. SO MUCH FOR MEDIA FREEDOM.

PRINCIPAL

E-TOLLS

HONK! HONK!

@#%%#@)!!

HOOT! HOOT!

A-TOLLS

@#%%#@)!!

AVENGERS FILMING CAUSES JOBURG TRAFFIC CHAOS

©RAPID PHASE · 2014

AND IN OTHER NEWS, NOW THAT THE **AVENGERS** SEQUEL HAS WRAPPED, PRODUCERS HAVE REVEALED THAT SOME OF THE SUPERHEROES WERE **AFFECTED** BY THEIR STAY IN **JOHANNESBURG**.

CAPTAIN AMERICA IS BUYING A **HOUSE** IN CAPE TOWN... PARTS OF **IRON MAN** WERE STOLEN BY THIEVES AND SOLD AS **SCRAP METAL**...

www.madamandeve.co.za

©RAPID PHASE · 2014

...AND THE INCREDIBLE **HULK** HAS MYSTERIOUSLY GONE **MISSING**.

HULK WANT **LAND** WITH NO REPARATION.

I LIKE HIM. SIGN HIM UP.

EFF   EFF

OSCAR TELECAST TO RUN FOR MONTHS

IT'S SO **CONFUSING!** HOW CAN YOU **TELL** IF THEY'RE TALKING ABOUT THE OSCAR **AWARDS**... OR THE OSCAR PISTORIUS **TRIAL?**

ELLEN DeGENERES READY FOR BIG OSCAR NIGHT

OSCAR PARTIES SET ALL OVER HOLLYWOOD

OSCAR RACE HEATING UP

DESIGNER DRESSES FOR OSCAR

©RAPID PHASE · 2014

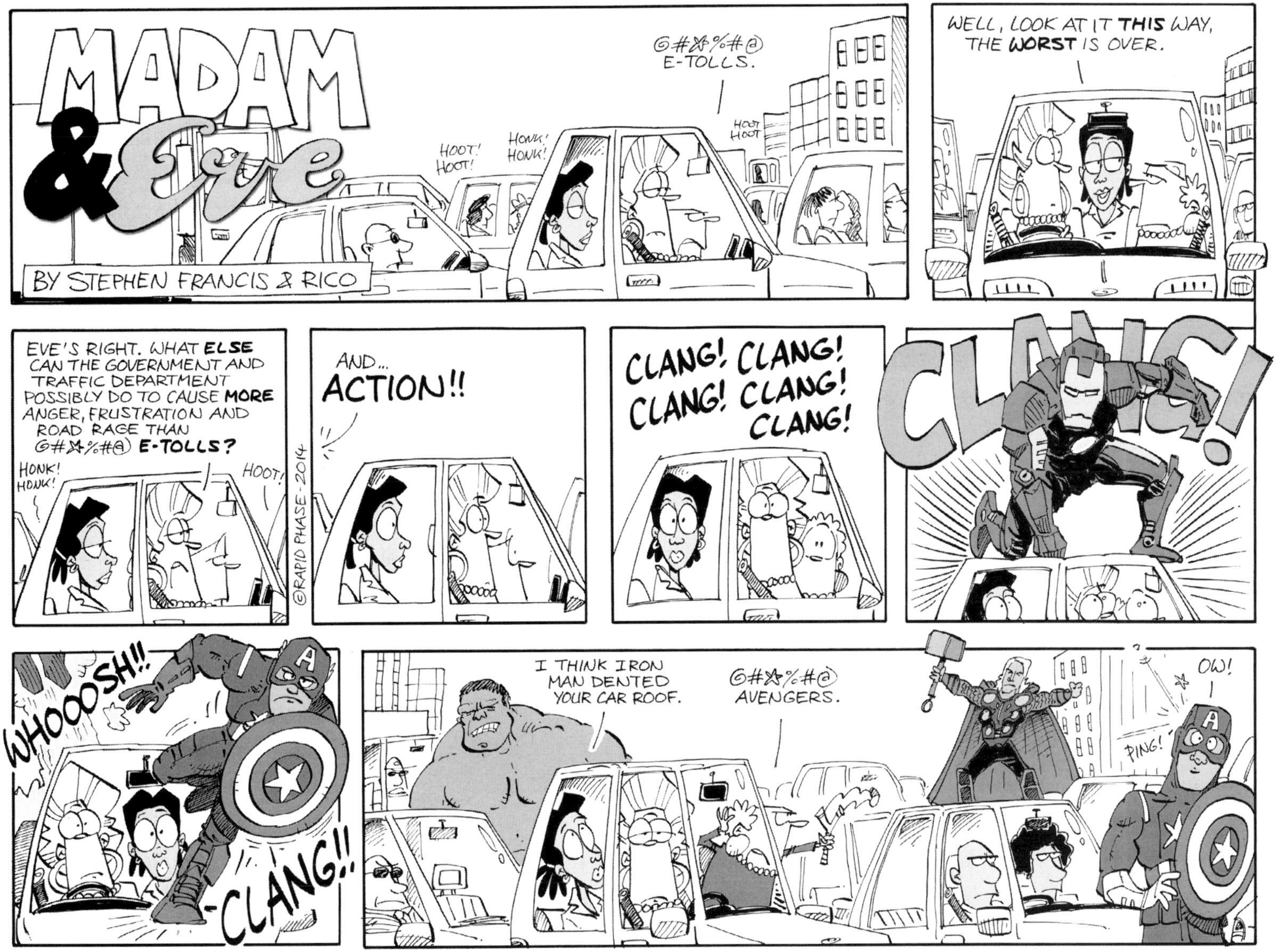
MADAM & Eve
BY STEPHEN FRANCIS & RICO
HOOT! HOOT!
HONK! HONK!
G#%#@ E-TOLLS.
HOOT HOOT
WELL, LOOK AT IT THIS WAY, THE WORST IS OVER.
EVE'S RIGHT. WHAT ELSE CAN THE GOVERNMENT AND TRAFFIC DEPARTMENT POSSIBLY DO TO CAUSE MORE ANGER, FRUSTRATION AND ROAD RAGE THAN G#%#@ E-TOLLS?
HONK! HONK!
HOOT!
©RAPID PHASE · 2014
AND... ACTION!!
CLANG! CLANG! CLANG! CLANG! CLANG!
CLANG!
WHOOOSH!!
-CLANG!!
I THINK IRON MAN DENTED YOUR CAR ROOF.
G#%#@ AVENGERS.
OW!
PING!

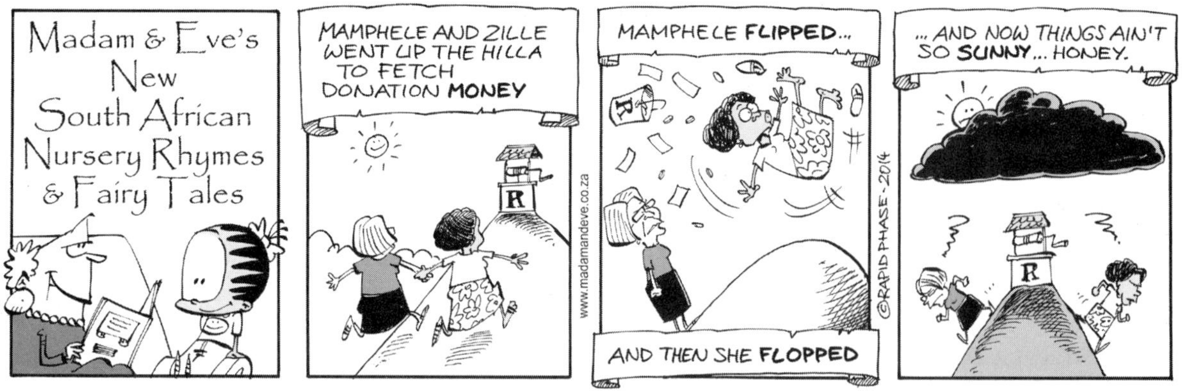
Madam & Eve's
New
South African
Nursery Rhymes
& Fairy Tales
MAMPHELE AND ZILLE WENT UP THE HILLA TO FETCH DONATION MONEY
R
www.madamandeve.co.za
MAMPHELE FLIPPED...
AND THEN SHE FLOPPED
©RAPID PHASE - 2014
... AND NOW THINGS AIN'T SO SUNNY... HONEY.
R

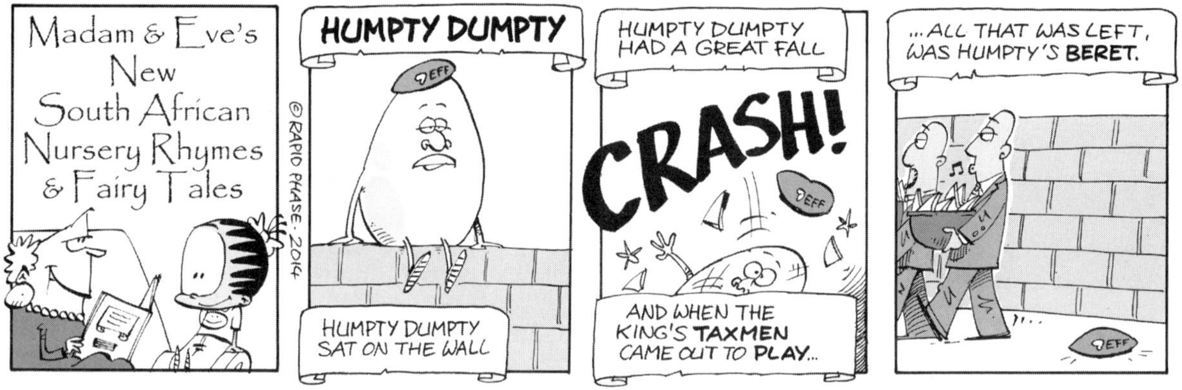
Madam & Eve's
New
South African
Nursery Rhymes
& Fairy Tales
© RAPID PHASE - 2014
HUMPTY DUMPTY
EFF
HUMPTY DUMPTY SAT ON THE WALL
HUMPTY DUMPTY HAD A GREAT FALL
CRASH!
EFF
AND WHEN THE KING'S TAXMEN CAME OUT TO PLAY...
...ALL THAT WAS LEFT, WAS HUMPTY'S BERET.
EFF

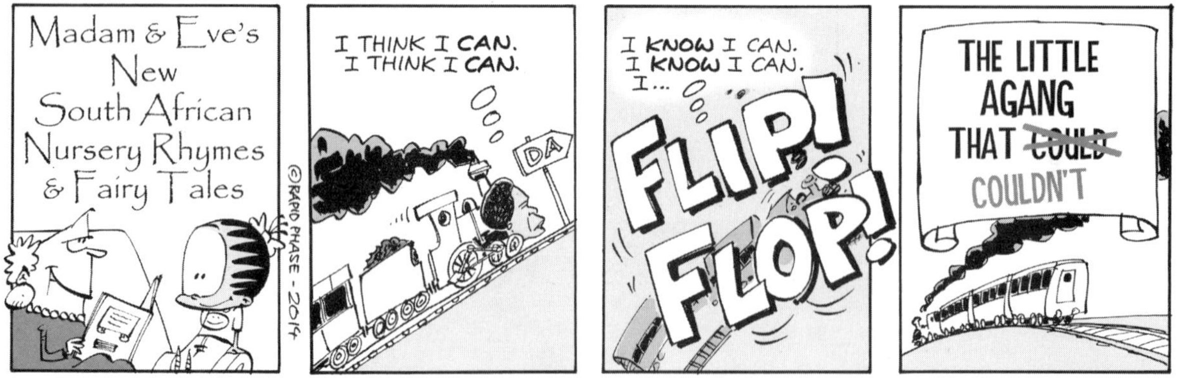
Madam & Eve's
New
South African
Nursery Rhymes
& Fairy Tales
©RAPID PHASE - 2014
I THINK I CAN.
I THINK I CAN.
DA
I KNOW I CAN.
I KNOW I CAN.
I...
FLIP!
FLOP!
THE LITTLE
AGANG
THAT COULD
COULDN'T

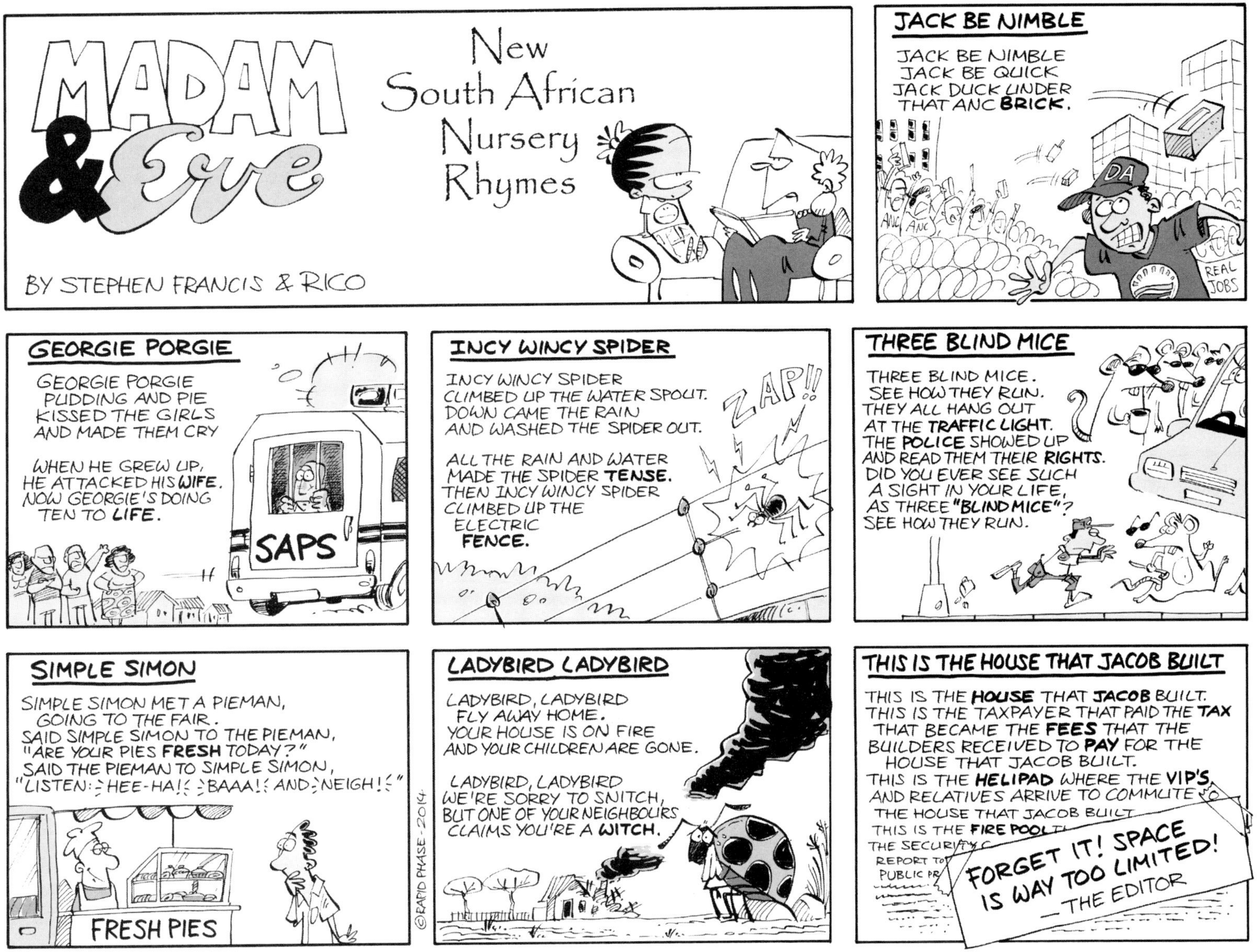
MADAM & Eve
New South African Nursery Rhymes
BY STEPHEN FRANCIS & RICO
JACK BE NIMBLE
JACK BE NIMBLE
JACK BE QUICK
JACK DUCK UNDER
THAT ANC BRICK.
DA
ANC
ANC
REAL JOBS
GEORGIE PORGIE
GEORGIE PORGIE
PUDDING AND PIE
KISSED THE GIRLS
AND MADE THEM CRY
WHEN HE GREW UP,
HE ATTACKED HIS WIFE.
NOW GEORGIE'S DOING
TEN TO LIFE.
SAPS
INCY WINCY SPIDER
INCY WINCY SPIDER
CLIMBED UP THE WATER SPOUT.
DOWN CAME THE RAIN
AND WASHED THE SPIDER OUT.
ALL THE RAIN AND WATER
MADE THE SPIDER TENSE.
THEN INCY WINCY SPIDER
CLIMBED UP THE
ELECTRIC
FENCE.
ZAP!!
THREE BLIND MICE
THREE BLIND MICE.
SEE HOW THEY RUN.
THEY ALL HANG OUT
AT THE TRAFFIC LIGHT.
THE POLICE SHOWED UP
AND READ THEM THEIR RIGHTS.
DID YOU EVER SEE SUCH
A SIGHT IN YOUR LIFE,
AS THREE "BLIND MICE"?
SEE HOW THEY RUN.
SIMPLE SIMON
SIMPLE SIMON MET A PIEMAN,
GOING TO THE FAIR.
SAID SIMPLE SIMON TO THE PIEMAN,
"ARE YOUR PIES FRESH TODAY?"
SAID THE PIEMAN TO SIMPLE SIMON,
"LISTEN: HEE-HA! BAAA! AND NEIGH!"
FRESH PIES
©RAPID PHASE · 2014
LADYBIRD LADYBIRD
LADYBIRD, LADYBIRD
FLY AWAY HOME.
YOUR HOUSE IS ON FIRE
AND YOUR CHILDREN ARE GONE.
LADYBIRD, LADYBIRD
WE'RE SORRY TO SNITCH,
BUT ONE OF YOUR NEIGHBOURS
CLAIMS YOU'RE A WITCH.
THIS IS THE HOUSE THAT JACOB BUILT
THIS IS THE HOUSE THAT JACOB BUILT.
THIS IS THE TAXPAYER THAT PAID THE TAX
THAT BECAME THE FEES THAT THE
BUILDERS RECEIVED TO PAY FOR THE
HOUSE THAT JACOB BUILT.
THIS IS THE HELIPAD WHERE THE VIP'S,
AND RELATIVES ARRIVE TO COMMUTE TO
THE HOUSE THAT JACOB BUILT
THIS IS THE FIRE POOL
THE SECURITY
REPORT TO
PUBLIC
FORGET IT! SPACE
IS WAY TOO LIMITED!
— THE EDITOR

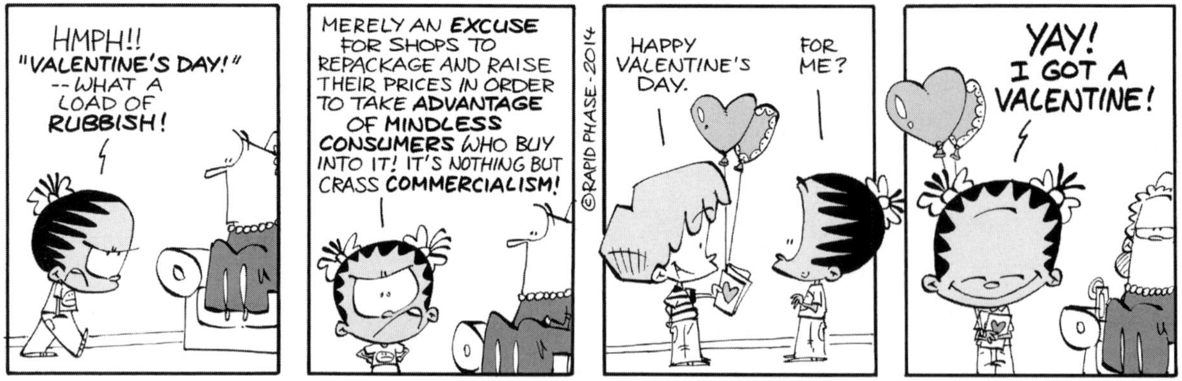
HMPH!! "VALENTINE'S DAY!" --WHAT A LOAD OF RUBBISH!
MERELY AN EXCUSE FOR SHOPS TO REPACKAGE AND RAISE THEIR PRICES IN ORDER TO TAKE ADVANTAGE OF MINDLESS CONSUMERS WHO BUY INTO IT! IT'S NOTHING BUT CRASS COMMERCIALISM!
©RAPID PHASE - 2014
HAPPY VALENTINE'S DAY.
FOR ME?
YAY! I GOT A VALENTINE!

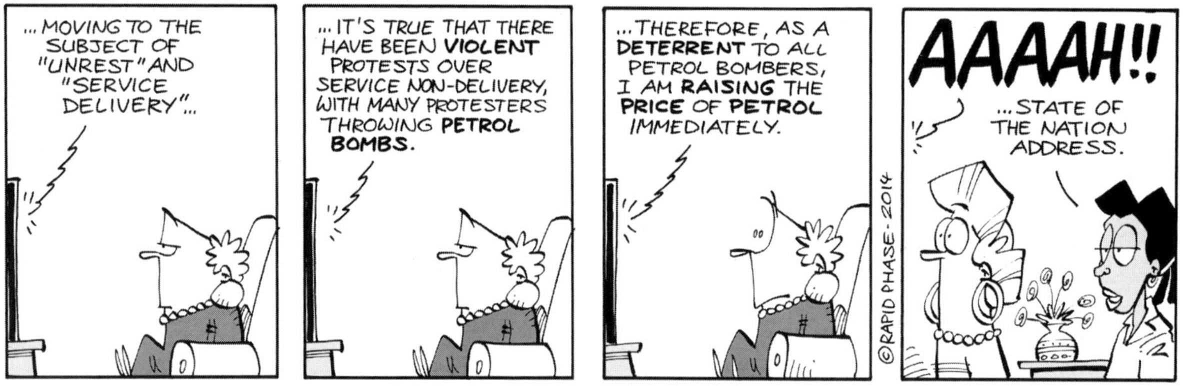
...MOVING TO THE SUBJECT OF "UNREST" AND "SERVICE DELIVERY"...
...IT'S TRUE THAT THERE HAVE BEEN VIOLENT PROTESTS OVER SERVICE NON-DELIVERY, WITH MANY PROTESTERS THROWING PETROL BOMBS.
...THEREFORE, AS A DETERRENT TO ALL PETROL BOMBERS, I AM RAISING THE PRICE OF PETROL IMMEDIATELY.
©RAPID PHASE - 2014
AAAAH!!
...STATE OF THE NATION ADDRESS.

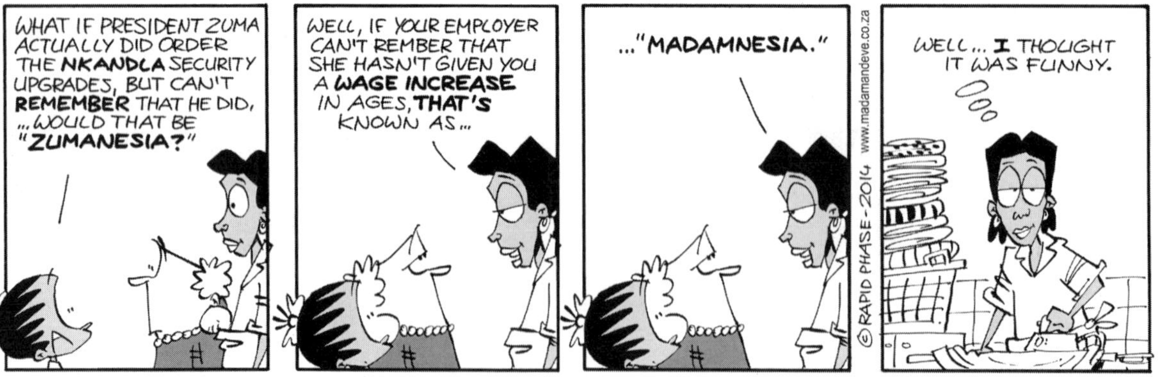
WHAT IF PRESIDENT ZUMA ACTUALLY DID ORDER THE NKANDLA SECURITY UPGRADES, BUT CAN'T REMEMBER THAT HE DID, ...WOULD THAT BE "ZUMANESIA?"
WELL, IF YOUR EMPLOYER CAN'T REMBER THAT SHE HASN'T GIVEN YOU A WAGE INCREASE IN AGES, THAT'S KNOWN AS...
..."MADAMNESIA."
© RAPID PHASE - 2014 www.madamandeve.co.za
WELL... I THOUGHT IT WAS FUNNY.

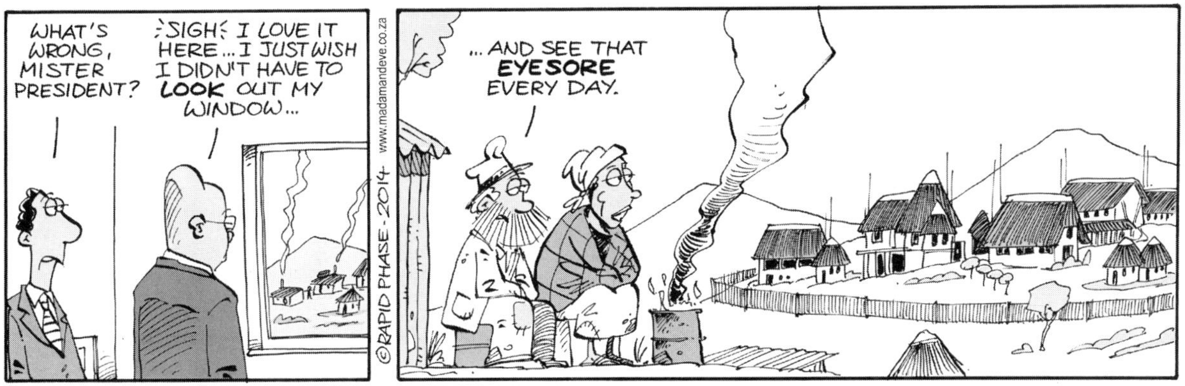
WHAT'S WRONG, MISTER PRESIDENT?
SIGH I LOVE IT HERE... I JUST WISH I DIDN'T HAVE TO LOOK OUT MY WINDOW...
©RAPID PHASE - 2014 www.madamandeve.co.za
... AND SEE THAT EYESORE EVERY DAY.

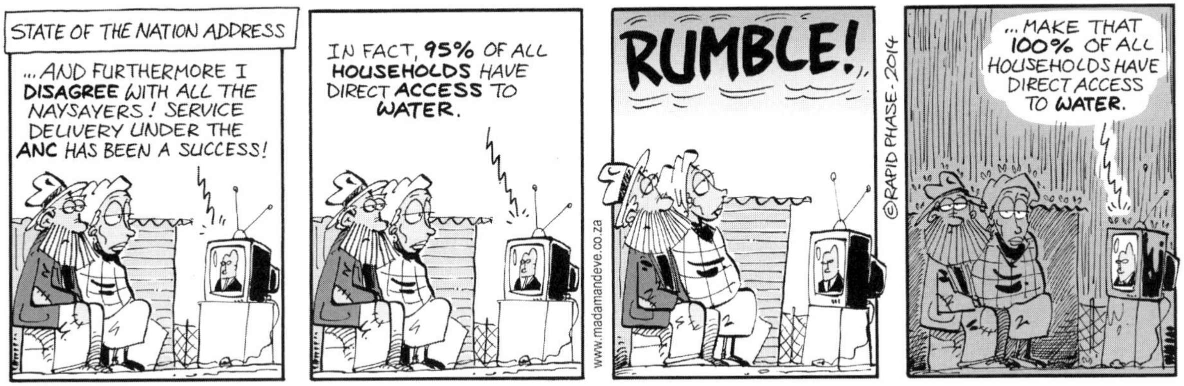
STATE OF THE NATION ADDRESS
... AND FURTHERMORE I DISAGREE WITH ALL THE NAYSAYERS! SERVICE DELIVERY UNDER THE ANC HAS BEEN A SUCCESS!
IN FACT, 95% OF ALL HOUSEHOLDS HAVE DIRECT ACCESS TO WATER.
www.madamandeve.co.za
RUMBLE!
©RAPID PHASE - 2014
... MAKE THAT 100% OF ALL HOUSEHOLDS HAVE DIRECT ACCESS TO WATER.

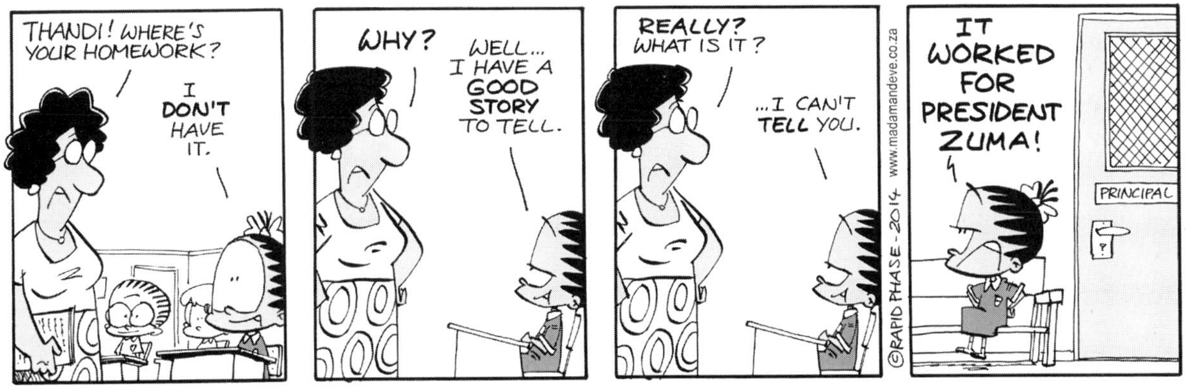
THANDI! WHERE'S YOUR HOMEWORK?
I DON'T HAVE IT.
WHY?
WELL... I HAVE A GOOD STORY TO TELL.
REALLY? WHAT IS IT?
... I CAN'T TELL YOU.
©RAPID PHASE - 2014 www.madamandeve.co.za
IT WORKED FOR PRESIDENT ZUMA!
PRINCIPAL

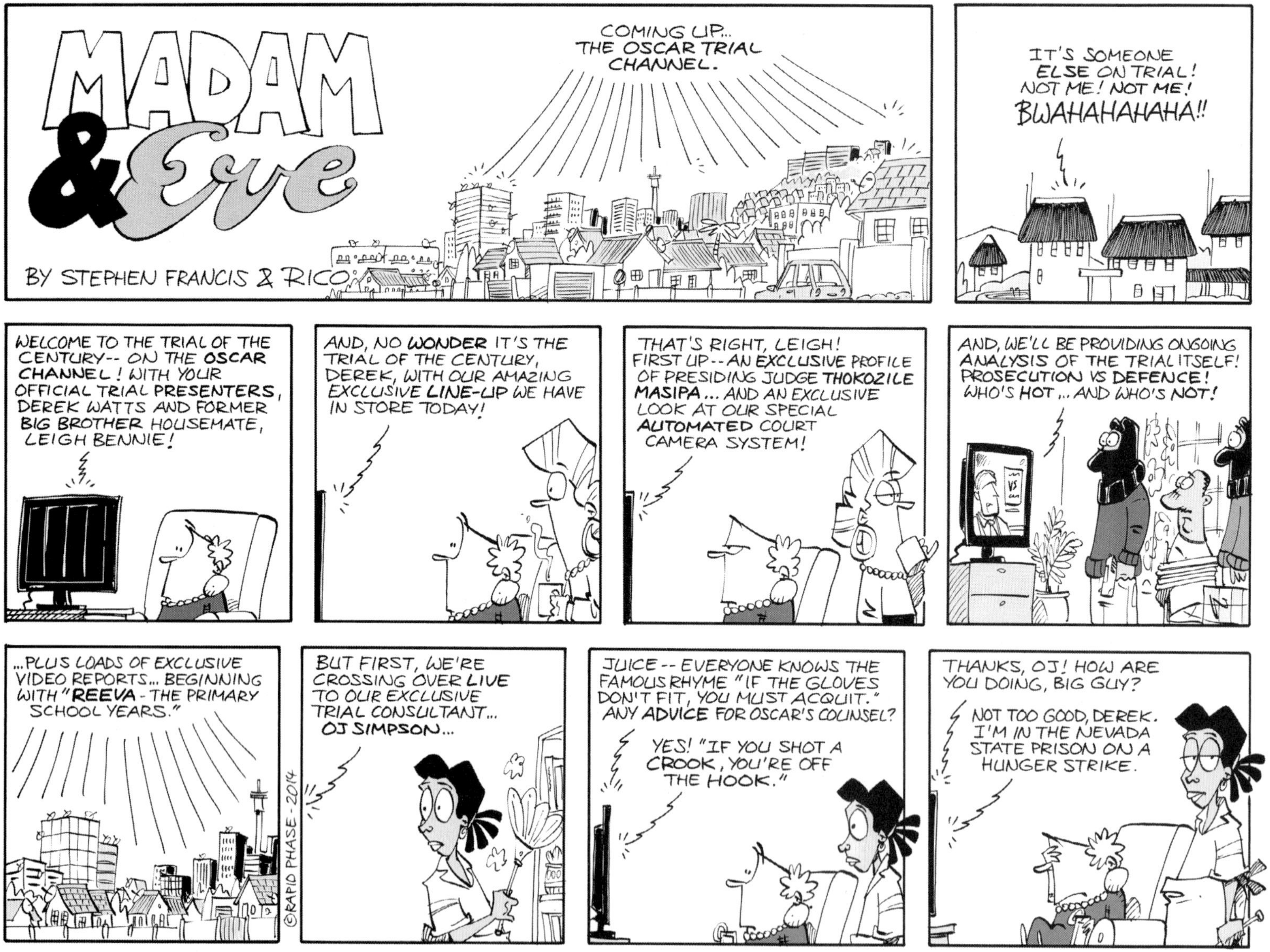
MADAM & Eve
BY STEPHEN FRANCIS & RICO
COMING UP... THE OSCAR TRIAL CHANNEL.
IT'S SOMEONE ELSE ON TRIAL! NOT ME! NOT ME! BWAHAHAHAHA!!
WELCOME TO THE TRIAL OF THE CENTURY-- ON THE OSCAR CHANNEL! WITH YOUR OFFICIAL TRIAL PRESENTERS, DEREK WATTS AND FORMER BIG BROTHER HOUSEMATE, LEIGH BENNIE!
AND, NO WONDER IT'S THE TRIAL OF THE CENTURY, DEREK, WITH OUR AMAZING EXCLUSIVE LINE-UP WE HAVE IN STORE TODAY!
THAT'S RIGHT, LEIGH! FIRST UP-- AN EXCLUSIVE PROFILE OF PRESIDING JUDGE THOKOZILE MASIPA... AND AN EXCLUSIVE LOOK AT OUR SPECIAL AUTOMATED COURT CAMERA SYSTEM!
AND, WE'LL BE PROVIDING ONGOING ANALYSIS OF THE TRIAL ITSELF! PROSECUTION VS DEFENCE! WHO'S HOT... AND WHO'S NOT!
...PLUS LOADS OF EXCLUSIVE VIDEO REPORTS... BEGINNING WITH "REEVA - THE PRIMARY SCHOOL YEARS."
©RAPID PHASE - 2014
BUT FIRST, WE'RE CROSSING OVER LIVE TO OUR EXCLUSIVE TRIAL CONSULTANT... OJ SIMPSON...
JUICE -- EVERYONE KNOWS THE FAMOUS RHYME "IF THE GLOVES DON'T FIT, YOU MUST ACQUIT." ANY ADVICE FOR OSCAR'S COUNSEL?
YES! "IF YOU SHOT A CROOK, YOU'RE OFF THE HOOK."
THANKS, OJ! HOW ARE YOU DOING, BIG GUY?
NOT TOO GOOD, DEREK. I'M IN THE NEVADA STATE PRISON ON A HUNGER STRIKE.

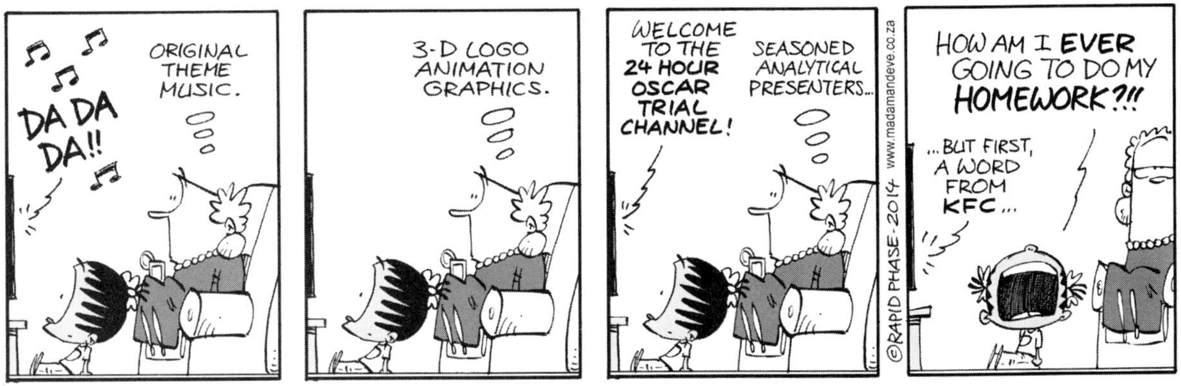
ORIGINAL THEME MUSIC.
DA DA DA!!
3-D LOGO ANIMATION GRAPHICS.
WELCOME TO THE 24 HOUR OSCAR TRIAL CHANNEL!
SEASONED ANALYTICAL PRESENTERS...
©RAPID PHASE - 2014 www.madamandeve.co.za
HOW AM I EVER GOING TO DO MY HOMEWORK?!!
...BUT FIRST, A WORD FROM KFC...

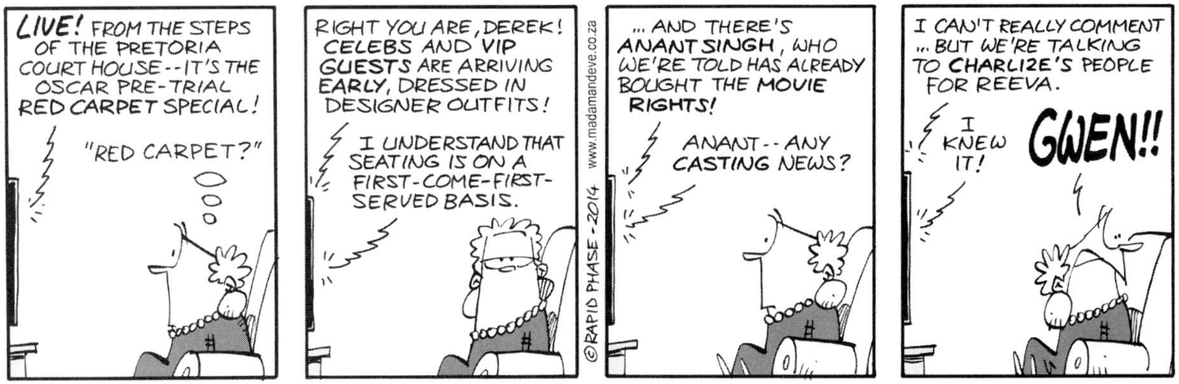
LIVE! FROM THE STEPS OF THE PRETORIA COURT HOUSE--IT'S THE OSCAR PRE-TRIAL RED CARPET SPECIAL!
"RED CARPET?"
RIGHT YOU ARE, DEREK! CELEBS AND VIP GUESTS ARE ARRIVING EARLY, DRESSED IN DESIGNER OUTFITS!
I UNDERSTAND THAT SEATING IS ON A FIRST-COME-FIRST-SERVED BASIS.
©RAPID PHASE - 2014 www.madamandeve.co.za
...AND THERE'S ANANT SINGH, WHO WE'RE TOLD HAS ALREADY BOUGHT THE MOVIE RIGHTS!
ANANT--ANY CASTING NEWS?
I CAN'T REALLY COMMENT ...BUT WE'RE TALKING TO CHARLIZE'S PEOPLE FOR REEVA.
I KNEW IT!
GWEN!!

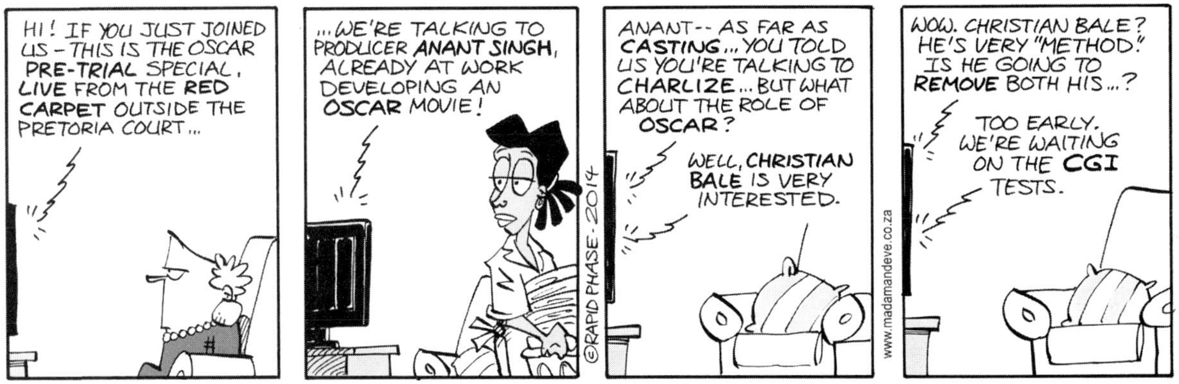
HI! IF YOU JUST JOINED US - THIS IS THE OSCAR PRE-TRIAL SPECIAL, LIVE FROM THE RED CARPET OUTSIDE THE PRETORIA COURT...
...WE'RE TALKING TO PRODUCER ANANT SINGH, ALREADY AT WORK DEVELOPING AN OSCAR MOVIE!
©RAPID PHASE - 2014
ANANT-- AS FAR AS CASTING... YOU TOLD US YOU'RE TALKING TO CHARLIZE... BUT WHAT ABOUT THE ROLE OF OSCAR?
WELL, CHRISTIAN BALE IS VERY INTERESTED.
www.madamandeve.co.za
WOW. CHRISTIAN BALE? HE'S VERY "METHOD." IS HE GOING TO REMOVE BOTH HIS...?
TOO EARLY. WE'RE WAITING ON THE CGI TESTS.

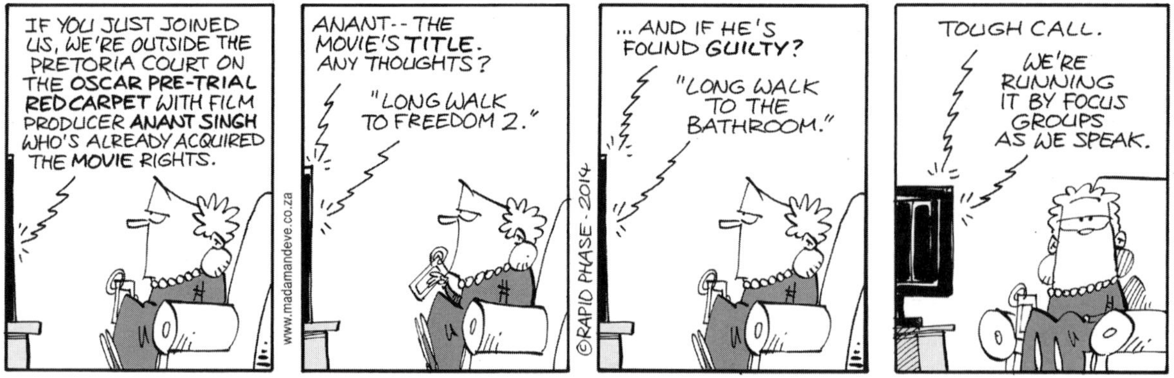
IF YOU JUST JOINED US, WE'RE OUTSIDE THE PRETORIA COURT ON THE OSCAR PRE-TRIAL RED CARPET WITH FILM PRODUCER ANANT SINGH WHO'S ALREADY ACQUIRED THE MOVIE RIGHTS.
www.madamandeve.co.za
ANANT-- THE MOVIE'S TITLE. ANY THOUGHTS?
"LONG WALK TO FREEDOM 2."
©RAPID PHASE-2014
... AND IF HE'S FOUND GUILTY?
"LONG WALK TO THE BATHROOM."
TOUGH CALL.
WE'RE RUNNING IT BY FOCUS GROUPS AS WE SPEAK.

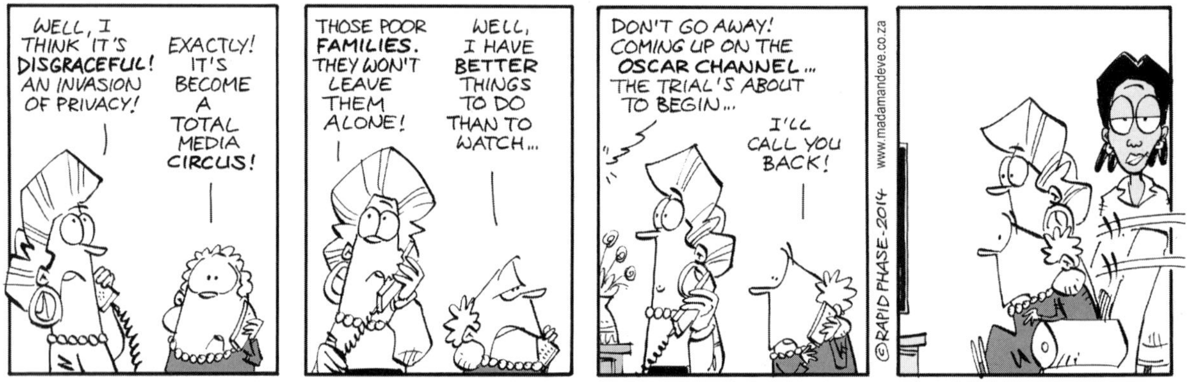
WELL, I THINK IT'S DISGRACEFUL! AN INVASION OF PRIVACY!
EXACTLY! IT'S BECOME A TOTAL MEDIA CIRCUS!
THOSE POOR FAMILIES. THEY WON'T LEAVE THEM ALONE!
WELL, I HAVE BETTER THINGS TO DO THAN TO WATCH...
DON'T GO AWAY! COMING UP ON THE OSCAR CHANNEL... THE TRIAL'S ABOUT TO BEGIN...
I'LL CALL YOU BACK!
©RAPID PHASE-2014
www.madamandeve.co.za

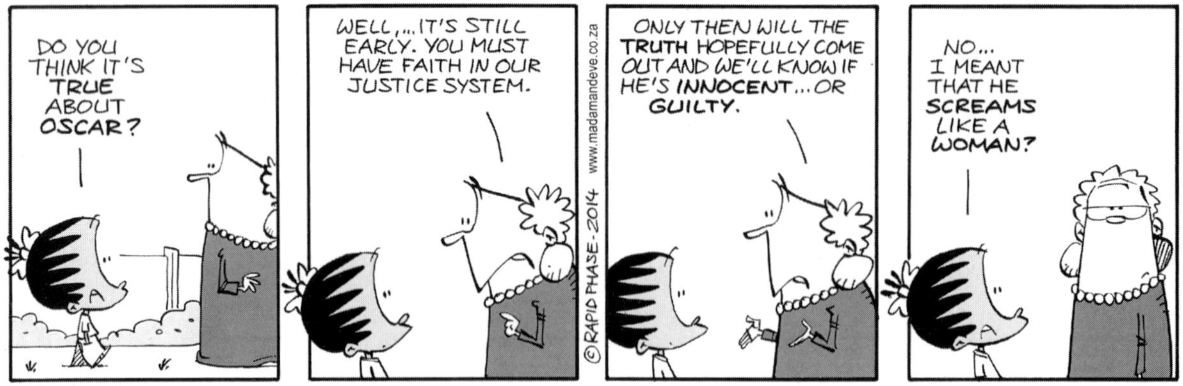
DO YOU THINK IT'S TRUE ABOUT OSCAR?
WELL,... IT'S STILL EARLY. YOU MUST HAVE FAITH IN OUR JUSTICE SYSTEM.
©RAPID PHASE-2014
www.madamandeve.co.za
ONLY THEN WILL THE TRUTH HOPEFULLY COME OUT AND WE'LL KNOW IF HE'S INNOCENT... OR GUILTY.
NO... I MEANT THAT HE SCREAMS LIKE A WOMAN?

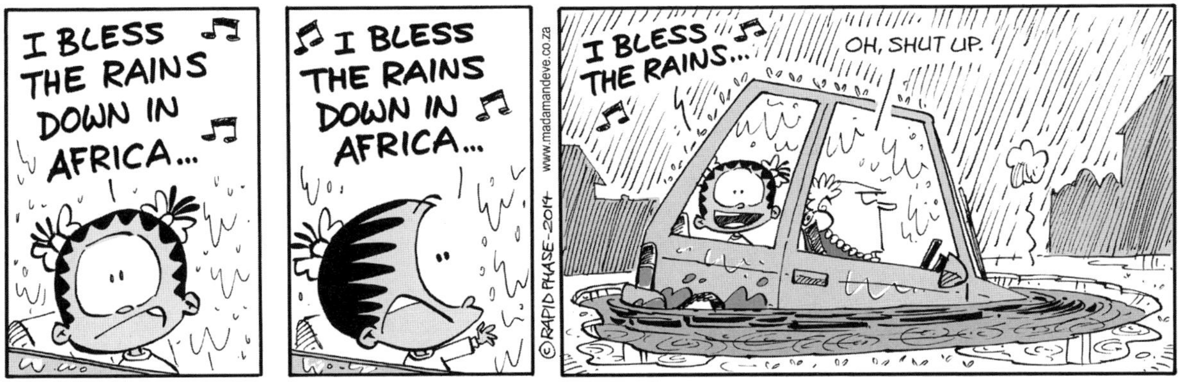
I BLESS THE RAINS DOWN IN AFRICA...
I BLESS THE RAINS DOWN IN AFRICA...
I BLESS THE RAINS...
OH, SHUT UP.
© RAPID PHASE-2014 www.madamandeve.co.za

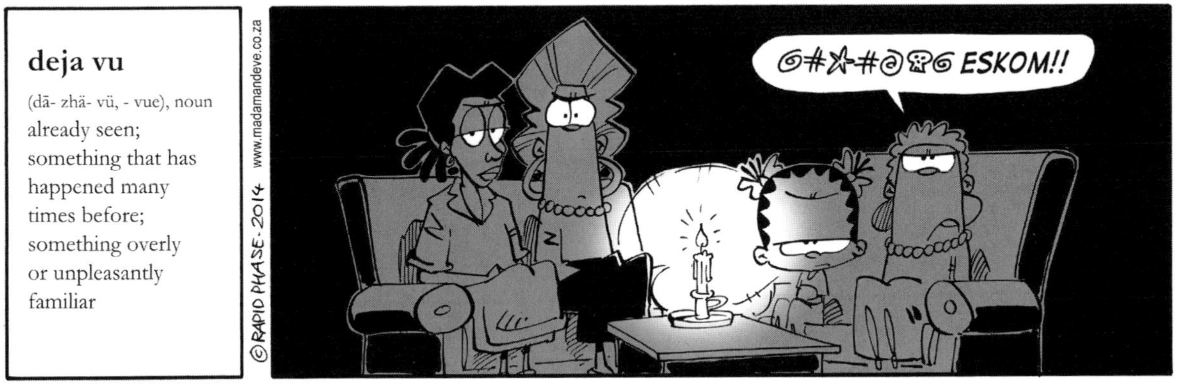
deja vu
(dā- zhä- vü, - vue), noun
already seen;
something that has
happened many
times before;
something overly
or unpleasantly
familiar
© RAPID PHASE-2014 www.madamandeve.co.za
@#✲#@☠@ ESKOM!!

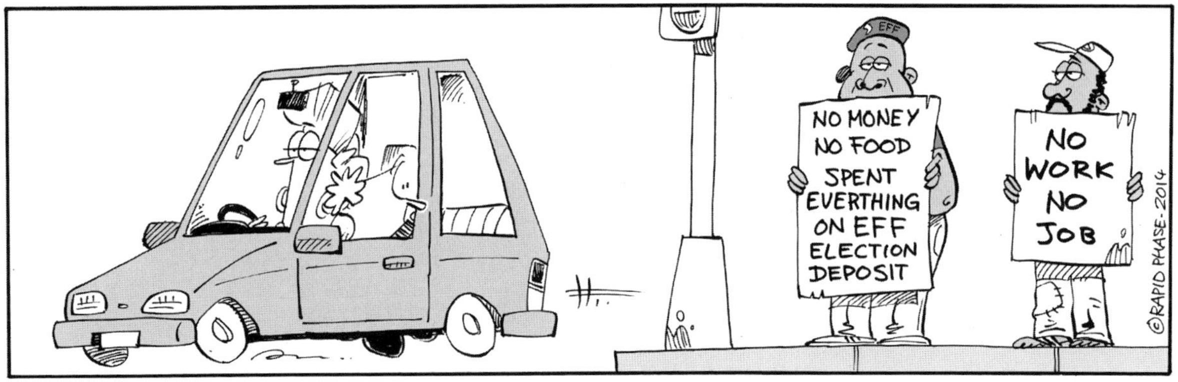
NO MONEY
NO FOOD
SPENT
EVERTHING
ON EFF
ELECTION
DEPOSIT
NO
WORK
NO
JOB
EFF
© RAPID PHASE-2014

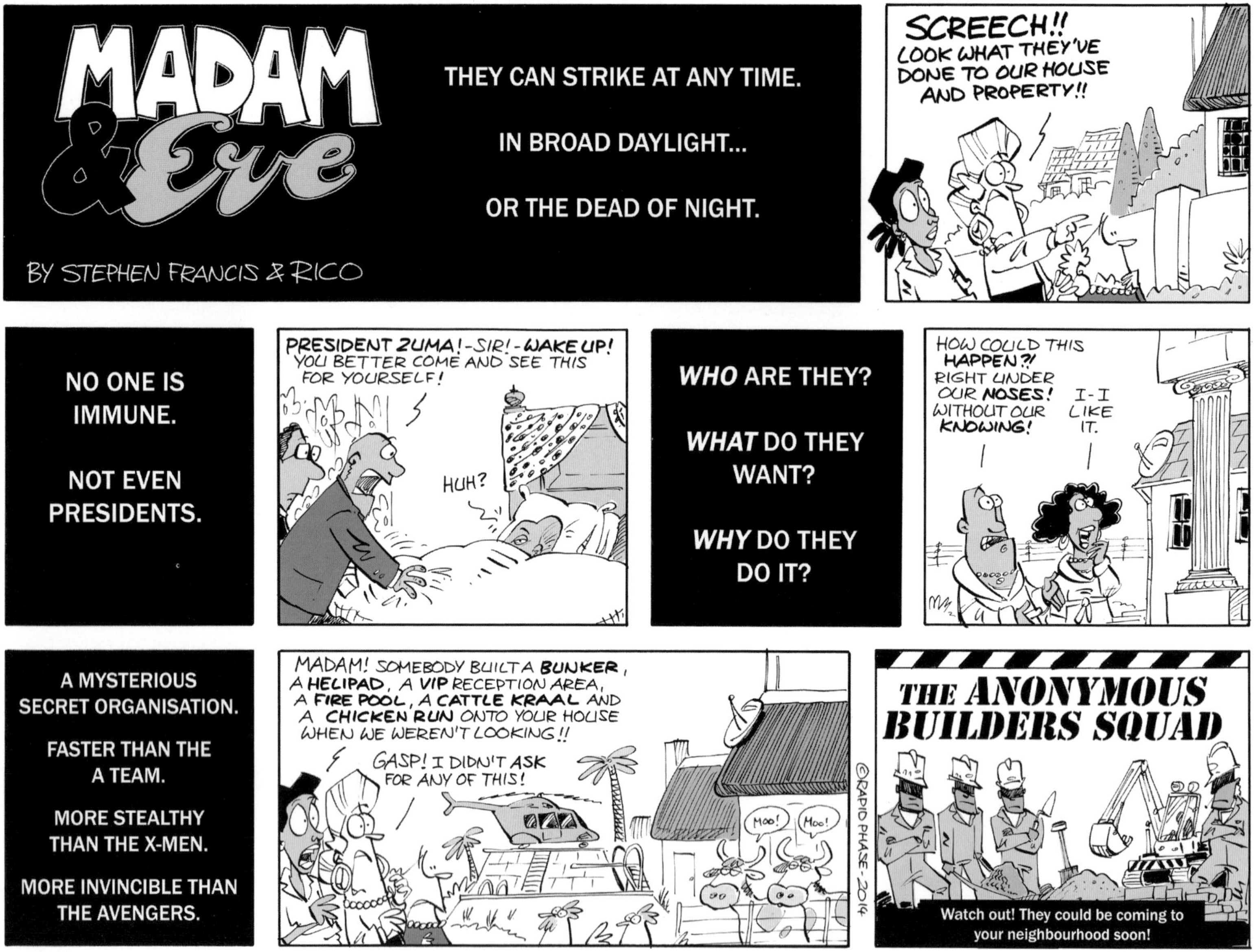
MADAM & Eve
BY STEPHEN FRANCIS & RICO
THEY CAN STRIKE AT ANY TIME.
IN BROAD DAYLIGHT...
OR THE DEAD OF NIGHT.
SCREECH!! LOOK WHAT THEY'VE DONE TO OUR HOUSE AND PROPERTY!!
NO ONE IS IMMUNE.
NOT EVEN PRESIDENTS.
PRESIDENT ZUMA! - SIR! - WAKE UP! YOU BETTER COME AND SEE THIS FOR YOURSELF!
HUH?
WHO ARE THEY?
WHAT DO THEY WANT?
WHY DO THEY DO IT?
HOW COULD THIS HAPPEN?! RIGHT UNDER OUR NOSES! WITHOUT OUR KNOWING!
I-I LIKE IT.
A MYSTERIOUS SECRET ORGANISATION.
FASTER THAN THE A TEAM.
MORE STEALTHY THAN THE X-MEN.
MORE INVINCIBLE THAN THE AVENGERS.
MADAM! SOMEBODY BUILT A BUNKER, A HELIPAD, A VIP RECEPTION AREA, A FIRE POOL, A CATTLE KRAAL AND A CHICKEN RUN ONTO YOUR HOUSE WHEN WE WEREN'T LOOKING!!
GASP! I DIDN'T ASK FOR ANY OF THIS!
MOO!
MOO!
©RAPID PHASE - 2014
THE ANONYMOUS BUILDERS SQUAD
Watch out! They could be coming to your neighbourhood soon!

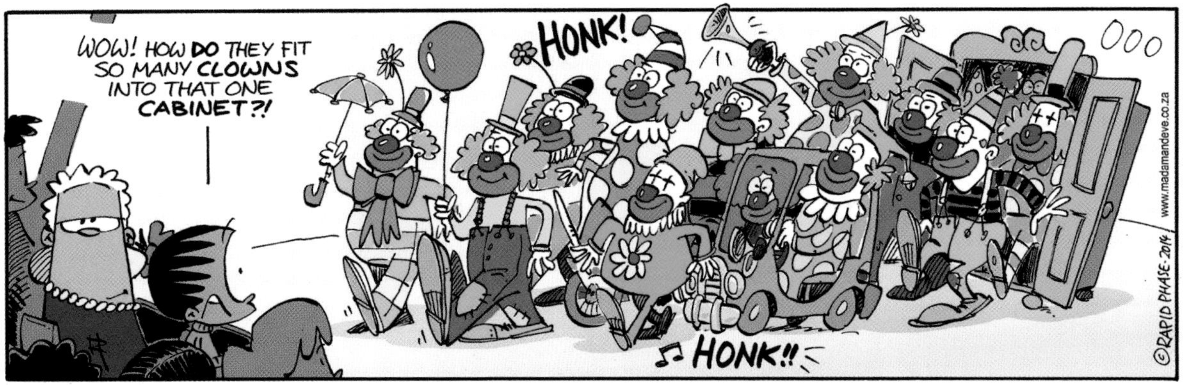
WOW! HOW DO THEY FIT SO MANY CLOWNS INTO THAT ONE CABINET?!
HONK!
OOO
HONK!!
©RAPID PHASE-2014 www.madamandeve.co.za

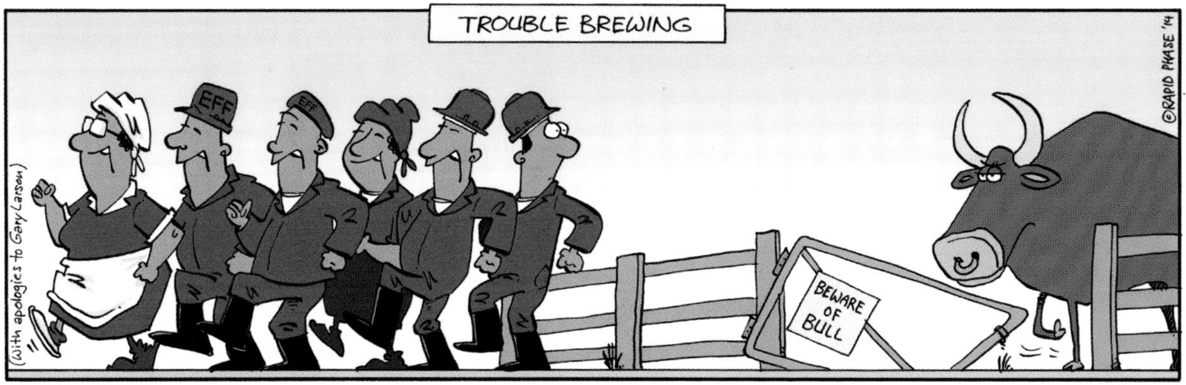
TROUBLE BREWING
(With apologies to Gary Larson)
EFF
EFF
BEWARE OF BULL
©RAPID PHASE '14

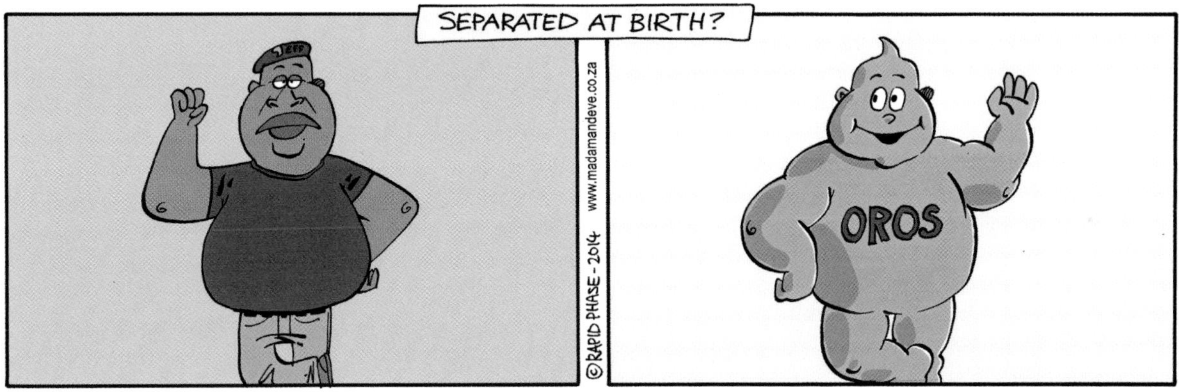
SEPARATED AT BIRTH?
EFF
©RAPID PHASE-2014 www.madamandeve.co.za
OROS

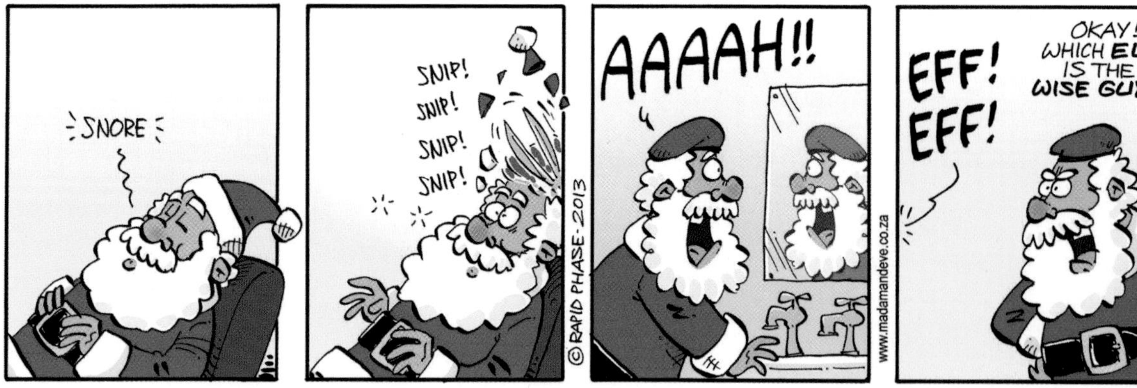
SNORE
SNIP!
SNIP!
SNIP!
SNIP!
©RAPID PHASE-2013
AAAAH!!
www.madamandeve.co.za
EFF!
EFF!
OKAY! WHICH **ELF** IS THE **WISE GUY**?!

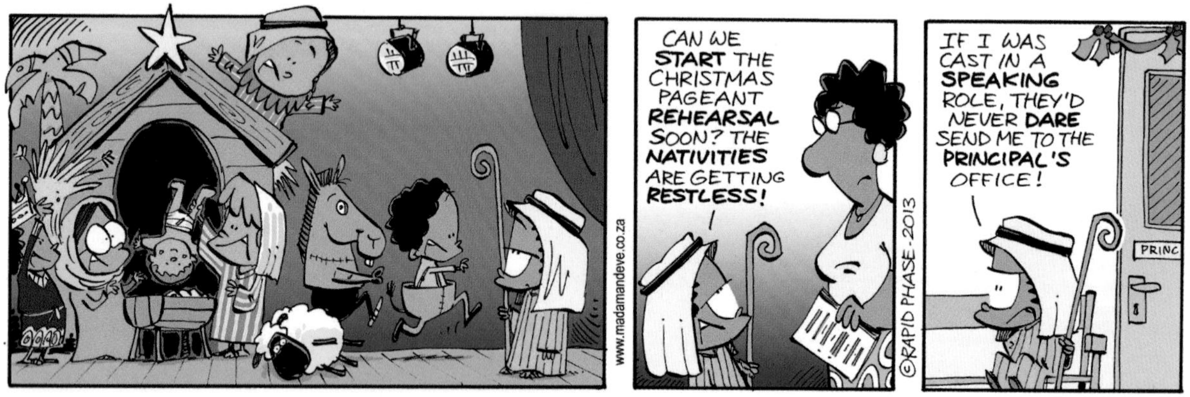
www.madamandeve.co.za
CAN WE **START** THE CHRISTMAS PAGEANT **REHEARSAL** SOON? THE **NATIVITIES** ARE GETTING **RESTLESS**!
©RAPID PHASE-2013
IF I WAS CAST IN A **SPEAKING** ROLE, THEY'D NEVER **DARE** SEND ME TO THE **PRINCIPAL'S** OFFICE!
PRINC

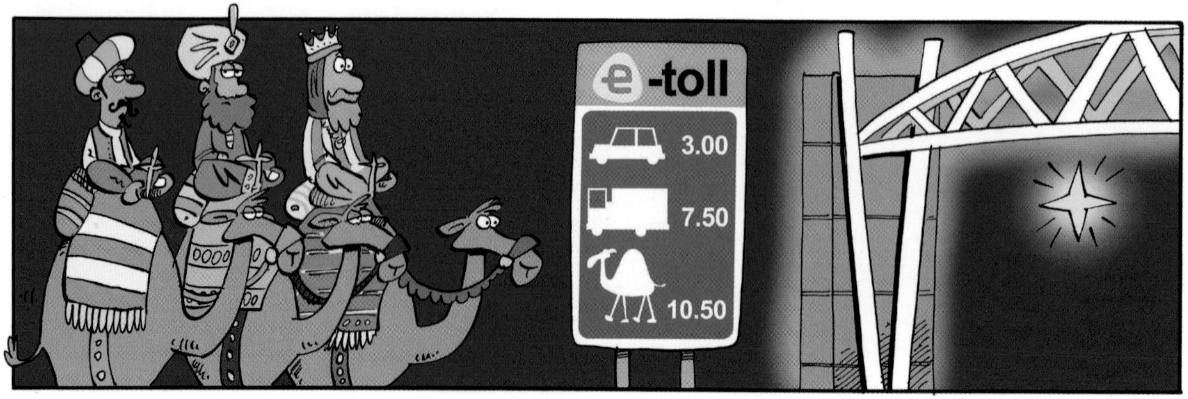
e-toll
3.00
7.50
10.50

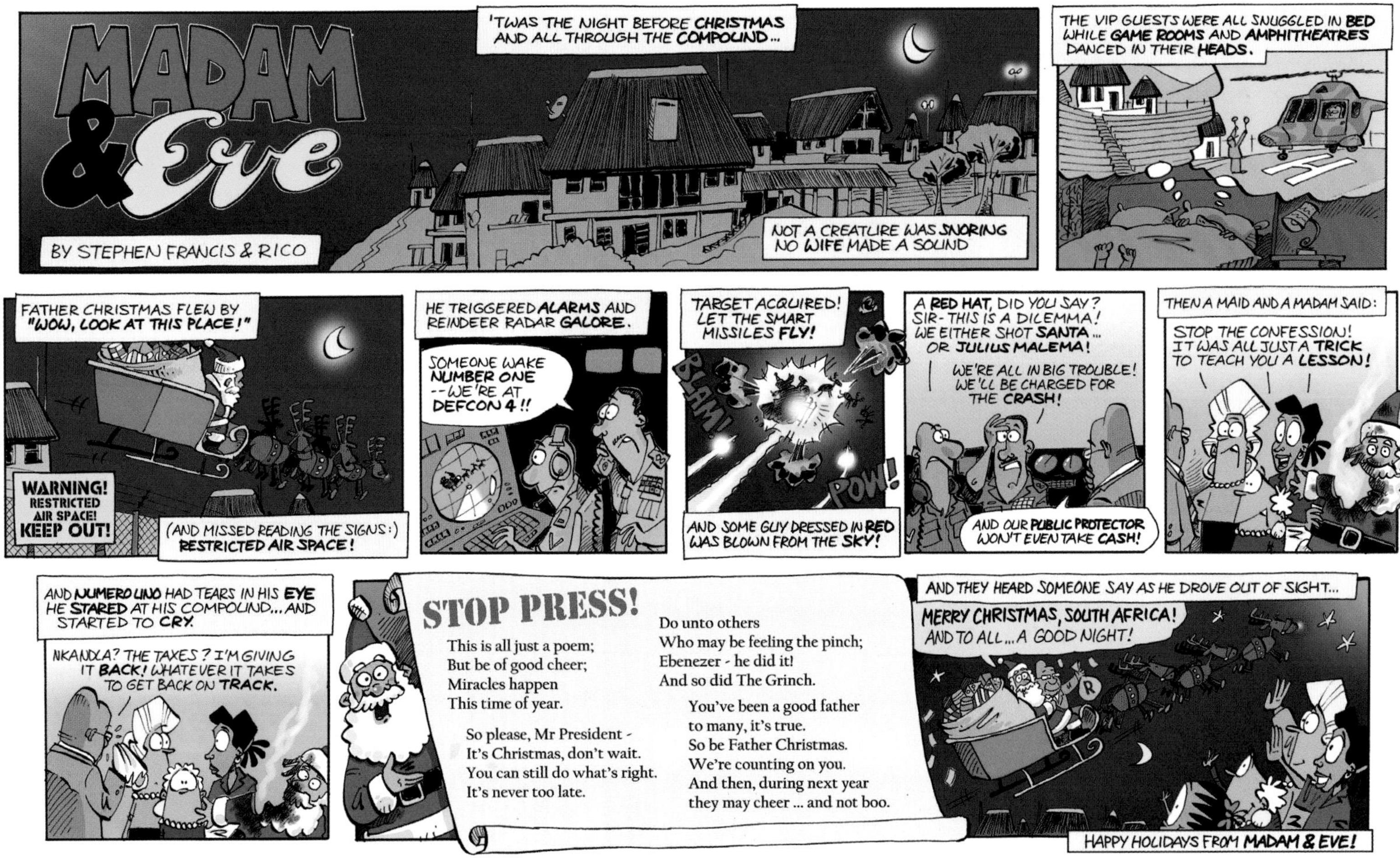
MADAM & Eve
BY STEPHEN FRANCIS & RICO
'TWAS THE NIGHT BEFORE CHRISTMAS AND ALL THROUGH THE COMPOUND...
NOT A CREATURE WAS SNORING NO WIFE MADE A SOUND
THE VIP GUESTS WERE ALL SNUGGLED IN BED WHILE GAME ROOMS AND AMPHITHEATRES DANCED IN THEIR HEADS.
FATHER CHRISTMAS FLEW BY "WOW, LOOK AT THIS PLACE!"
WARNING! RESTRICTED AIR SPACE! KEEP OUT!
(AND MISSED READING THE SIGNS:) RESTRICTED AIR SPACE!
HE TRIGGERED ALARMS AND REINDEER RADAR GALORE.
SOMEONE WAKE NUMBER ONE --WE'RE AT DEFCON 4!!
TARGET ACQUIRED! LET THE SMART MISSILES FLY!
BLAM!
POW!
AND SOME GUY DRESSED IN RED WAS BLOWN FROM THE SKY!
A RED HAT, DID YOU SAY? SIR- THIS IS A DILEMMA! WE EITHER SHOT SANTA... OR JULIUS MALEMA!
WE'RE ALL IN BIG TROUBLE! WE'LL BE CHARGED FOR THE CRASH!
AND OUR PUBLIC PROTECTOR WON'T EVEN TAKE CASH!
THEN A MAID AND A MADAM SAID:
STOP THE CONFESSION! IT WAS ALL JUST A TRICK TO TEACH YOU A LESSON!
AND NUMERO UNO HAD TEARS IN HIS EYE HE STARED AT HIS COMPOUND... AND STARTED TO CRY.
NKANDLA? THE TAXES? I'M GIVING IT BACK! WHATEVER IT TAKES TO GET BACK ON TRACK.
STOP PRESS!
This is all just a poem;
But be of good cheer;
Miracles happen
This time of year.
So please, Mr President -
It's Christmas, don't wait.
You can still do what's right.
It's never too late.
Do unto others
Who may be feeling the pinch;
Ebenezer - he did it!
And so did The Grinch.
You've been a good father
to many, it's true.
So be Father Christmas.
We're counting on you.
And then, during next year
they may cheer ... and not boo.
AND THEY HEARD SOMEONE SAY AS HE DROVE OUT OF SIGHT...
MERRY CHRISTMAS, SOUTH AFRICA! AND TO ALL... A GOOD NIGHT!
HAPPY HOLIDAYS FROM MADAM & EVE!

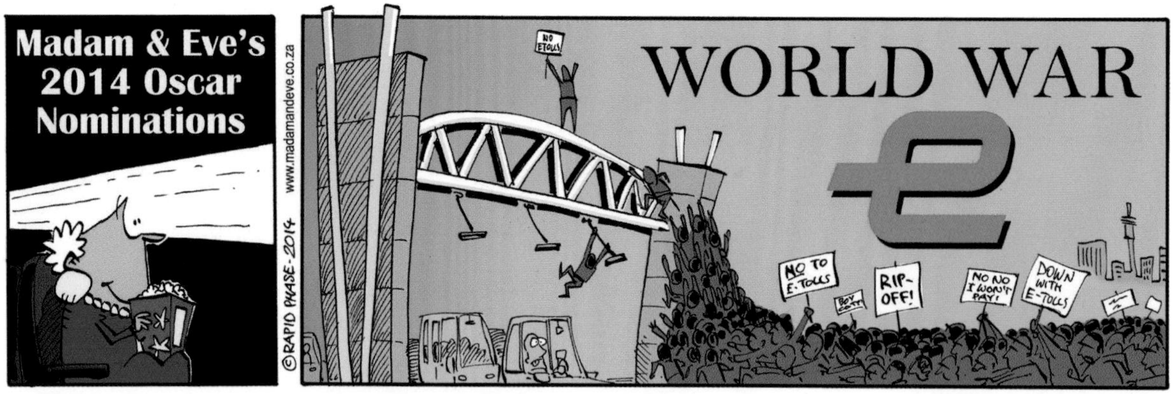
Madam & Eve's 2014 Oscar Nominations
www.madamandeve.co.za
©RAPID PHASE-2014
WORLD WAR
NO ETOLLS
NO TO E-TOLLS
RIP-OFF!
NO NO I WON'T PAY!
DOWN WITH E-TOLLS

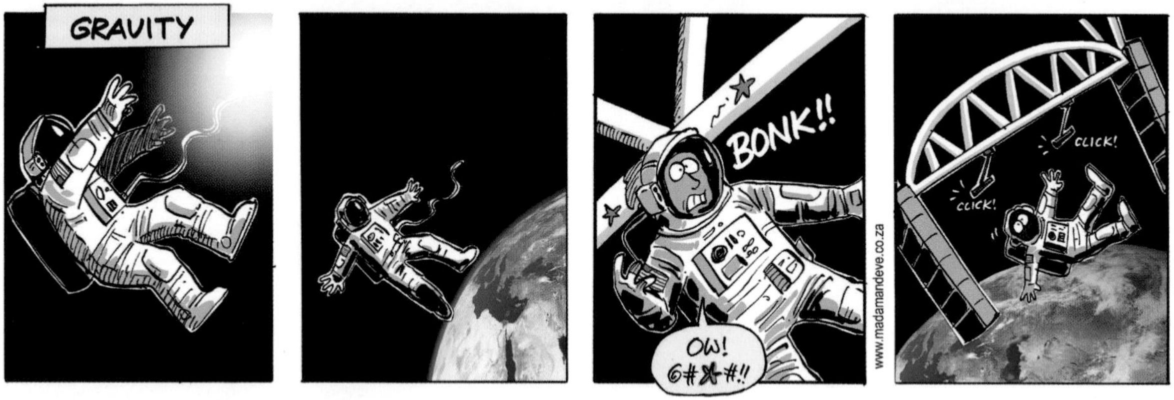
GRAVITY
BONK!!
OW!
CLICK!
CLICK!
www.madamandeve.co.za

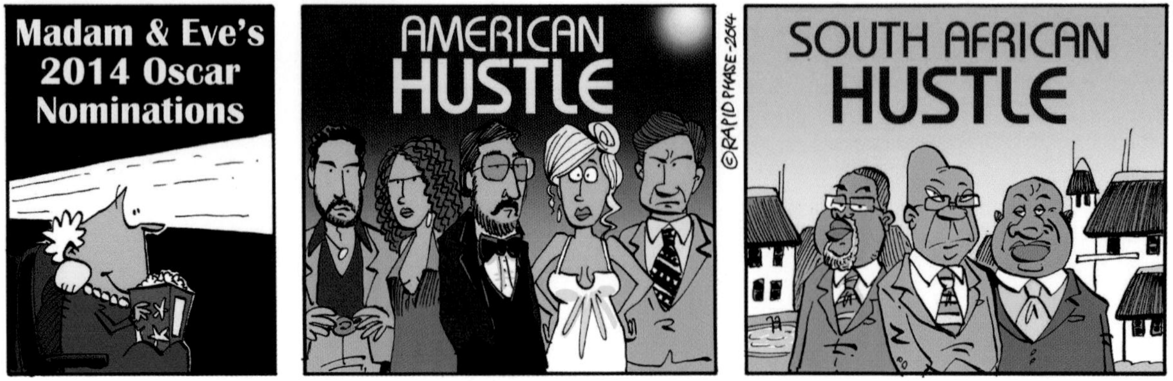
Madam & Eve's 2014 Oscar Nominations
AMERICAN HUSTLE
©RAPID PHASE-2014
SOUTH AFRICAN HUSTLE

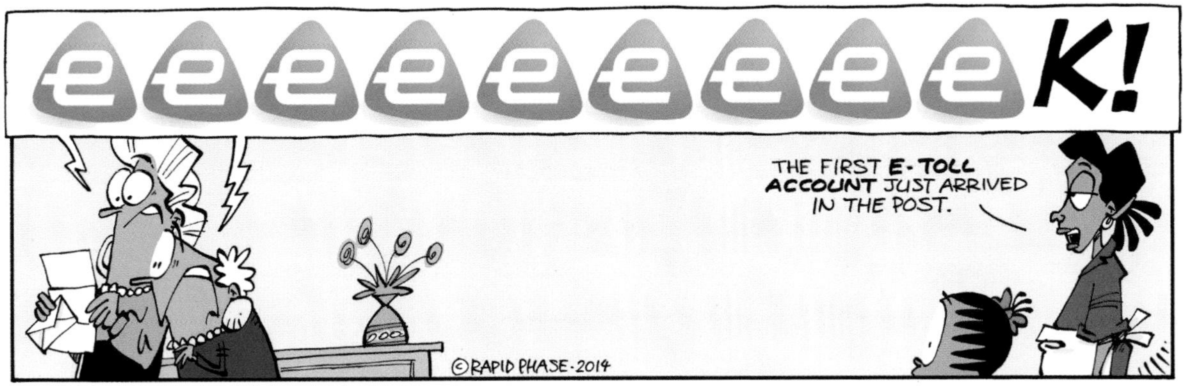
eeeeeeeeeK!
THE FIRST E-TOLL ACCOUNT JUST ARRIVED IN THE POST.
©RAPID PHASE-2014

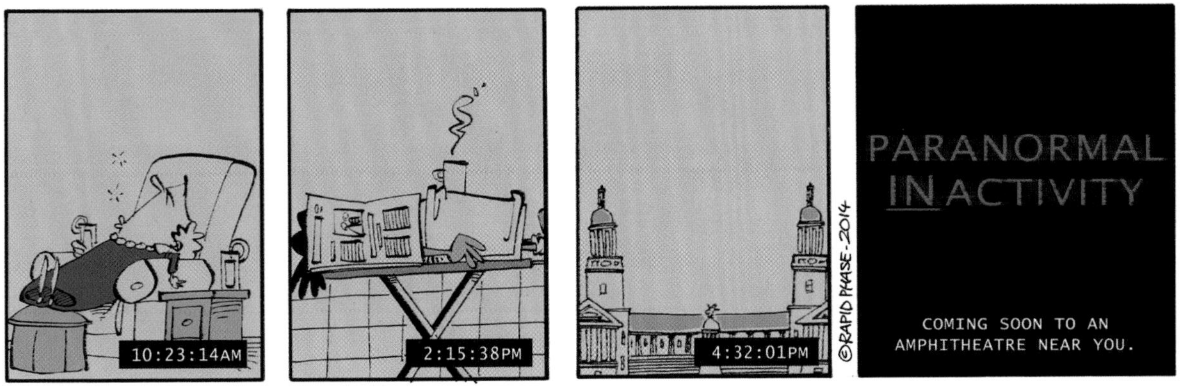
10:23:14AM
2:15:38PM
4:32:01PM
©RAPID PHASE-2014
PARANORMAL INACTIVITY
COMING SOON TO AN AMPHITHEATRE NEAR YOU.

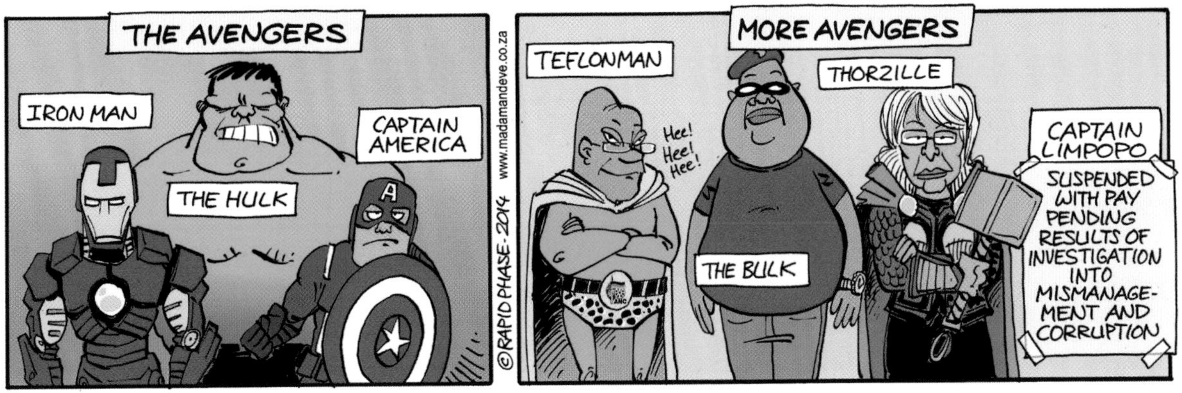
THE AVENGERS
IRON MAN
THE HULK
CAPTAIN AMERICA
©RAPID PHASE-2014 www.madamandeve.co.za
MORE AVENGERS
TEFLONMAN
Hee! Hee! Hee!
THE BULK
THORZILLE
CAPTAIN LIMPOPO
SUSPENDED WITH PAY PENDING RESULTS OF INVESTIGATION INTO MISMANAGEMENT AND CORRUPTION

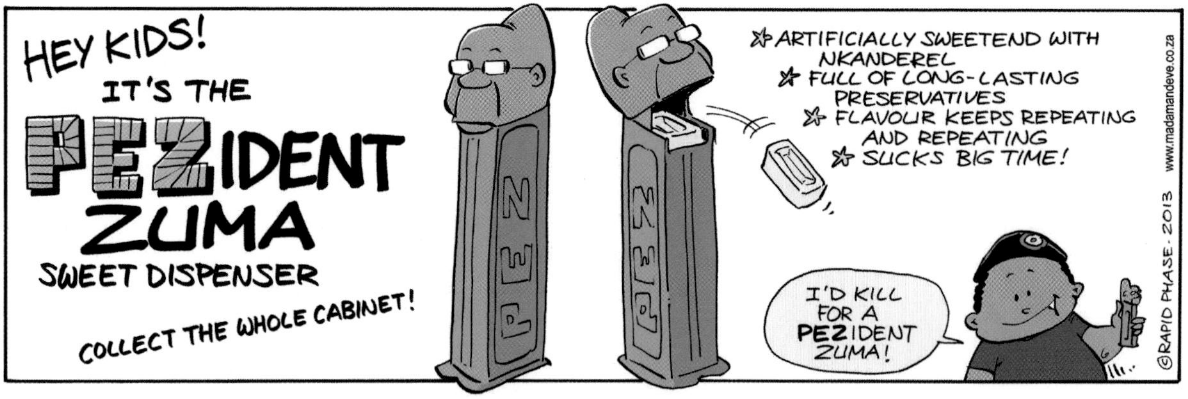
HEY KIDS!
IT'S THE
PEZIDENT
ZUMA
SWEET DISPENSER
COLLECT THE WHOLE CABINET!
PEZ
PEZ
ARTIFICIALLY SWEETEND WITH NKANDEREL
FULL OF LONG-LASTING PRESERVATIVES
FLAVOUR KEEPS REPEATING AND REPEATING
SUCKS BIG TIME!
I'D KILL FOR A PEZIDENT ZUMA!
©RAPID PHASE - 2013 www.madamandeve.co.za

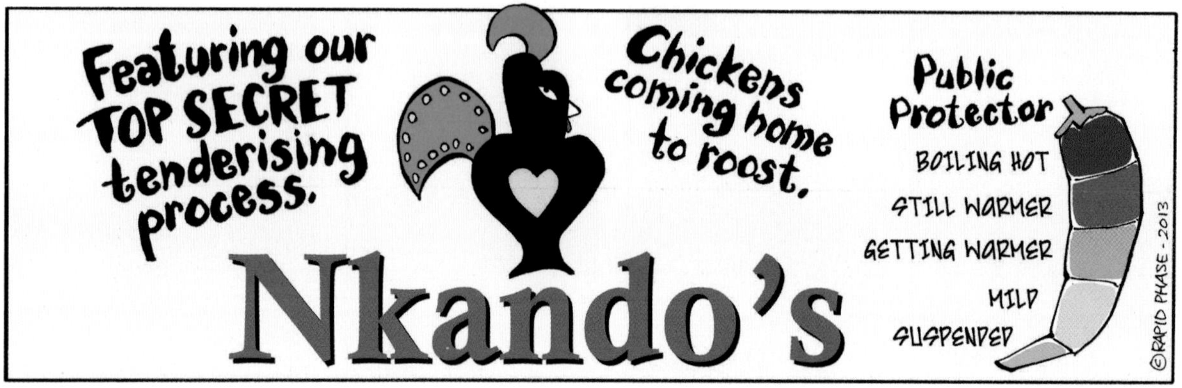
Featuring our TOP SECRET tenderising process.
Chickens coming home to roost.
Nkando's
Public Protector
BOILING HOT
STILL WARMER
GETTING WARMER
MILD
SUSPENDED
©RAPID PHASE - 2013

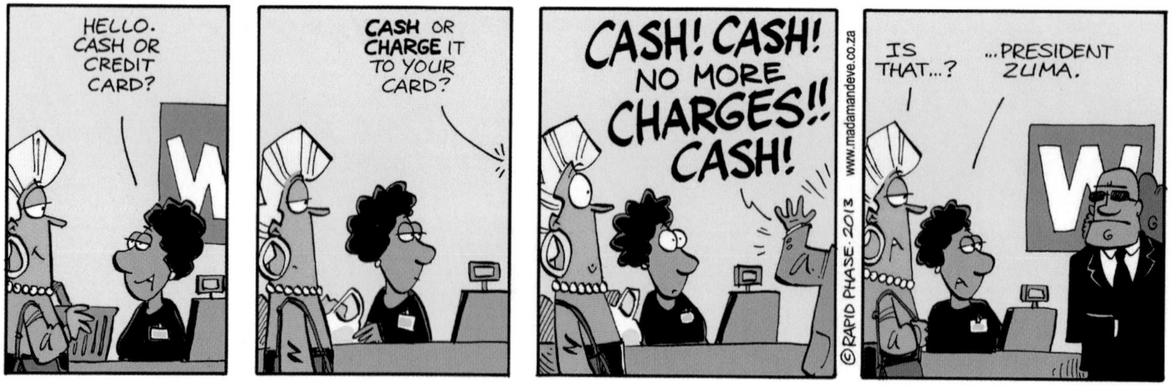
HELLO. CASH OR CREDIT CARD?
CASH OR CHARGE IT TO YOUR CARD?
CASH! CASH! NO MORE CHARGES!! CASH!
©RAPID PHASE: 2013 www.madamandeve.co.za
IS THAT...?
...PRESIDENT ZUMA.

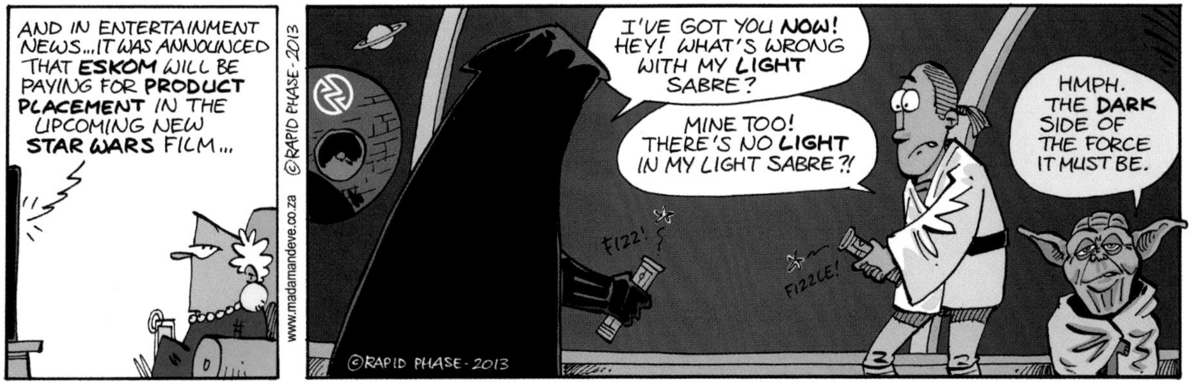
AND IN ENTERTAINMENT NEWS...IT WAS ANNOUNCED THAT **ESKOM** WILL BE PAYING FOR **PRODUCT PLACEMENT** IN THE UPCOMING NEW **STAR WARS** FILM...
www.madamandeve.co.za
©RAPID PHASE-2013
I'VE GOT YOU **NOW**! HEY! WHAT'S WRONG WITH MY **LIGHT** SABRE?
MINE TOO! THERE'S NO **LIGHT** IN MY LIGHT SABRE?!
FIZZ!
FIZZLE!
HMPH. THE **DARK** SIDE OF THE FORCE IT MUST BE.
©RAPID PHASE-2013

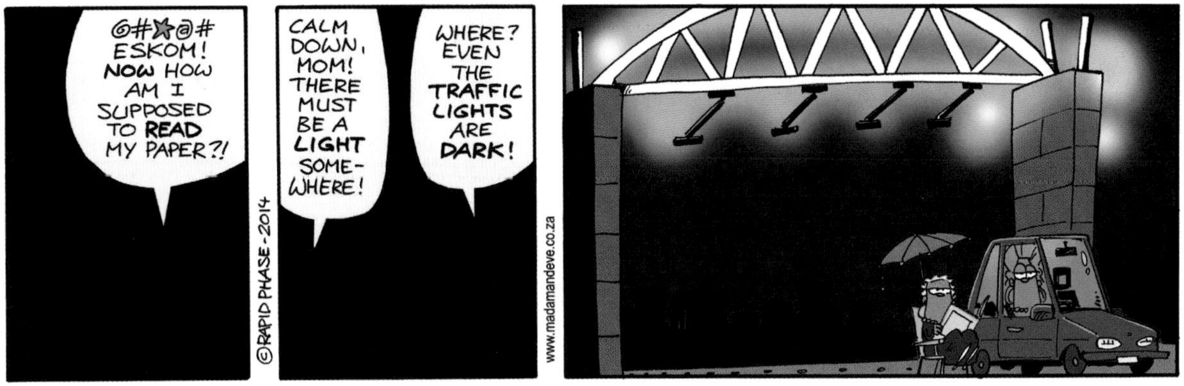
@#*@# ESKOM! **NOW** HOW AM I SUPPOSED TO **READ** MY PAPER?!
©RAPID PHASE-2014
CALM DOWN, MOM! THERE MUST BE A **LIGHT** SOMEWHERE!
WHERE? EVEN THE **TRAFFIC LIGHTS** ARE **DARK**!
www.madamandeve.co.za

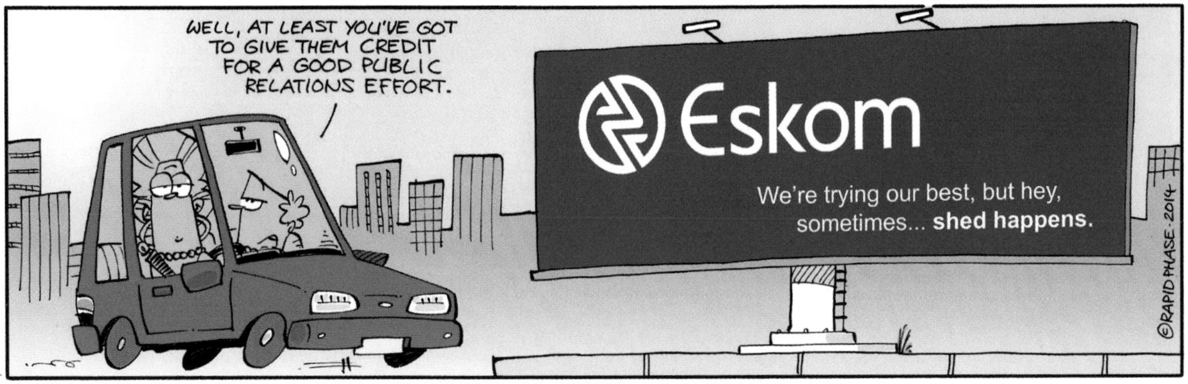
WELL, AT LEAST YOU'VE GOT TO GIVE THEM CREDIT FOR A GOOD PUBLIC RELATIONS EFFORT.
Eskom
We're trying our best, but hey, sometimes... **shed happens.**
©RAPID PHASE-2014

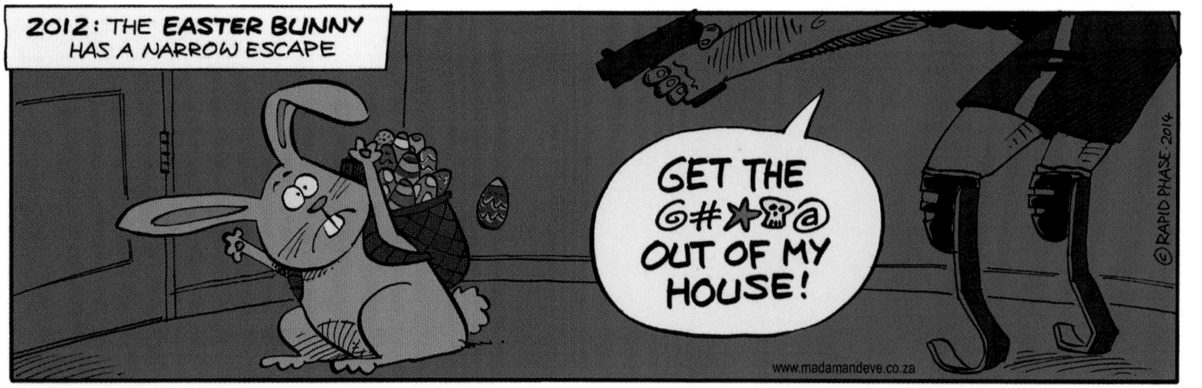
2012: THE EASTER BUNNY HAS A NARROW ESCAPE
GET THE G#*?@ OUT OF MY HOUSE!
©RAPID PHASE-2014
www.madamandeve.co.za

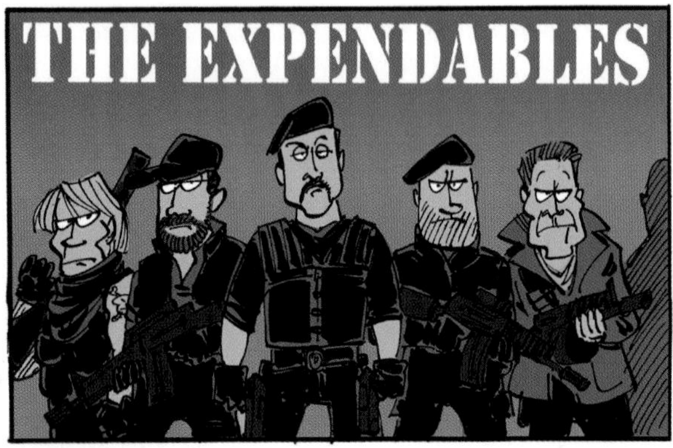
THE EXPENDABLES
©RAPID PHASE-2014 www.madamandeve.co.za

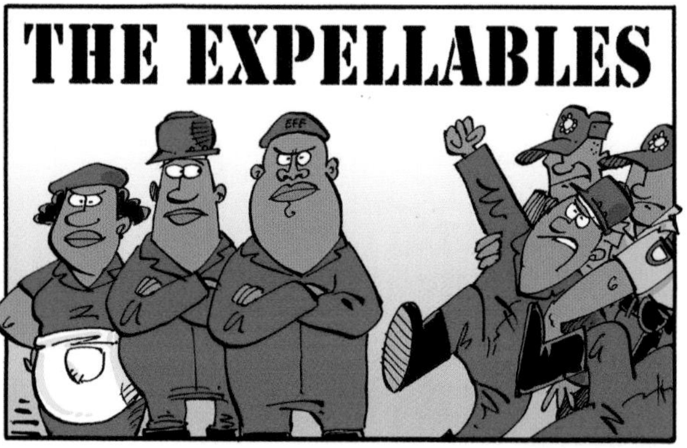
THE EXPELLABLES
EFF

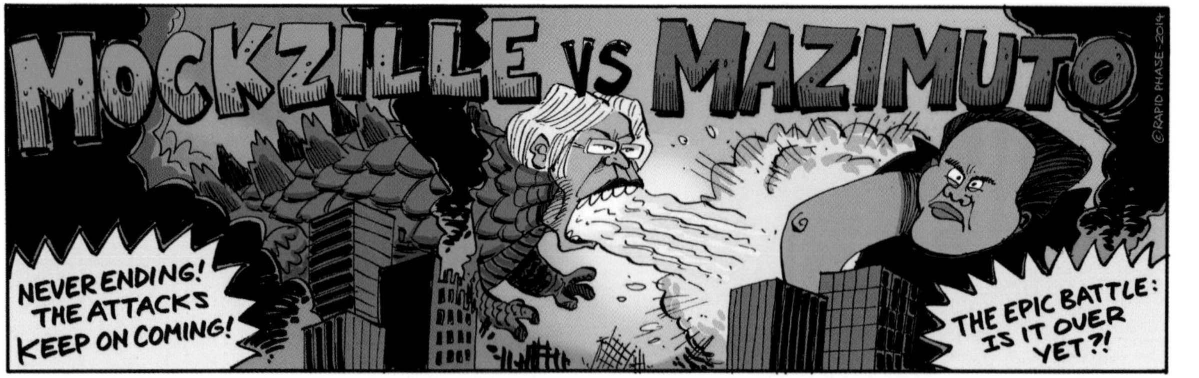
MOCKZILLE VS MAZIMUTO
©RAPID PHASE-2014
NEVER ENDING! THE ATTACKS KEEP ON COMING!
THE EPIC BATTLE: IS IT OVER YET?!

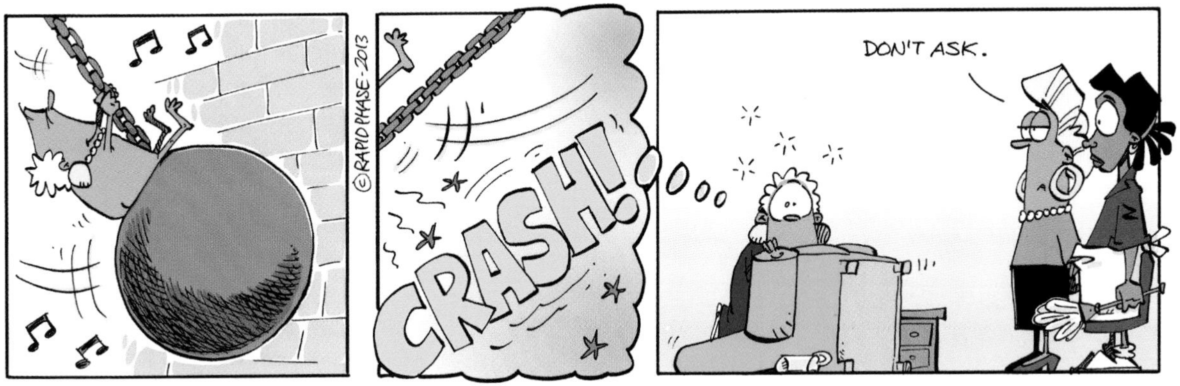
©RAPID PHASE-2013
CRASH!
DON'T ASK.

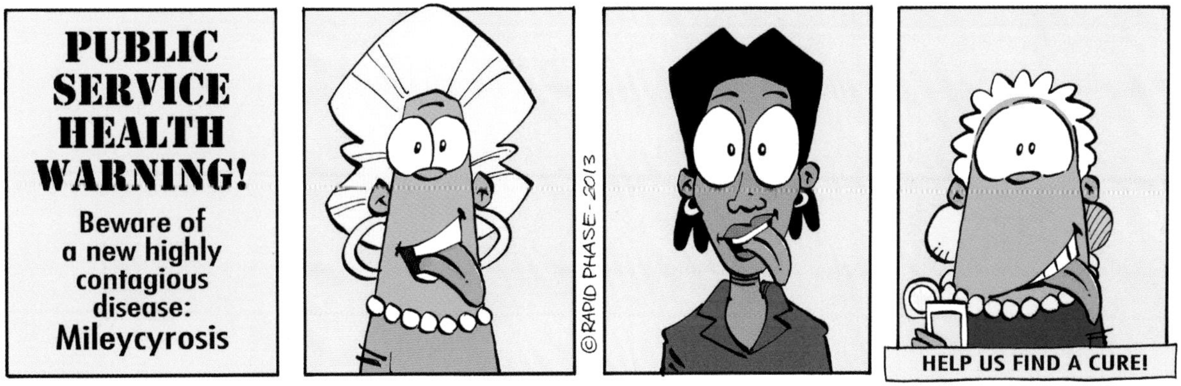
PUBLIC SERVICE HEALTH WARNING!
Beware of a new highly contagious disease:
Mileycyrosis
©RAPID PHASE-2013
HELP US FIND A CURE!

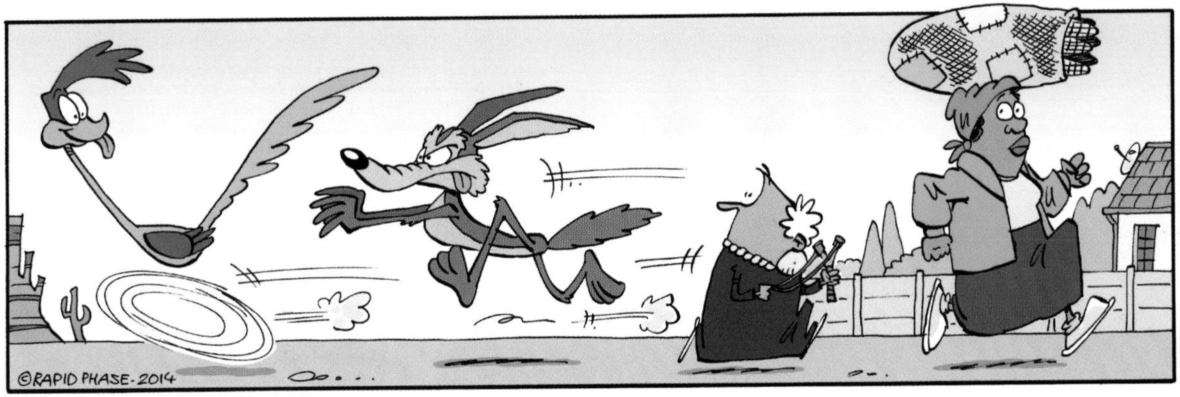
©RAPID PHASE-2014

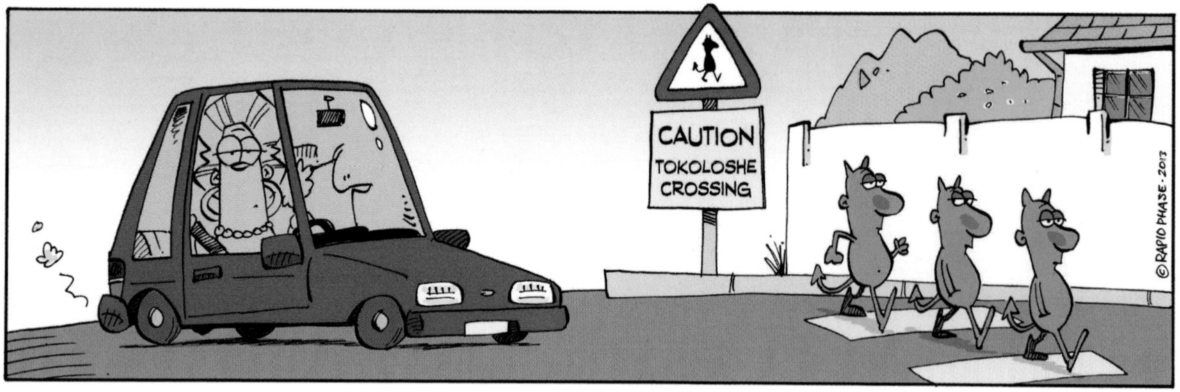
CAUTION
TOKOLOSHE
CROSSING
©RAPID PHASE-2013

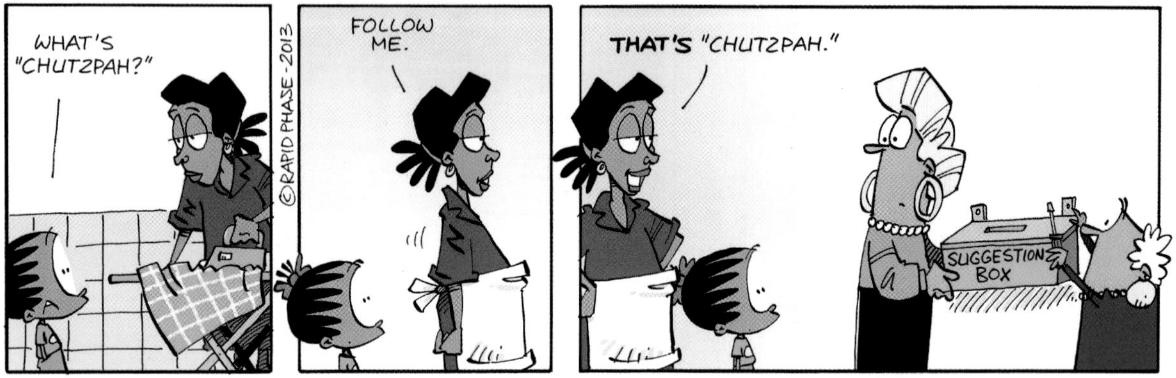
WHAT'S "CHUTZPAH?"
©RAPID PHASE-2013
FOLLOW ME.
THAT'S "CHUTZPAH."
SUGGESTION BOX

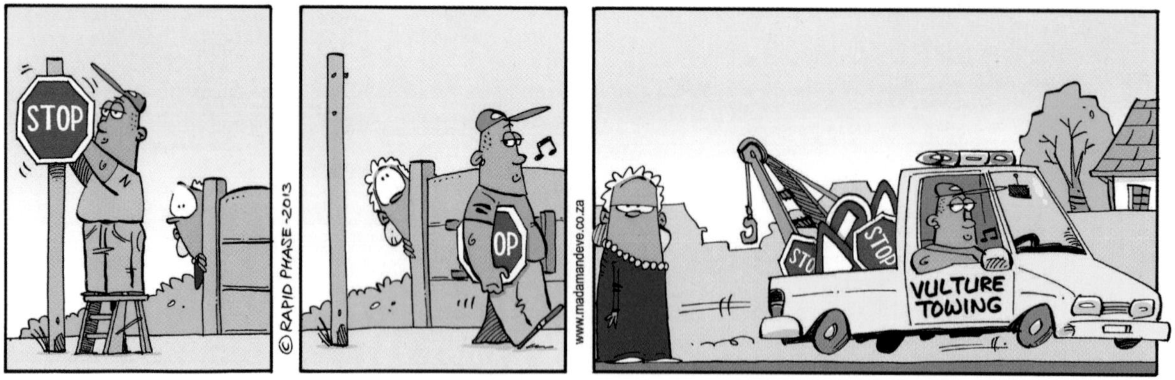
STOP
©RAPID PHASE-2013
OP
www.madamandeve.co.za
STOP
STOP
VULTURE TOWING

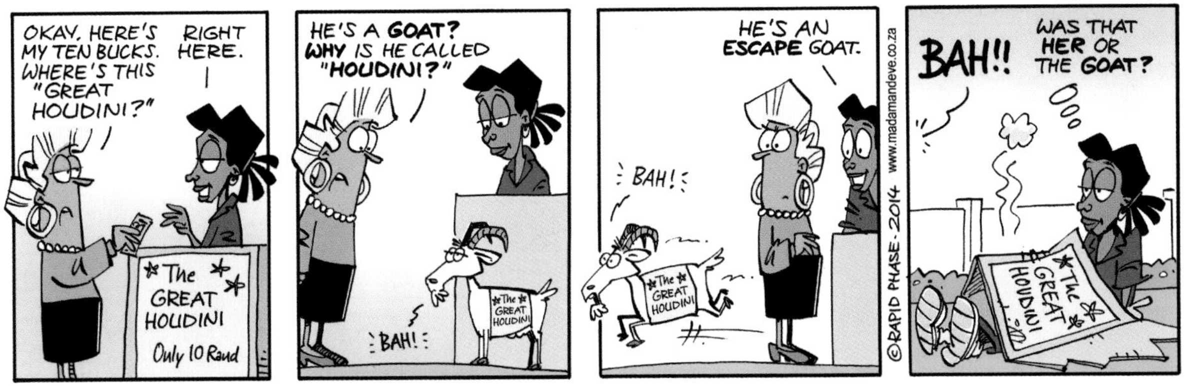
OKAY, HERE'S MY TEN BUCKS. WHERE'S THIS "GREAT HOUDINI?"
RIGHT HERE.
The GREAT HOUDINI Only 10 Rand
HE'S A GOAT? WHY IS HE CALLED "HOUDINI?"
BAH!
The GREAT HOUDINI
HE'S AN ESCAPE GOAT.
BAH!
The GREAT HOUDINI
©RAPID PHASE · 2014 www.madamandeve.co.za
BAH!!
WAS THAT HER OR THE GOAT?
THE GREAT HOUDINI

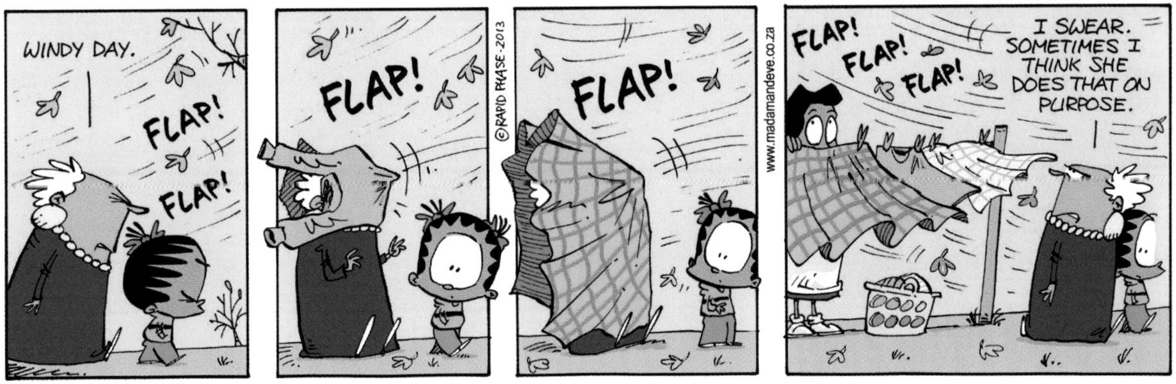
WINDY DAY.
FLAP!
FLAP!
FLAP!
©RAPID PHASE · 2013
FLAP!
www.madamandeve.co.za
FLAP!
FLAP!
FLAP!
I SWEAR. SOMETIMES I THINK SHE DOES THAT ON PURPOSE.

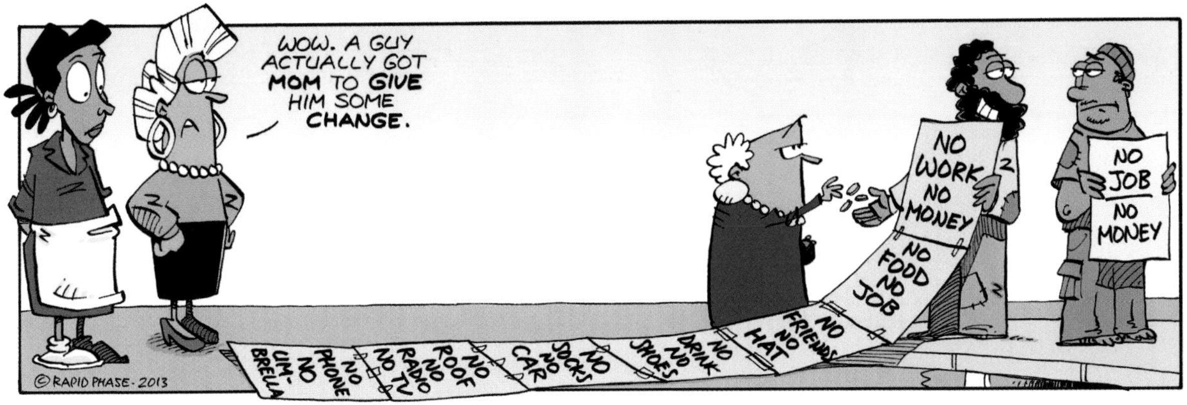
WOW. A GUY ACTUALLY GOT MOM TO GIVE HIM SOME CHANGE.
NO WORK NO MONEY
NO FOOD NO JOB
NO FRIENDS
NO HAT
NO DRINK NO SHOES
NO SOCKS NO CAR
NO ROOF NO RADIO NO TV
NO PHONE NO UM-BRELLA
NO JOB NO MONEY
©RAPID PHASE · 2013

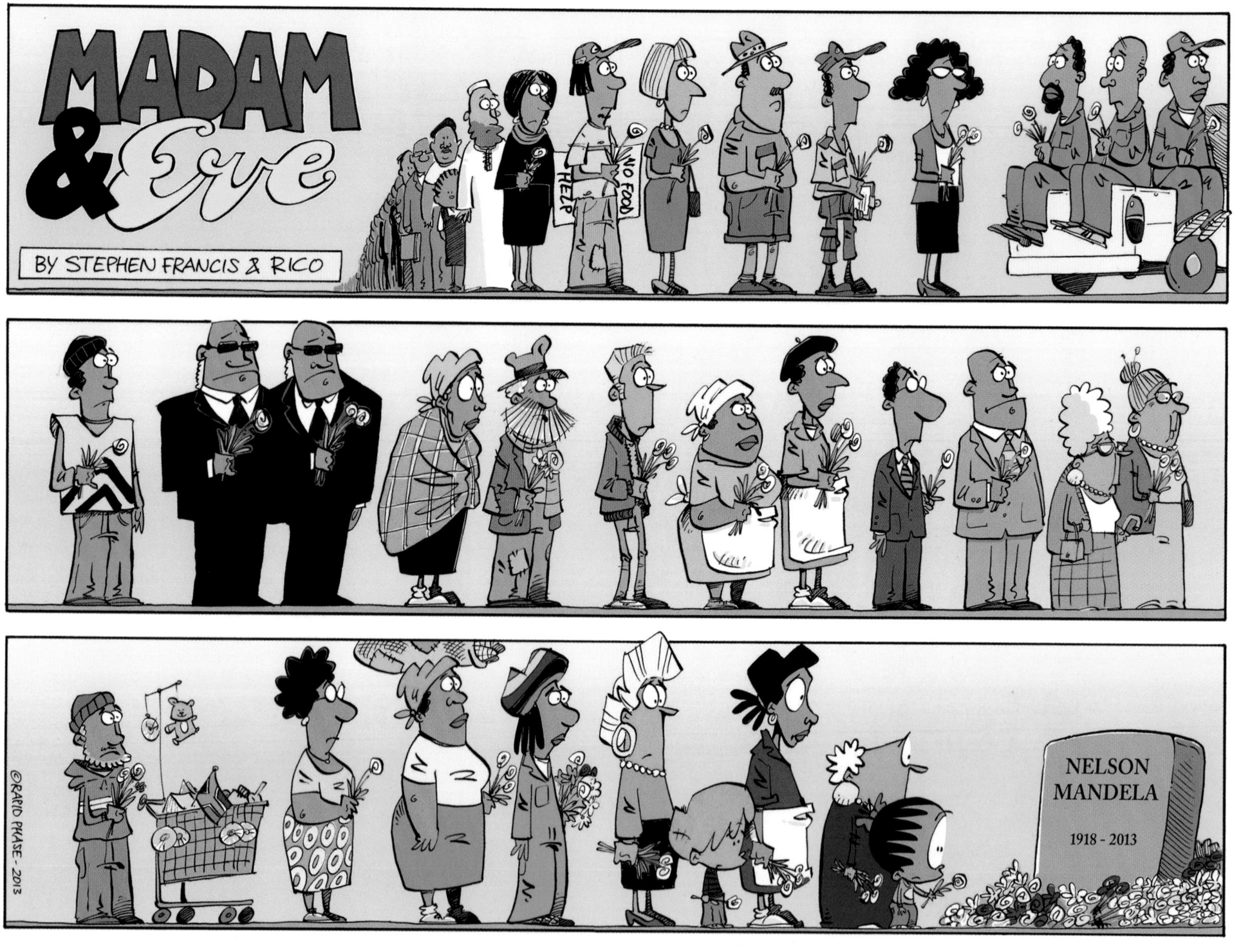

MADAM & Eve
BY STEPHEN FRANCIS & RICO
HELP
NO FOOD
©RAPID PHASE - 2013
NELSON MANDELA
1918 - 2013

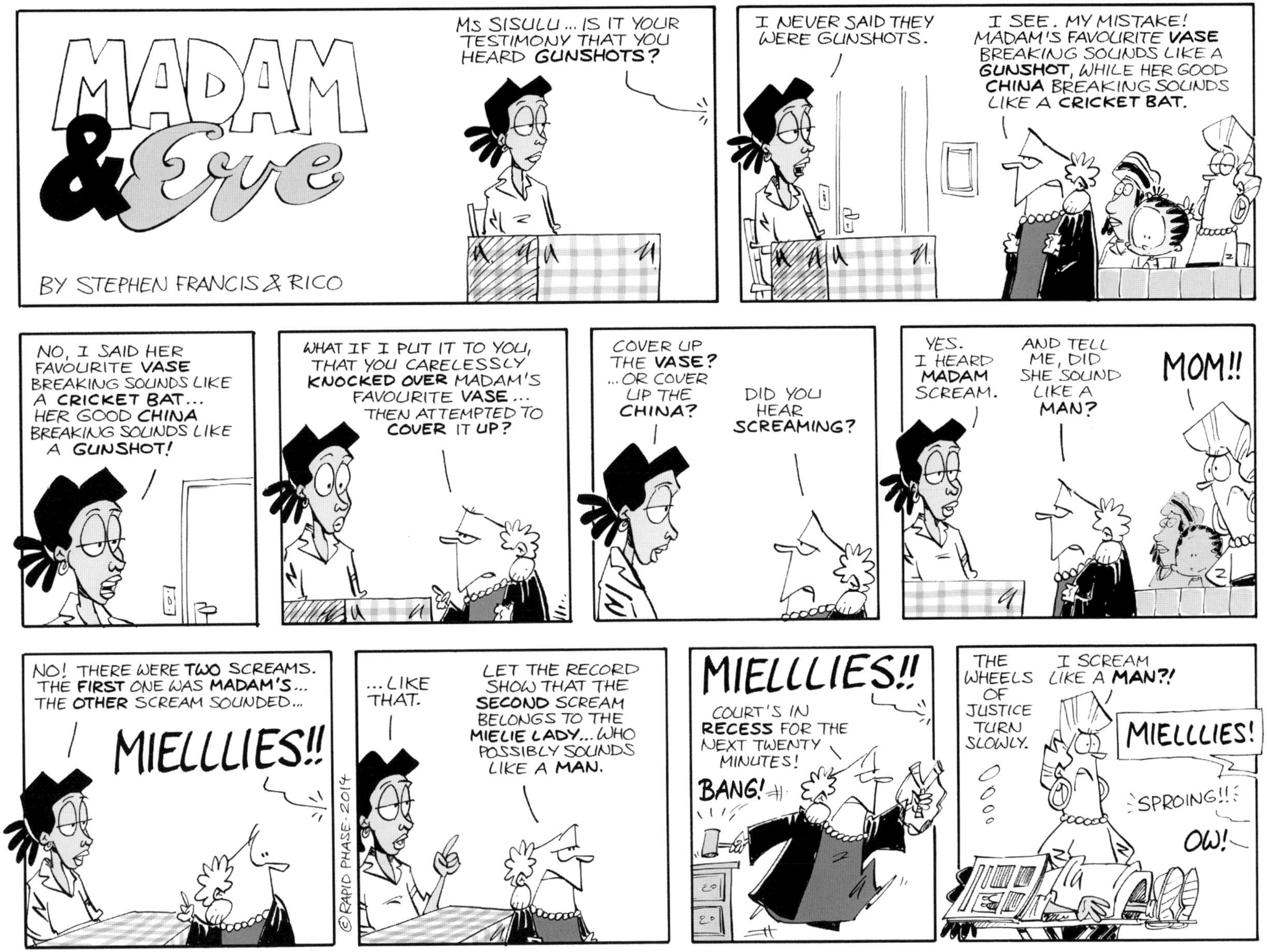
MADAM & Eve
BY STEPHEN FRANCIS & RICO
Ms SISULU... IS IT YOUR TESTIMONY THAT YOU HEARD GUNSHOTS?
I NEVER SAID THEY WERE GUNSHOTS.
I SEE. MY MISTAKE! MADAM'S FAVOURITE VASE BREAKING SOUNDS LIKE A GUNSHOT, WHILE HER GOOD CHINA BREAKING SOUNDS LIKE A CRICKET BAT.
NO, I SAID HER FAVOURITE VASE BREAKING SOUNDS LIKE A CRICKET BAT... HER GOOD CHINA BREAKING SOUNDS LIKE A GUNSHOT!
WHAT IF I PUT IT TO YOU, THAT YOU CARELESSLY KNOCKED OVER MADAM'S FAVOURITE VASE... THEN ATTEMPTED TO COVER IT UP?
COVER UP THE VASE? ...OR COVER UP THE CHINA?
DID YOU HEAR SCREAMING?
YES. I HEARD MADAM SCREAM.
AND TELL ME, DID SHE SOUND LIKE A MAN?
MOM!!
NO! THERE WERE TWO SCREAMS. THE FIRST ONE WAS MADAM'S... THE OTHER SCREAM SOUNDED...
MIELLLIES!!
...LIKE THAT.
LET THE RECORD SHOW THAT THE SECOND SCREAM BELONGS TO THE MIELIE LADY... WHO POSSIBLY SOUNDS LIKE A MAN.
© RAPID PHASE · 2014
MIELLLIES!!
COURT'S IN RECESS FOR THE NEXT TWENTY MINUTES!
BANG!
THE WHEELS OF JUSTICE TURN SLOWLY.
I SCREAM LIKE A MAN?!
MIELLLIES!
SPROING!!
OW!

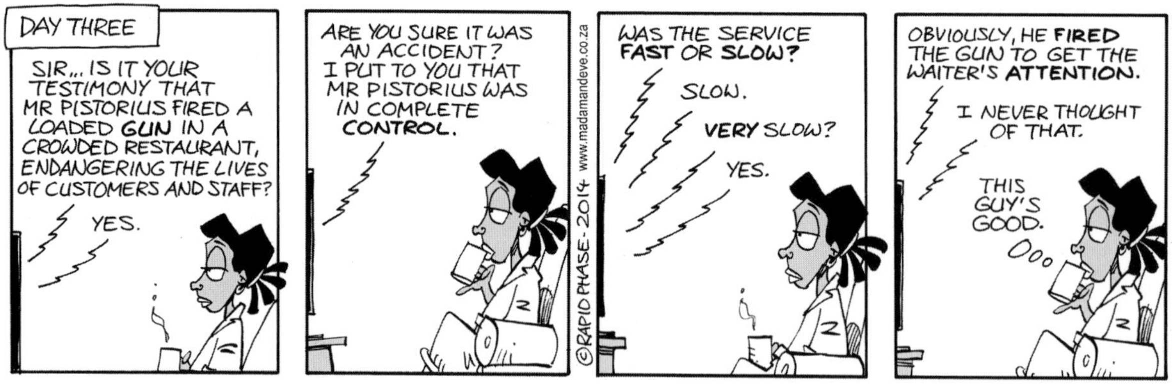
DAY THREE
SIR... IS IT YOUR TESTIMONY THAT MR PISTORIUS FIRED A LOADED GUN IN A CROWDED RESTAURANT, ENDANGERING THE LIVES OF CUSTOMERS AND STAFF?
YES.
ARE YOU SURE IT WAS AN ACCIDENT? I PUT TO YOU THAT MR PISTORIUS WAS IN COMPLETE CONTROL.
©RAPID PHASE - 2014 www.madamandeve.co.za
WAS THE SERVICE FAST OR SLOW?
SLOW.
VERY SLOW?
YES.
OBVIOUSLY, HE FIRED THE GUN TO GET THE WAITER'S ATTENTION.
I NEVER THOUGHT OF THAT.
THIS GUY'S GOOD.

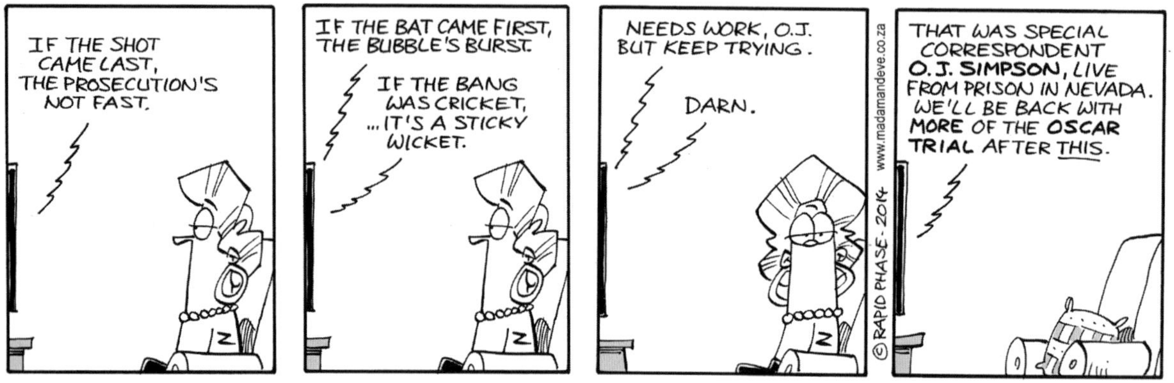
IF THE SHOT CAME LAST, THE PROSECUTION'S NOT FAST.
IF THE BAT CAME FIRST, THE BUBBLE'S BURST.
IF THE BANG WAS CRICKET, ...IT'S A STICKY WICKET.
NEEDS WORK, O.J. BUT KEEP TRYING.
DARN.
©RAPID PHASE - 2014 www.madamandeve.co.za
THAT WAS SPECIAL CORRESPONDENT O.J. SIMPSON, LIVE FROM PRISON IN NEVADA. WE'LL BE BACK WITH MORE OF THE OSCAR TRIAL AFTER THIS.

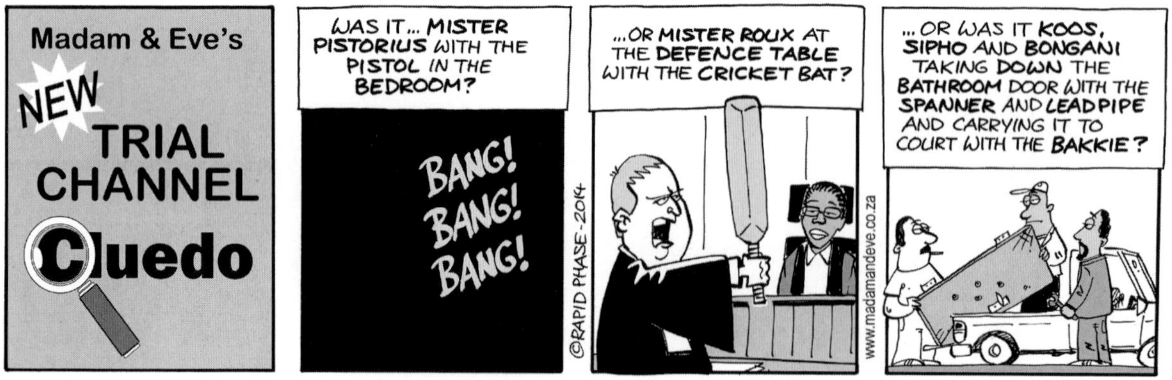
Madam & Eve's
NEW
TRIAL CHANNEL
Cluedo
WAS IT... MISTER PISTORIUS WITH THE PISTOL IN THE BEDROOM?
BANG! BANG! BANG!
©RAPID PHASE - 2014
...OR MISTER ROUX AT THE DEFENCE TABLE WITH THE CRICKET BAT?
www.madamandeve.co.za
...OR WAS IT KOOS, SIPHO AND BONGANI TAKING DOWN THE BATHROOM DOOR WITH THE SPANNER AND LEADPIPE AND CARRYING IT TO COURT WITH THE BAKKIE?

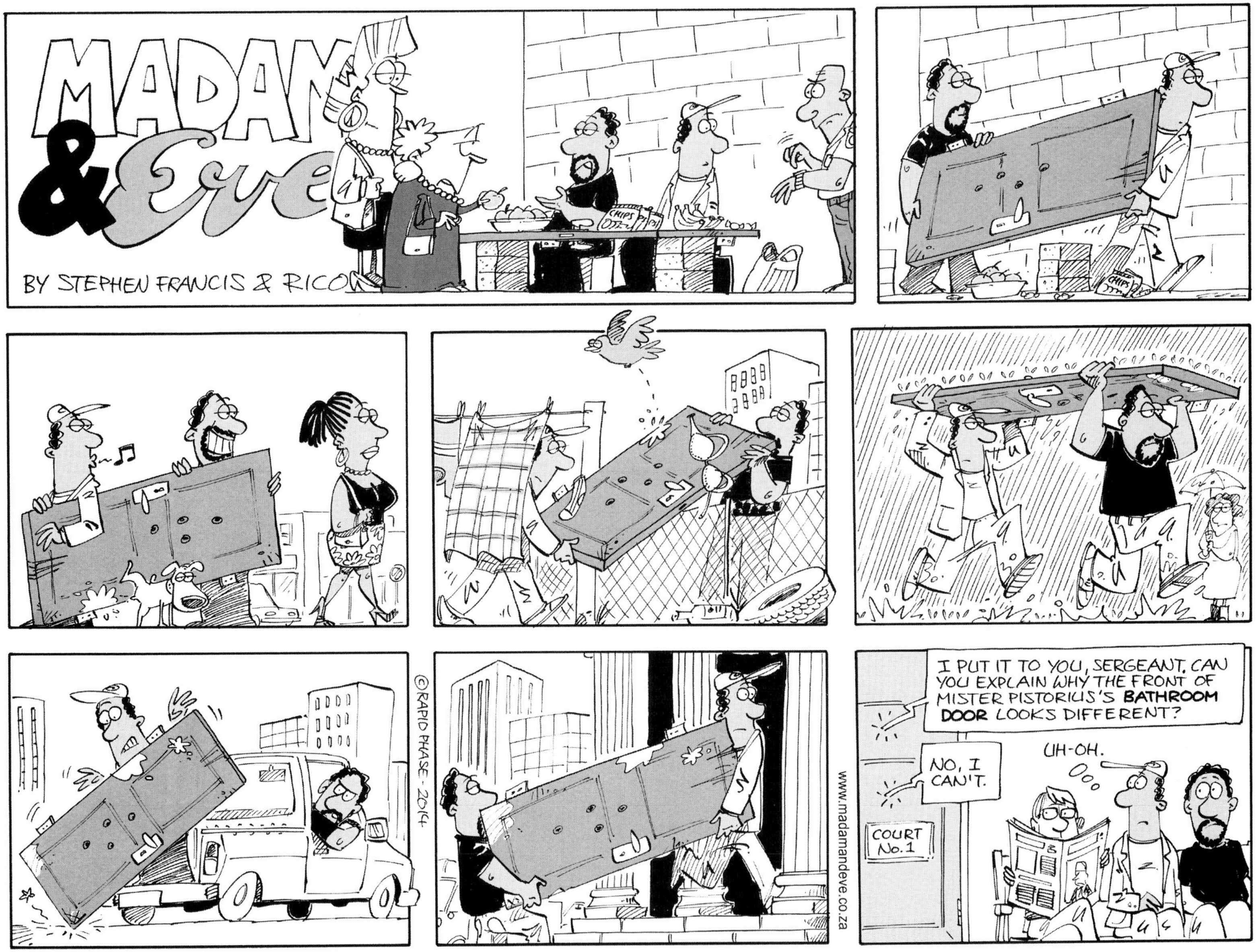
MADAM & Eve
BY STEPHEN FRANCIS & RICO
CHIPS
CHIPS
© RAPID PHASE - 2014
www.madamandeve.co.za
I PUT IT TO YOU, SERGEANT. CAN YOU EXPLAIN WHY THE FRONT OF MISTER PISTORIUS'S **BATHROOM DOOR** LOOKS DIFFERENT?
NO, I CAN'T.
UH-OH.
COURT No. 1

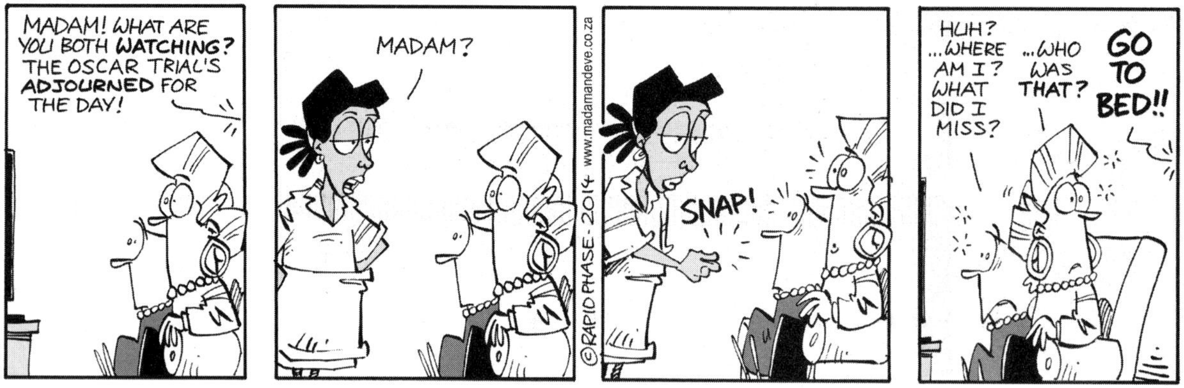
MADAM! WHAT ARE YOU BOTH WATCHING? THE OSCAR TRIAL'S ADJOURNED FOR THE DAY!
MADAM?
©RAPID PHASE·2014 www.madamandeve.co.za
SNAP!
HUH? ...WHERE AM I? WHAT DID I MISS?
...WHO WAS THAT?
GO TO BED!!

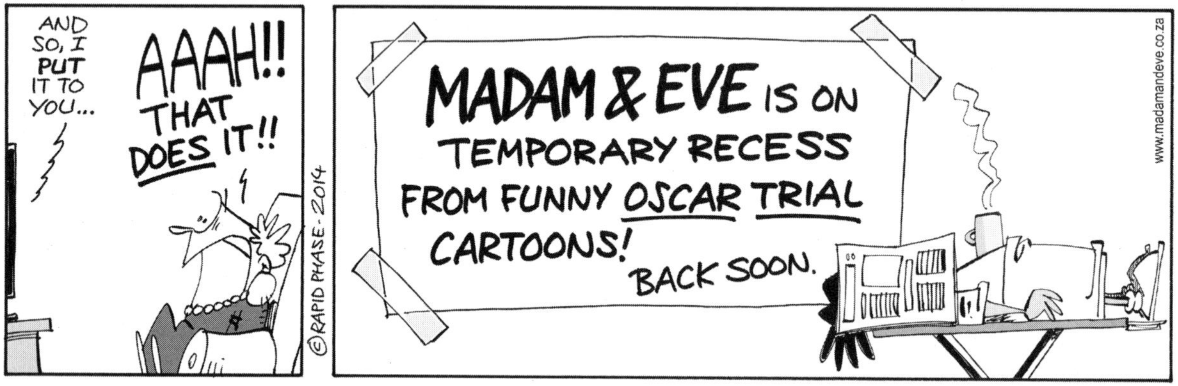
AND SO, I PUT IT TO YOU...
AAAH!! THAT DOES IT!!
©RAPID PHASE·2014
MADAM & EVE IS ON TEMPORARY RECESS FROM FUNNY OSCAR TRIAL CARTOONS!
BACK SOON.
www.madamandeve.co.za

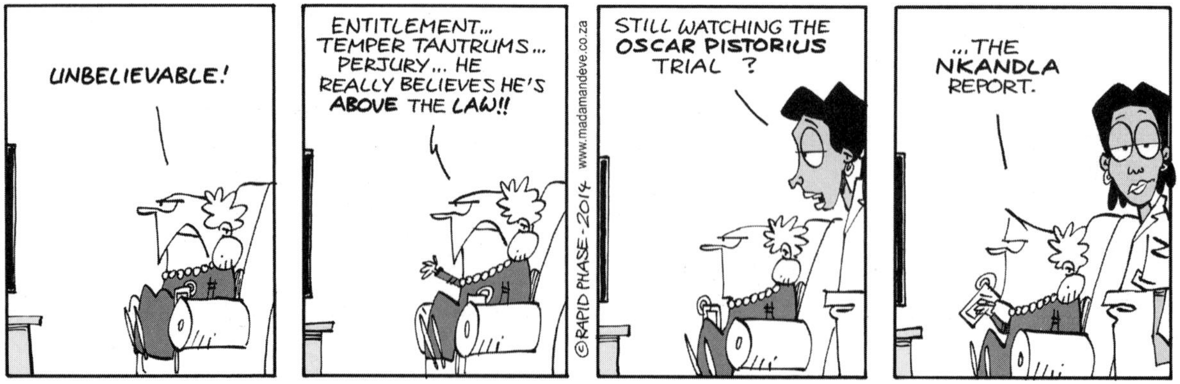
UNBELIEVABLE!
ENTITLEMENT... TEMPER TANTRUMS... PERJURY... HE REALLY BELIEVES HE'S ABOVE THE LAW!!
©RAPID PHASE·2014 www.madamandeve.co.za
STILL WATCHING THE OSCAR PISTORIUS TRIAL ?
...THE NKANDLA REPORT.

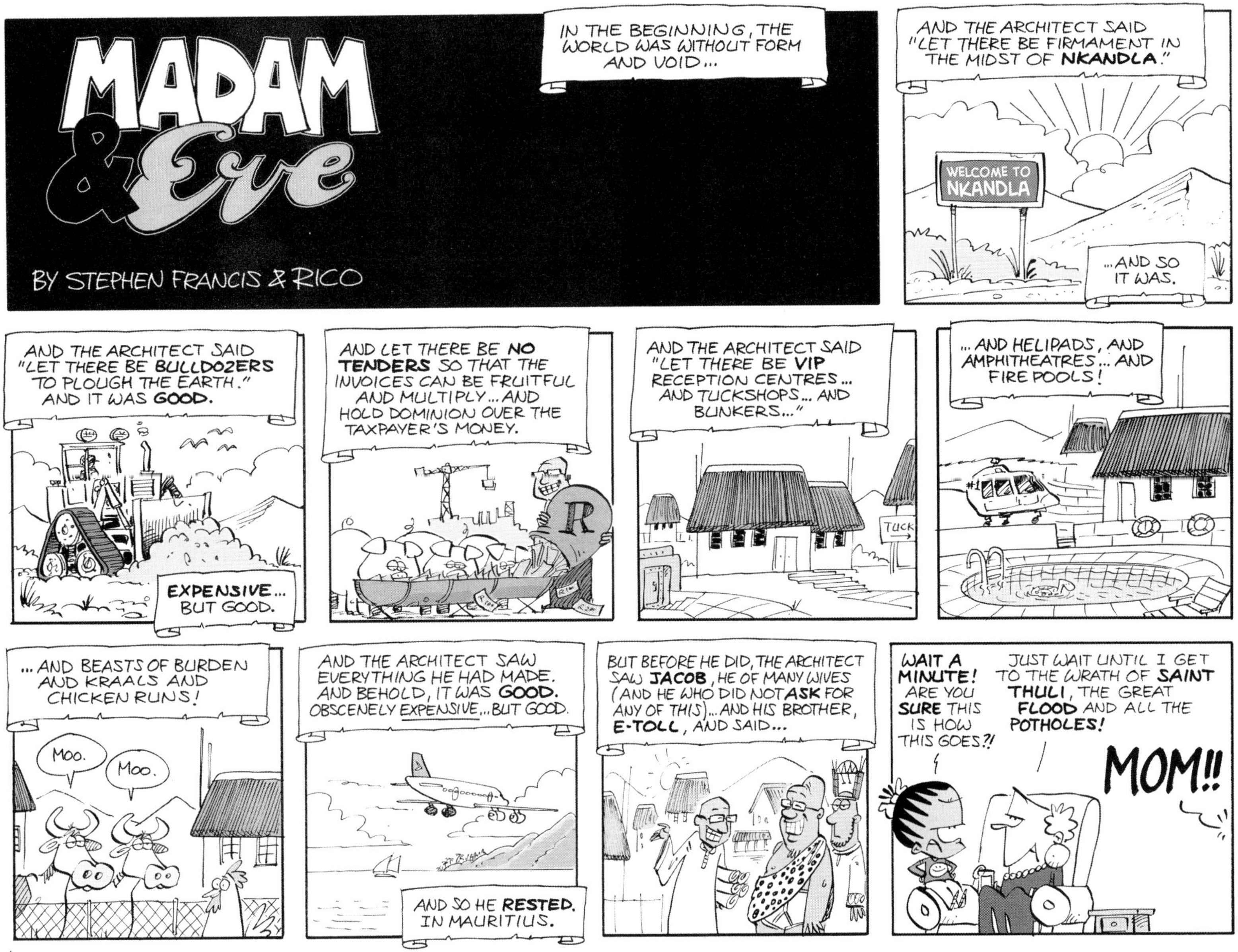
MADAM & Eve
BY STEPHEN FRANCIS & RICO
IN THE BEGINNING, THE WORLD WAS WITHOUT FORM AND VOID...
AND THE ARCHITECT SAID "LET THERE BE FIRMAMENT IN THE MIDST OF NKANDLA."
WELCOME TO NKANDLA
...AND SO IT WAS.
AND THE ARCHITECT SAID "LET THERE BE BULLDOZERS TO PLOUGH THE EARTH." AND IT WAS GOOD.
EXPENSIVE... BUT GOOD.
AND LET THERE BE NO TENDERS SO THAT THE INVOICES CAN BE FRUITFUL AND MULTIPLY... AND HOLD DOMINION OVER THE TAXPAYER'S MONEY.
R
AND THE ARCHITECT SAID "LET THERE BE VIP RECEPTION CENTRES... AND TUCKSHOPS... AND BUNKERS..."
TUCK
...AND HELIPADS, AND AMPHITHEATRES... AND FIRE POOLS!
...AND BEASTS OF BURDEN AND KRAALS AND CHICKEN RUNS!
Moo.
Moo.
AND THE ARCHITECT SAW EVERYTHING HE HAD MADE. AND BEHOLD, IT WAS GOOD. OBSCENELY EXPENSIVE... BUT GOOD.
AND SO HE RESTED. IN MAURITIUS.
BUT BEFORE HE DID, THE ARCHITECT SAW JACOB, HE OF MANY WIVES (AND HE WHO DID NOT ASK FOR ANY OF THIS)... AND HIS BROTHER, E-TOLL, AND SAID...
WAIT A MINUTE! ARE YOU SURE THIS IS HOW THIS GOES?!
JUST WAIT UNTIL I GET TO THE WRATH OF SAINT THULI, THE GREAT FLOOD AND ALL THE POTHOLES!
MOM!!

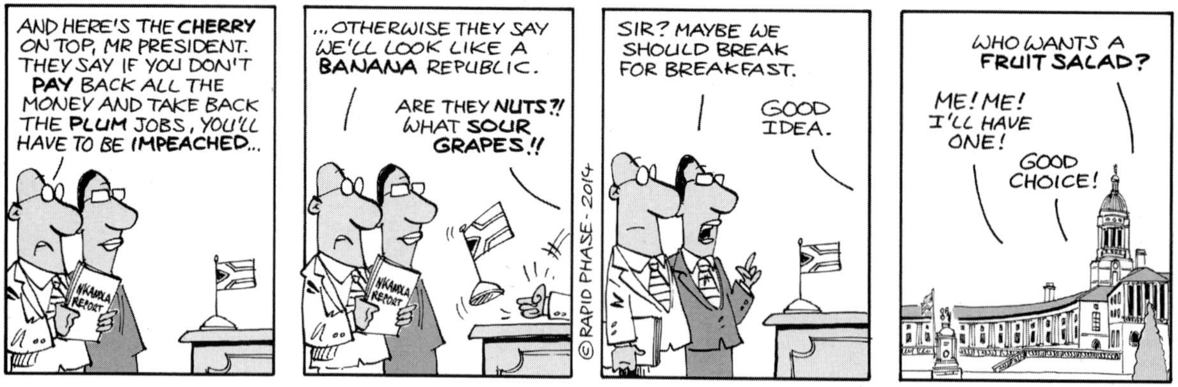
AND HERE'S THE CHERRY ON TOP, MR PRESIDENT. THEY SAY IF YOU DON'T PAY BACK ALL THE MONEY AND TAKE BACK THE PLUM JOBS, YOU'LL HAVE TO BE IMPEACHED...
NKANDLA REPORT
...OTHERWISE THEY SAY WE'LL LOOK LIKE A BANANA REPUBLIC.
ARE THEY NUTS?! WHAT SOUR GRAPES!!
NKANDLA REPORT
© RAPID PHASE · 2014
SIR? MAYBE WE SHOULD BREAK FOR BREAKFAST.
GOOD IDEA.
WHO WANTS A FRUIT SALAD?
ME! ME! I'LL HAVE ONE!
GOOD CHOICE!

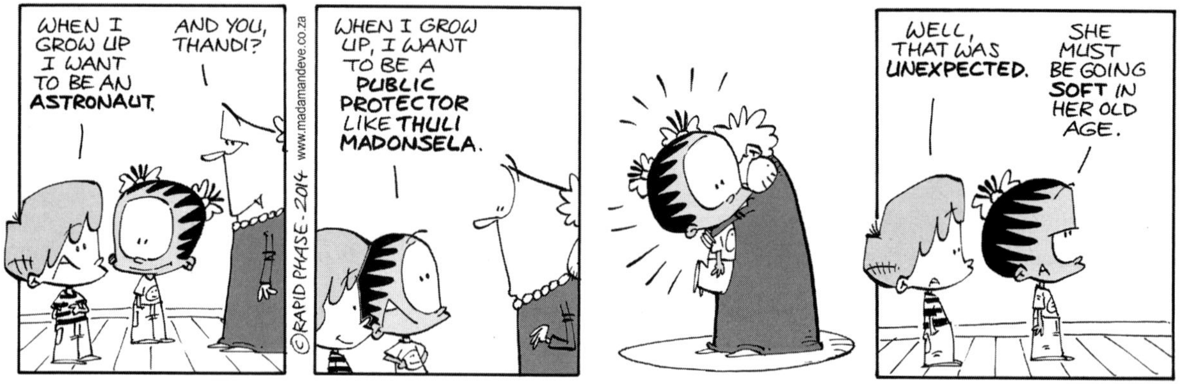
WHEN I GROW UP I WANT TO BE AN ASTRONAUT.
AND YOU, THANDI?
© RAPID PHASE · 2014 www.madamandeve.co.za
WHEN I GROW UP, I WANT TO BE A PUBLIC PROTECTOR LIKE THULI MADONSELA.
WELL, THAT WAS UNEXPECTED.
SHE MUST BE GOING SOFT IN HER OLD AGE.

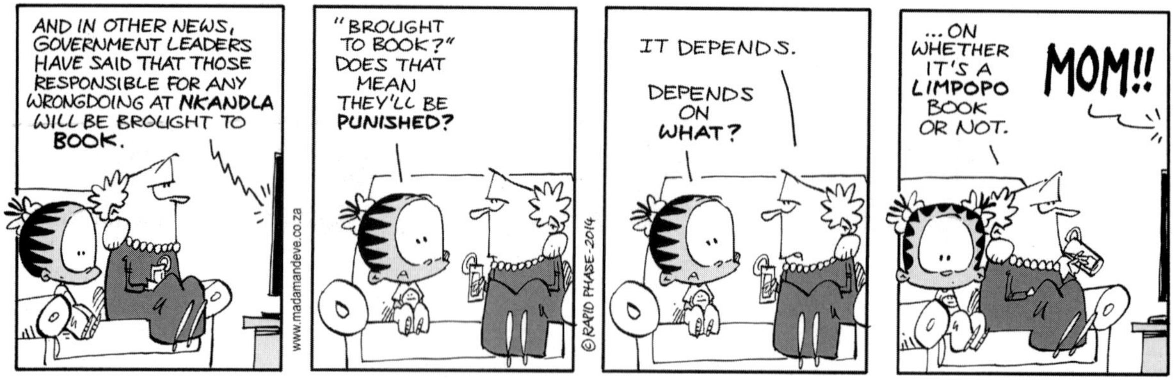
AND IN OTHER NEWS, GOVERNMENT LEADERS HAVE SAID THAT THOSE RESPONSIBLE FOR ANY WRONGDOING AT NKANDLA WILL BE BROUGHT TO BOOK.
www.madamandeve.co.za
"BROUGHT TO BOOK?" DOES THAT MEAN THEY'LL BE PUNISHED?
© RAPID PHASE · 2014
IT DEPENDS.
DEPENDS ON WHAT?
...ON WHETHER IT'S A LIMPOPO BOOK OR NOT.
MOM!!

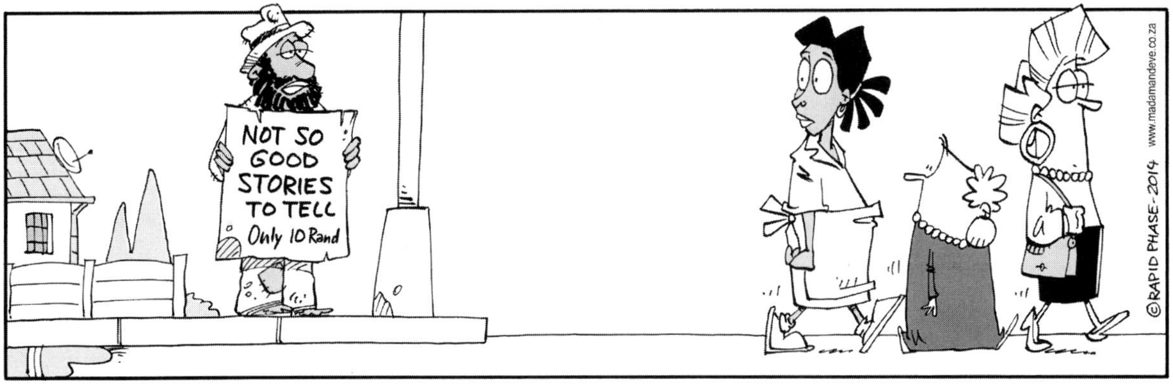
NOT SO GOOD STORIES TO TELL
Only 10 Rand
©RAPID PHASE-2014 www.madamandeve.co.za

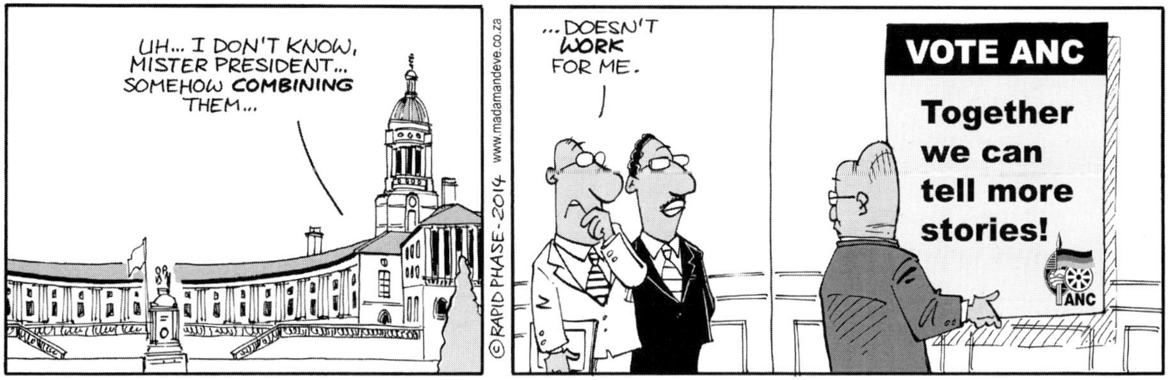
UH... I DON'T KNOW, MISTER PRESIDENT... SOMEHOW COMBINING THEM...
©RAPID PHASE-2014 www.madamandeve.co.za
...DOESN'T WORK FOR ME.
VOTE ANC
Together we can tell more stories!
ANC

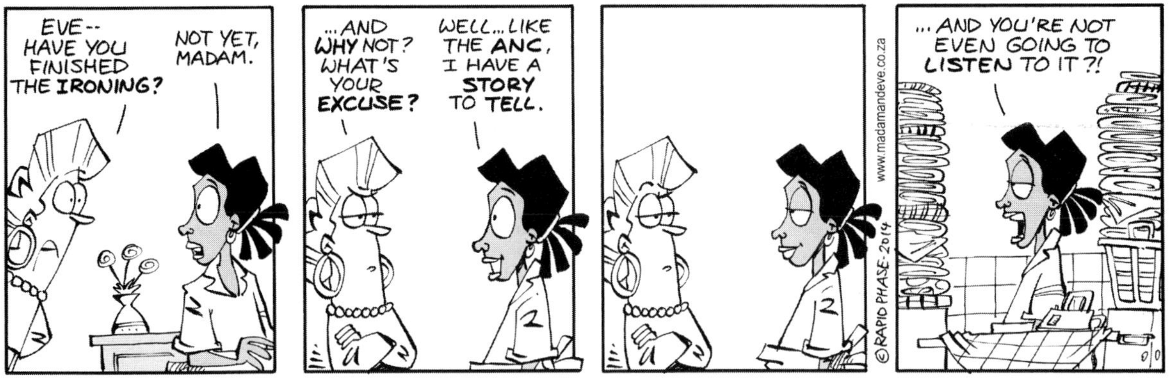
EVE-- HAVE YOU FINISHED THE IRONING?
NOT YET, MADAM.
...AND WHY NOT? WHAT'S YOUR EXCUSE?
WELL... LIKE THE ANC, I HAVE A STORY TO TELL.
©RAPID PHASE-2014 www.madamandeve.co.za
...AND YOU'RE NOT EVEN GOING TO LISTEN TO IT?!

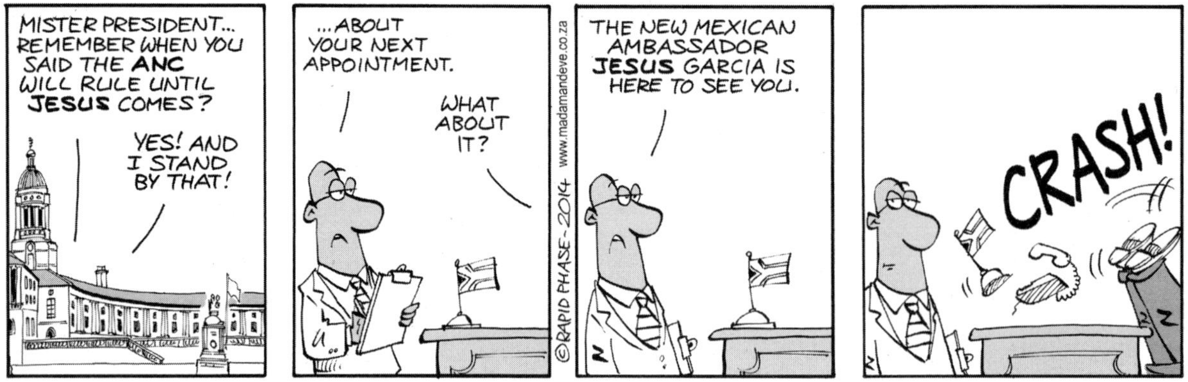
MISTER PRESIDENT... REMEMBER WHEN YOU SAID THE ANC WILL RULE UNTIL JESUS COMES?
YES! AND I STAND BY THAT!
...ABOUT YOUR NEXT APPOINTMENT.
WHAT ABOUT IT?
THE NEW MEXICAN AMBASSADOR JESUS GARCIA IS HERE TO SEE YOU.
CRASH!
©RAPID PHASE-2014 www.madamandeve.co.za

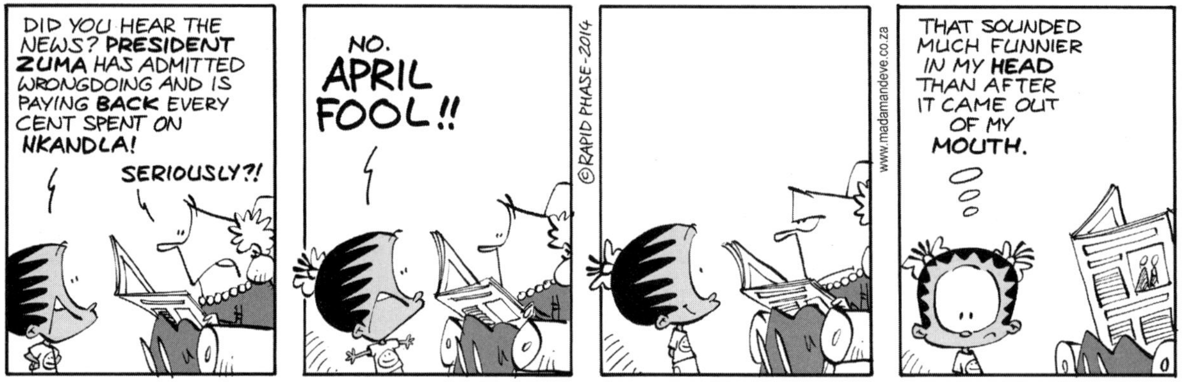
DID YOU HEAR THE NEWS? PRESIDENT ZUMA HAS ADMITTED WRONGDOING AND IS PAYING BACK EVERY CENT SPENT ON NKANDLA!
SERIOUSLY?!
NO. APRIL FOOL!!
THAT SOUNDED MUCH FUNNIER IN MY HEAD THAN AFTER IT CAME OUT OF MY MOUTH.
©RAPID PHASE-2014 www.madamandeve.co.za

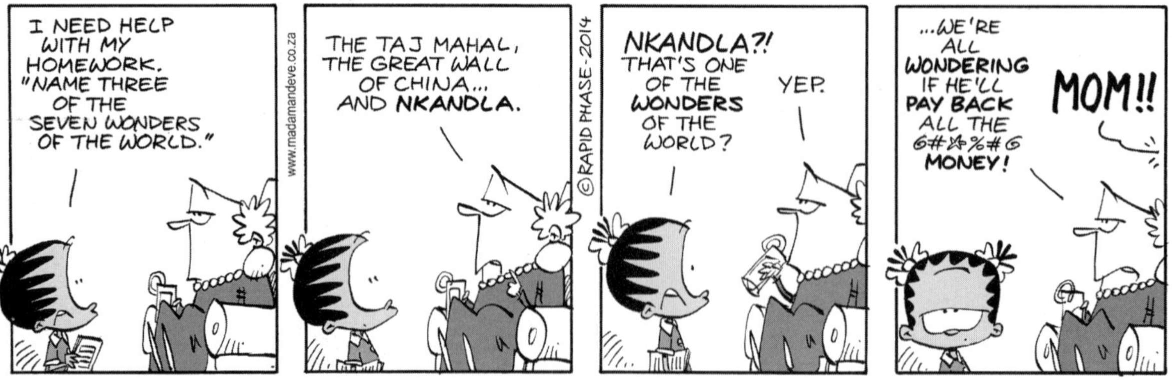
I NEED HELP WITH MY HOMEWORK. "NAME THREE OF THE SEVEN WONDERS OF THE WORLD."
THE TAJ MAHAL, THE GREAT WALL OF CHINA... AND NKANDLA.
NKANDLA?! THAT'S ONE OF THE WONDERS OF THE WORLD?
YEP.
...WE'RE ALL WONDERING IF HE'LL PAY BACK ALL THE 6#☆%#6 MONEY!
MOM!!
©RAPID PHASE-2014 www.madamandeve.co.za

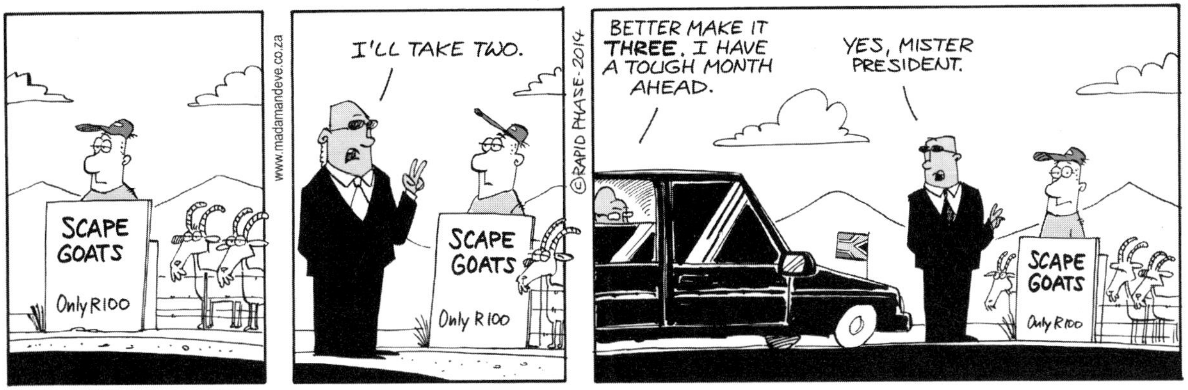
SCAPE GOATS
Only R100
www.madamandeve.co.za
I'LL TAKE TWO.
SCAPE GOATS
Only R100
©RAPID PHASE · 2014
BETTER MAKE IT THREE. I HAVE A TOUGH MONTH AHEAD.
YES, MISTER PRESIDENT.
SCAPE GOATS
Only R100

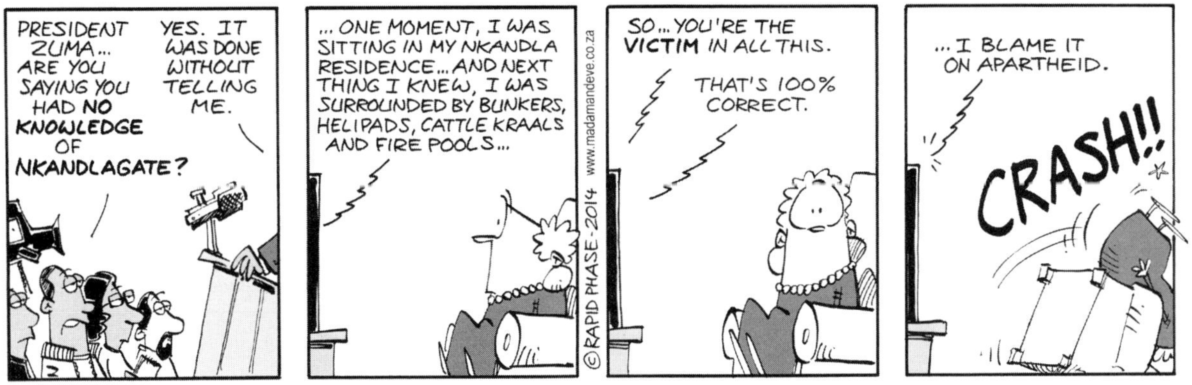
PRESIDENT ZUMA... ARE YOU SAYING YOU HAD NO KNOWLEDGE OF NKANDLAGATE?
YES. IT WAS DONE WITHOUT TELLING ME.
... ONE MOMENT, I WAS SITTING IN MY NKANDLA RESIDENCE... AND NEXT THING I KNEW, I WAS SURROUNDED BY BUNKERS, HELIPADS, CATTLE KRAALS AND FIRE POOLS...
www.madamandeve.co.za
©RAPID PHASE · 2014
SO... YOU'RE THE VICTIM IN ALL THIS.
THAT'S 100% CORRECT.
... I BLAME IT ON APARTHEID.
CRASH!!

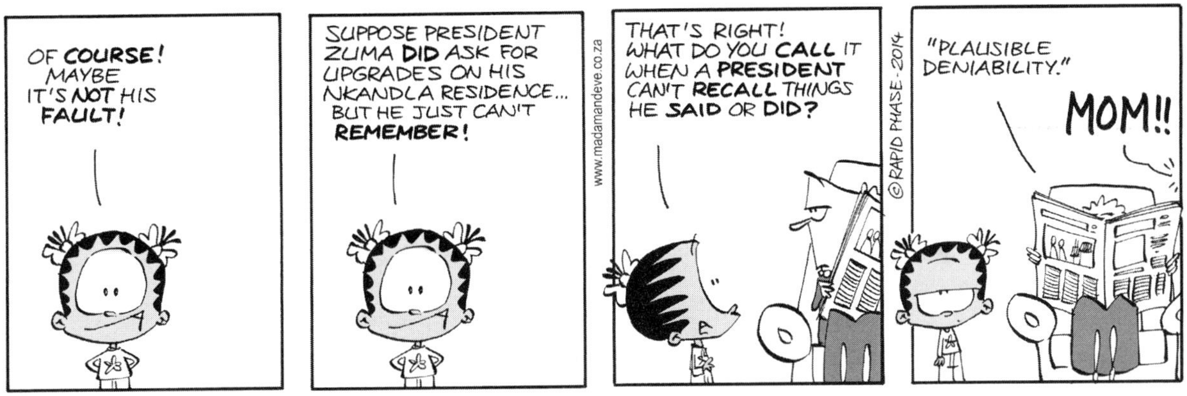
OF COURSE! MAYBE IT'S NOT HIS FAULT!
SUPPOSE PRESIDENT ZUMA DID ASK FOR UPGRADES ON HIS NKANDLA RESIDENCE... BUT HE JUST CAN'T REMEMBER!
www.madamandeve.co.za
THAT'S RIGHT! WHAT DO YOU CALL IT WHEN A PRESIDENT CAN'T RECALL THINGS HE SAID OR DID?
©RAPID PHASE · 2014
"PLAUSIBLE DENIABILITY."
MOM!!

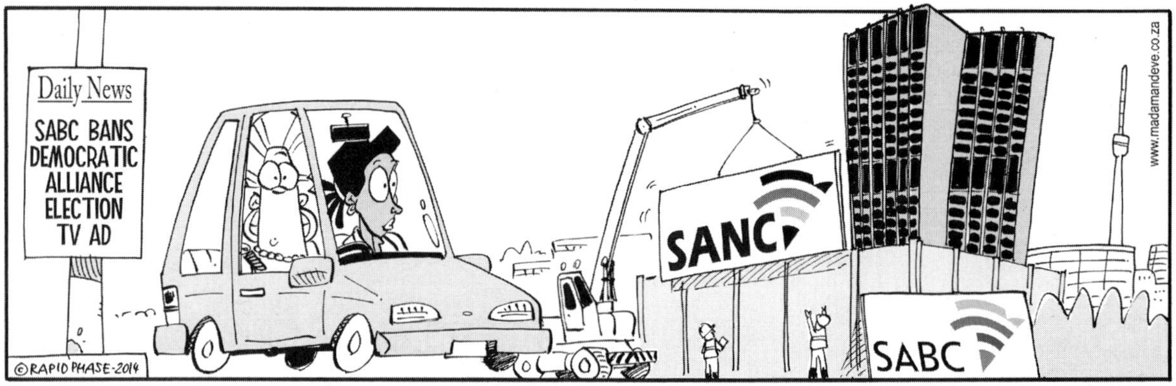
Daily News
SABC BANS DEMOCRATIC ALLIANCE ELECTION TV AD
SANC
SABC
©RAPID PHASE-2014
www.madamandeve.co.za

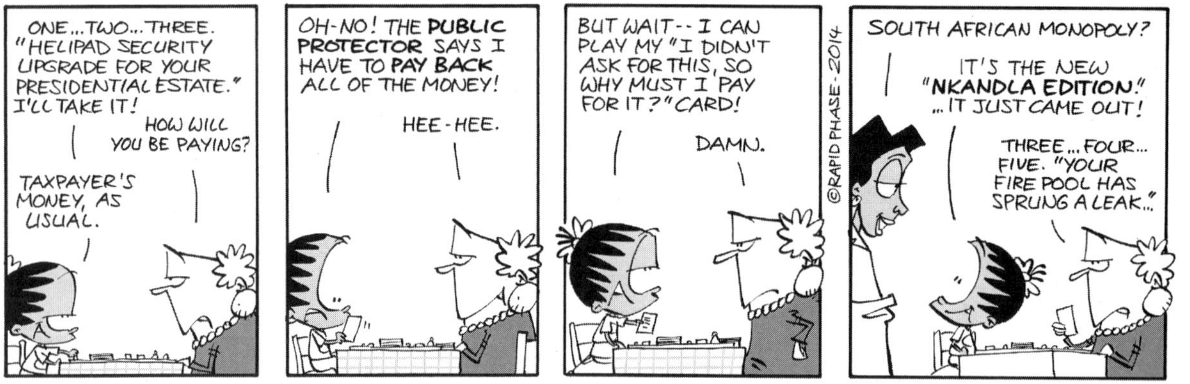
ONE...TWO...THREE. "HELIPAD SECURITY UPGRADE FOR YOUR PRESIDENTIAL ESTATE." I'LL TAKE IT!
HOW WILL YOU BE PAYING?
TAXPAYER'S MONEY, AS USUAL.
OH-NO! THE PUBLIC PROTECTOR SAYS I HAVE TO PAY BACK ALL OF THE MONEY!
HEE-HEE.
BUT WAIT-- I CAN PLAY MY "I DIDN'T ASK FOR THIS, SO WHY MUST I PAY FOR IT?" CARD!
DAMN.
©RAPID PHASE-2014
SOUTH AFRICAN MONOPOLY?
IT'S THE NEW "NKANDLA EDITION." ... IT JUST CAME OUT!
THREE... FOUR... FIVE. "YOUR FIRE POOL HAS SPRUNG A LEAK..."

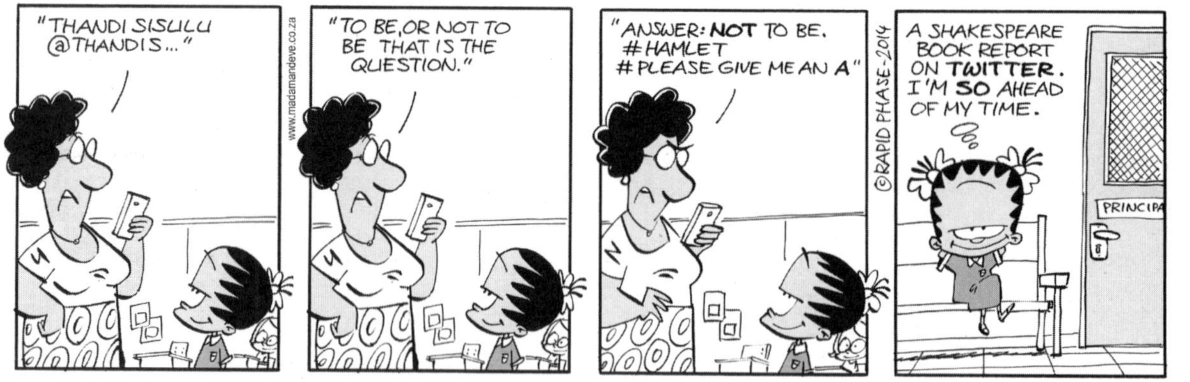
"THANDI SISULU @THANDIS..."
www.madamandeve.co.za
"TO BE, OR NOT TO BE THAT IS THE QUESTION."
"ANSWER: NOT TO BE. #HAMLET #PLEASE GIVE ME AN A"
©RAPID PHASE-2014
A SHAKESPEARE BOOK REPORT ON TWITTER. I'M SO AHEAD OF MY TIME.
PRINCIPA

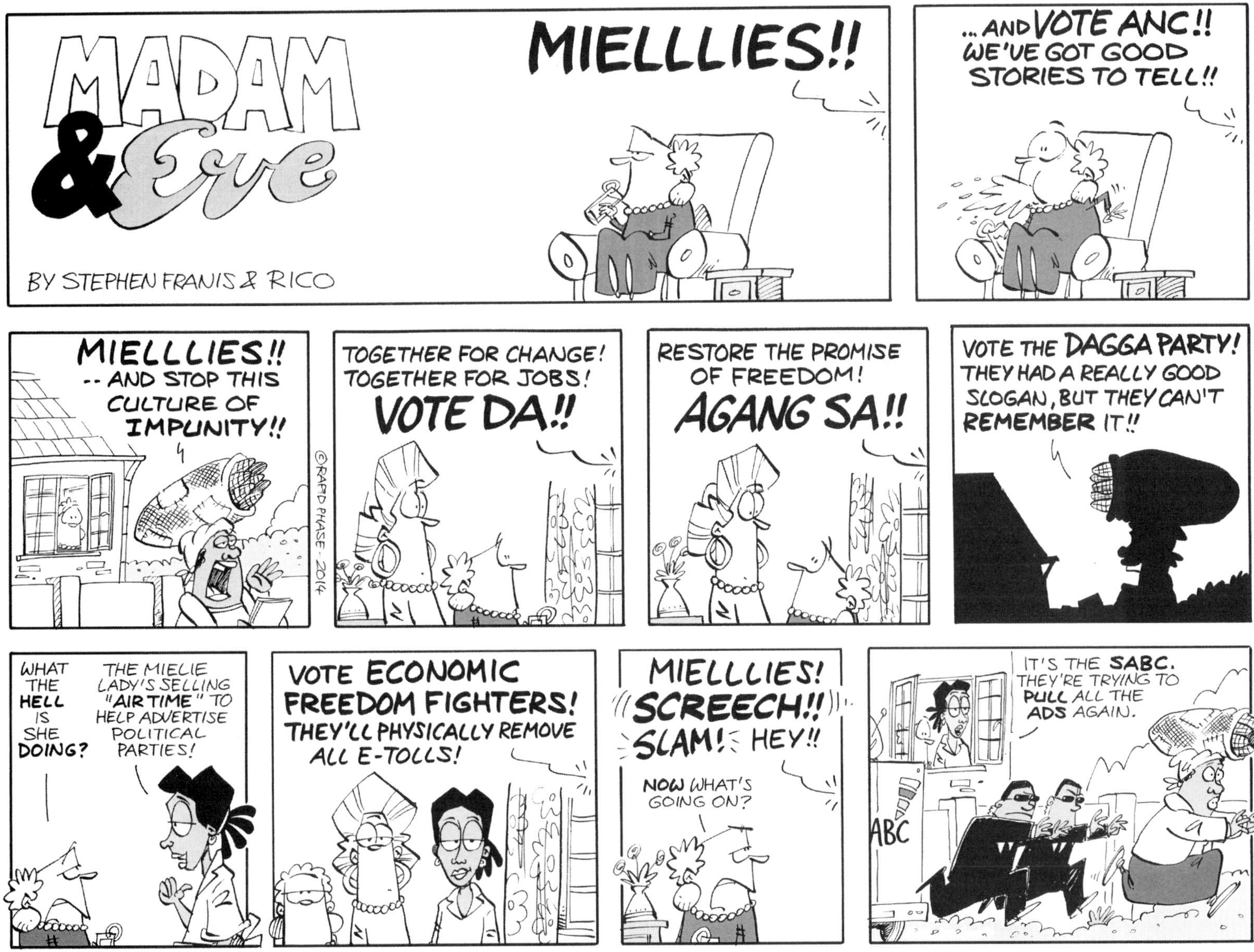
MADAM & Eve
BY STEPHEN FRANIS & RICO
MIELLLIES!!
...AND VOTE ANC!! WE'VE GOT GOOD STORIES TO TELL!!
MIELLLIES!! -- AND STOP THIS CULTURE OF IMPUNITY!!
© RAPID PHASE · 2014
TOGETHER FOR CHANGE! TOGETHER FOR JOBS! VOTE DA!!
RESTORE THE PROMISE OF FREEDOM! AGANG SA!!
VOTE THE DAGGA PARTY! THEY HAD A REALLY GOOD SLOGAN, BUT THEY CAN'T REMEMBER IT!!
WHAT THE HELL IS SHE DOING?
THE MIELIE LADY'S SELLING "AIR TIME" TO HELP ADVERTISE POLITICAL PARTIES!
VOTE ECONOMIC FREEDOM FIGHTERS! THEY'LL PHYSICALLY REMOVE ALL E-TOLLS!
MIELLLIES!
SCREECH!!
SLAM!
HEY!!
NOW WHAT'S GOING ON?
IT'S THE SABC. THEY'RE TRYING TO PULL ALL THE ADS AGAIN.
ABC

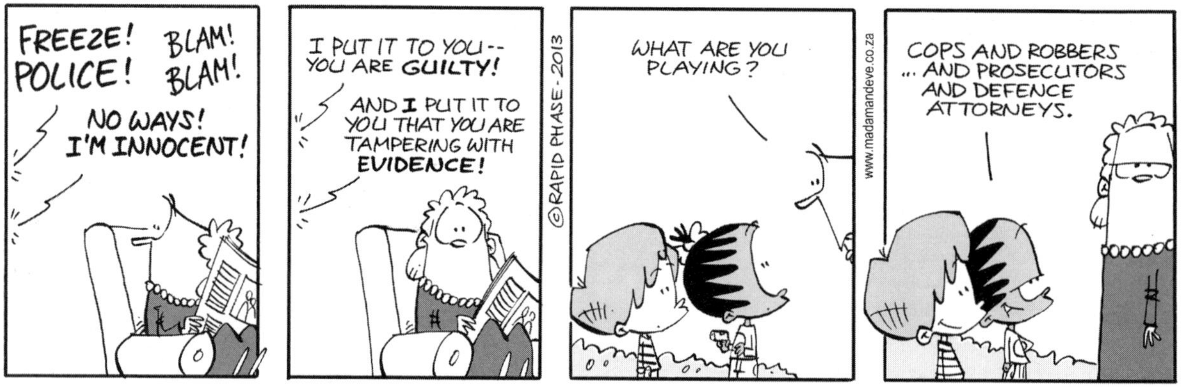
FREEZE! POLICE!
BLAM! BLAM!
NO WAYS! I'M INNOCENT!
I PUT IT TO YOU -- YOU ARE GUILTY!
AND I PUT IT TO YOU THAT YOU ARE TAMPERING WITH EVIDENCE!
©RAPID PHASE - 2013
WHAT ARE YOU PLAYING?
www.madamandeve.co.za
COPS AND ROBBERS ... AND PROSECUTORS AND DEFENCE ATTORNEYS.

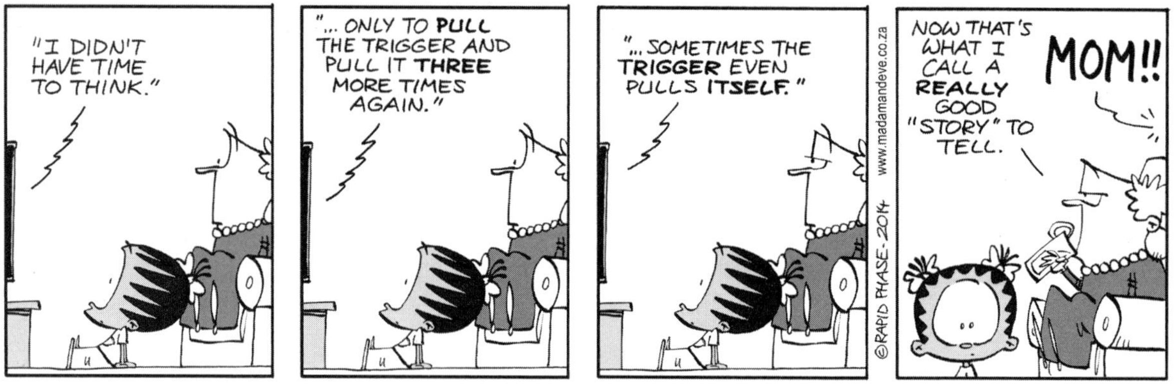
"I DIDN'T HAVE TIME TO THINK."
"... ONLY TO PULL THE TRIGGER AND PULL IT THREE MORE TIMES AGAIN."
"... SOMETIMES THE TRIGGER EVEN PULLS ITSELF."
©RAPID PHASE - 2014 www.madamandeve.co.za
NOW THAT'S WHAT I CALL A REALLY GOOD "STORY" TO TELL.
MOM!!

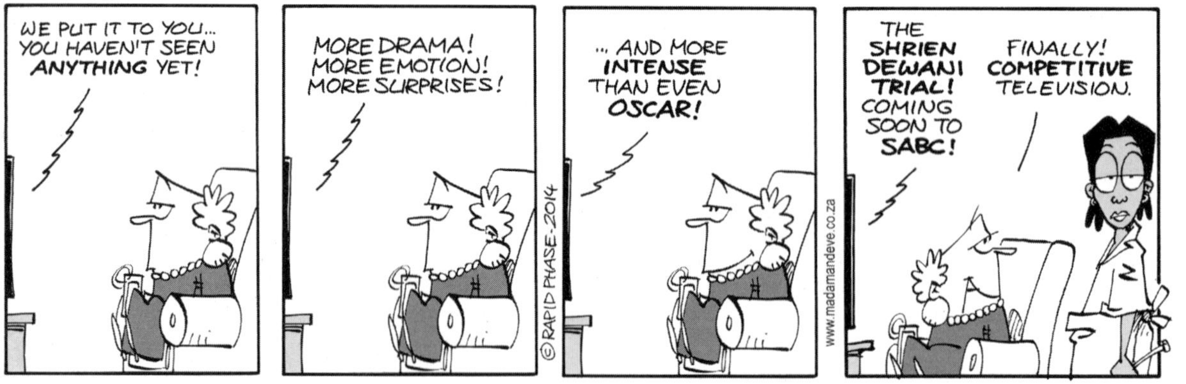
WE PUT IT TO YOU... YOU HAVEN'T SEEN ANYTHING YET!
MORE DRAMA! MORE EMOTION! MORE SURPRISES!
©RAPID PHASE-2014
... AND MORE INTENSE THAN EVEN OSCAR!
www.madamandeve.co.za
THE SHRIEN DEWANI TRIAL! COMING SOON TO SABC!
FINALLY! COMPETITIVE TELEVISION.

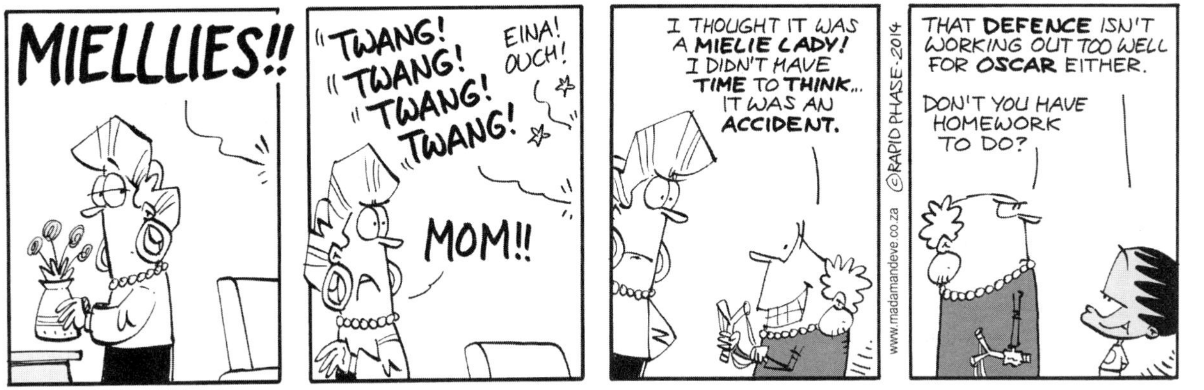
MIELLLIES!!
TWANG! TWANG! TWANG! TWANG!
EINA! OUCH!
MOM!!
I THOUGHT IT WAS A MIELIE LADY! I DIDN'T HAVE TIME TO THINK... IT WAS AN ACCIDENT.
©RAPID PHASE·2014
www.madamandeve.co.za
THAT DEFENCE ISN'T WORKING OUT TOO WELL FOR OSCAR EITHER.
DON'T YOU HAVE HOMEWORK TO DO?

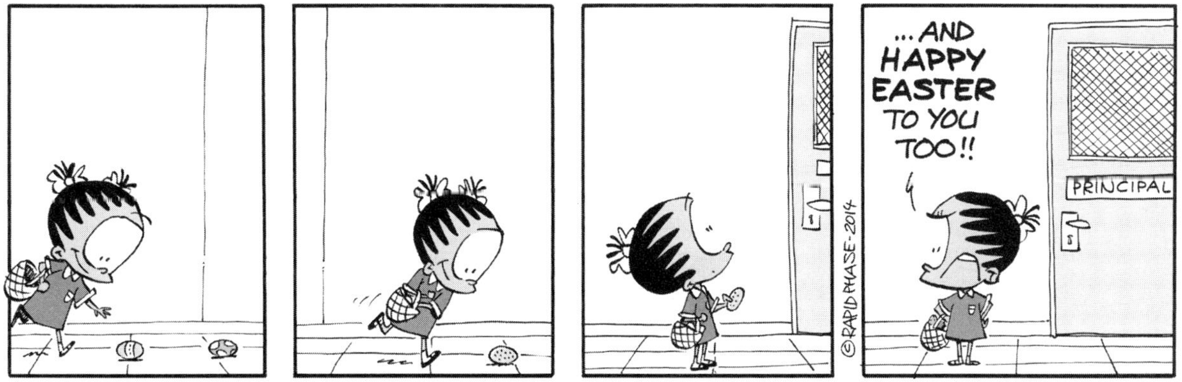
©RAPID PHASE·2014
...AND HAPPY EASTER TO YOU TOO!!
PRINCIPAL

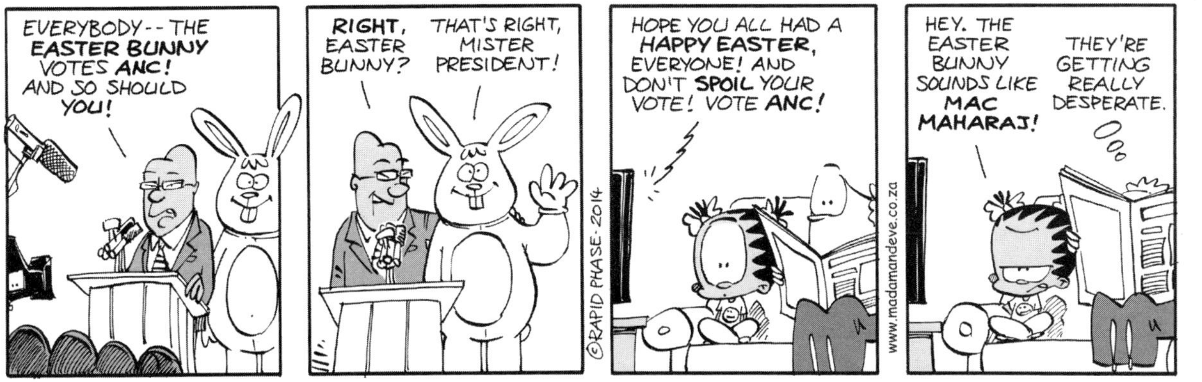
EVERYBODY -- THE EASTER BUNNY VOTES ANC! AND SO SHOULD YOU!
RIGHT, EASTER BUNNY?
THAT'S RIGHT, MISTER PRESIDENT!
©RAPID PHASE·2014
HOPE YOU ALL HAD A HAPPY EASTER, EVERYONE! AND DON'T SPOIL YOUR VOTE! VOTE ANC!
www.madamandeve.co.za
HEY. THE EASTER BUNNY SOUNDS LIKE MAC MAHARAJ!
THEY'RE GETTING REALLY DESPERATE.

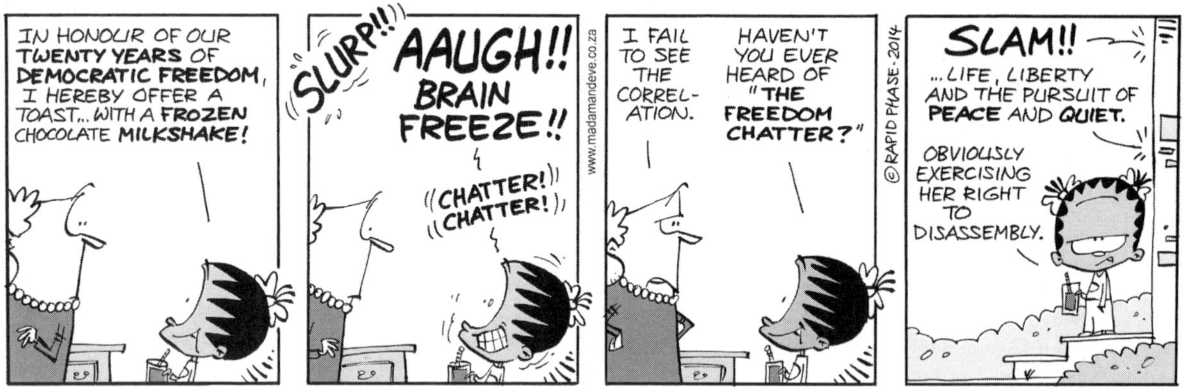
IN HONOUR OF OUR **TWENTY YEARS** OF **DEMOCRATIC FREEDOM**, I HEREBY OFFER A TOAST... WITH A **FROZEN** CHOCOLATE **MILKSHAKE!**
SLURP!!
AAUGH!! BRAIN FREEZE!!
CHATTER! CHATTER!
www.madamandeve.co.za
I FAIL TO SEE THE CORRELATION.
HAVEN'T YOU EVER HEARD OF **"THE FREEDOM CHATTER?"**
©RAPID PHASE-2014
SLAM!!
...LIFE, LIBERTY AND THE PURSUIT OF **PEACE** AND **QUIET.**
OBVIOUSLY EXERCISING HER RIGHT TO DISASSEMBLY.

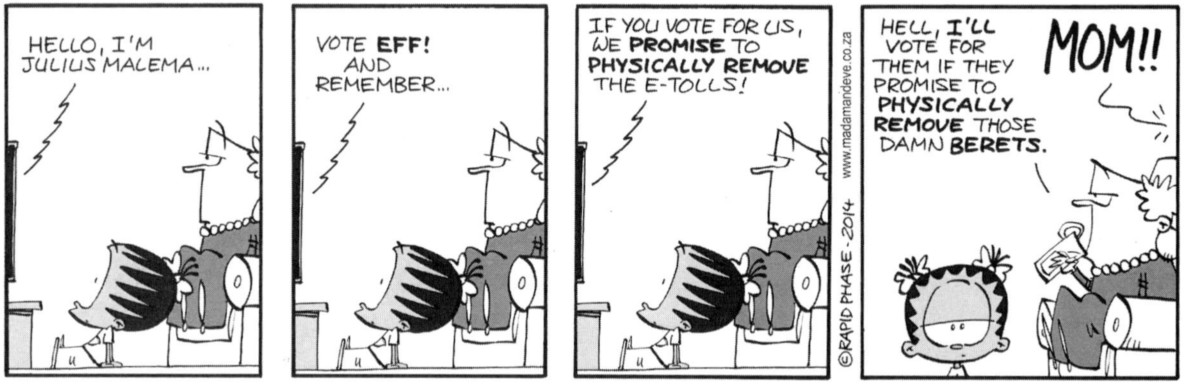
HELLO, I'M JULIUS MALEMA...
VOTE **EFF!** AND REMEMBER...
IF YOU VOTE FOR US, WE **PROMISE** TO **PHYSICALLY REMOVE** THE E-TOLLS!
www.madamandeve.co.za
©RAPID PHASE-2014
HELL, **I'LL** VOTE FOR THEM IF THEY PROMISE TO **PHYSICALLY REMOVE** THOSE DAMN **BERETS.**
MOM!!

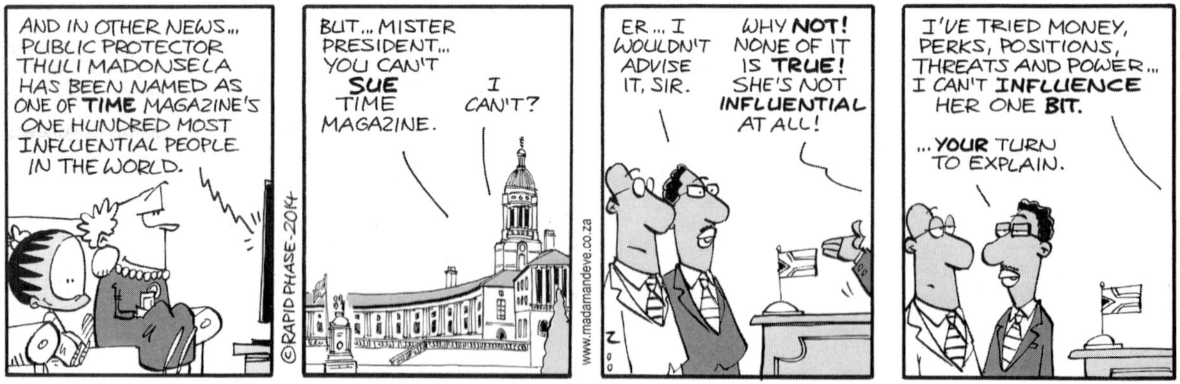
AND IN OTHER NEWS... PUBLIC PROTECTOR THULI MADONSELA HAS BEEN NAMED AS ONE OF **TIME** MAGAZINE'S ONE HUNDRED MOST INFLUENTIAL PEOPLE IN THE WORLD.
©RAPID PHASE-2014
BUT... MISTER PRESIDENT... YOU CAN'T **SUE** TIME MAGAZINE.
I CAN'T?
www.madamandeve.co.za
ER... I WOULDN'T ADVISE IT, SIR.
WHY **NOT!** NONE OF IT IS **TRUE!** SHE'S NOT **INFLUENTIAL** AT ALL!
I'VE TRIED MONEY, PERKS, POSITIONS, THREATS AND POWER... I CAN'T **INFLUENCE** HER ONE **BIT.**
...**YOUR** TURN TO EXPLAIN.

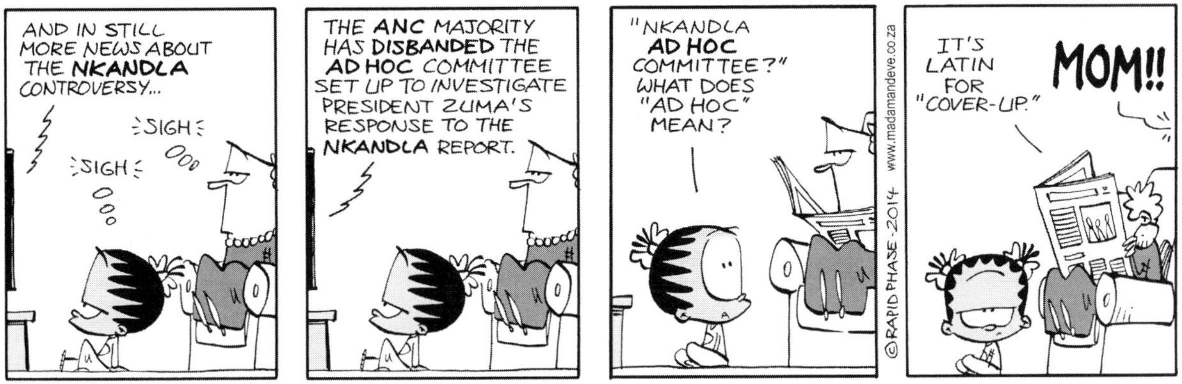
AND IN STILL MORE NEWS ABOUT THE NKANDLA CONTROVERSY...
SIGH
SIGH
THE ANC MAJORITY HAS DISBANDED THE AD HOC COMMITTEE SET UP TO INVESTIGATE PRESIDENT ZUMA'S RESPONSE TO THE NKANDLA REPORT.
"NKANDLA AD HOC COMMITTEE?" WHAT DOES "AD HOC" MEAN?
©RAPID PHASE-2014 www.madamandeve.co.za
IT'S LATIN FOR "COVER-UP."
MOM!!

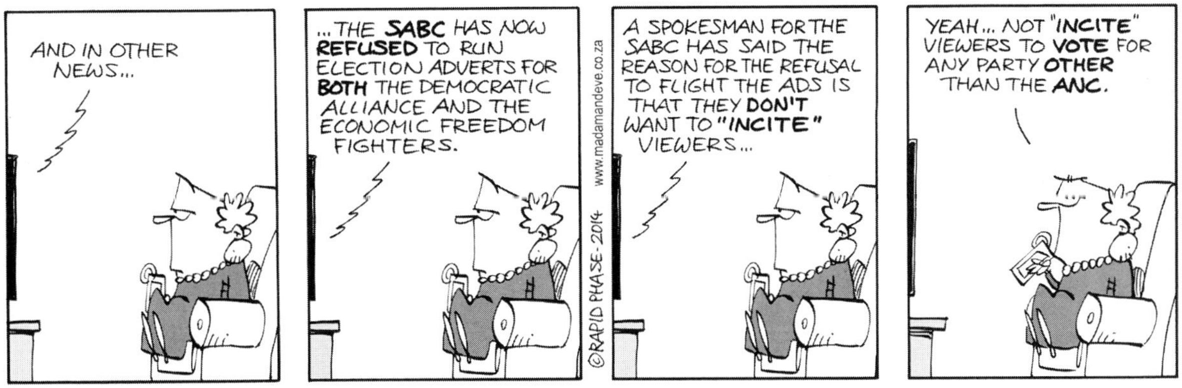
AND IN OTHER NEWS...
...THE SABC HAS NOW REFUSED TO RUN ELECTION ADVERTS FOR BOTH THE DEMOCRATIC ALLIANCE AND THE ECONOMIC FREEDOM FIGHTERS.
©RAPID PHASE-2014 www.madamandeve.co.za
A SPOKESMAN FOR THE SABC HAS SAID THE REASON FOR THE REFUSAL TO FLIGHT THE ADS IS THAT THEY DON'T WANT TO "INCITE" VIEWERS...
YEAH... NOT "INCITE" VIEWERS TO VOTE FOR ANY PARTY OTHER THAN THE ANC.

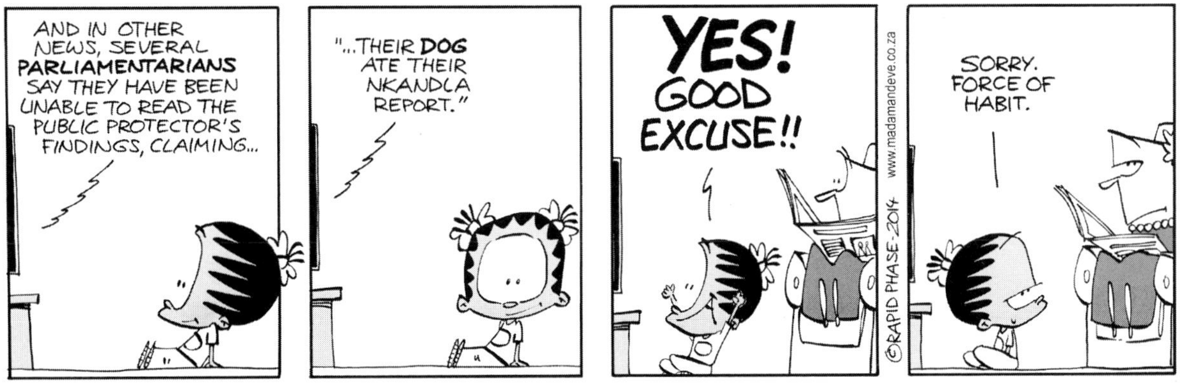
AND IN OTHER NEWS, SEVERAL PARLIAMENTARIANS SAY THEY HAVE BEEN UNABLE TO READ THE PUBLIC PROTECTOR'S FINDINGS, CLAIMING...
"...THEIR DOG ATE THEIR NKANDLA REPORT."
YES! GOOD EXCUSE!!
©RAPID PHASE-2014 www.madamandeve.co.za
SORRY. FORCE OF HABIT.

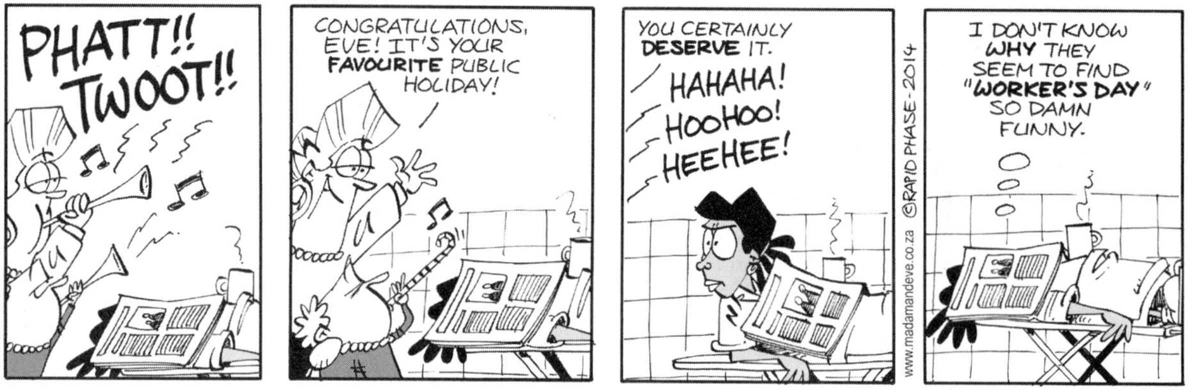
PHATT!! TWOOT!!
CONGRATULATIONS, EVE! IT'S YOUR FAVOURITE PUBLIC HOLIDAY!
YOU CERTAINLY DESERVE IT.
HAHAHA! HOOHOO! HEEHEE!
©RAPID PHASE - 2014 www.madamandeve.co.za
I DON'T KNOW WHY THEY SEEM TO FIND "WORKER'S DAY" SO DAMN FUNNY.

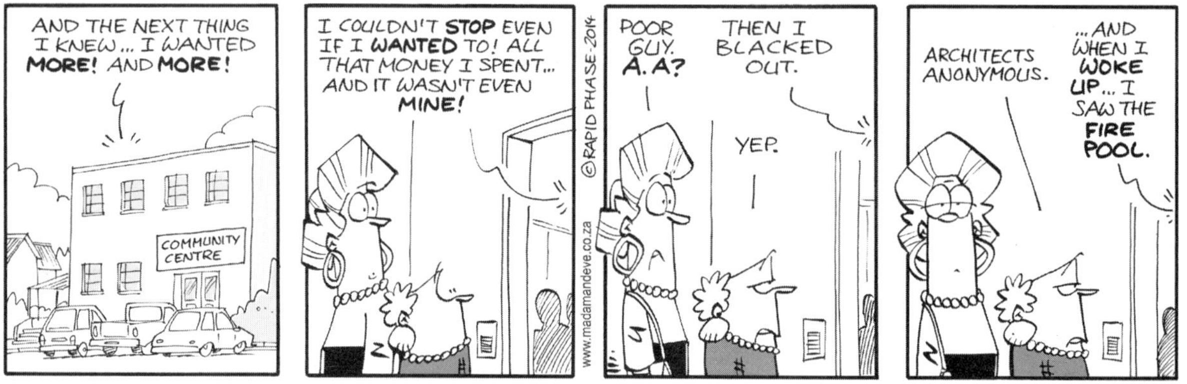
AND THE NEXT THING I KNEW... I WANTED MORE! AND MORE!
COMMUNITY CENTRE
I COULDN'T STOP EVEN IF I WANTED TO! ALL THAT MONEY I SPENT... AND IT WASN'T EVEN MINE!
©RAPID PHASE - 2014 www.madamandeve.co.za
POOR GUY. A.A?
THEN I BLACKED OUT.
YEP.
ARCHITECTS ANONYMOUS.
...AND WHEN I WOKE UP... I SAW THE FIRE POOL.

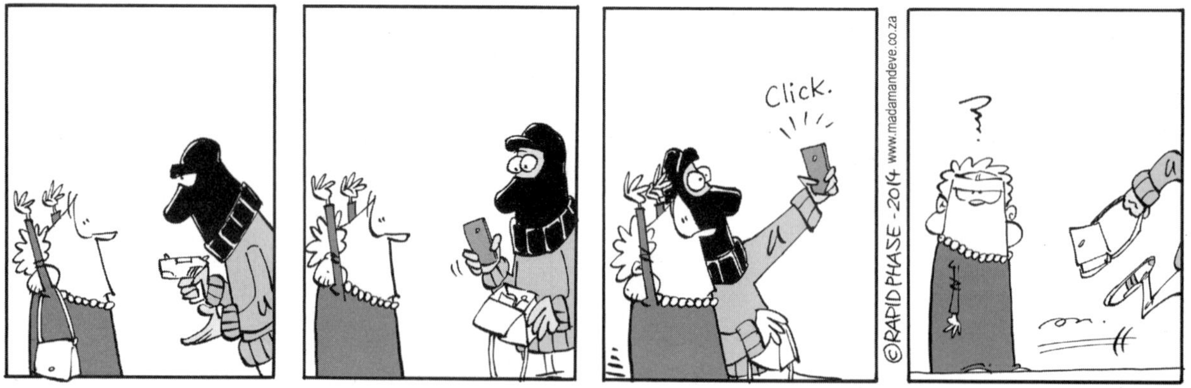
Click.
©RAPID PHASE - 2014 www.madamandeve.co.za

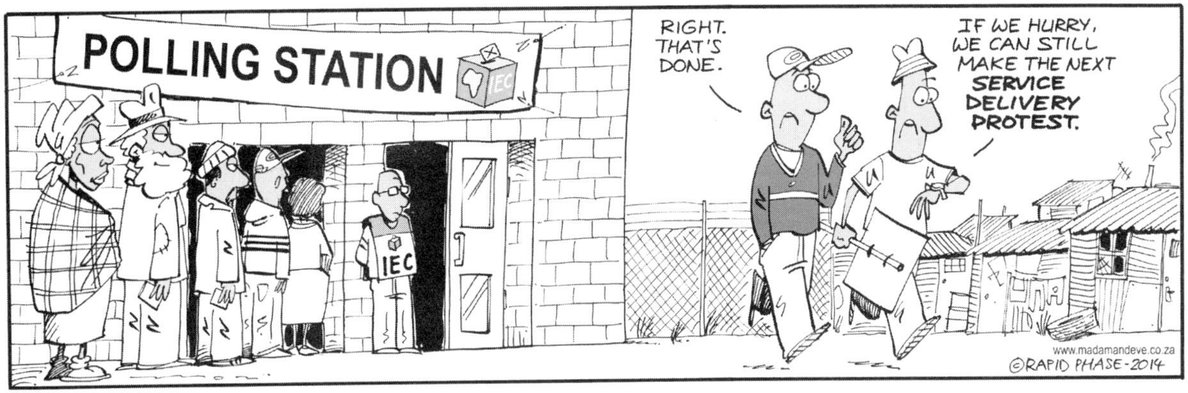
POLLING STATION
IEC
IEC
RIGHT. THAT'S DONE.
IF WE HURRY, WE CAN STILL MAKE THE NEXT SERVICE DELIVERY PROTEST.
www.madamandeve.co.za
©RAPID PHASE-2014

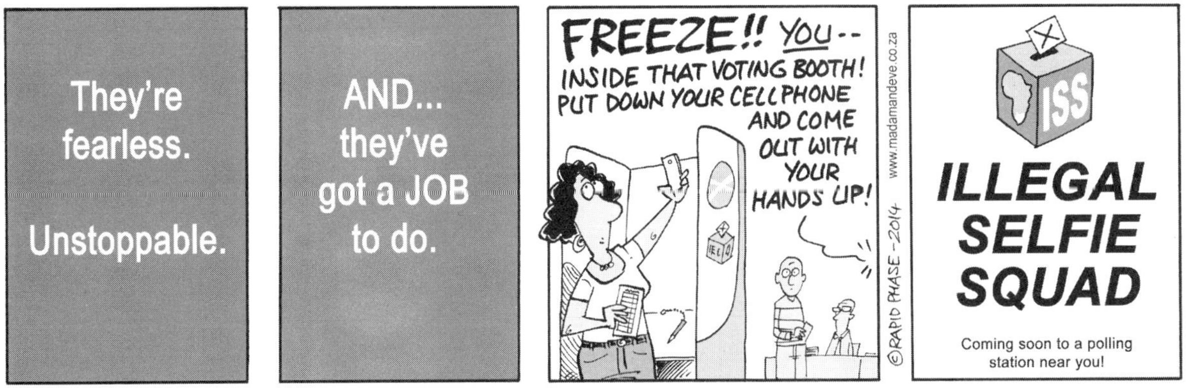
They're fearless.
Unstoppable.
AND... they've got a JOB to do.
FREEZE!! YOU-- INSIDE THAT VOTING BOOTH! PUT DOWN YOUR CELLPHONE AND COME OUT WITH YOUR HANDS UP!
www.madamandeve.co.za
©RAPID PHASE-2014
ISS
ILLEGAL SELFIE SQUAD
Coming soon to a polling station near you!

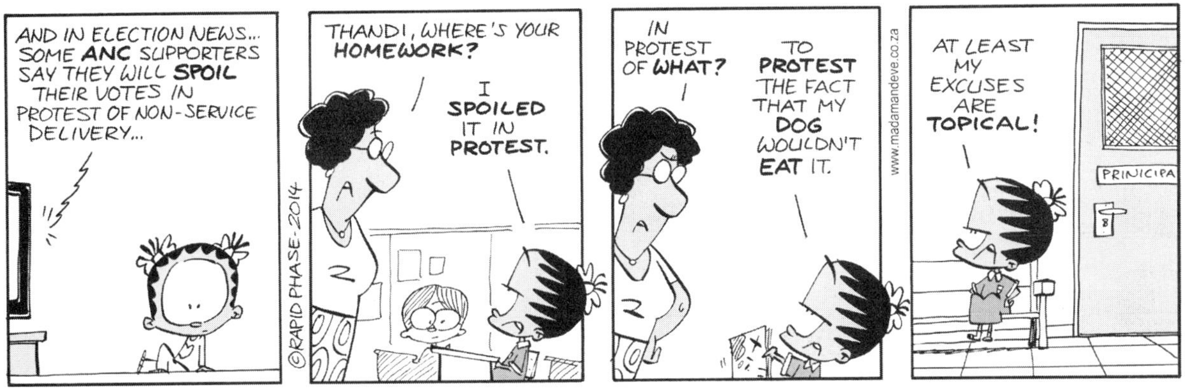
AND IN ELECTION NEWS... SOME ANC SUPPORTERS SAY THEY WILL SPOIL THEIR VOTES IN PROTEST OF NON-SERVICE DELIVERY...
©RAPID PHASE-2014
THANDI, WHERE'S YOUR HOMEWORK?
I SPOILED IT IN PROTEST.
IN PROTEST OF WHAT?
TO PROTEST THE FACT THAT MY DOG WOULDN'T EAT IT.
www.madamandeve.co.za
AT LEAST MY EXCUSES ARE TOPICAL!
PRINICIPA

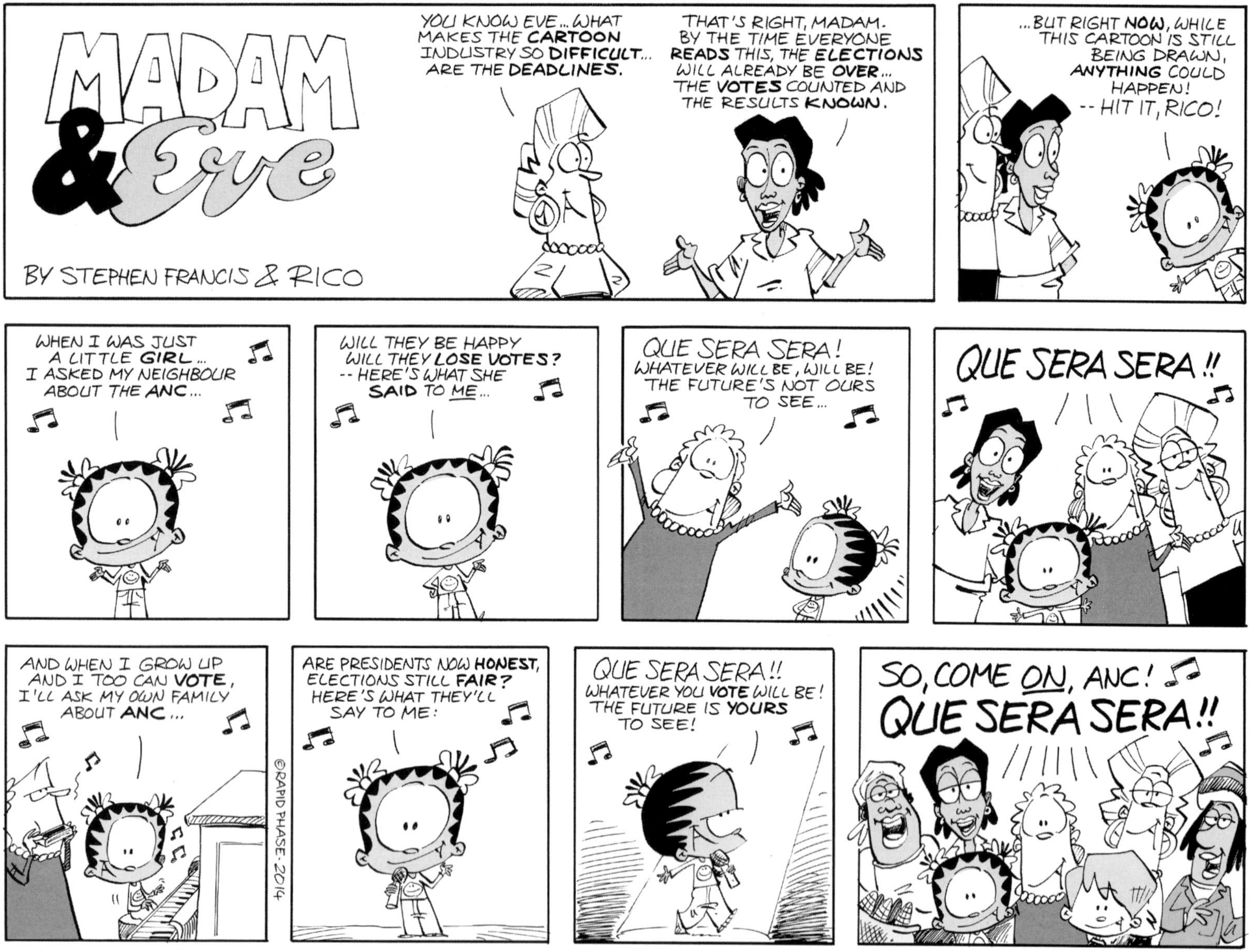
MADAM & Eve
BY STEPHEN FRANCIS & RICO
YOU KNOW EVE... WHAT MAKES THE CARTOON INDUSTRY SO DIFFICULT... ARE THE DEADLINES.
THAT'S RIGHT, MADAM. BY THE TIME EVERYONE READS THIS, THE ELECTIONS WILL ALREADY BE OVER... THE VOTES COUNTED AND THE RESULTS KNOWN.
...BUT RIGHT NOW, WHILE THIS CARTOON IS STILL BEING DRAWN, ANYTHING COULD HAPPEN!
-- HIT IT, RICO!
WHEN I WAS JUST A LITTLE GIRL... I ASKED MY NEIGHBOUR ABOUT THE ANC...
WILL THEY BE HAPPY WILL THEY LOSE VOTES? -- HERE'S WHAT SHE SAID TO ME...
QUE SERA SERA! WHATEVER WILL BE, WILL BE! THE FUTURE'S NOT OURS TO SEE...
QUE SERA SERA!!
AND WHEN I GROW UP AND I TOO CAN VOTE, I'LL ASK MY OWN FAMILY ABOUT ANC...
©RAPID PHASE 2014
ARE PRESIDENTS NOW HONEST, ELECTIONS STILL FAIR? HERE'S WHAT THEY'LL SAY TO ME:
QUE SERA SERA!! WHATEVER YOU VOTE WILL BE! THE FUTURE IS YOURS TO SEE!
SO, COME ON, ANC! QUE SERA SERA!!

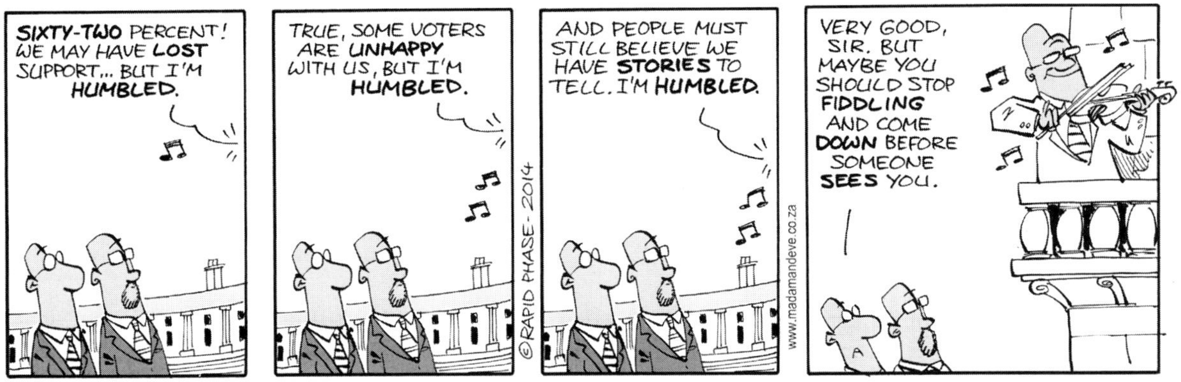
SIXTY-TWO PERCENT! WE MAY HAVE LOST SUPPORT... BUT I'M HUMBLED.
TRUE, SOME VOTERS ARE UNHAPPY WITH US, BUT I'M HUMBLED.
©RAPID PHASE-2014
AND PEOPLE MUST STILL BELIEVE WE HAVE STORIES TO TELL. I'M HUMBLED.
www.madamandeve.co.za
VERY GOOD, SIR. BUT MAYBE YOU SHOULD STOP FIDDLING AND COME DOWN BEFORE SOMEONE SEES YOU.

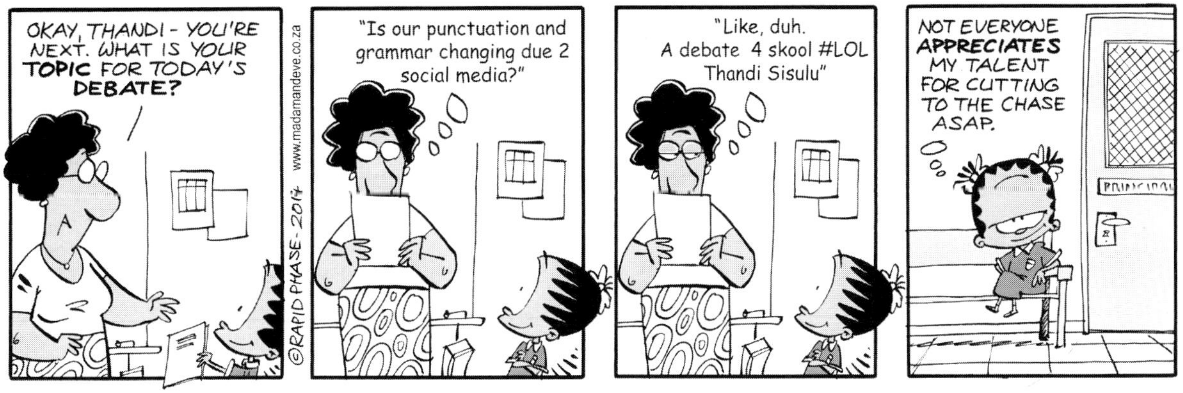
OKAY, THANDI - YOU'RE NEXT. WHAT IS YOUR TOPIC FOR TODAY'S DEBATE?
©RAPID PHASE-2014 www.madamandeve.co.za
"Is our punctuation and grammar changing due 2 social media?"
"Like, duh. A debate 4 skool #LOL Thandi Sisulu"
NOT EVERYONE APPRECIATES MY TALENT FOR CUTTING TO THE CHASE ASAP.

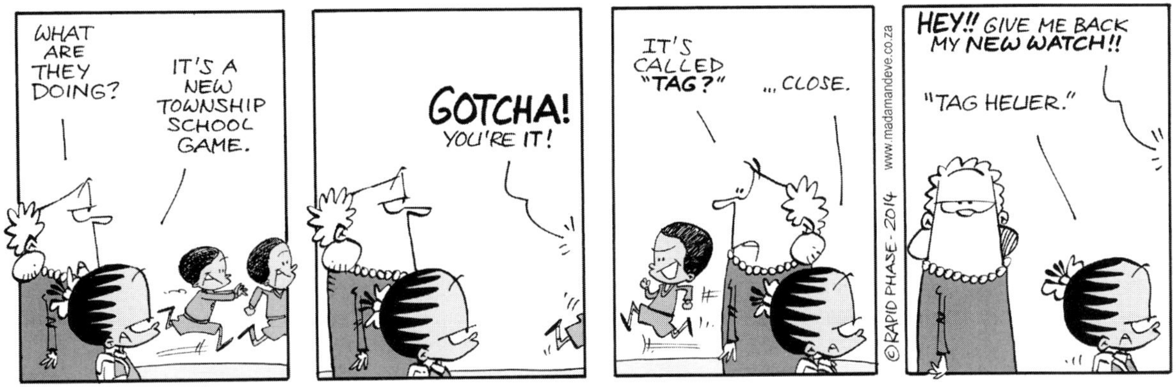
WHAT ARE THEY DOING?
IT'S A NEW TOWNSHIP SCHOOL GAME.
GOTCHA! YOU'RE IT!
IT'S CALLED "TAG?"
... CLOSE.
©RAPID PHASE-2014 www.madamandeve.co.za
HEY!! GIVE ME BACK MY NEW WATCH!!
"TAG HEUER."

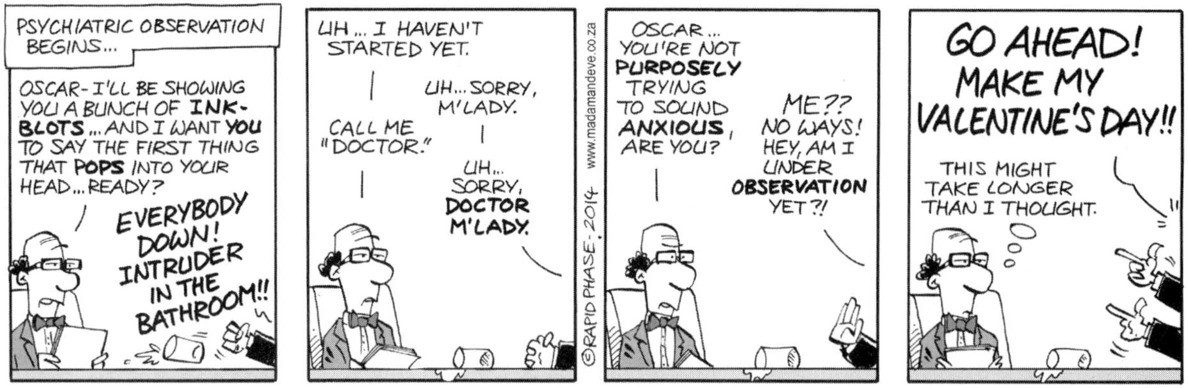
PSYCHIATRIC OBSERVATION BEGINS...
OSCAR- I'LL BE SHOWING YOU A BUNCH OF INK-BLOTS... AND I WANT YOU TO SAY THE FIRST THING THAT POPS INTO YOUR HEAD... READY?
EVERYBODY DOWN! INTRUDER IN THE BATHROOM!!
UH... I HAVEN'T STARTED YET.
UH... SORRY, M'LADY.
CALL ME "DOCTOR."
UH... SORRY, DOCTOR M'LADY.
©RAPID PHASE-2014 www.madamandeve.co.za
OSCAR... YOU'RE NOT PURPOSELY TRYING TO SOUND ANXIOUS, ARE YOU?
ME?? NO WAYS! HEY, AM I UNDER OBSERVATION YET?!
GO AHEAD! MAKE MY VALENTINE'S DAY!!
THIS MIGHT TAKE LONGER THAN I THOUGHT.

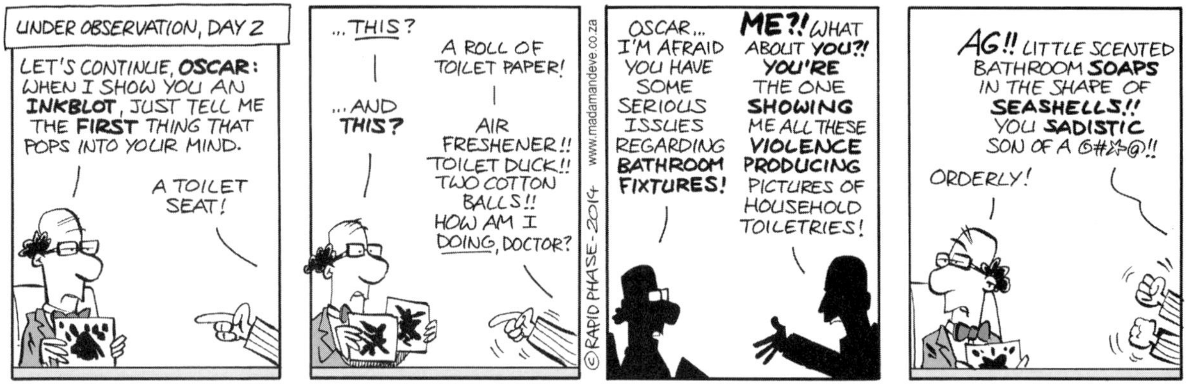
UNDER OBSERVATION, DAY 2
LET'S CONTINUE, OSCAR: WHEN I SHOW YOU AN INKBLOT, JUST TELL ME THE FIRST THING THAT POPS INTO YOUR MIND.
A TOILET SEAT!
...THIS?
A ROLL OF TOILET PAPER!
...AND THIS?
AIR FRESHENER!! TOILET DUCK!! TWO COTTON BALLS!! HOW AM I DOING, DOCTOR?
©RAPID PHASE-2014 www.madamandeve.co.za
OSCAR... I'M AFRAID YOU HAVE SOME SERIOUS ISSUES REGARDING BATHROOM FIXTURES!
ME?! WHAT ABOUT YOU?! YOU'RE THE ONE SHOWING ME ALL THESE VIOLENCE PRODUCING PICTURES OF HOUSEHOLD TOILETRIES!
AG!! LITTLE SCENTED BATHROOM SOAPS IN THE SHAPE OF SEASHELLS!! YOU SADISTIC SON OF A @#*@!!
ORDERLY!

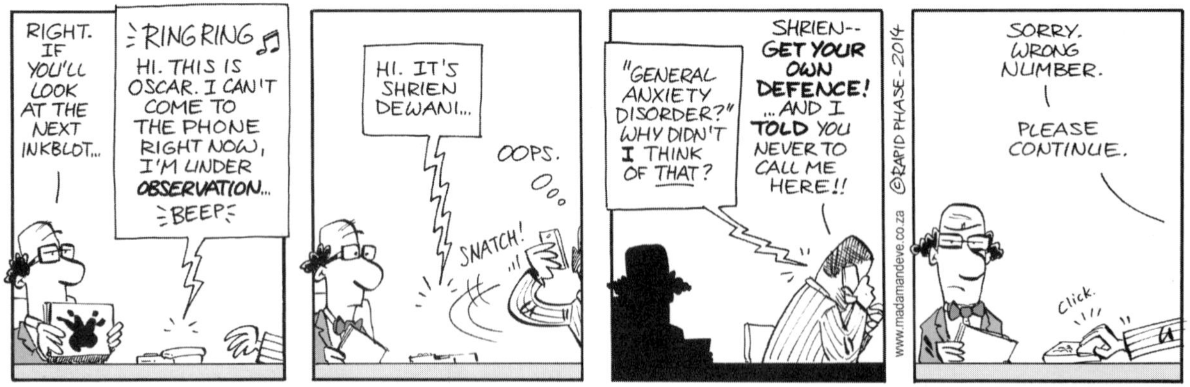
RIGHT. IF YOU'LL LOOK AT THE NEXT INKBLOT...
RING RING
HI. THIS IS OSCAR. I CAN'T COME TO THE PHONE RIGHT NOW, I'M UNDER OBSERVATION...
BEEP
HI. IT'S SHRIEN DEWANI...
OOPS.
SNATCH!
"GENERAL ANXIETY DISORDER?" WHY DIDN'T I THINK OF THAT?
SHRIEN-- GET YOUR OWN DEFENCE! ...AND I TOLD YOU NEVER TO CALL ME HERE!!
©RAPID PHASE-2014 www.madamandeve.co.za
SORRY. WRONG NUMBER.
PLEASE CONTINUE.
CLICK.

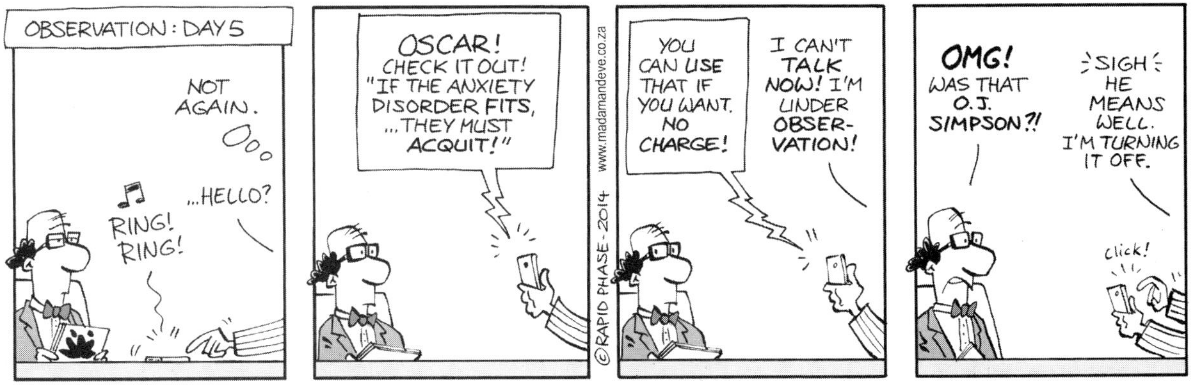
OBSERVATION : DAY 5
NOT AGAIN.
RING! RING!
...HELLO?
OSCAR! CHECK IT OUT! "IF THE ANXIETY DISORDER FITS, ...THEY MUST ACQUIT!"
© RAPID PHASE - 2014 www.madamandeve.co.za
YOU CAN USE THAT IF YOU WANT. NO CHARGE!
I CAN'T TALK NOW! I'M UNDER OBSERVATION!
OMG! WAS THAT O.J. SIMPSON?!
SIGH HE MEANS WELL. I'M TURNING IT OFF.
click!

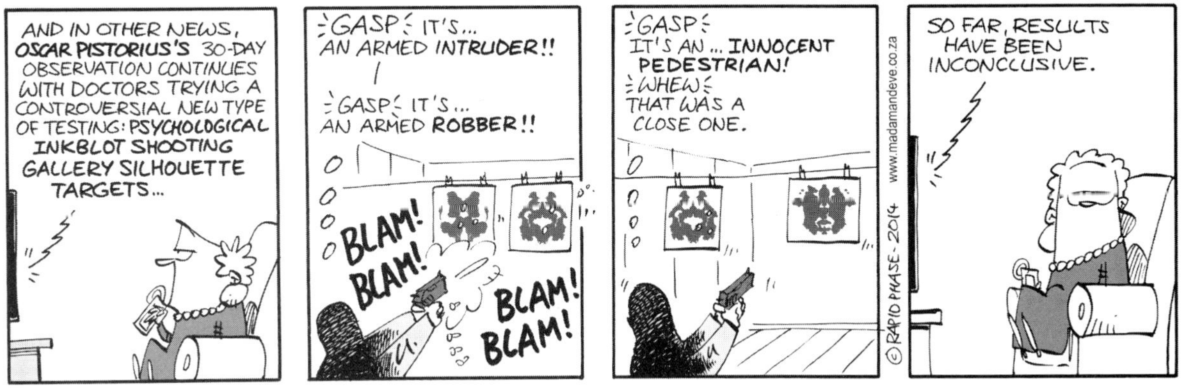
AND IN OTHER NEWS, OSCAR PISTORIUS'S 30-DAY OBSERVATION CONTINUES WITH DOCTORS TRYING A CONTROVERSIAL NEW TYPE OF TESTING: PSYCHOLOGICAL INKBLOT SHOOTING GALLERY SILHOUETTE TARGETS...
GASP IT'S... AN ARMED INTRUDER!!
GASP IT'S... AN ARMED ROBBER!!
BLAM! BLAM!
BLAM! BLAM!
GASP IT'S AN... INNOCENT PEDESTRIAN!
WHEW THAT WAS A CLOSE ONE.
© RAPID PHASE - 2014 www.madamandeve.co.za
SO FAR, RESULTS HAVE BEEN INCONCLUSIVE.

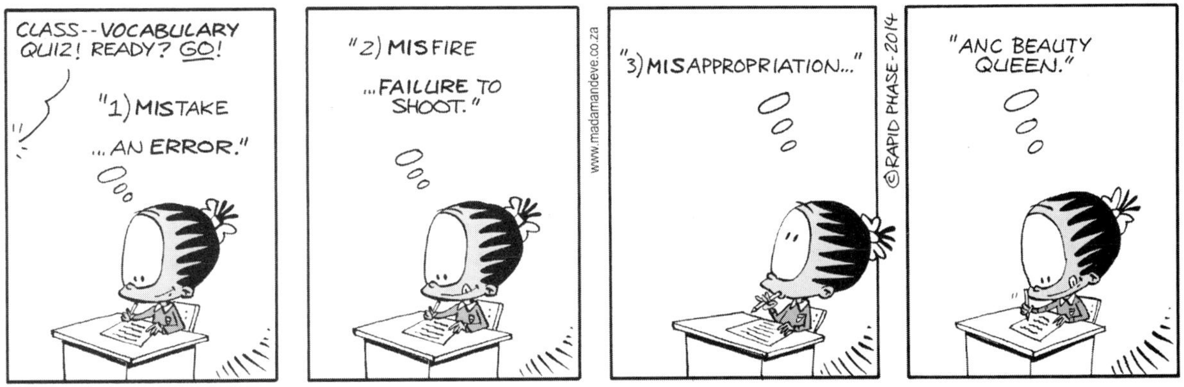
CLASS--VOCABULARY QUIZ! READY? GO!
"1) MISTAKE ...AN ERROR."
"2) MISFIRE ...FAILURE TO SHOOT."
www.madamandeve.co.za
"3) MISAPPROPRIATION..."
© RAPID PHASE - 2014
"ANC BEAUTY QUEEN."

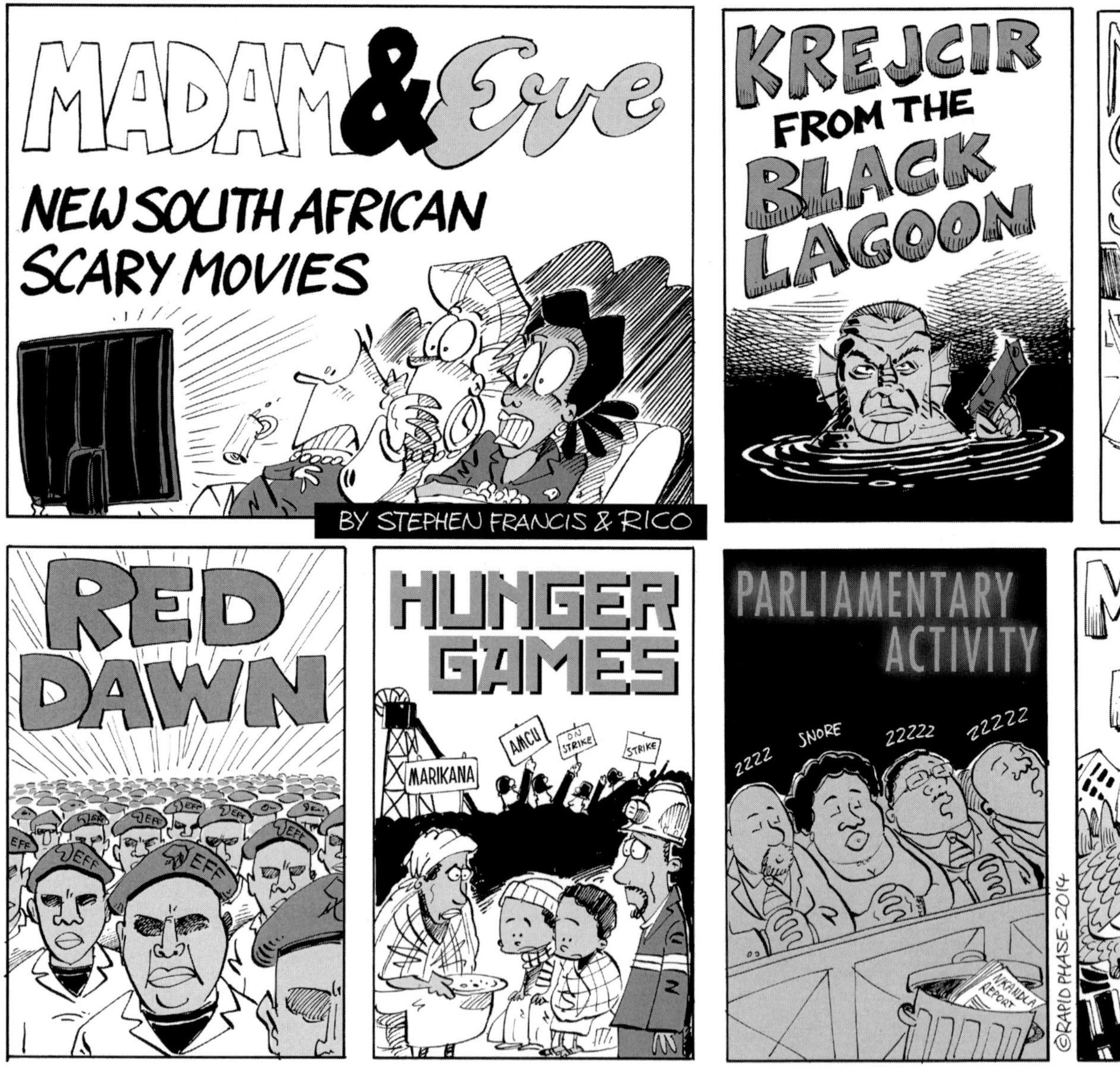

MADAM & Eve
NEW SOUTH AFRICAN SCARY MOVIES
BY STEPHEN FRANCIS & RICO
KREJCIR FROM THE BLACK LAGOON
NIGHTMARE ON NKANDLA STREET
NKANDLA REPORT
PUBLIC PROTECTOR
RED DAWN
EFF
HUNGER GAMES
MARIKANA
AMCU
ON STRIKE
STRIKE
PARLIAMENTARY ACTIVITY
ZZZZ
SNORE
ZZZZZ
ZZZZZ
NKANDLA REPORT
©RAPID PHASE · 2014
MADAMZILLA VS EVE-UTO
WAGE NEGOTIATIONS OF THE GARGANTUANS!

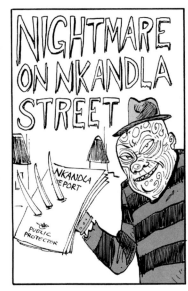

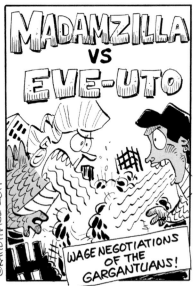

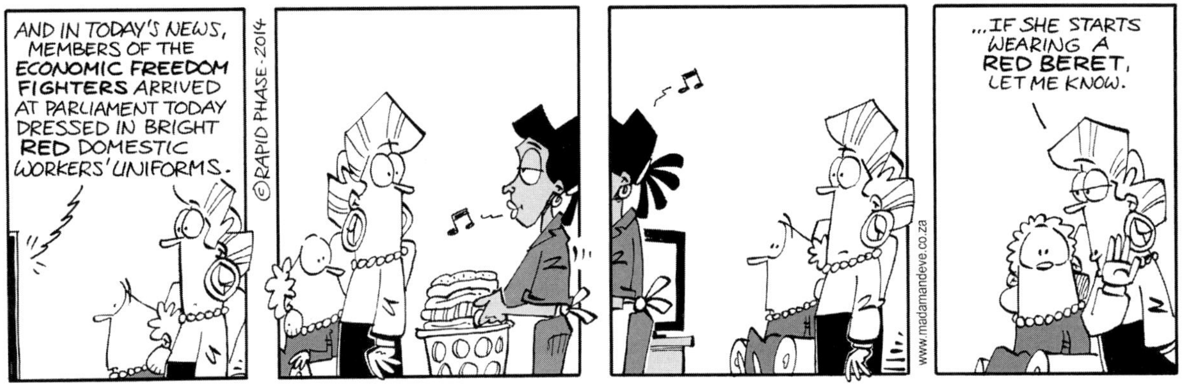
AND IN TODAY'S NEWS, MEMBERS OF THE **ECONOMIC FREEDOM FIGHTERS** ARRIVED AT PARLIAMENT TODAY DRESSED IN BRIGHT **RED** DOMESTIC WORKERS' UNIFORMS.
©RAPID PHASE · 2014
...IF SHE STARTS WEARING A **RED BERET**, LET ME KNOW.
www.madamandeve.co.za

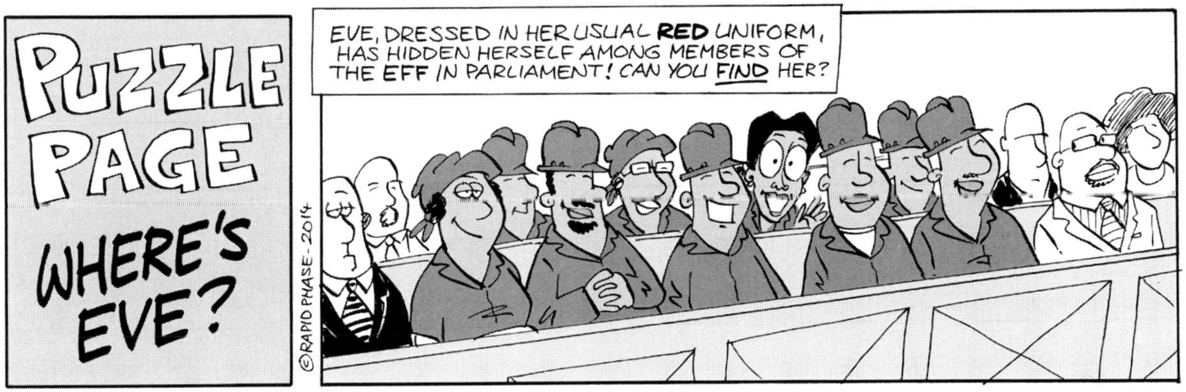
PUZZLE PAGE
WHERE'S EVE?
©RAPID PHASE · 2014
EVE, DRESSED IN HER USUAL **RED** UNIFORM, HAS HIDDEN HERSELF AMONG MEMBERS OF THE **EFF** IN PARLIAMENT! CAN YOU FIND HER?

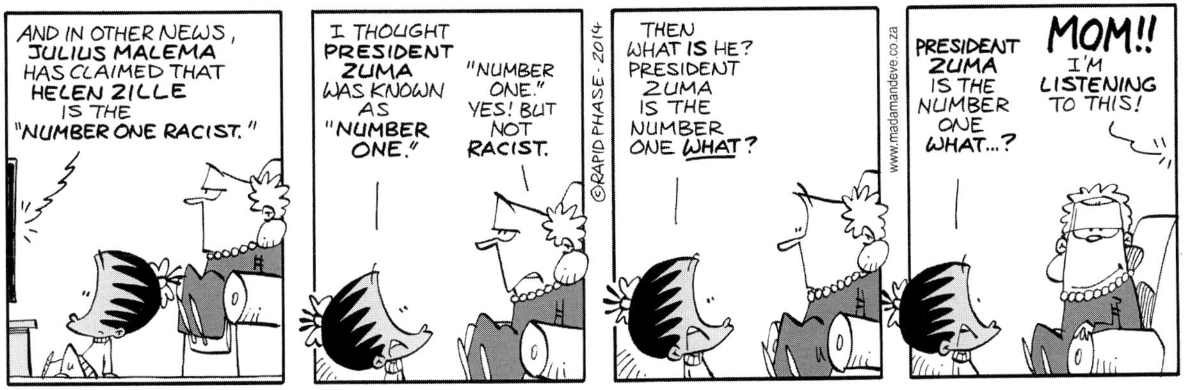
AND IN OTHER NEWS, **JULIUS MALEMA** HAS CLAIMED THAT **HELEN ZILLE** IS THE "**NUMBER ONE RACIST.**"
I THOUGHT **PRESIDENT ZUMA** WAS KNOWN AS "**NUMBER ONE.**"
"NUMBER ONE." YES! BUT NOT **RACIST.**
©RAPID PHASE · 2014
THEN WHAT **IS** HE? PRESIDENT ZUMA IS THE NUMBER ONE **WHAT**?
www.madamandeve.co.za
PRESIDENT ZUMA IS THE NUMBER ONE **WHAT...?**
MOM!! I'M **LISTENING** TO THIS!

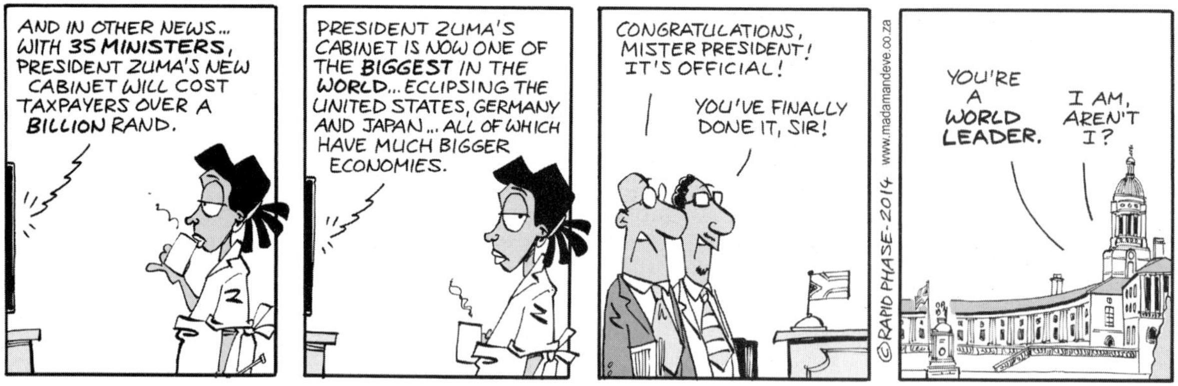
AND IN OTHER NEWS... WITH 35 MINISTERS, PRESIDENT ZUMA'S NEW CABINET WILL COST TAXPAYERS OVER A BILLION RAND.
PRESIDENT ZUMA'S CABINET IS NOW ONE OF THE BIGGEST IN THE WORLD... ECLIPSING THE UNITED STATES, GERMANY AND JAPAN... ALL OF WHICH HAVE MUCH BIGGER ECONOMIES.
CONGRATULATIONS, MISTER PRESIDENT! IT'S OFFICIAL!
YOU'VE FINALLY DONE IT, SIR!
©RAPID PHASE-2014 www.madamandeve.co.za
YOU'RE A WORLD LEADER.
I AM, AREN'T I?

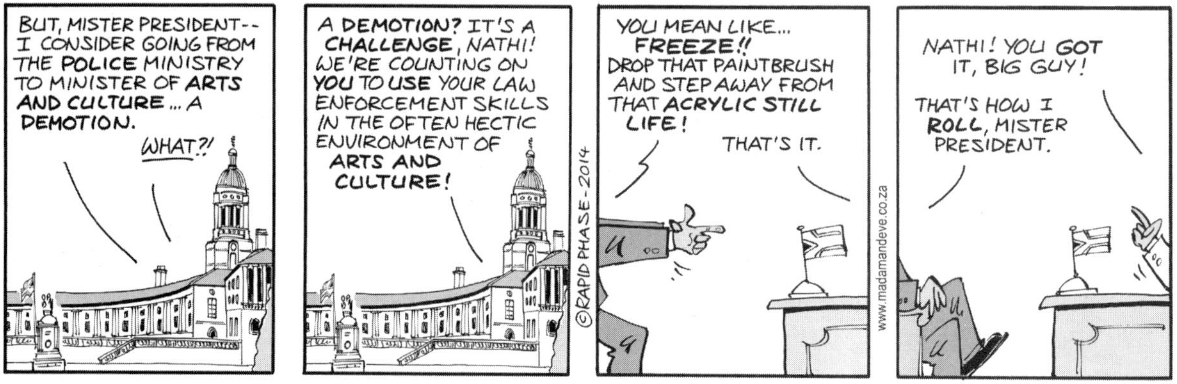
BUT, MISTER PRESIDENT-- I CONSIDER GOING FROM THE POLICE MINISTRY TO MINISTER OF ARTS AND CULTURE... A DEMOTION.
WHAT?!
A DEMOTION? IT'S A CHALLENGE, NATHI! WE'RE COUNTING ON YOU TO USE YOUR LAW ENFORCEMENT SKILLS IN THE OFTEN HECTIC ENVIRONMENT OF ARTS AND CULTURE!
©RAPID PHASE-2014
YOU MEAN LIKE... FREEZE!! DROP THAT PAINTBRUSH AND STEP AWAY FROM THAT ACRYLIC STILL LIFE!
THAT'S IT.
www.madamandeve.co.za
NATHI! YOU GOT IT, BIG GUY!
THAT'S HOW I ROLL, MISTER PRESIDENT.

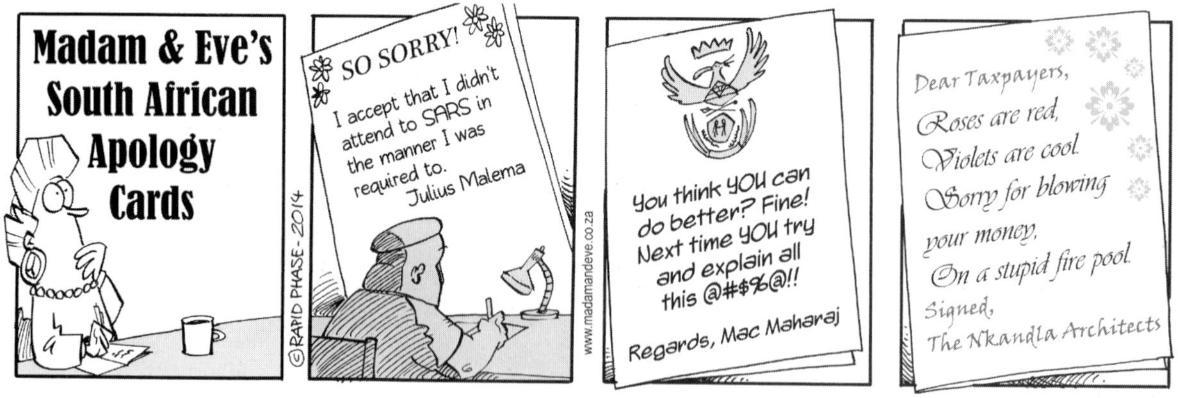
Madam & Eve's South African Apology Cards
©RAPID PHASE-2014
SO SORRY!
I accept that I didn't attend to SARS in the manner I was required to.
Julius Malema
www.madamandeve.co.za
You think YOU can do better? Fine! Next time YOU try and explain all this @#$%@!!
Regards, Mac Maharaj
Dear Taxpayers,
Roses are red,
Violets are cool.
Sorry for blowing
your money,
On a stupid fire pool.
Signed,
The Nkandla Architects

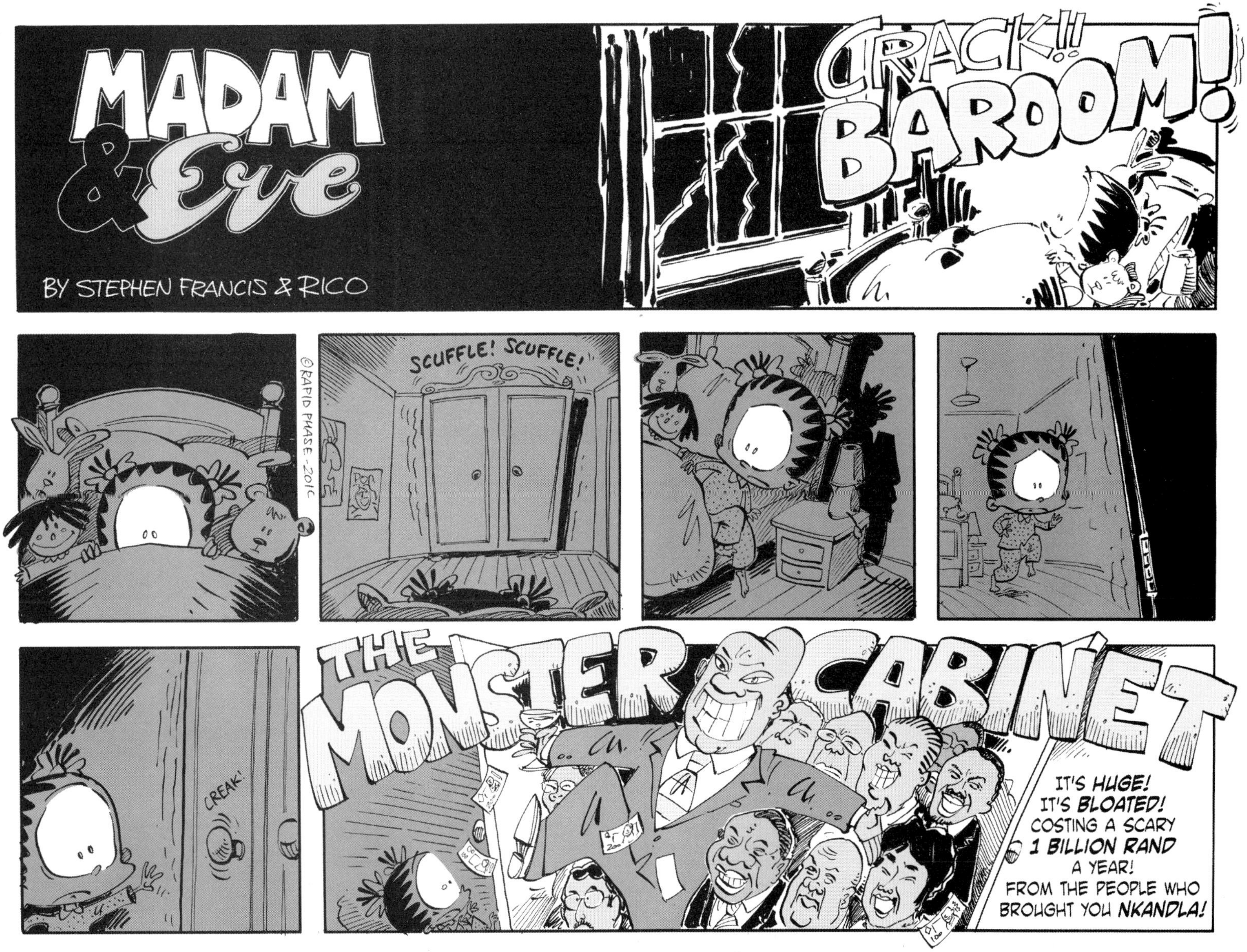
MADAM & Eve
BY STEPHEN FRANCIS & RICO
CRACK!! BAROOM!
©RAPID PHASE - 2016
SCUFFLE! SCUFFLE!
CREAK!
THE MONSTER CABINET
IT'S HUGE!
IT'S BLOATED!
COSTING A SCARY
1 BILLION RAND
A YEAR!
FROM THE PEOPLE WHO
BROUGHT YOU NKANDLA!

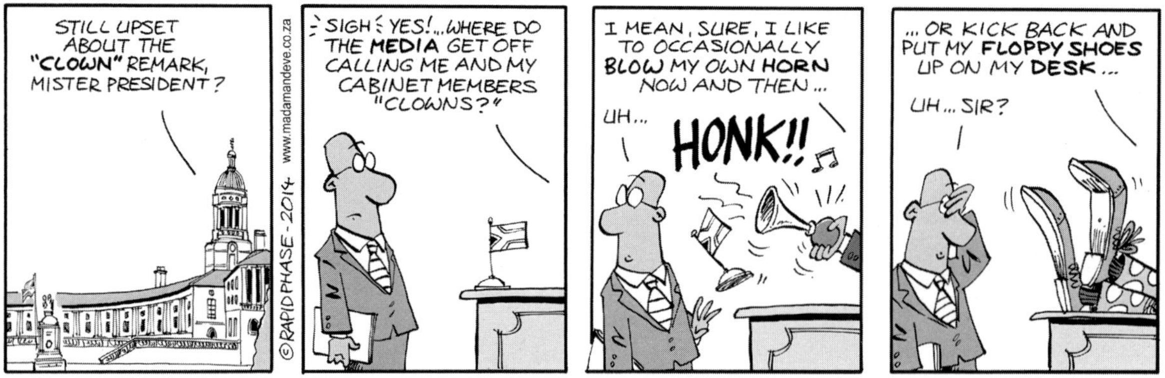
STILL UPSET ABOUT THE "CLOWN" REMARK, MISTER PRESIDENT?
www.madamandeve.co.za
© RAPID PHASE - 2014
:SIGH: YES!... WHERE DO THE MEDIA GET OFF CALLING ME AND MY CABINET MEMBERS "CLOWNS?"
I MEAN, SURE, I LIKE TO OCCASIONALLY BLOW MY OWN HORN NOW AND THEN...
UH...
HONK!!
... OR KICK BACK AND PUT MY FLOPPY SHOES UP ON MY DESK...
UH... SIR?

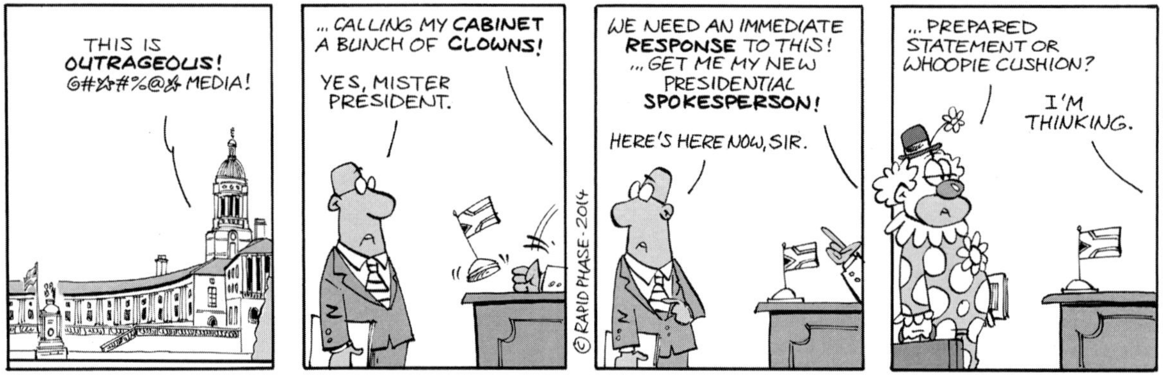
THIS IS OUTRAGEOUS! @#%#%@% MEDIA!
... CALLING MY CABINET A BUNCH OF CLOWNS!
YES, MISTER PRESIDENT.
© RAPID PHASE - 2014
WE NEED AN IMMEDIATE RESPONSE TO THIS! ...GET ME MY NEW PRESIDENTIAL SPOKESPERSON!
HERE'S HERE NOW, SIR.
... PREPARED STATEMENT OR WHOOPIE CUSHION?
I'M THINKING.

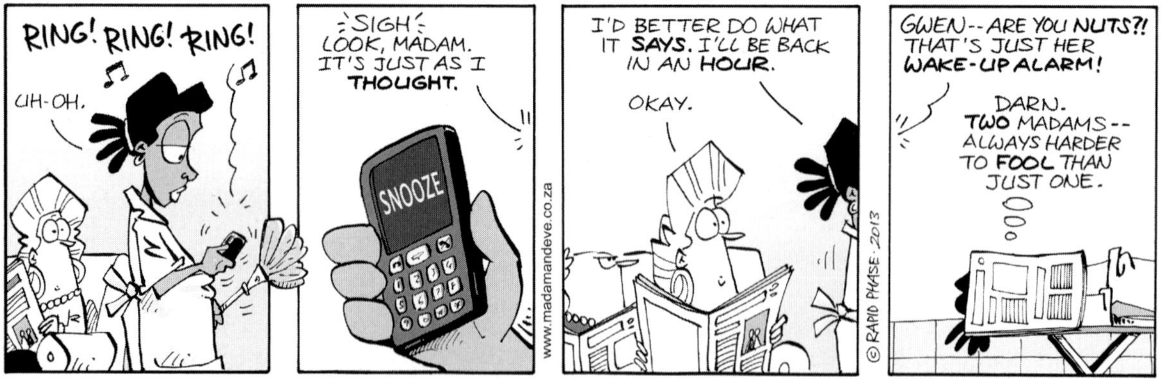
RING! RING! RING!
UH-OH.
:SIGH: LOOK, MADAM. IT'S JUST AS I THOUGHT.
SNOOZE
www.madamandeve.co.za
I'D BETTER DO WHAT IT SAYS. I'LL BE BACK IN AN HOUR.
OKAY.
© RAPID PHASE - 2013
GWEN -- ARE YOU NUTS?! THAT'S JUST HER WAKE-UP ALARM!
DARN. TWO MADAMS -- ALWAYS HARDER TO FOOL THAN JUST ONE.

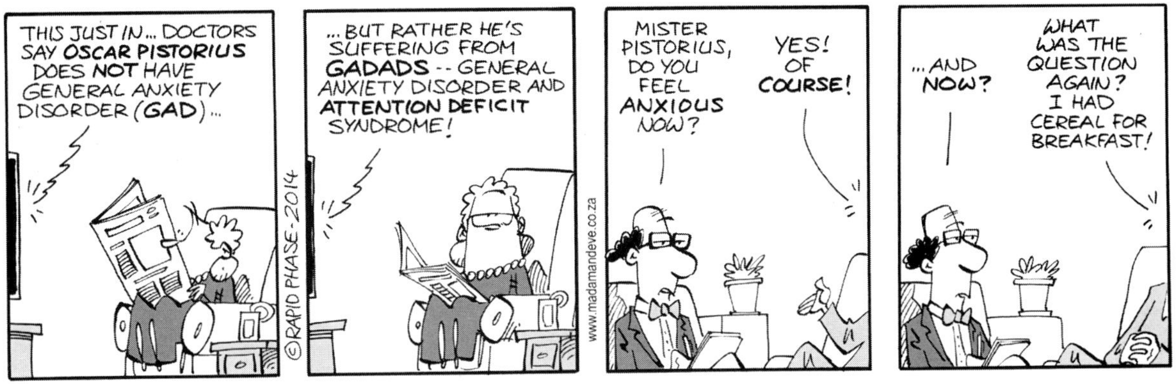
THIS JUST IN... DOCTORS SAY OSCAR PISTORIUS DOES NOT HAVE GENERAL ANXIETY DISORDER (GAD)...
©RAPID PHASE-2014
...BUT RATHER HE'S SUFFERING FROM GADADS -- GENERAL ANXIETY DISORDER AND ATTENTION DEFICIT SYNDROME!
www.madamandeve.co.za
MISTER PISTORIUS, DO YOU FEEL ANXIOUS NOW?
YES! OF COURSE!
...AND NOW?
WHAT WAS THE QUESTION AGAIN? I HAD CEREAL FOR BREAKFAST!

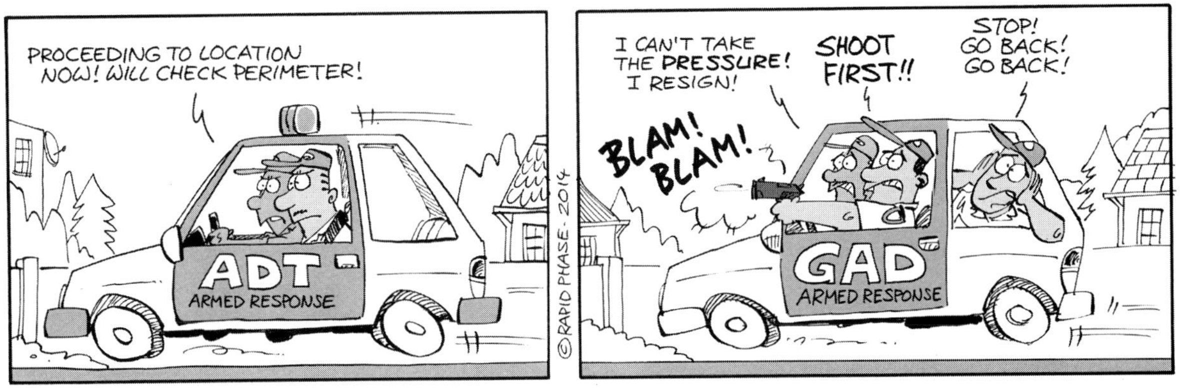
PROCEEDING TO LOCATION NOW! WILL CHECK PERIMETER!
ADT
ARMED RESPONSE
©RAPID PHASE-2014
I CAN'T TAKE THE PRESSURE! I RESIGN!
SHOOT FIRST!!
STOP! GO BACK! GO BACK!
BLAM! BLAM!
GAD
ARMED RESPONSE

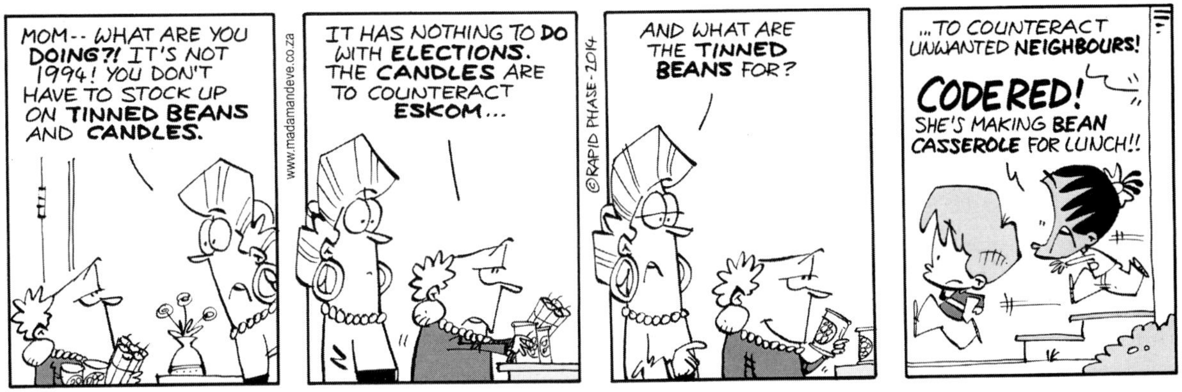
MOM-- WHAT ARE YOU DOING?! IT'S NOT 1994! YOU DON'T HAVE TO STOCK UP ON TINNED BEANS AND CANDLES.
www.madamandeve.co.za
IT HAS NOTHING TO DO WITH ELECTIONS. THE CANDLES ARE TO COUNTERACT ESKOM...
©RAPID PHASE-2014
AND WHAT ARE THE TINNED BEANS FOR?
...TO COUNTERACT UNWANTED NEIGHBOURS!
CODE RED!
SHE'S MAKING BEAN CASSEROLE FOR LUNCH!!

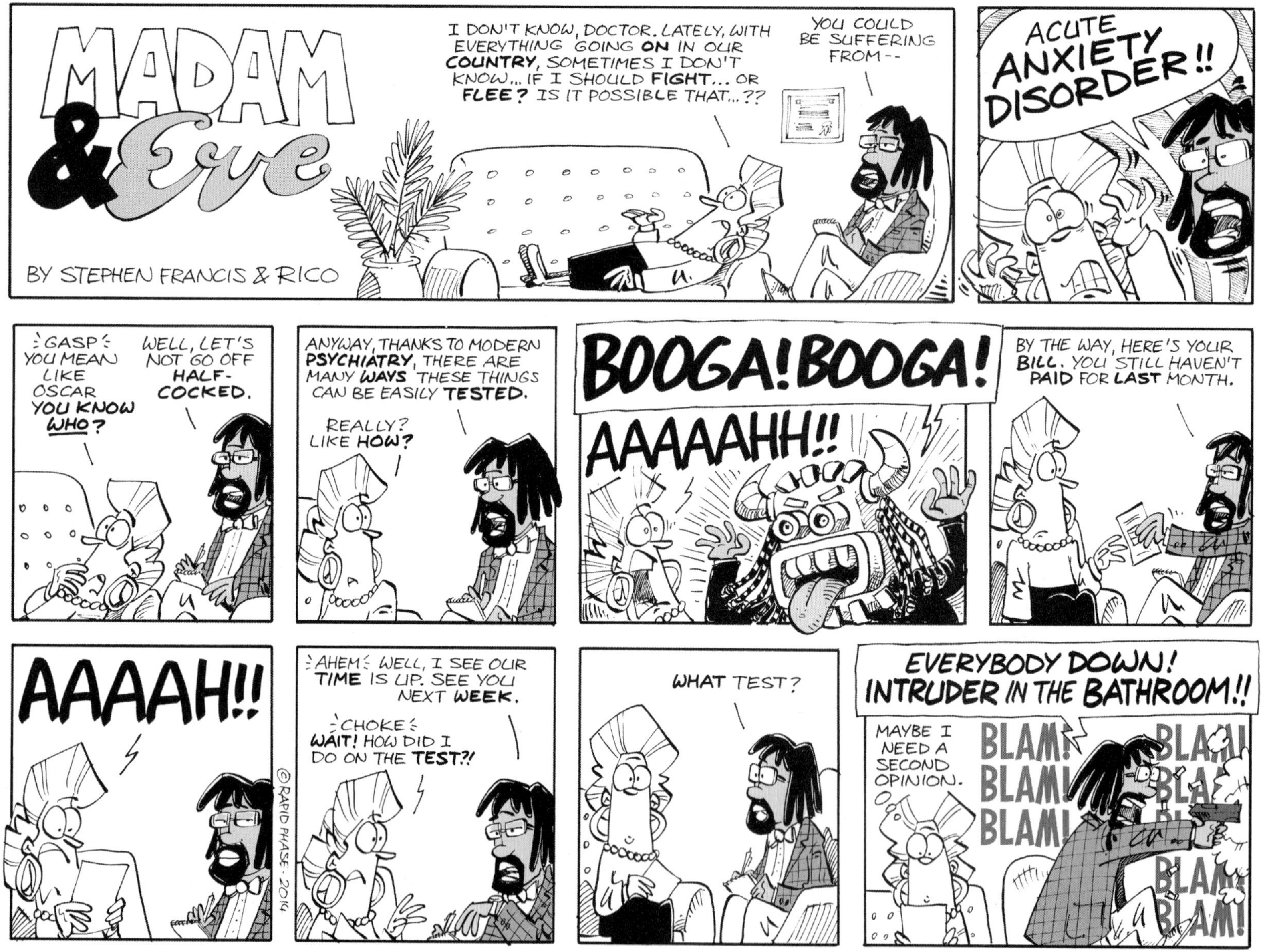
MADAM & Eve
BY STEPHEN FRANCIS & RICO
I DON'T KNOW, DOCTOR. LATELY, WITH EVERYTHING GOING ON IN OUR COUNTRY, SOMETIMES I DON'T KNOW... IF I SHOULD FIGHT... OR FLEE? IS IT POSSIBLE THAT...??
YOU COULD BE SUFFERING FROM--
ACUTE ANXIETY DISORDER!!
:GASP: YOU MEAN LIKE OSCAR YOU KNOW WHO?
WELL, LET'S NOT GO OFF HALF-COCKED.
ANYWAY, THANKS TO MODERN PSYCHIATRY, THERE ARE MANY WAYS THESE THINGS CAN BE EASILY TESTED.
REALLY? LIKE HOW?
BOOGA! BOOGA!
AAAAAHH!!
BY THE WAY, HERE'S YOUR BILL. YOU STILL HAVEN'T PAID FOR LAST MONTH.
AAAAH!!
© RAPID PHASE 2014
:AHEM: WELL, I SEE OUR TIME IS UP. SEE YOU NEXT WEEK.
:CHOKE: WAIT! HOW DID I DO ON THE TEST?!
WHAT TEST?
EVERYBODY DOWN! INTRUDER IN THE BATHROOM!!
MAYBE I NEED A SECOND OPINION.
BLAM! BLAM! BLAM!
BLAM! BLAM! BLAM! BLAM! BLAM!

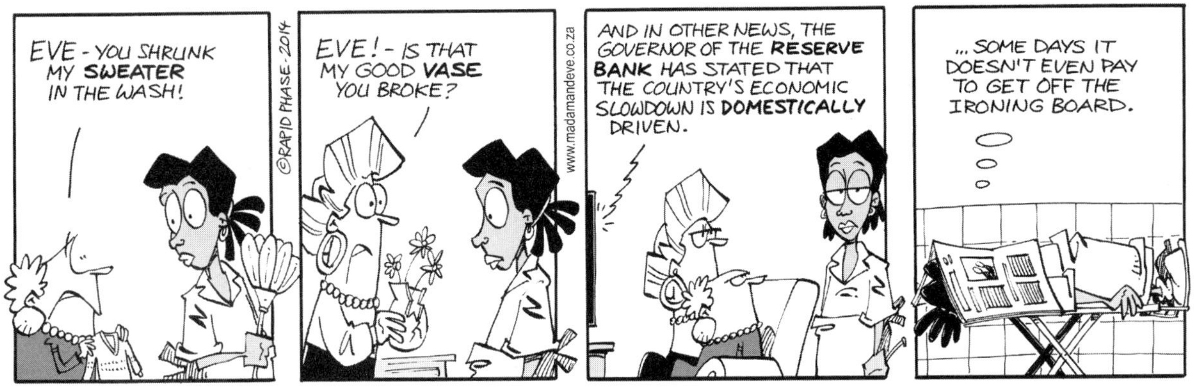
EVE - YOU SHRUNK MY SWEATER IN THE WASH!
©RAPID PHASE · 2014
EVE! - IS THAT MY GOOD VASE YOU BROKE?
www.madamandeve.co.za
AND IN OTHER NEWS, THE GOVERNOR OF THE RESERVE BANK HAS STATED THAT THE COUNTRY'S ECONOMIC SLOWDOWN IS DOMESTICALLY DRIVEN.
... SOME DAYS IT DOESN'T EVEN PAY TO GET OFF THE IRONING BOARD.

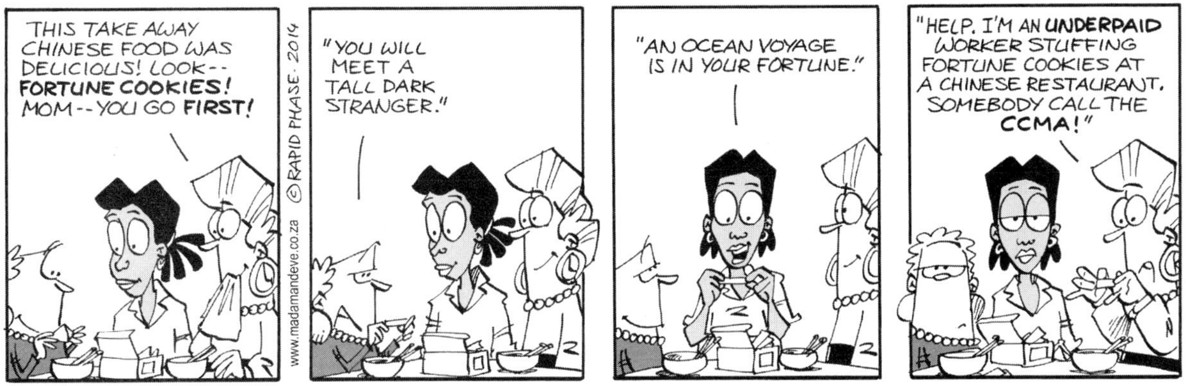
THIS TAKE AWAY CHINESE FOOD WAS DELICIOUS! LOOK-- FORTUNE COOKIES! MOM--YOU GO FIRST!
© RAPID PHASE · 2014
www.madamandeve.co.za
"YOU WILL MEET A TALL DARK STRANGER."
"AN OCEAN VOYAGE IS IN YOUR FORTUNE."
"HELP. I'M AN UNDERPAID WORKER STUFFING FORTUNE COOKIES AT A CHINESE RESTAURANT. SOMEBODY CALL THE CCMA!"

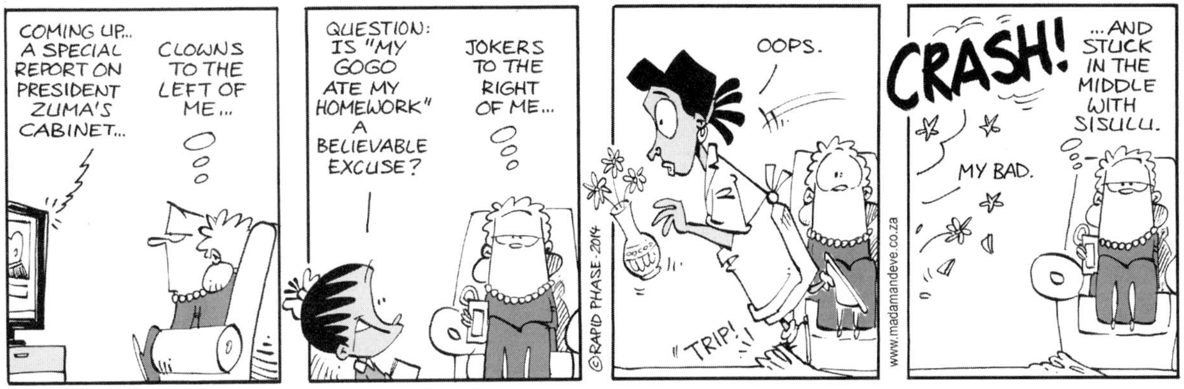
COMING UP... A SPECIAL REPORT ON PRESIDENT ZUMA'S CABINET...
CLOWNS TO THE LEFT OF ME...
QUESTION: IS "MY GOGO ATE MY HOMEWORK" A BELIEVABLE EXCUSE?
JOKERS TO THE RIGHT OF ME...
OOPS.
TRIP!
©RAPID PHASE · 2014
www.madamandeve.co.za
CRASH!
MY BAD.
...AND STUCK IN THE MIDDLE WITH SISULU.

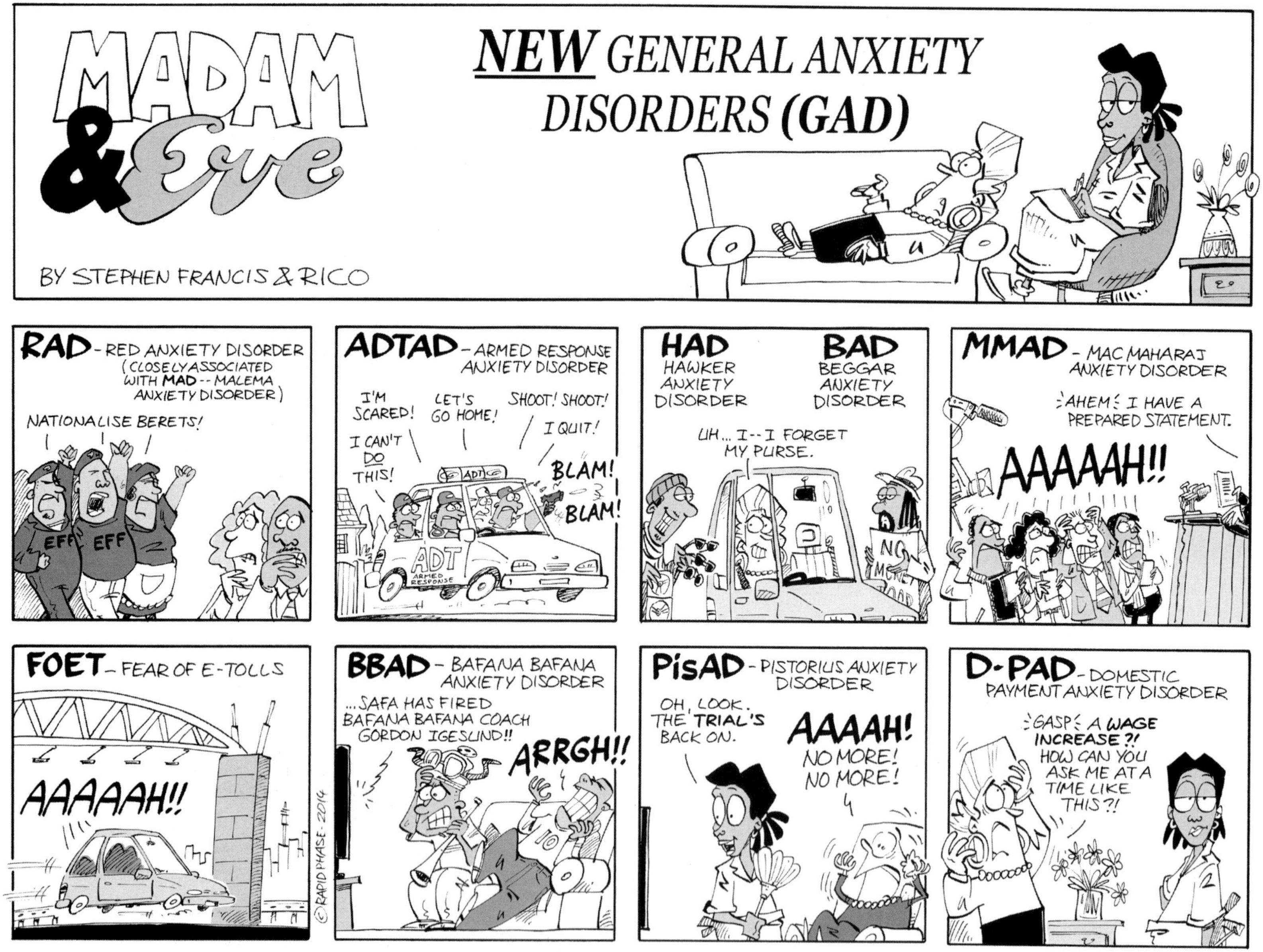
MADAM & Eve
NEW GENERAL ANXIETY DISORDERS (GAD)
BY STEPHEN FRANCIS & RICO
RAD - RED ANXIETY DISORDER (CLOSELY ASSOCIATED WITH MAD -- MALEMA ANXIETY DISORDER)
NATIONALISE BERETS!
EFF
EFF
ADTAD - ARMED RESPONSE ANXIETY DISORDER
I'M SCARED!
LET'S GO HOME!
SHOOT! SHOOT!
I CAN'T DO THIS!
I QUIT!
BLAM!
BLAM!
ADT
ADT ARMED RESPONSE
HAD HAWKER ANXIETY DISORDER
BAD BEGGAR ANXIETY DISORDER
UH... I-- I FORGET MY PURSE.
MMAD - MAC MAHARAJ ANXIETY DISORDER
AHEM I HAVE A PREPARED STATEMENT.
AAAAAH!!
FOET - FEAR OF E-TOLLS
AAAAAH!!
BBAD - BAFANA BAFANA ANXIETY DISORDER
...SAFA HAS FIRED BAFANA BAFANA COACH GORDON IGESUND!!
ARRGH!!
PisAD - PISTORIUS ANXIETY DISORDER
OH, LOOK. THE TRIAL'S BACK ON.
AAAAH! NO MORE! NO MORE!
D-PAD - DOMESTIC PAYMENT ANXIETY DISORDER
GASP A WAGE INCREASE?! HOW CAN YOU ASK ME AT A TIME LIKE THIS?!
© RAPID PHASE - 2014

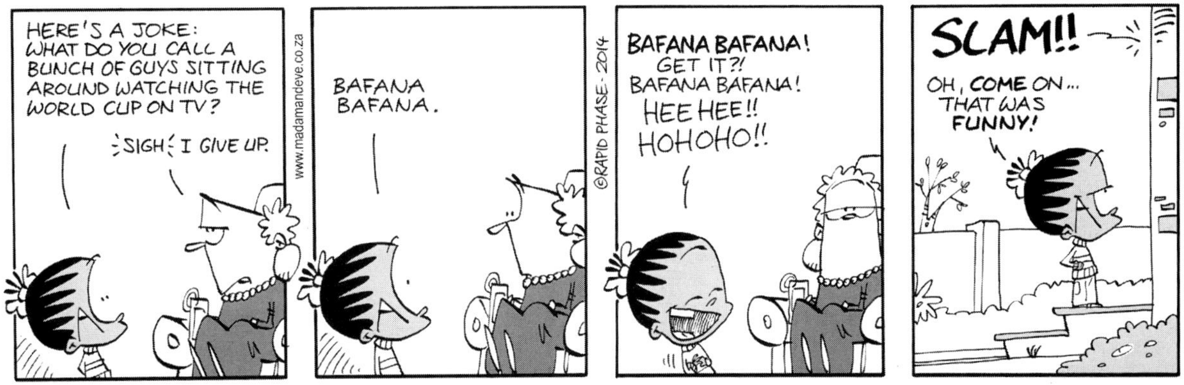
HERE'S A JOKE: WHAT DO YOU CALL A BUNCH OF GUYS SITTING AROUND WATCHING THE WORLD CUP ON TV?
SIGH I GIVE UP.
www.madamandeve.co.za
BAFANA BAFANA.
©RAPID PHASE - 2014
BAFANA BAFANA! GET IT?! BAFANA BAFANA!
HEE HEE!! HOHOHO!!
SLAM!!
OH, COME ON... THAT WAS FUNNY!

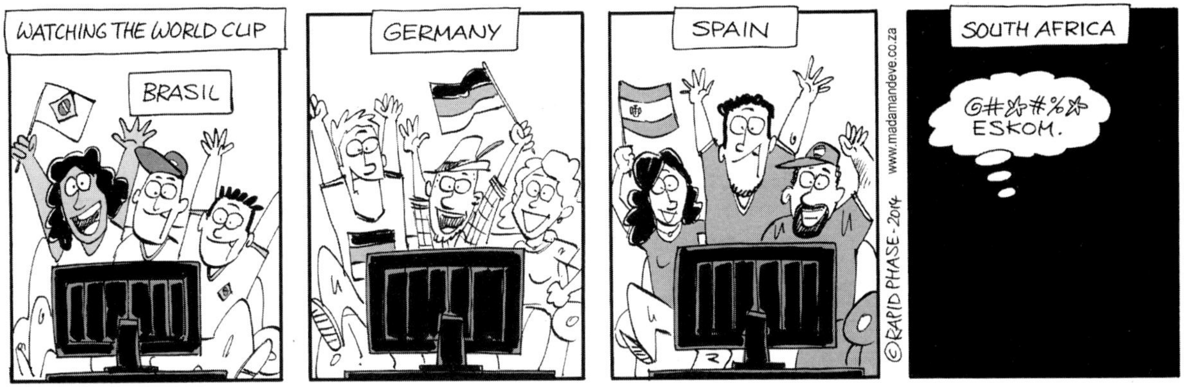
WATCHING THE WORLD CUP
BRASIL
GERMANY
SPAIN
www.madamandeve.co.za
©RAPID PHASE - 2014
SOUTH AFRICA
@#✲✲#%✲ ESKOM.

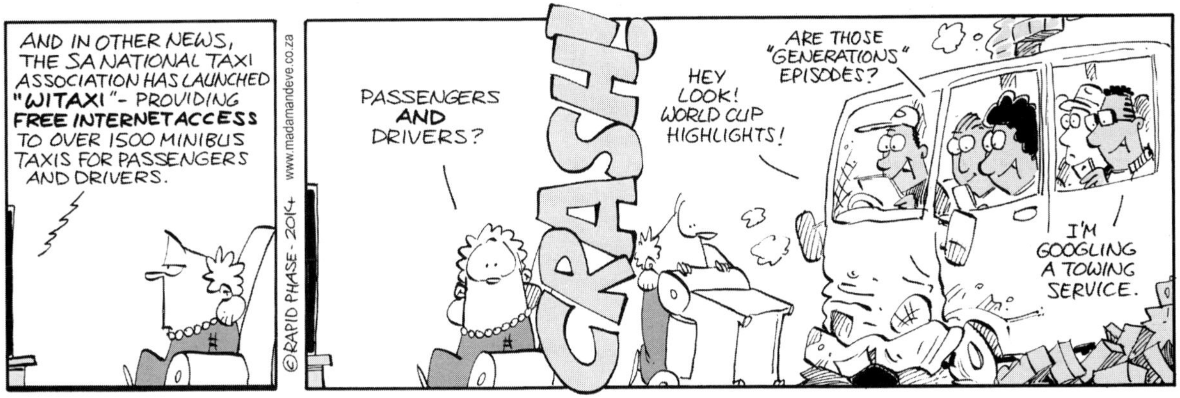
AND IN OTHER NEWS, THE SA NATIONAL TAXI ASSOCIATION HAS LAUNCHED "WITAXI" - PROVIDING FREE INTERNET ACCESS TO OVER 1500 MINIBUS TAXIS FOR PASSENGERS AND DRIVERS.
www.madamandeve.co.za
©RAPID PHASE - 2014
PASSENGERS AND DRIVERS?
CRASH!
HEY LOOK! WORLD CUP HIGHLIGHTS!
ARE THOSE "GENERATIONS" EPISODES?
I'M GOOGLING A TOWING SERVICE.

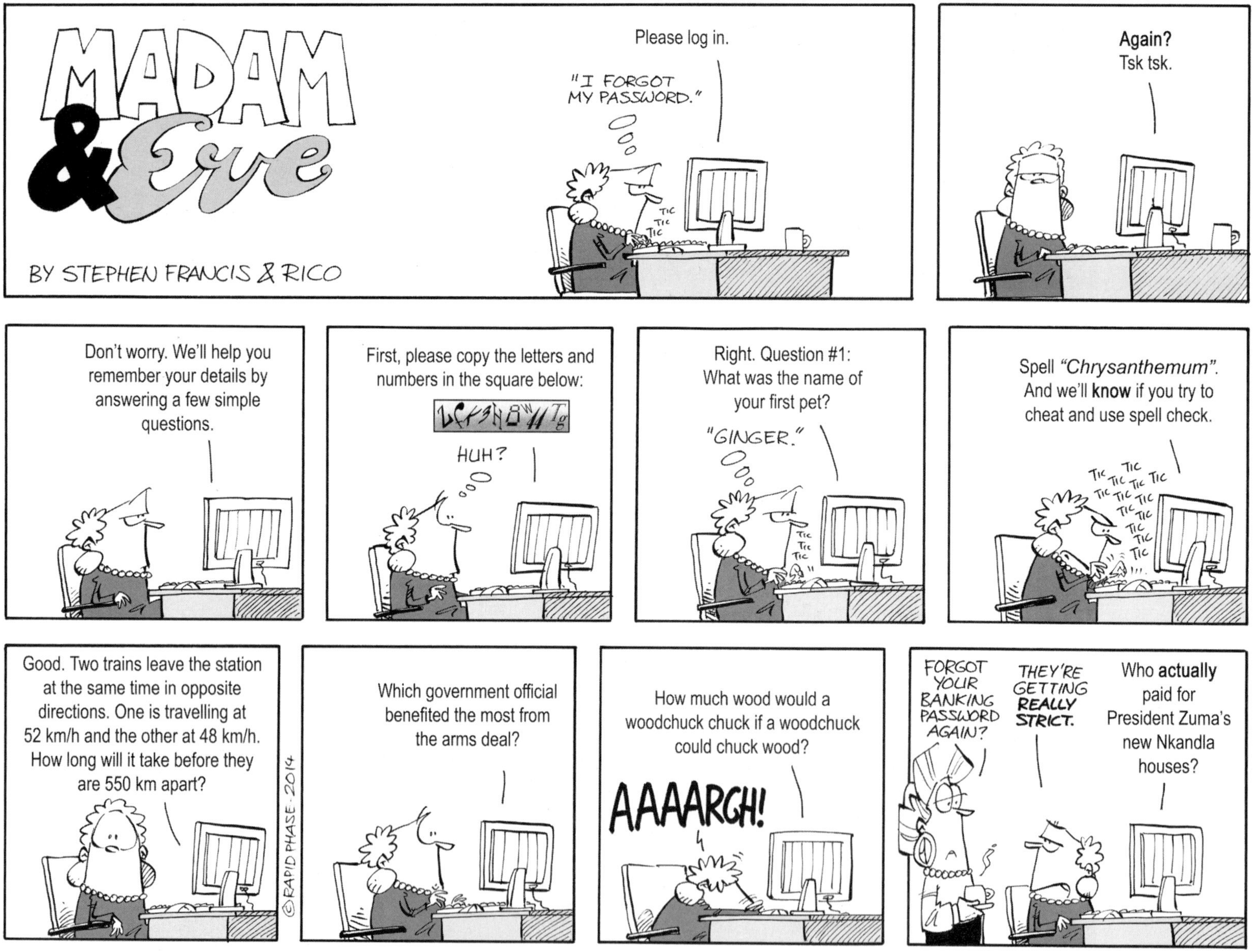

MADAM & Eve
BY STEPHEN FRANCIS & RICO
Please log in.
"I FORGOT MY PASSWORD."
TIC TIC TIC
Again?
Tsk tsk.
Don't worry. We'll help you remember your details by answering a few simple questions.
First, please copy the letters and numbers in the square below:
HUH?
Right. Question #1: What was the name of your first pet?
"GINGER."
TIC TIC TIC
Spell *"Chrysanthemum"*. And we'll **know** if you try to cheat and use spell check.
TIC TIC TIC TIC TIC TIC TIC TIC TIC TIC TIC TIC TIC TIC
Good. Two trains leave the station at the same time in opposite directions. One is travelling at 52 km/h and the other at 48 km/h. How long will it take before they are 550 km apart?
©RAPID PHASE 2014
Which government official benefited the most from the arms deal?
How much wood would a woodchuck chuck if a woodchuck could chuck wood?
AAAARGH!
FORGOT YOUR BANKING PASSWORD AGAIN?
THEY'RE GETTING **REALLY STRICT.**
Who **actually** paid for President Zuma's new Nkandla houses?

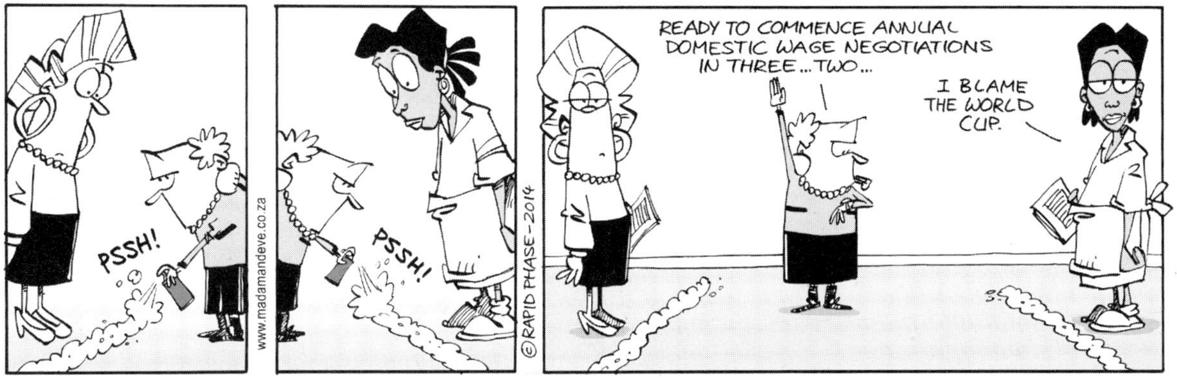
PSSH!
www.madamandeve.co.za
PSSH!
©RAPID PHASE-2014
READY TO COMMENCE ANNUAL DOMESTIC WAGE NEGOTIATIONS IN THREE...TWO...
I BLAME THE WORLD CUP.

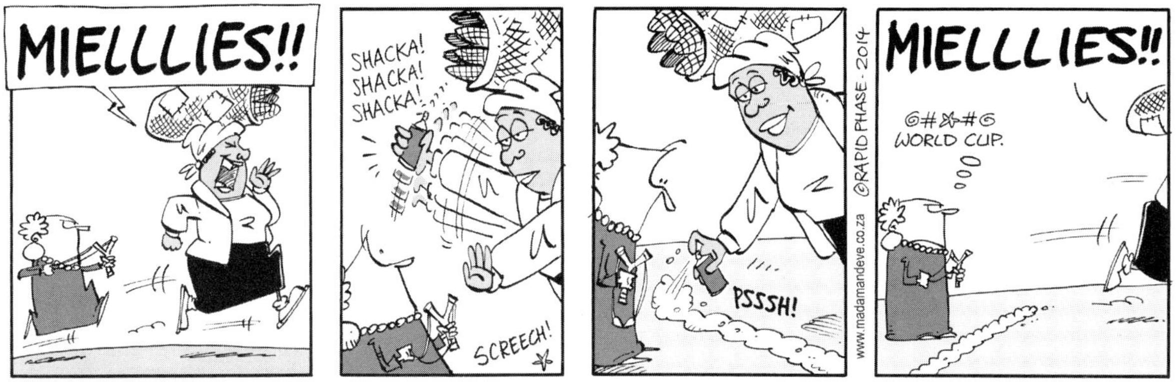
MIELLLIES!!
SHACKA! SHACKA! SHACKA!
SCREECH!
PSSSH!
©RAPID PHASE-2014
www.madamandeve.co.za
MIELLLIES!!
@#*#@ WORLD CUP.

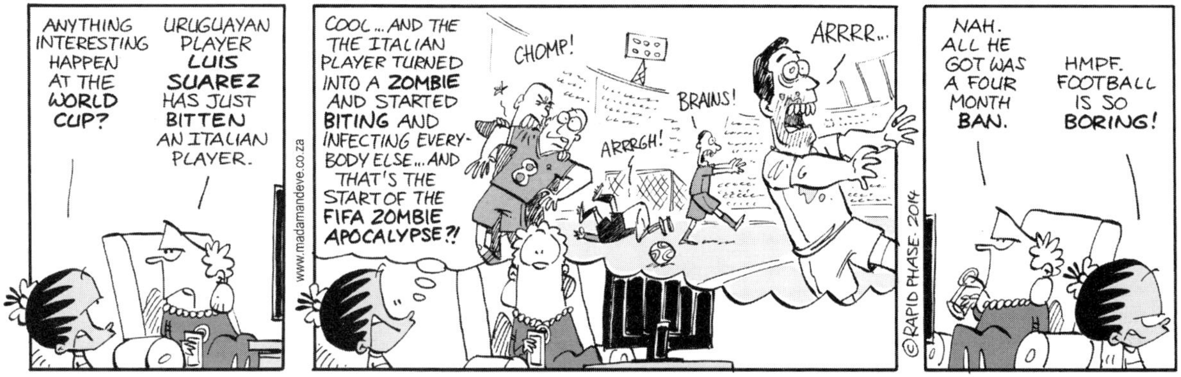
ANYTHING INTERESTING HAPPEN AT THE **WORLD CUP?**
URUGUAYAN PLAYER **LUIS SUAREZ** HAS JUST **BITTEN** AN ITALIAN PLAYER.
www.madamandeve.co.za
COOL...AND THE THE ITALIAN PLAYER TURNED INTO A **ZOMBIE** AND STARTED **BITING** AND INFECTING EVERY-BODY ELSE...AND THAT'S THE START OF THE **FIFA ZOMBIE APOCALYPSE?!**
CHOMP!
BRAINS!
ARRRGH!
ARRRR...
©RAPID PHASE-2014
NAH. ALL HE GOT WAS A FOUR MONTH **BAN.**
HMPF. FOOTBALL IS SO **BORING!**

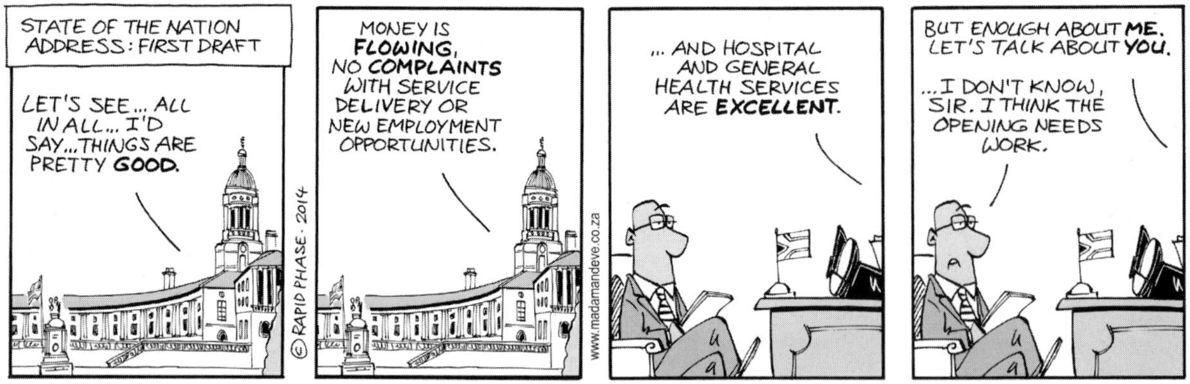
STATE OF THE NATION ADDRESS: FIRST DRAFT
LET'S SEE... ALL IN ALL... I'D SAY... THINGS ARE PRETTY **GOOD**.
© RAPID PHASE · 2014
MONEY IS **FLOWING**, NO **COMPLAINTS** WITH SERVICE DELIVERY OR NEW EMPLOYMENT OPPORTUNITIES.
www.madamandeve.co.za
... AND HOSPITAL AND GENERAL HEALTH SERVICES ARE **EXCELLENT**.
BUT ENOUGH ABOUT **ME**. LET'S TALK ABOUT **YOU**.
... I DON'T KNOW, SIR. I THINK THE OPENING NEEDS WORK.

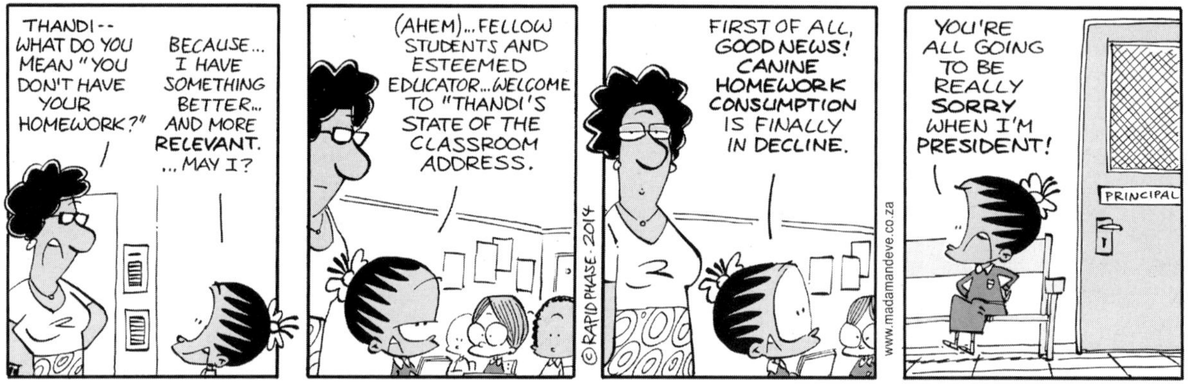
THANDI -- WHAT DO YOU MEAN "YOU DON'T HAVE YOUR HOMEWORK?"
BECAUSE... I HAVE SOMETHING BETTER... AND MORE **RELEVANT**. ... MAY I?
(AHEM)... FELLOW STUDENTS AND ESTEEMED EDUCATOR... WELCOME TO "THANDI'S STATE OF THE CLASSROOM ADDRESS.
© RAPID PHASE · 2014
FIRST OF ALL, **GOOD NEWS**! **CANINE HOMEWORK CONSUMPTION** IS FINALLY IN **DECLINE**.
www.madamandeve.co.za
YOU'RE ALL GOING TO BE REALLY **SORRY** WHEN I'M **PRESIDENT**!
PRINCIPAL

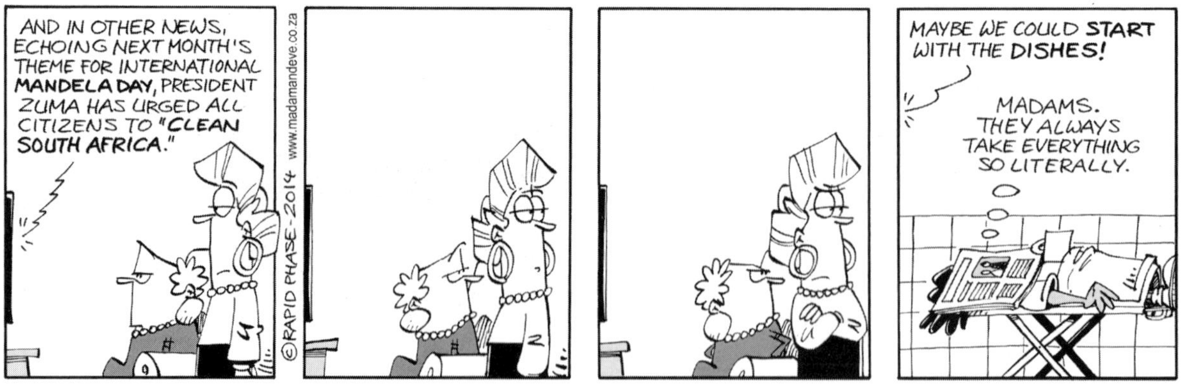
AND IN OTHER NEWS, ECHOING NEXT MONTH'S THEME FOR INTERNATIONAL **MANDELA DAY**, PRESIDENT ZUMA HAS URGED ALL CITIZENS TO "**CLEAN SOUTH AFRICA**."
© RAPID PHASE · 2014 www.madamandeve.co.za
MAYBE WE COULD **START** WITH THE **DISHES**!
MADAMS. THEY ALWAYS TAKE EVERYTHING SO LITERALLY.

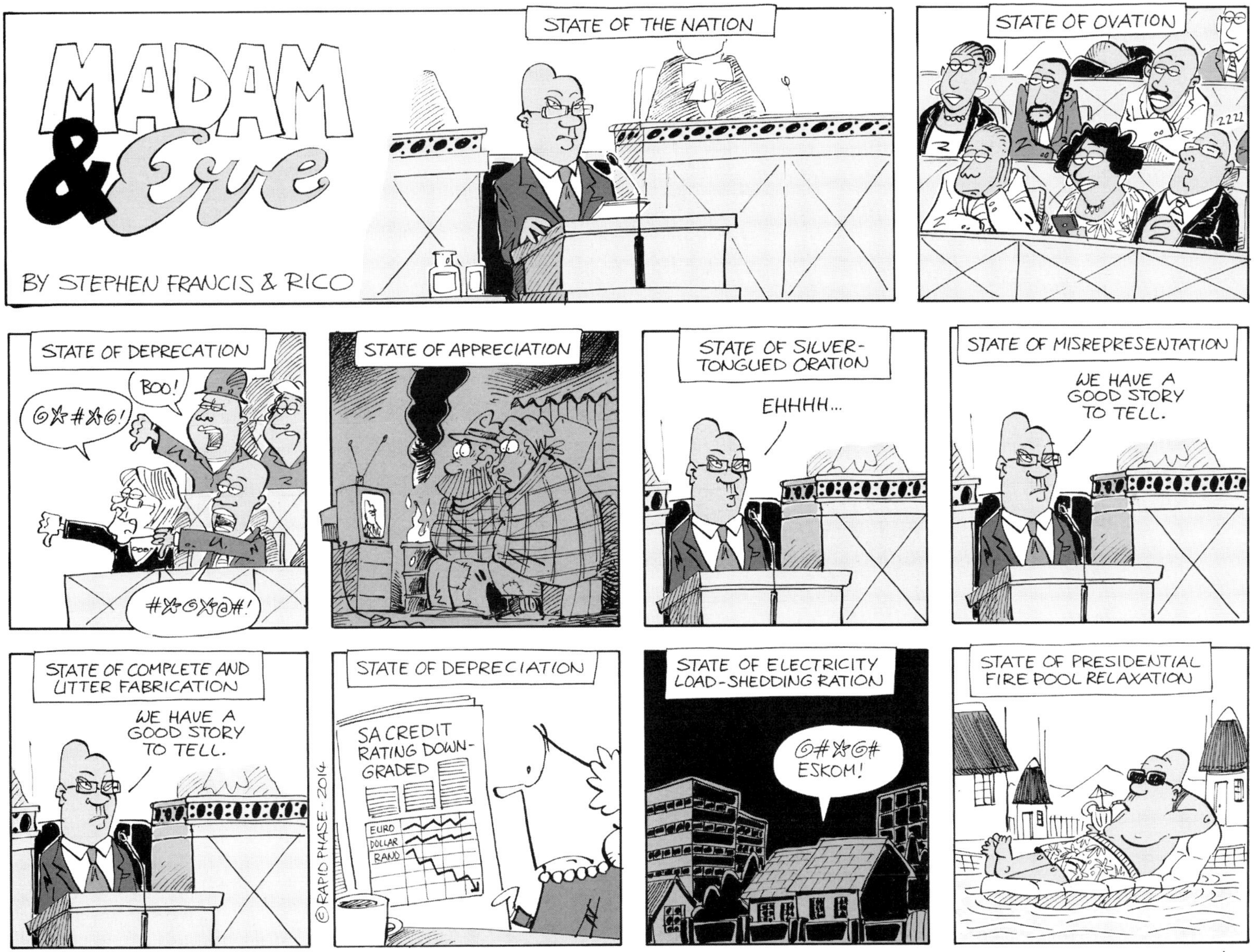
MADAM & Eve
BY STEPHEN FRANCIS & RICO
STATE OF THE NATION
STATE OF OVATION
ZZZZ
STATE OF DEPRECATION
BOO!
@*#*@!
#*@*@#!
STATE OF APPRECIATION
STATE OF SILVER-TONGUED ORATION
EHHHH...
STATE OF MISREPRESENTATION
WE HAVE A GOOD STORY TO TELL.
STATE OF COMPLETE AND UTTER FABRICATION
WE HAVE A GOOD STORY TO TELL.
© RAPID PHASE · 2014
STATE OF DEPRECIATION
SA CREDIT RATING DOWN-GRADED
EURO
DOLLAR
RAND
STATE OF ELECTRICITY LOAD-SHEDDING RATION
@#*@# ESKOM!
STATE OF PRESIDENTIAL FIRE POOL RELAXATION

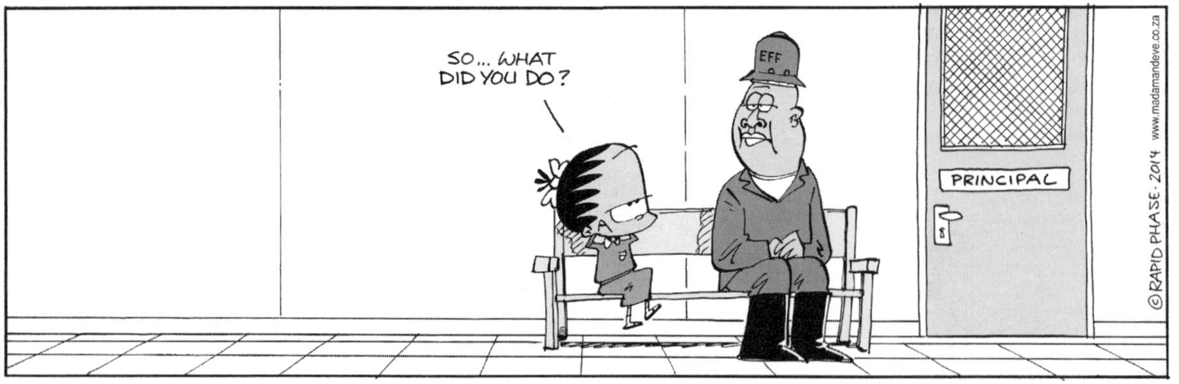
SO... WHAT DID YOU DO?
EFF
PRINCIPAL
© RAPID PHASE · 2014 www.madamandeve.co.za

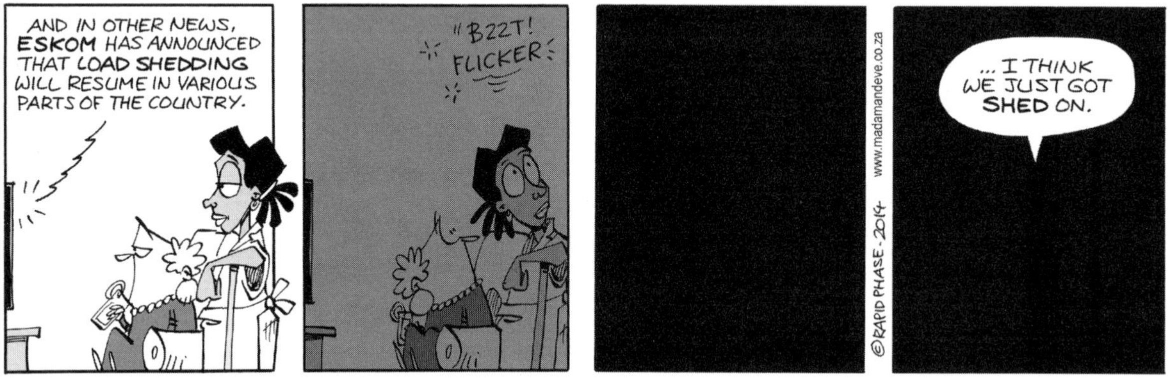
AND IN OTHER NEWS, ESKOM HAS ANNOUNCED THAT LOAD SHEDDING WILL RESUME IN VARIOUS PARTS OF THE COUNTRY.
"BZZT! FLICKER"
© RAPID PHASE · 2014 www.madamandeve.co.za
... I THINK WE JUST GOT SHED ON.

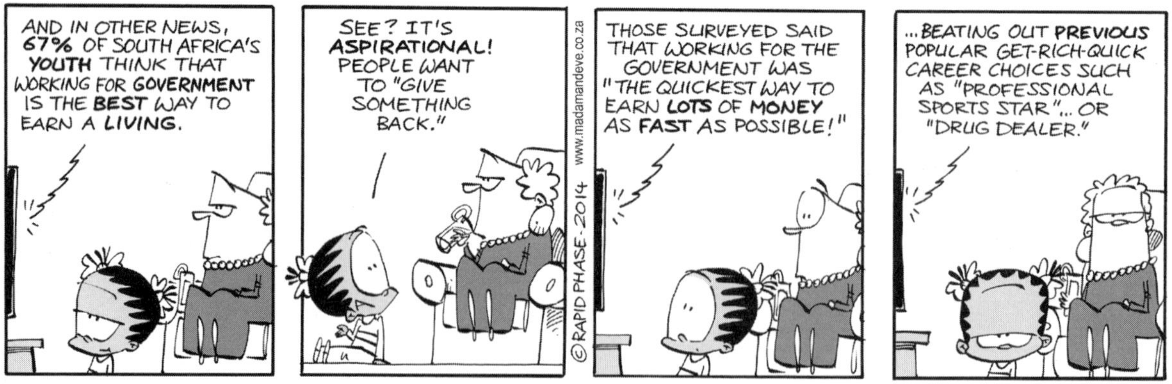
AND IN OTHER NEWS, 67% OF SOUTH AFRICA'S YOUTH THINK THAT WORKING FOR GOVERNMENT IS THE BEST WAY TO EARN A LIVING.
SEE? IT'S ASPIRATIONAL! PEOPLE WANT TO "GIVE SOMETHING BACK."
© RAPID PHASE · 2014 www.madamandeve.co.za
THOSE SURVEYED SAID THAT WORKING FOR THE GOVERNMENT WAS "THE QUICKEST WAY TO EARN LOTS OF MONEY AS FAST AS POSSIBLE!"
...BEATING OUT PREVIOUS POPULAR GET-RICH-QUICK CAREER CHOICES SUCH AS "PROFESSIONAL SPORTS STAR"... OR "DRUG DEALER."

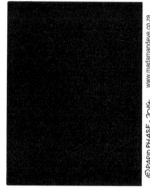

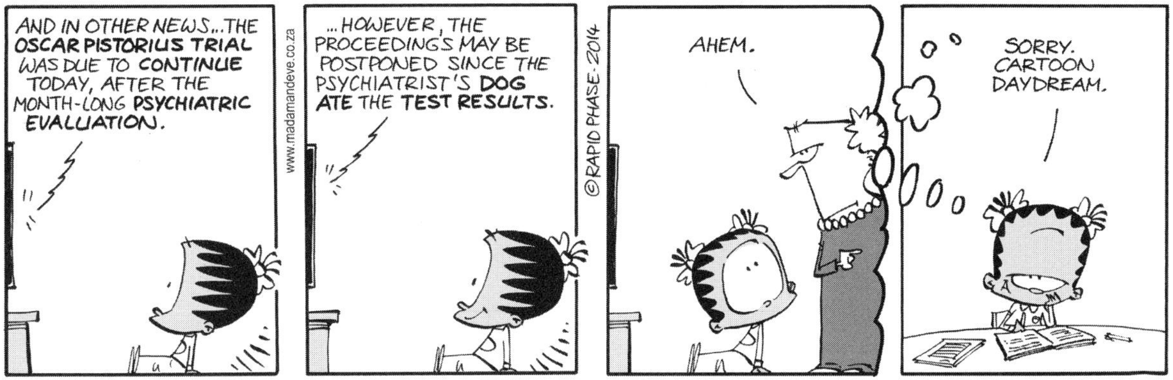

AND IN OTHER NEWS... THE OSCAR PISTORIUS TRIAL WAS DUE TO CONTINUE TODAY, AFTER THE MONTH-LONG PSYCHIATRIC EVALUATION.
www.madamandeve.co.za
... HOWEVER, THE PROCEEDINGS MAY BE POSTPONED SINCE THE PSYCHIATRIST'S DOG ATE THE TEST RESULTS.
©RAPID PHASE·2014
AHEM.
SORRY. CARTOON DAYDREAM.

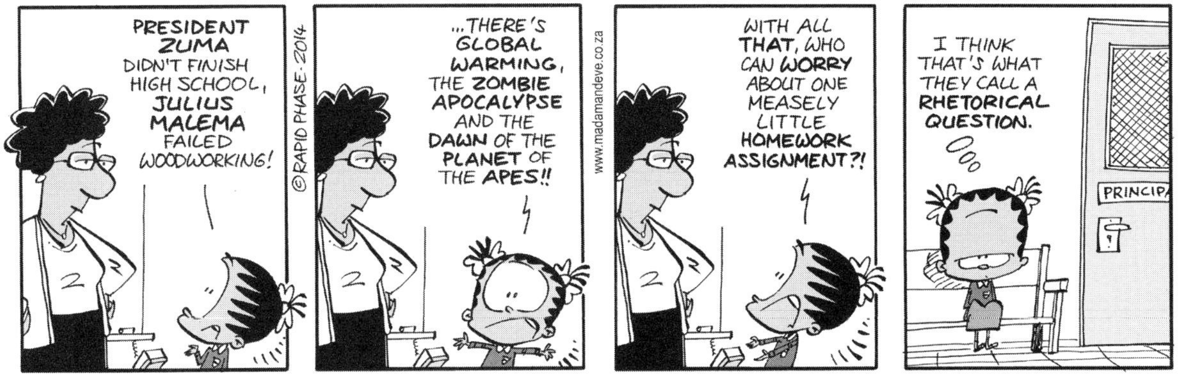

PRESIDENT ZUMA DIDN'T FINISH HIGH SCHOOL, JULIUS MALEMA FAILED WOODWORKING!
©RAPID PHASE·2014
... THERE'S GLOBAL WARMING, THE ZOMBIE APOCALYPSE AND THE DAWN OF THE PLANET OF THE APES!!
www.madamandeve.co.za
WITH ALL THAT, WHO CAN WORRY ABOUT ONE MEASELY LITTLE HOMEWORK ASSIGNMENT?!
I THINK THAT'S WHAT THEY CALL A RHETORICAL QUESTION.
PRINCIPA

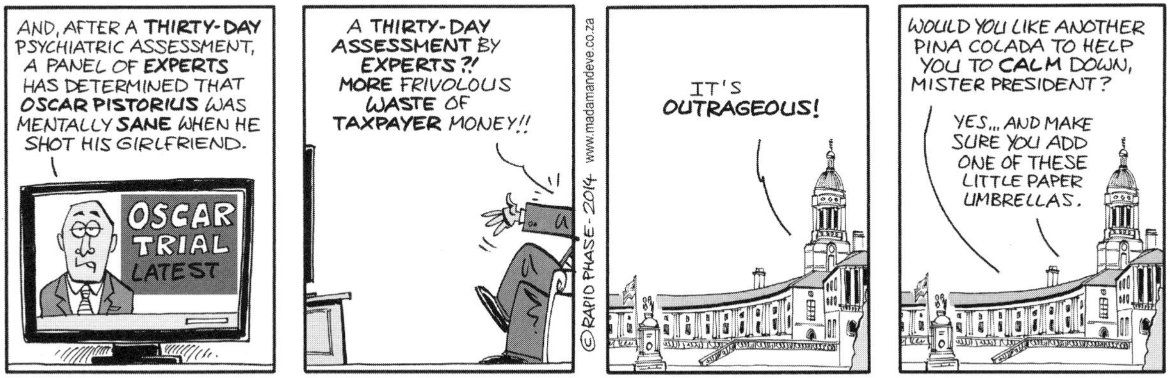

AND, AFTER A THIRTY-DAY PSYCHIATRIC ASSESSMENT, A PANEL OF EXPERTS HAS DETERMINED THAT OSCAR PISTORIUS WAS MENTALLY SANE WHEN HE SHOT HIS GIRLFRIEND.
OSCAR TRIAL LATEST
A THIRTY-DAY ASSESSMENT BY EXPERTS?! MORE FRIVOLOUS WASTE OF TAXPAYER MONEY!!
©RAPID PHASE·2014 www.madamandeve.co.za
IT'S OUTRAGEOUS!
WOULD YOU LIKE ANOTHER PINA COLADA TO HELP YOU TO CALM DOWN, MISTER PRESIDENT?
YES... AND MAKE SURE YOU ADD ONE OF THESE LITTLE PAPER UMBRELLAS.

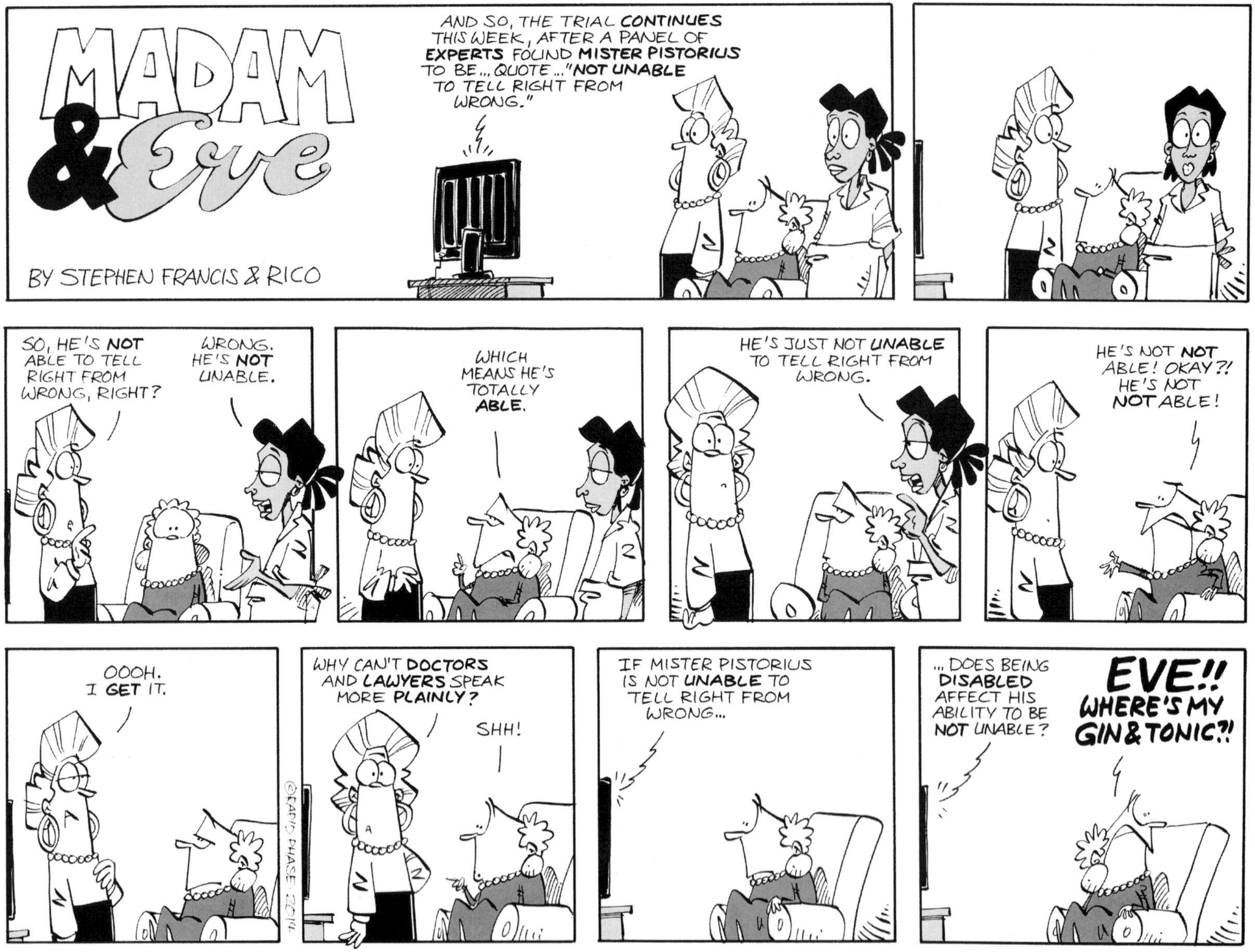
MADAM & Eve
BY STEPHEN FRANCIS & RICO
AND SO, THE TRIAL CONTINUES THIS WEEK, AFTER A PANEL OF EXPERTS FOUND MISTER PISTORIUS TO BE... QUOTE..."NOT UNABLE TO TELL RIGHT FROM WRONG."
SO, HE'S NOT ABLE TO TELL RIGHT FROM WRONG, RIGHT?
WRONG. HE'S NOT UNABLE.
WHICH MEANS HE'S TOTALLY ABLE.
HE'S JUST NOT UNABLE TO TELL RIGHT FROM WRONG.
HE'S NOT NOT ABLE! OKAY?! HE'S NOT NOT ABLE!
OOOH. I GET IT.
©RAPID PHASE 2014
WHY CAN'T DOCTORS AND LAWYERS SPEAK MORE PLAINLY?
SHH!
IF MISTER PISTORIUS IS NOT UNABLE TO TELL RIGHT FROM WRONG...
...DOES BEING DISABLED AFFECT HIS ABILITY TO BE NOT UNABLE?
EVE!! WHERE'S MY GIN & TONIC?!

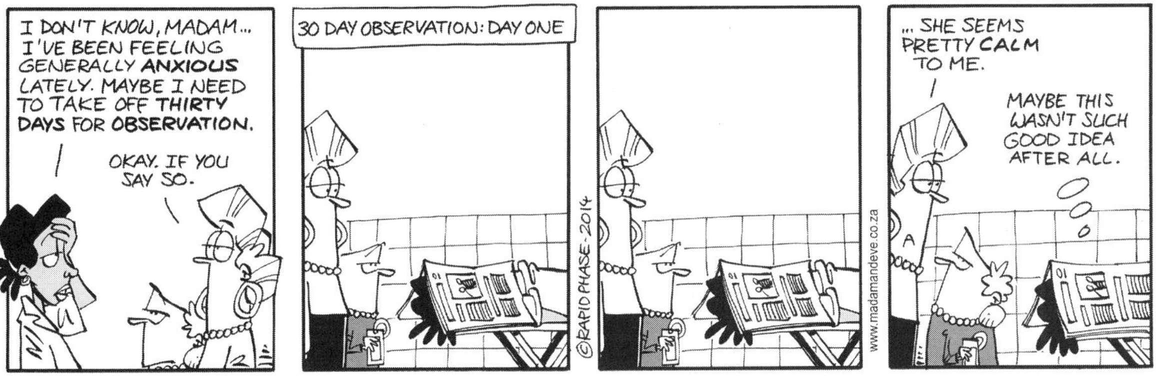

I DON'T KNOW, MADAM... I'VE BEEN FEELING GENERALLY **ANXIOUS** LATELY. MAYBE I NEED TO TAKE OFF **THIRTY DAYS** FOR **OBSERVATION.**
OKAY. IF YOU SAY SO.
30 DAY OBSERVATION: DAY ONE
©RAPID PHASE - 2014
www.madamandeve.co.za
... SHE SEEMS PRETTY **CALM** TO ME.
MAYBE THIS WASN'T SUCH GOOD IDEA AFTER ALL.

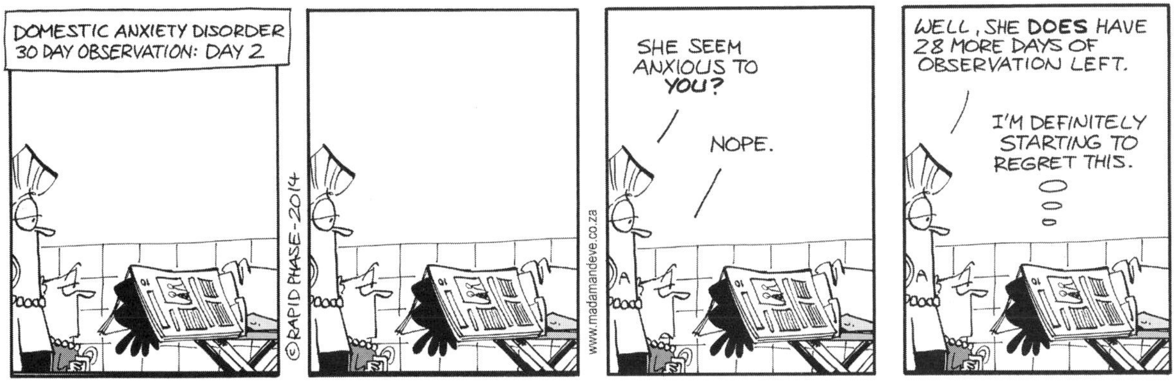

DOMESTIC ANXIETY DISORDER 30 DAY OBSERVATION: DAY 2
©RAPID PHASE - 2014
www.madamandeve.co.za
SHE SEEM ANXIOUS TO **YOU?**
NOPE.
WELL, SHE **DOES** HAVE 28 MORE DAYS OF OBSERVATION LEFT.
I'M DEFINITELY STARTING TO REGRET THIS.

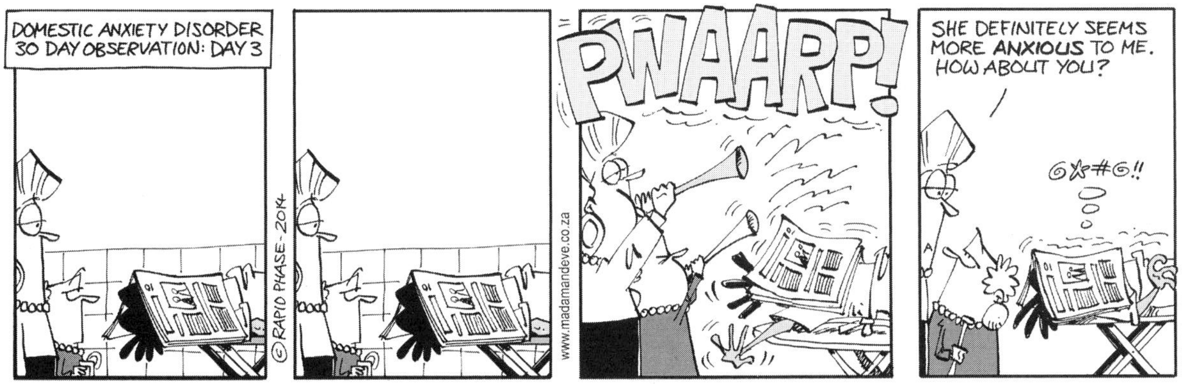

DOMESTIC ANXIETY DISORDER 30 DAY OBSERVATION: DAY 3
©RAPID PHASE - 2014
www.madamandeve.co.za
PWAARP!
SHE DEFINITELY SEEMS MORE **ANXIOUS** TO ME. HOW ABOUT YOU?

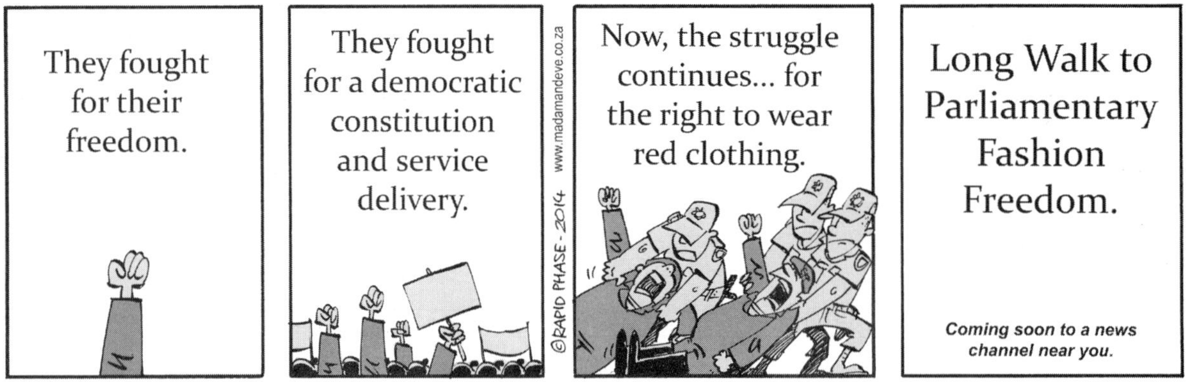
They fought for their freedom.
They fought for a democratic constitution and service delivery.
www.madamandeve.co.za
©RAPID PHASE-2014
Now, the struggle continues... for the right to wear red clothing.
Long Walk to Parliamentary Fashion Freedom.
Coming soon to a news channel near you.

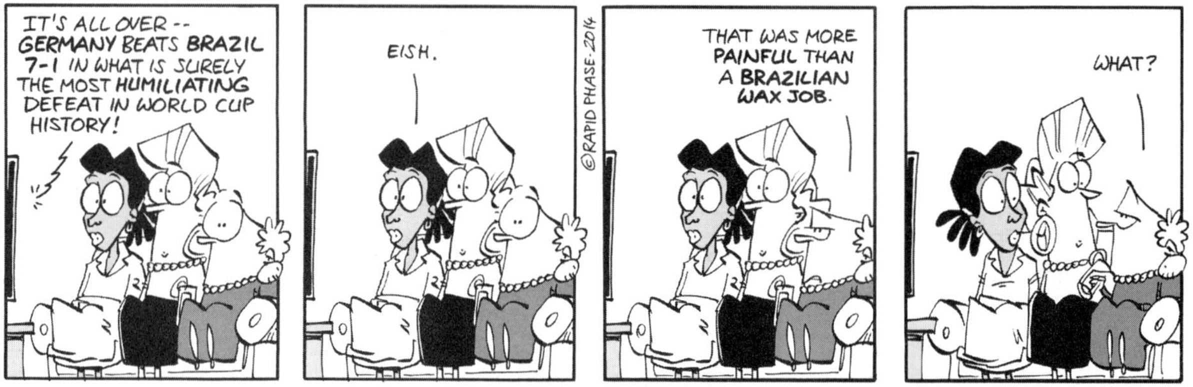
IT'S ALL OVER -- GERMANY BEATS BRAZIL 7-1 IN WHAT IS SURELY THE MOST HUMILIATING DEFEAT IN WORLD CUP HISTORY!
EISH.
©RAPID PHASE-2014
THAT WAS MORE PAINFUL THAN A BRAZILIAN WAX JOB.
WHAT?

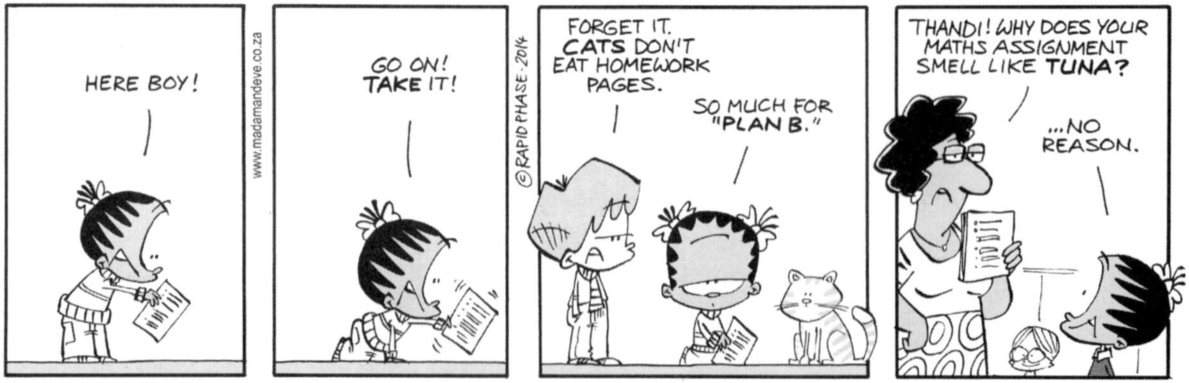
HERE BOY!
www.madamandeve.co.za
GO ON! TAKE IT!
©RAPID PHASE-2014
FORGET IT. CATS DON'T EAT HOMEWORK PAGES.
SO MUCH FOR "PLAN B."
THANDI! WHY DOES YOUR MATHS ASSIGNMENT SMELL LIKE TUNA?
...NO REASON.

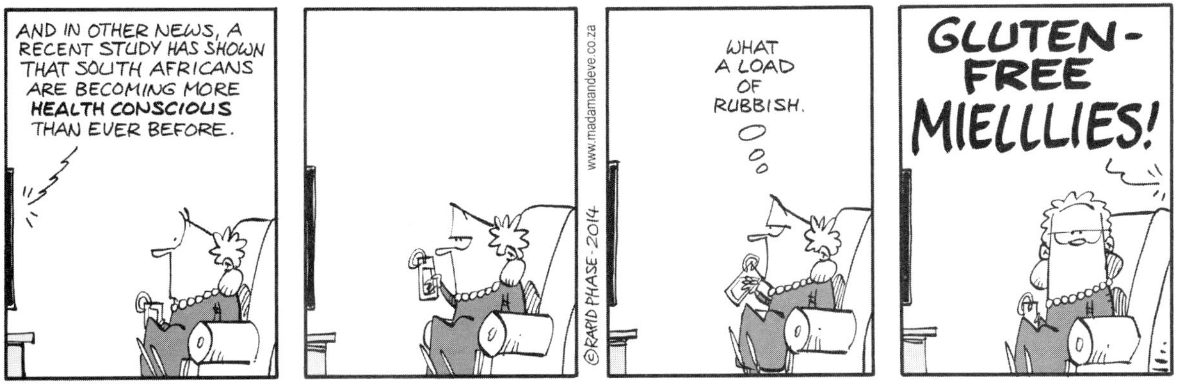
AND IN OTHER NEWS, A RECENT STUDY HAS SHOWN THAT SOUTH AFRICANS ARE BECOMING MORE **HEALTH CONSCIOUS** THAN EVER BEFORE.
www.madamandeve.co.za
©RAPID PHASE-2014
WHAT A LOAD OF RUBBISH.
GLUTEN-FREE MIELLLIES!

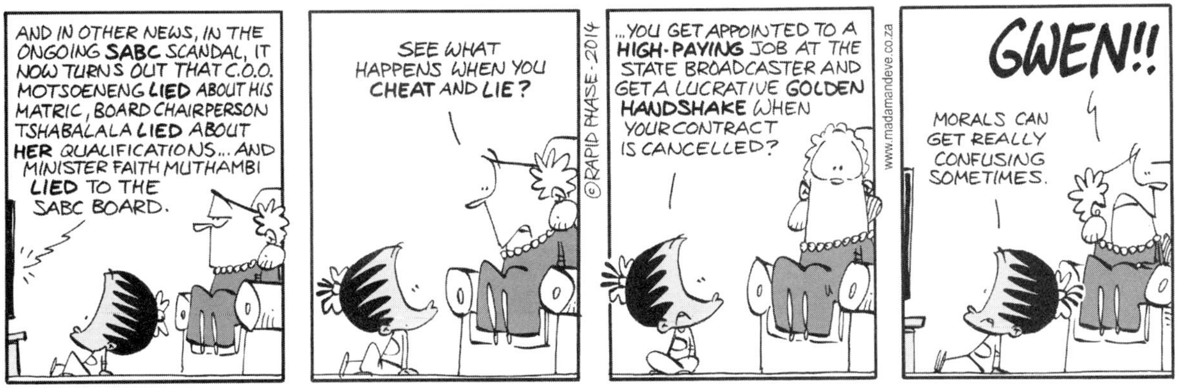
AND IN OTHER NEWS, IN THE ONGOING **SABC** SCANDAL, IT NOW TURNS OUT THAT C.O.O. MOTSOENENG **LIED** ABOUT HIS MATRIC, BOARD CHAIRPERSON TSHABALALA **LIED** ABOUT **HER** QUALIFICATIONS... AND MINISTER FAITH MUTHAMBI **LIED** TO THE SABC BOARD.
SEE WHAT HAPPENS WHEN YOU **CHEAT** AND **LIE**?
©RAPID PHASE-2014
...YOU GET APPOINTED TO A **HIGH-PAYING** JOB AT THE STATE BROADCASTER AND GET A LUCRATIVE **GOLDEN HANDSHAKE** WHEN YOUR CONTRACT IS CANCELLED?
www.madamandeve.co.za
GWEN!!
MORALS CAN GET REALLY CONFUSING SOMETIMES.

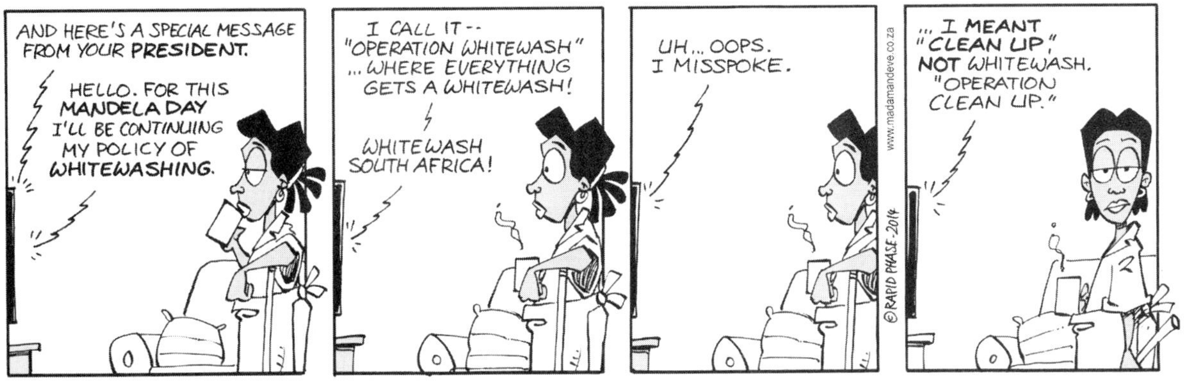
AND HERE'S A SPECIAL MESSAGE FROM YOUR **PRESIDENT**.
HELLO. FOR THIS **MANDELA DAY** I'LL BE CONTINUING MY POLICY OF **WHITEWASHING**.
I CALL IT -- "OPERATION WHITEWASH" ... WHERE EVERYTHING GETS A WHITEWASH!
WHITEWASH SOUTH AFRICA!
UH... OOPS. I MISSPOKE.
www.madamandeve.co.za
©RAPID PHASE-2014
... **I MEANT "CLEAN UP," NOT** WHITEWASH. "OPERATION CLEAN UP."

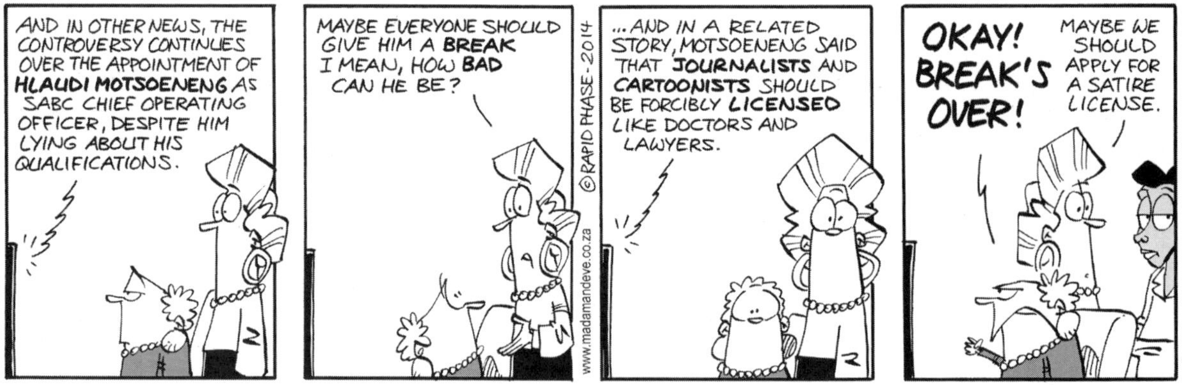
AND IN OTHER NEWS, THE CONTROVERSY CONTINUES OVER THE APPOINTMENT OF HLAUDI MOTSOENENG AS SABC CHIEF OPERATING OFFICER, DESPITE HIM LYING ABOUT HIS QUALIFICATIONS.
MAYBE EVERYONE SHOULD GIVE HIM A BREAK I MEAN, HOW BAD CAN HE BE?
© RAPID PHASE - 2014
www.madamandeve.co.za
...AND IN A RELATED STORY, MOTSOENENG SAID THAT JOURNALISTS AND CARTOONISTS SHOULD BE FORCIBLY LICENSED LIKE DOCTORS AND LAWYERS.
OKAY! BREAK'S OVER!
MAYBE WE SHOULD APPLY FOR A SATIRE LICENSE.

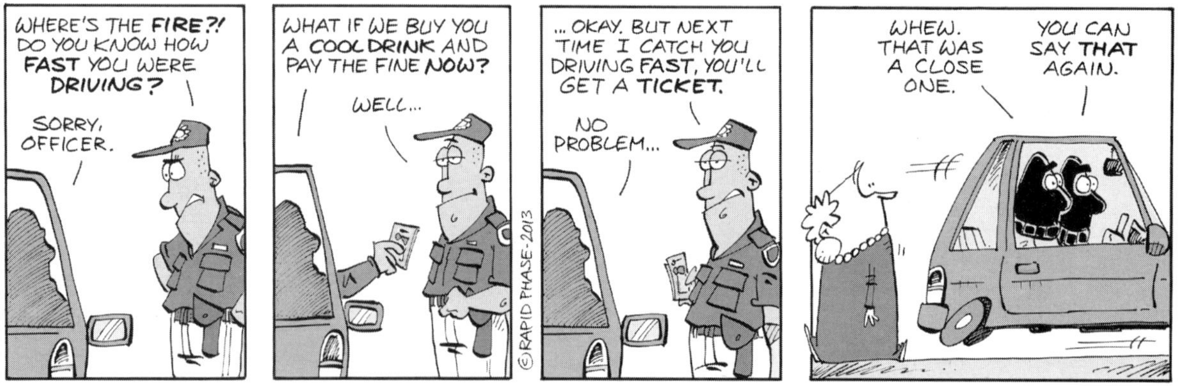
WHERE'S THE FIRE?! DO YOU KNOW HOW FAST YOU WERE DRIVING?
SORRY, OFFICER.
WHAT IF WE BUY YOU A COOLDRINK AND PAY THE FINE NOW?
WELL...
© RAPID PHASE - 2013
...OKAY. BUT NEXT TIME I CATCH YOU DRIVING FAST, YOU'LL GET A TICKET.
NO PROBLEM...
WHEW. THAT WAS A CLOSE ONE.
YOU CAN SAY THAT AGAIN.

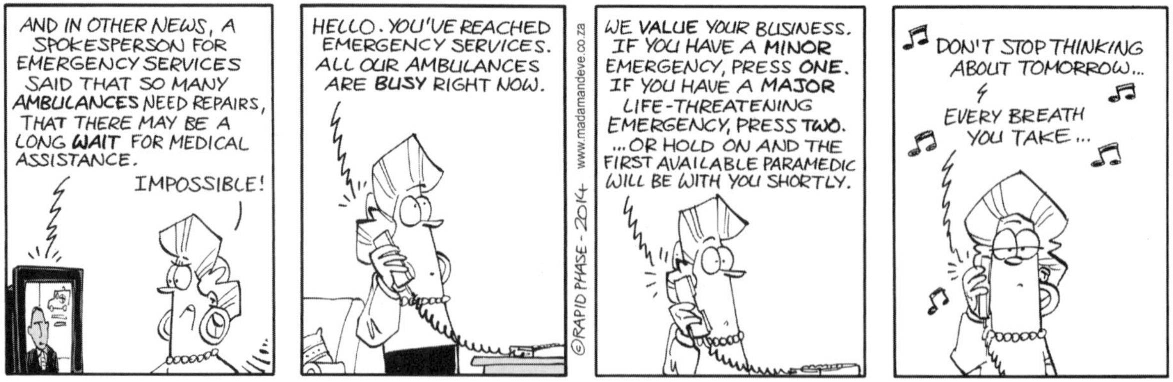
AND IN OTHER NEWS, A SPOKESPERSON FOR EMERGENCY SERVICES SAID THAT SO MANY AMBULANCES NEED REPAIRS, THAT THERE MAY BE A LONG WAIT FOR MEDICAL ASSISTANCE.
IMPOSSIBLE!
HELLO. YOU'VE REACHED EMERGENCY SERVICES. ALL OUR AMBULANCES ARE BUSY RIGHT NOW.
© RAPID PHASE - 2014
www.madamandeve.co.za
WE VALUE YOUR BUSINESS. IF YOU HAVE A MINOR EMERGENCY, PRESS ONE. IF YOU HAVE A MAJOR LIFE-THREATENING EMERGENCY, PRESS TWO. ...OR HOLD ON AND THE FIRST AVAILABLE PARAMEDIC WILL BE WITH YOU SHORTLY.
DON'T STOP THINKING ABOUT TOMORROW...
EVERY BREATH YOU TAKE...

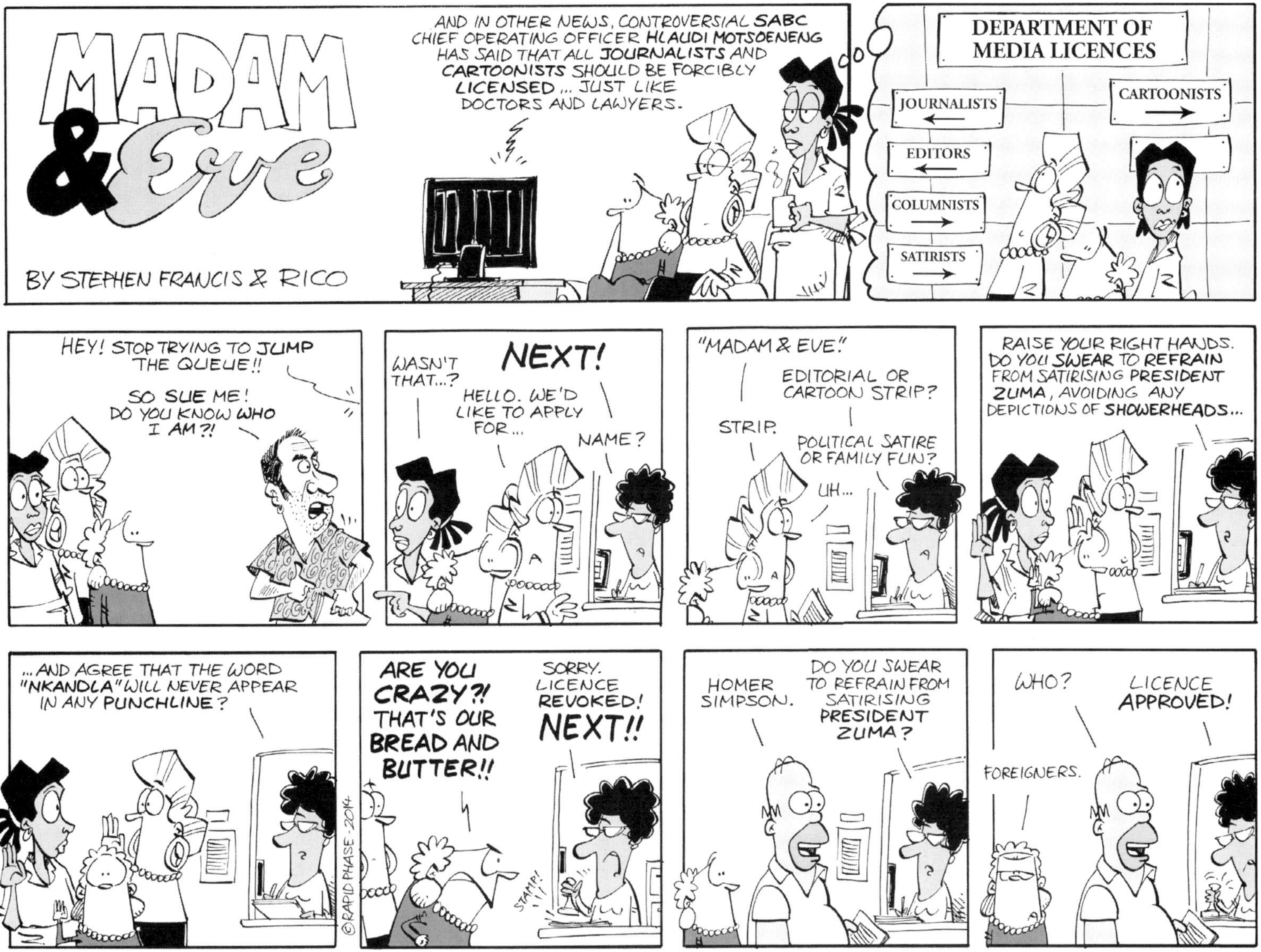
MADAM & Eve
BY STEPHEN FRANCIS & RICO
AND IN OTHER NEWS, CONTROVERSIAL SABC CHIEF OPERATING OFFICER HLAUDI MOTSOENENG HAS SAID THAT ALL JOURNALISTS AND CARTOONISTS SHOULD BE FORCIBLY LICENSED ... JUST LIKE DOCTORS AND LAWYERS.
DEPARTMENT OF MEDIA LICENCES
JOURNALISTS
CARTOONISTS
EDITORS
COLUMNISTS
SATIRISTS
HEY! STOP TRYING TO JUMP THE QUEUE!!
SO SUE ME! DO YOU KNOW WHO I AM?!
WASN'T THAT...?
NEXT!
HELLO. WE'D LIKE TO APPLY FOR...
NAME?
"MADAM & EVE."
EDITORIAL OR CARTOON STRIP?
STRIP.
POLITICAL SATIRE OR FAMILY FUN?
UH...
RAISE YOUR RIGHT HANDS. DO YOU SWEAR TO REFRAIN FROM SATIRISING PRESIDENT ZUMA, AVOIDING ANY DEPICTIONS OF SHOWERHEADS...
...AND AGREE THAT THE WORD "NKANDLA" WILL NEVER APPEAR IN ANY PUNCHLINE?
©RAPID PHASE · 2014
ARE YOU CRAZY?! THAT'S OUR BREAD AND BUTTER!!
SORRY. LICENCE REVOKED! NEXT!!
STAMP!
HOMER SIMPSON.
DO YOU SWEAR TO REFRAIN FROM SATIRISING PRESIDENT ZUMA?
WHO?
LICENCE APPROVED!
FOREIGNERS.

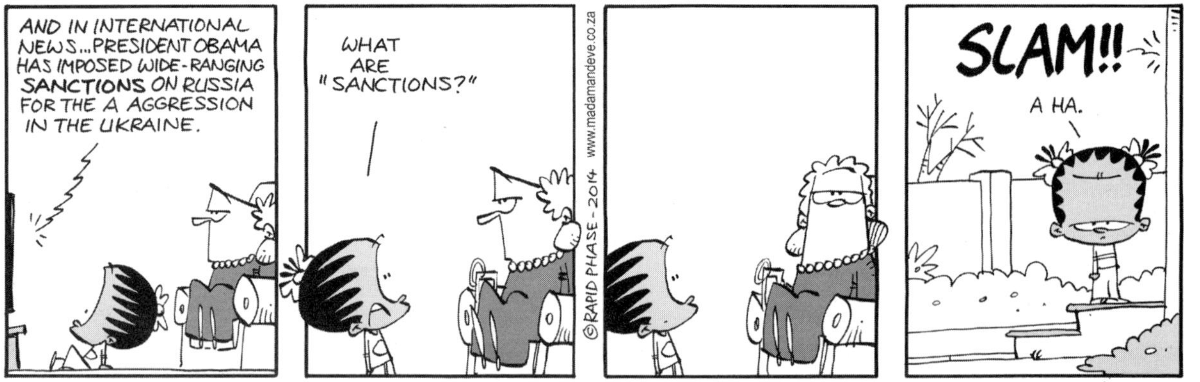
AND IN INTERNATIONAL NEWS... PRESIDENT OBAMA HAS IMPOSED WIDE-RANGING SANCTIONS ON RUSSIA FOR THE A AGGRESSION IN THE UKRAINE.
WHAT ARE "SANCTIONS?"
© RAPID PHASE - 2014 www.madamandeve.co.za
SLAM!!
A HA.

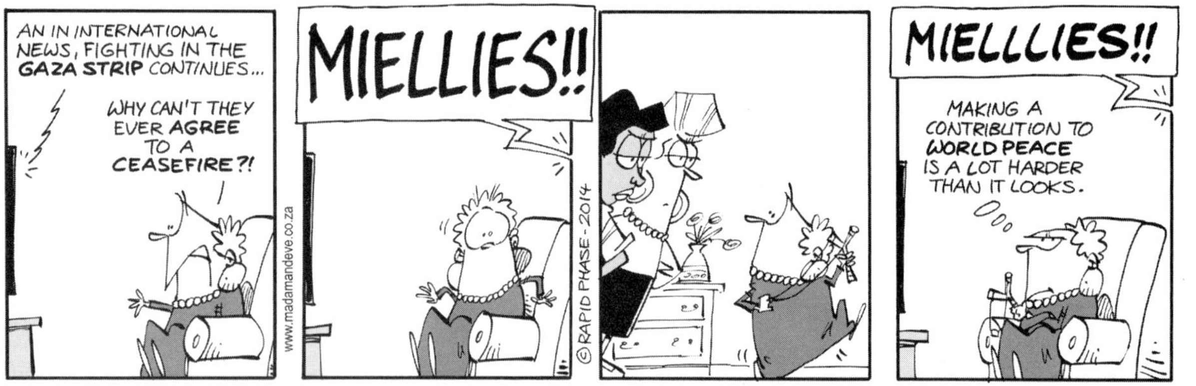
AN IN INTERNATIONAL NEWS, FIGHTING IN THE GAZA STRIP CONTINUES...
WHY CAN'T THEY EVER AGREE TO A CEASEFIRE?!
www.madamandeve.co.za
MIELLIES!!
© RAPID PHASE - 2014
MIELLLIES!!
MAKING A CONTRIBUTION TO WORLD PEACE IS A LOT HARDER THAN IT LOOKS.

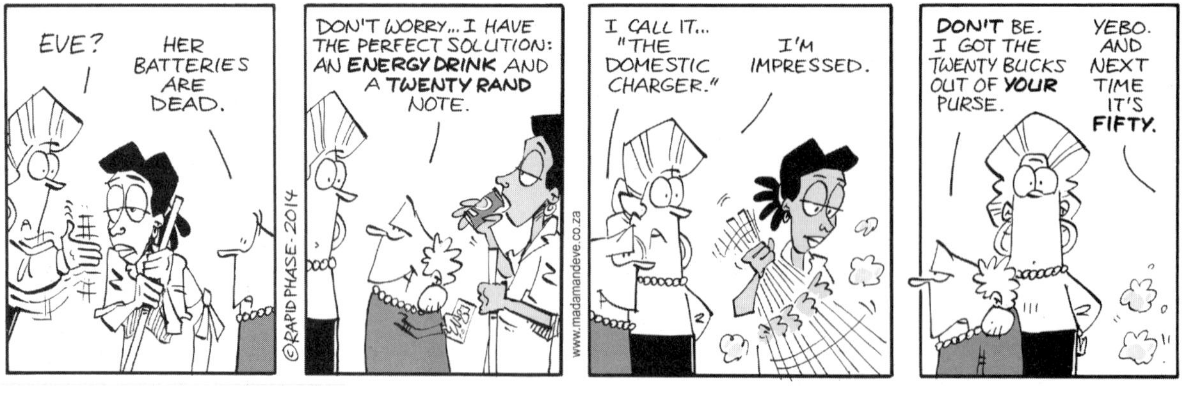
EVE?
HER BATTERIES ARE DEAD.
© RAPID PHASE - 2014
DON'T WORRY... I HAVE THE PERFECT SOLUTION: AN ENERGY DRINK AND A TWENTY RAND NOTE.
www.madamandeve.co.za
I CALL IT... "THE DOMESTIC CHARGER."
I'M IMPRESSED.
DON'T BE. I GOT THE TWENTY BUCKS OUT OF YOUR PURSE.
YEBO. AND NEXT TIME IT'S FIFTY.

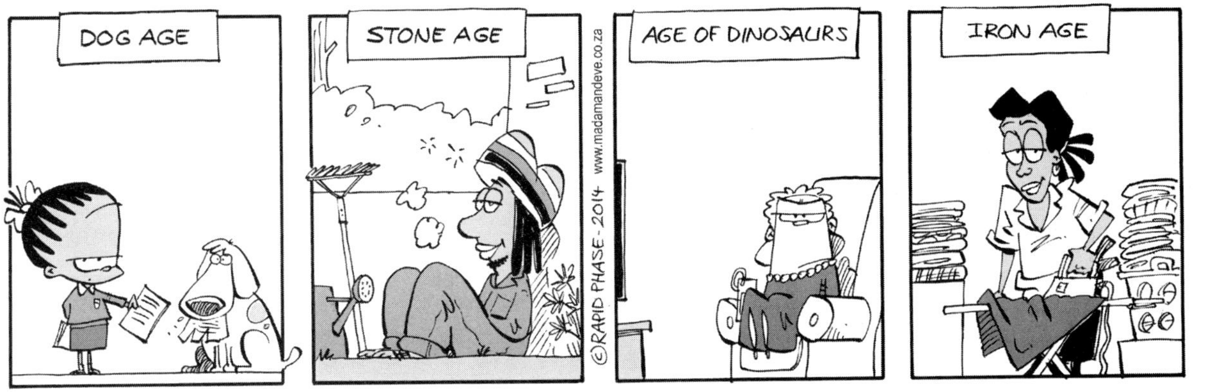
DOG AGE
STONE AGE
www.madamandeve.co.za
©RAPID PHASE-2014
AGE OF DINOSAURS
IRON AGE

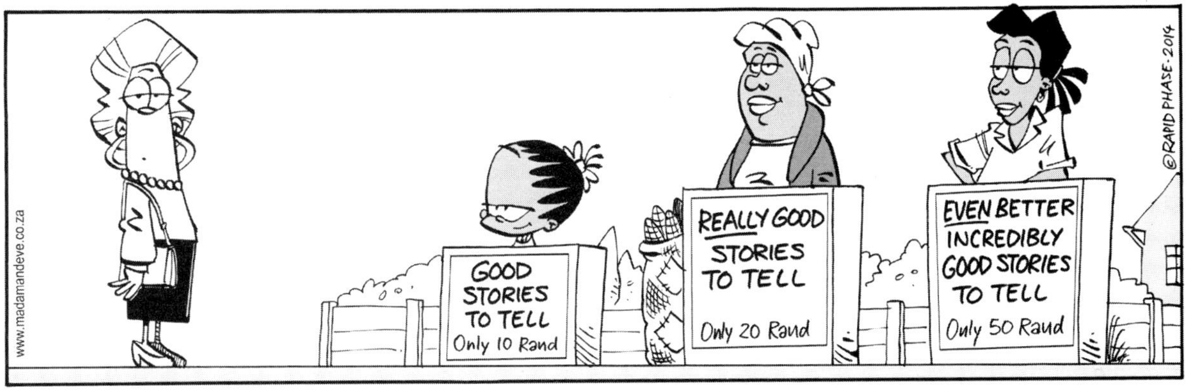
www.madamandeve.co.za
GOOD STORIES TO TELL
Only 10 Rand
REALLY GOOD STORIES TO TELL
Only 20 Rand
EVEN BETTER INCREDIBLY GOOD STORIES TO TELL
Only 50 Rand
©RAPID PHASE-2014

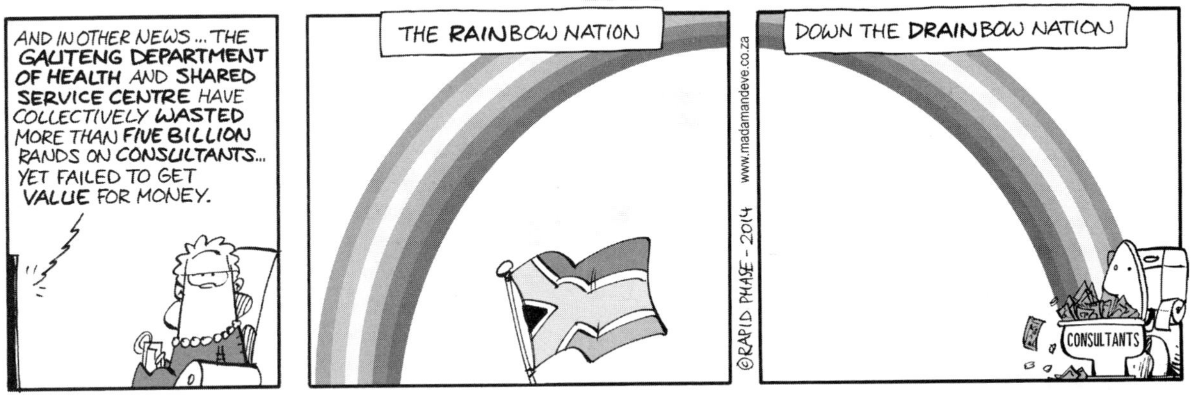
AND IN OTHER NEWS... THE GAUTENG DEPARTMENT OF HEALTH AND SHARED SERVICE CENTRE HAVE COLLECTIVELY WASTED MORE THAN FIVE BILLION RANDS ON CONSULTANTS... YET FAILED TO GET VALUE FOR MONEY.
THE RAINBOW NATION
www.madamandeve.co.za
©RAPID PHASE-2014
DOWN THE DRAINBOW NATION
CONSULTANTS

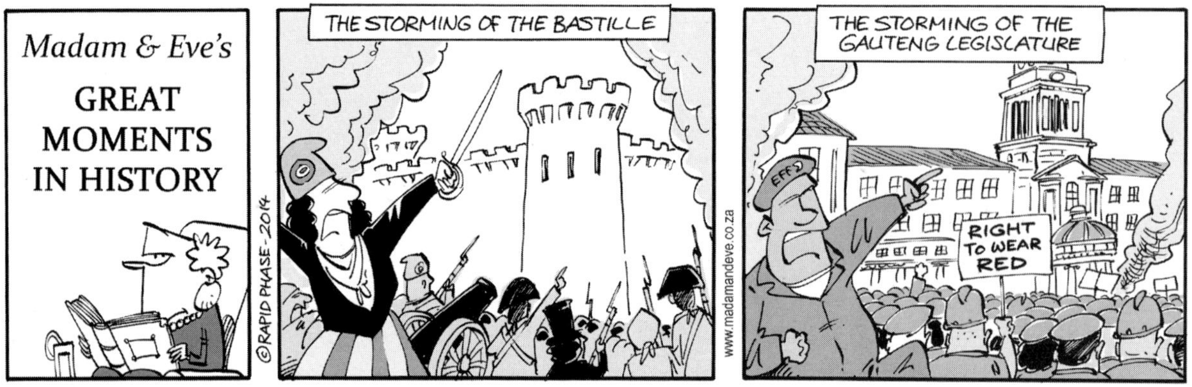
Madam & Eve's
GREAT MOMENTS IN HISTORY
THE STORMING OF THE BASTILLE
©RAPID PHASE · 2014
THE STORMING OF THE GAUTENG LEGISLATURE
www.madamandeve.co.za
RIGHT TO WEAR RED

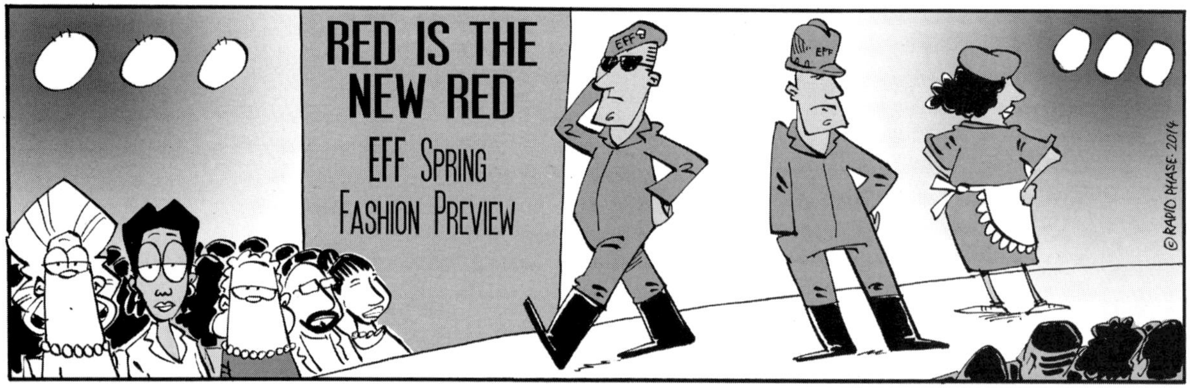
RED IS THE NEW RED
EFF Spring Fashion Preview
©RAPID PHASE · 2014

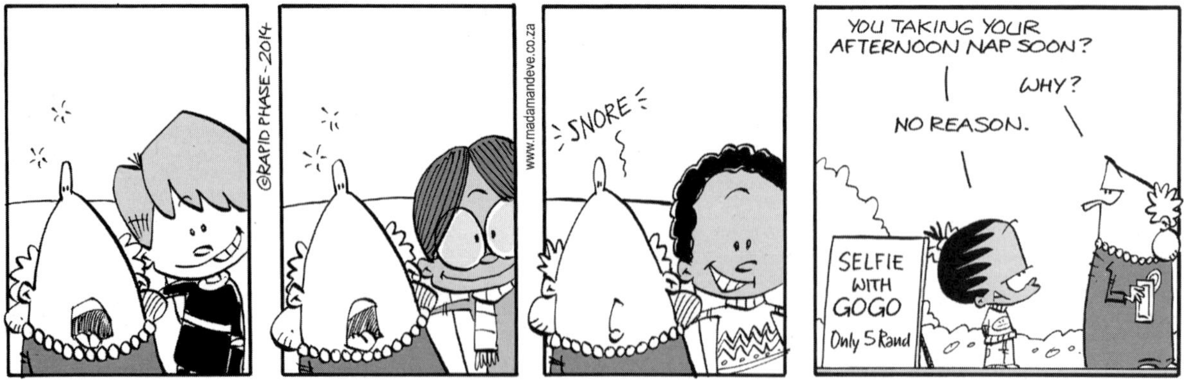
©RAPID PHASE · 2014
www.madamandeve.co.za
SNORE
YOU TAKING YOUR AFTERNOON NAP SOON?
WHY?
NO REASON.
SELFIE WITH GOGO Only 5 Rand

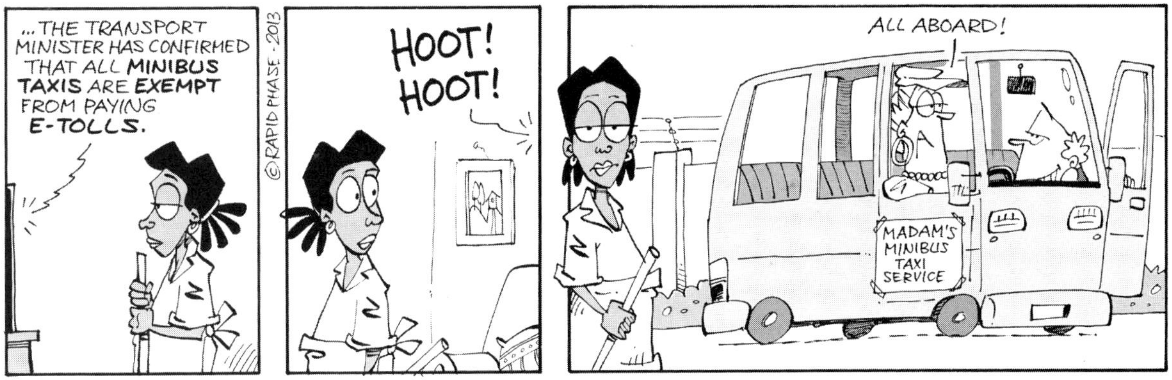
...THE TRANSPORT MINISTER HAS CONFIRMED THAT ALL **MINIBUS TAXIS** ARE **EXEMPT** FROM PAYING **E-TOLLS**.
©RAPID PHASE · 2013
HOOT! HOOT!
ALL ABOARD!
MADAM'S MINIBUS TAXI SERVICE

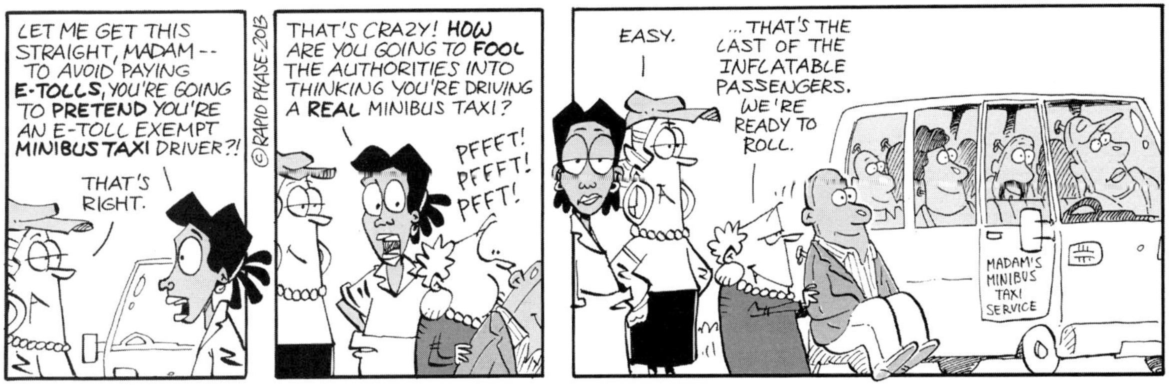
LET ME GET THIS STRAIGHT, MADAM -- TO AVOID PAYING **E-TOLLS**, YOU'RE GOING TO **PRETEND** YOU'RE AN E-TOLL EXEMPT **MINIBUS TAXI** DRIVER?!
THAT'S RIGHT.
©RAPID PHASE · 2013
THAT'S CRAZY! **HOW** ARE YOU GOING TO **FOOL** THE AUTHORITIES INTO THINKING YOU'RE DRIVING A **REAL** MINIBUS TAXI?
PFFFT! PFFFT! PFFT!
EASY.
...THAT'S THE LAST OF THE INFLATABLE PASSENGERS. WE'RE READY TO ROLL.
MADAM'S MINIBUS TAXI SERVICE

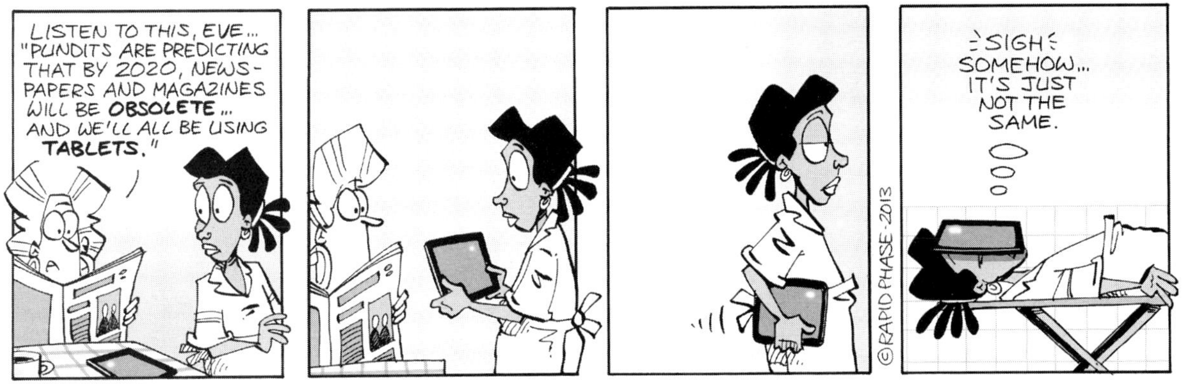
LISTEN TO THIS, EVE... "PUNDITS ARE PREDICTING THAT BY 2020, NEWS-PAPERS AND MAGAZINES WILL BE **OBSOLETE**... AND WE'LL ALL BE USING **TABLETS**."
©RAPID PHASE · 2013
SIGH
SOMEHOW... IT'S JUST NOT THE SAME.

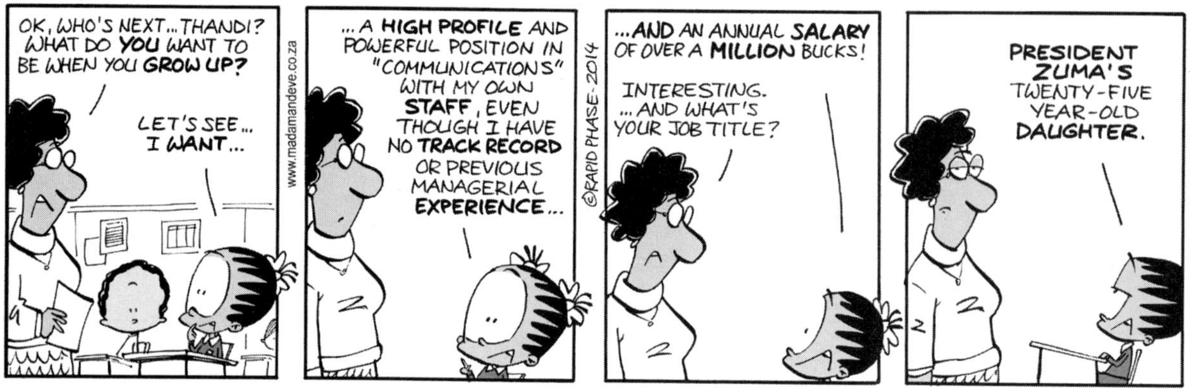
OK, WHO'S NEXT... THANDI? WHAT DO YOU WANT TO BE WHEN YOU GROW UP?
LET'S SEE... I WANT...
www.madamandeve.co.za
... A HIGH PROFILE AND POWERFUL POSITION IN "COMMUNICATIONS" WITH MY OWN STAFF, EVEN THOUGH I HAVE NO TRACK RECORD OR PREVIOUS MANAGERIAL EXPERIENCE...
©RAPID PHASE·2014
...AND AN ANNUAL SALARY OF OVER A MILLION BUCKS!
INTERESTING. ... AND WHAT'S YOUR JOB TITLE?
PRESIDENT ZUMA'S TWENTY-FIVE YEAR-OLD DAUGHTER.

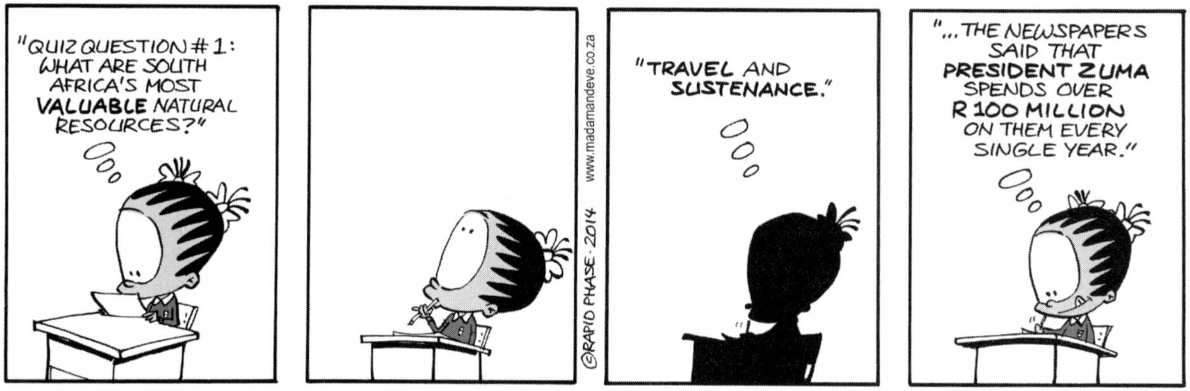
"QUIZ QUESTION #1: WHAT ARE SOUTH AFRICA'S MOST VALUABLE NATURAL RESOURCES?"
www.madamandeve.co.za
©RAPID PHASE·2014
"TRAVEL AND SUSTENANCE."
"... THE NEWSPAPERS SAID THAT PRESIDENT ZUMA SPENDS OVER R 100 MILLION ON THEM EVERY SINGLE YEAR."

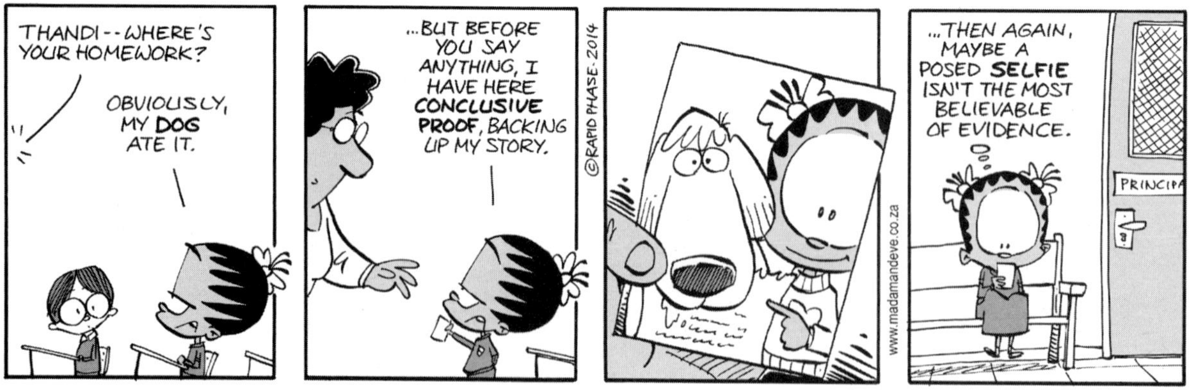
THANDI -- WHERE'S YOUR HOMEWORK?
OBVIOUSLY, MY DOG ATE IT.
... BUT BEFORE YOU SAY ANYTHING, I HAVE HERE CONCLUSIVE PROOF, BACKING UP MY STORY.
©RAPID PHASE·2014
www.madamandeve.co.za
... THEN AGAIN, MAYBE A POSED SELFIE ISN'T THE MOST BELIEVABLE OF EVIDENCE.
PRINCIPA

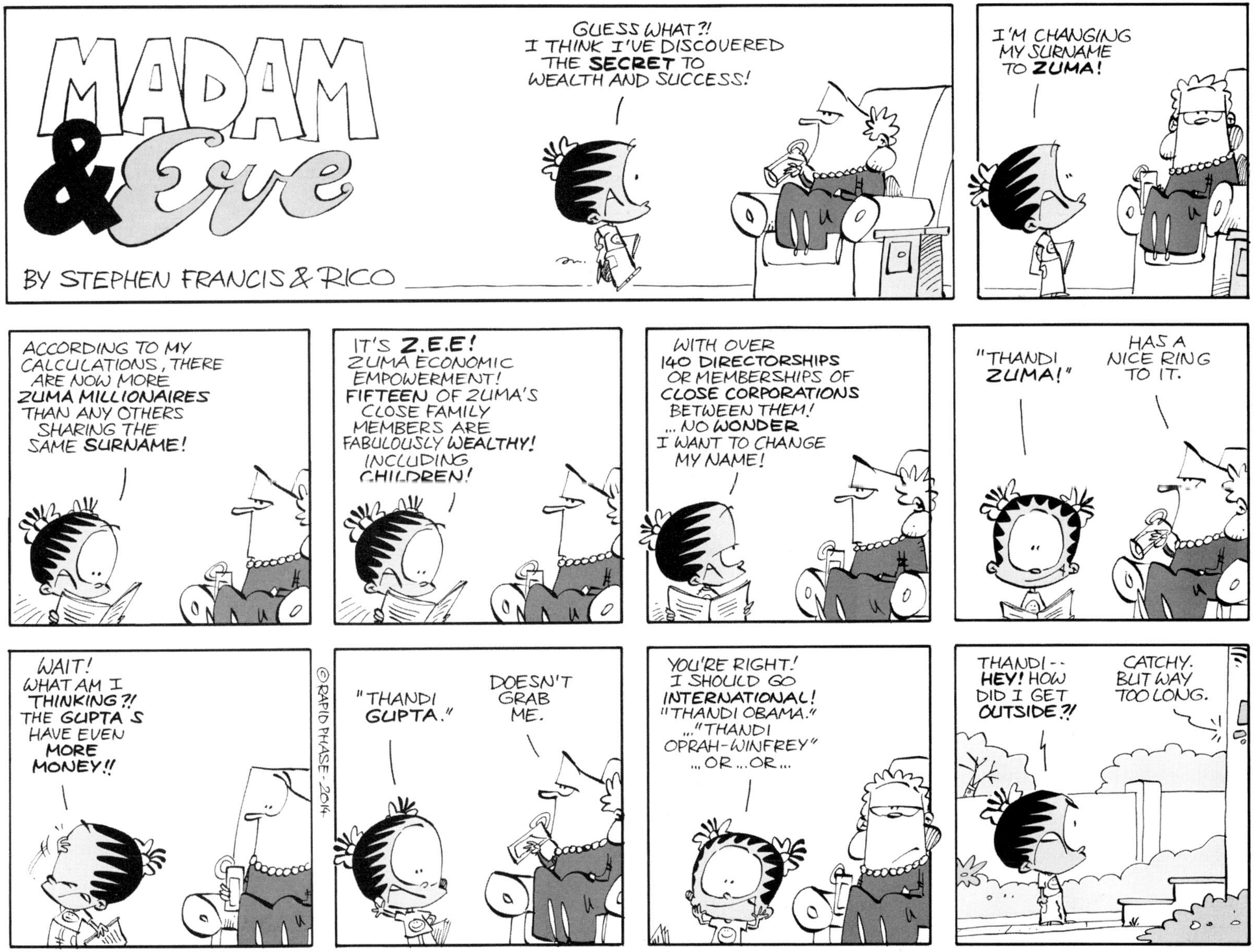
MADAM & Eve
BY STEPHEN FRANCIS & RICO
GUESS WHAT?! I THINK I'VE DISCOVERED THE SECRET TO WEALTH AND SUCCESS!
I'M CHANGING MY SURNAME TO ZUMA!
ACCORDING TO MY CALCULATIONS, THERE ARE NOW MORE ZUMA MILLIONAIRES THAN ANY OTHERS SHARING THE SAME SURNAME!
IT'S Z.E.E! ZUMA ECONOMIC EMPOWERMENT! FIFTEEN OF ZUMA'S CLOSE FAMILY MEMBERS ARE FABULOUSLY WEALTHY! INCLUDING CHILDREN!
WITH OVER 140 DIRECTORSHIPS OR MEMBERSHIPS OF CLOSE CORPORATIONS BETWEEN THEM! ...NO WONDER I WANT TO CHANGE MY NAME!
"THANDI ZUMA!"
HAS A NICE RING TO IT.
WAIT! WHAT AM I THINKING?! THE GUPTA'S HAVE EVEN MORE MONEY!!
© RAPID PHASE - 2014
"THANDI GUPTA."
DOESN'T GRAB ME.
YOU'RE RIGHT! I SHOULD GO INTERNATIONAL! "THANDI OBAMA." ..."THANDI OPRAH-WINFREY" ...OR...OR...
THANDI-- HEY! HOW DID I GET OUTSIDE?!
CATCHY. BUT WAY TOO LONG.

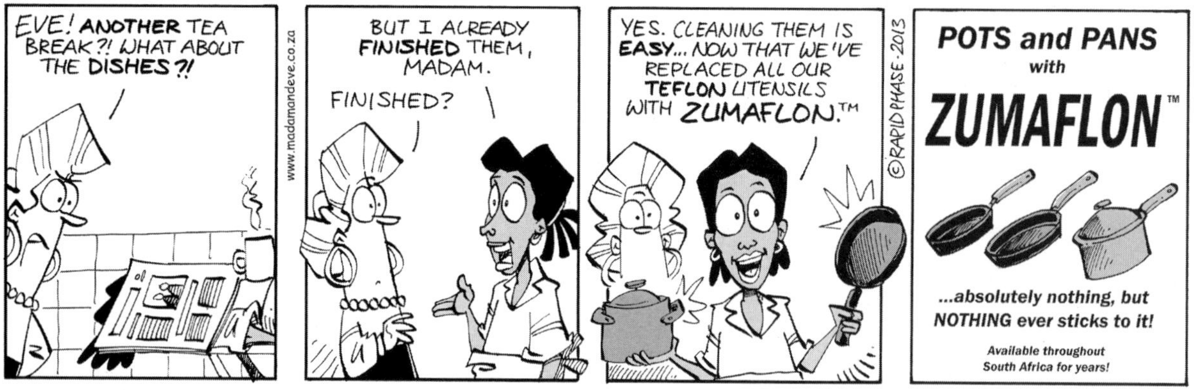
EVE! ANOTHER TEA BREAK?! WHAT ABOUT THE DISHES?!
www.madamandeve.co.za
BUT I ALREADY FINISHED THEM, MADAM.
FINISHED?
YES. CLEANING THEM IS EASY... NOW THAT WE'VE REPLACED ALL OUR TEFLON UTENSILS WITH ZUMAFLON.™
©RAPID PHASE · 2013
POTS and PANS with
ZUMAFLON™
...absolutely nothing, but NOTHING ever sticks to it!
Available throughout South Africa for years!

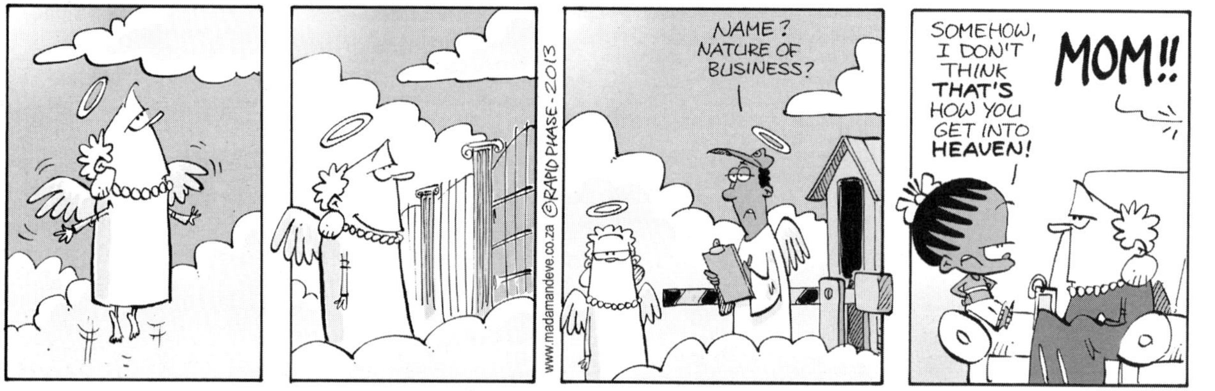
www.madamandeve.co.za ©RAPID PHASE · 2013
NAME? NATURE OF BUSINESS?
SOMEHOW, I DON'T THINK THAT'S HOW YOU GET INTO HEAVEN!
MOM!!

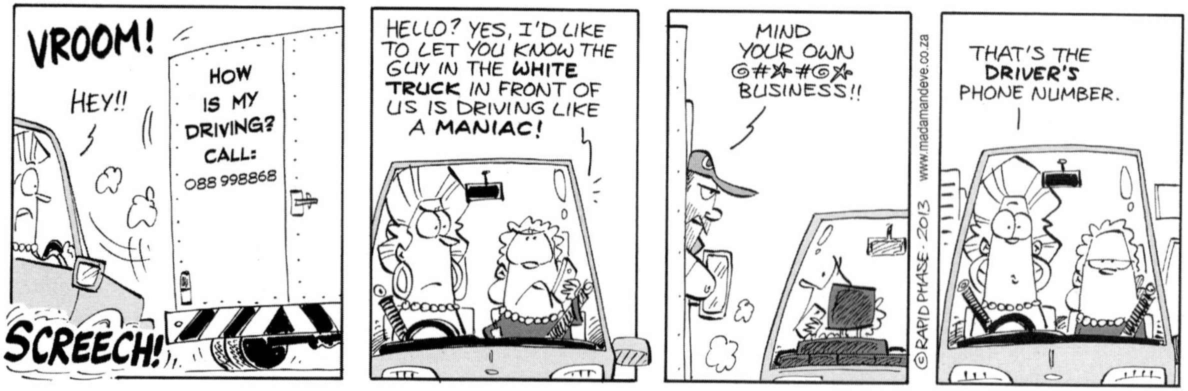
VROOM!
HEY!!
HOW IS MY DRIVING? CALL:
088 998868
SCREECH!
HELLO? YES, I'D LIKE TO LET YOU KNOW THE GUY IN THE WHITE TRUCK IN FRONT OF US IS DRIVING LIKE A MANIAC!
MIND YOUR OWN @#*#@* BUSINESS!!
©RAPID PHASE · 2013 www.madamandeve.co.za
THAT'S THE DRIVER'S PHONE NUMBER.

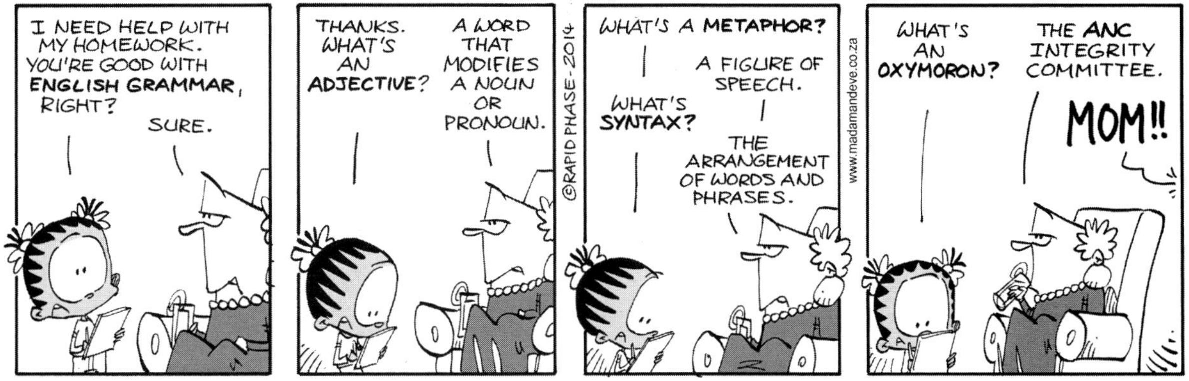
I NEED HELP WITH MY HOMEWORK. YOU'RE GOOD WITH ENGLISH GRAMMAR, RIGHT?
SURE.
THANKS. WHAT'S AN ADJECTIVE?
A WORD THAT MODIFIES A NOUN OR PRONOUN.
©RAPID PHASE-2014
WHAT'S A METAPHOR?
A FIGURE OF SPEECH.
WHAT'S SYNTAX?
THE ARRANGEMENT OF WORDS AND PHRASES.
www.madamandeve.co.za
WHAT'S AN OXYMORON?
THE ANC INTEGRITY COMMITTEE.
MOM!!

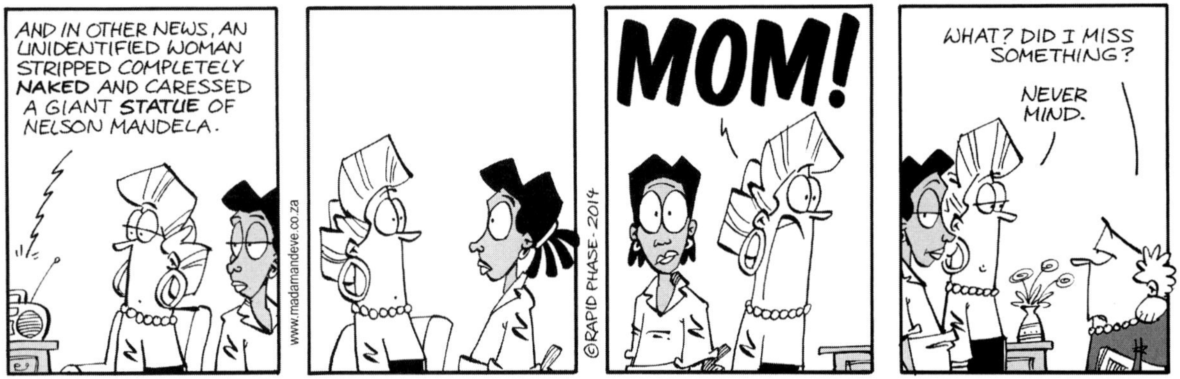
AND IN OTHER NEWS, AN UNIDENTIFIED WOMAN STRIPPED COMPLETELY NAKED AND CARESSED A GIANT STATUE OF NELSON MANDELA.
www.madamandeve.co.za
©RAPID PHASE-2014
MOM!
WHAT? DID I MISS SOMETHING?
NEVER MIND.

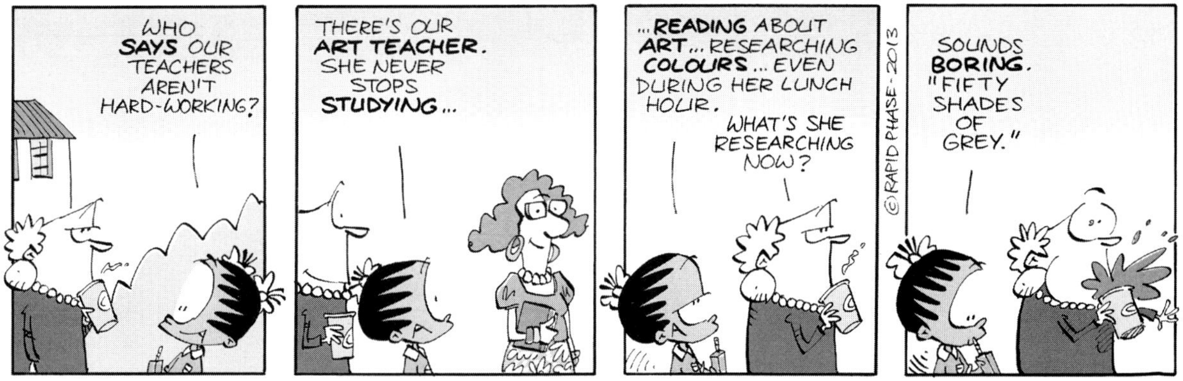
WHO SAYS OUR TEACHERS AREN'T HARD-WORKING?
THERE'S OUR ART TEACHER. SHE NEVER STOPS STUDYING...
...READING ABOUT ART... RESEARCHING COLOURS... EVEN DURING HER LUNCH HOUR.
WHAT'S SHE RESEARCHING NOW?
©RAPID PHASE-2013
SOUNDS BORING. "FIFTY SHADES OF GREY."

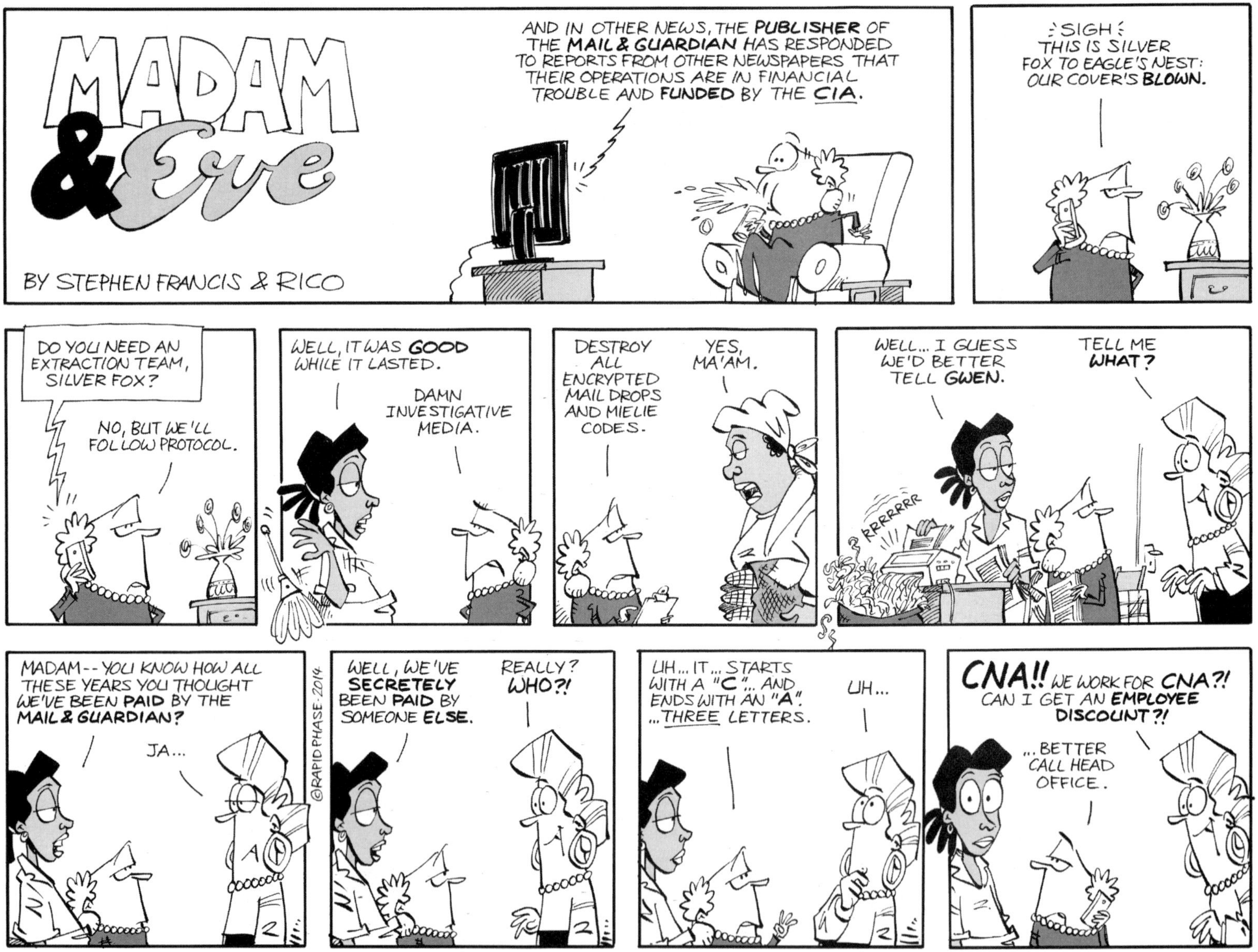
MADAM & Eve
BY STEPHEN FRANCIS & RICO
AND IN OTHER NEWS, THE PUBLISHER OF THE MAIL & GUARDIAN HAS RESPONDED TO REPORTS FROM OTHER NEWSPAPERS THAT THEIR OPERATIONS ARE IN FINANCIAL TROUBLE AND FUNDED BY THE CIA.
SIGH THIS IS SILVER FOX TO EAGLE'S NEST: OUR COVER'S BLOWN.
DO YOU NEED AN EXTRACTION TEAM, SILVER FOX?
NO, BUT WE'LL FOLLOW PROTOCOL.
WELL, IT WAS GOOD WHILE IT LASTED.
DAMN INVESTIGATIVE MEDIA.
DESTROY ALL ENCRYPTED MAIL DROPS AND MIELIE CODES.
YES, MA'AM.
WELL... I GUESS WE'D BETTER TELL GWEN.
TELL ME WHAT?
RRRRRRR
MADAM -- YOU KNOW HOW ALL THESE YEARS YOU THOUGHT WE'VE BEEN PAID BY THE MAIL & GUARDIAN?
JA...
©RAPID PHASE · 2014
WELL, WE'VE SECRETELY BEEN PAID BY SOMEONE ELSE.
REALLY? WHO?!
UH... IT... STARTS WITH A "C"... AND ENDS WITH AN "A". ...THREE LETTERS.
UH...
CNA!! WE WORK FOR CNA?! CAN I GET AN EMPLOYEE DISCOUNT?!
...BETTER CALL HEAD OFFICE.

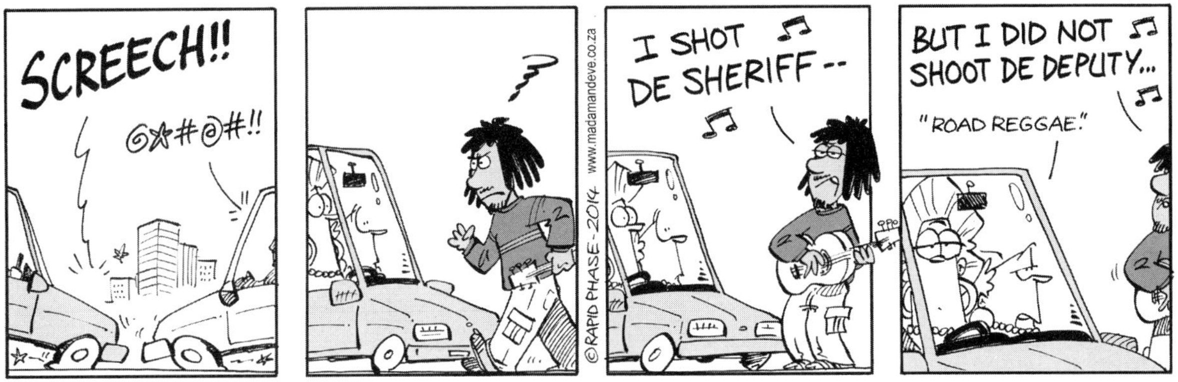
SCREECH!!
@*#@#!!
?
©RAPID PHASE·2014 www.madamandeve.co.za
I SHOT DE SHERIFF --
BUT I DID NOT SHOOT DE DEPUTY...
"ROAD REGGAE."

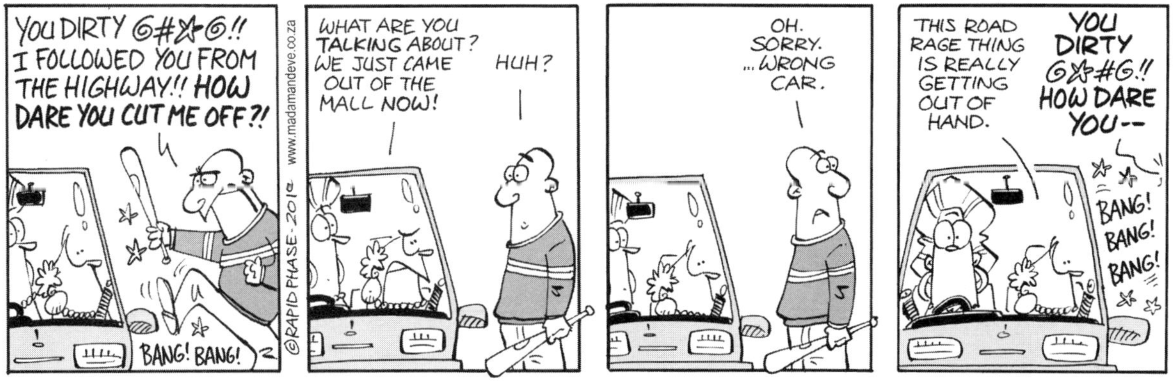
YOU DIRTY @#*@!! I FOLLOWED YOU FROM THE HIGHWAY!! HOW DARE YOU CUT ME OFF?!
BANG! BANG!
©RAPID PHASE·2014 www.madamandeve.co.za
WHAT ARE YOU TALKING ABOUT? WE JUST CAME OUT OF THE MALL NOW!
HUH?
OH. SORRY. ...WRONG CAR.
THIS ROAD RAGE THING IS REALLY GETTING OUT OF HAND.
YOU DIRTY @*#@!! HOW DARE YOU--
BANG! BANG! BANG!

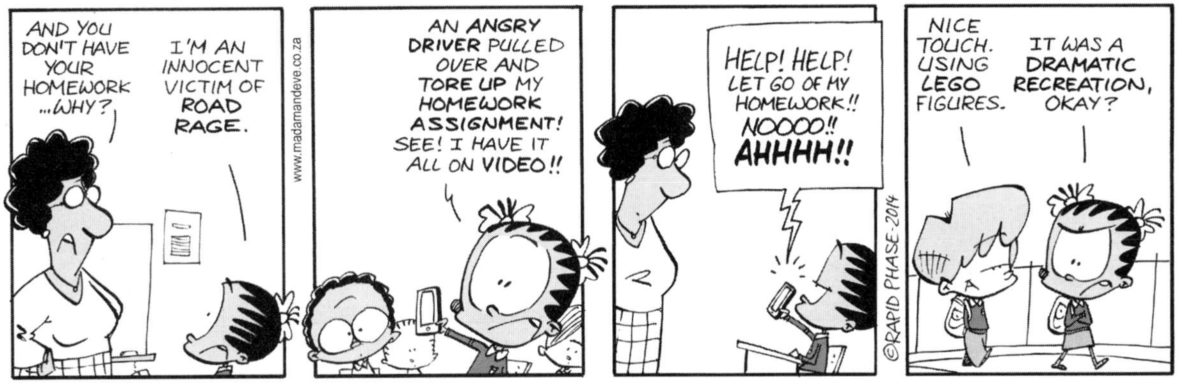
AND YOU DON'T HAVE YOUR HOMEWORK ...WHY?
I'M AN INNOCENT VICTIM OF ROAD RAGE.
www.madamandeve.co.za
AN ANGRY DRIVER PULLED OVER AND TORE UP MY HOMEWORK ASSIGNMENT! SEE! I HAVE IT ALL ON VIDEO!!
HELP! HELP! LET GO OF MY HOMEWORK!! NOOOO!! AHHHH!!
©RAPID PHASE·2014
NICE TOUCH. USING LEGO FIGURES.
IT WAS A DRAMATIC RECREATION, OKAY?

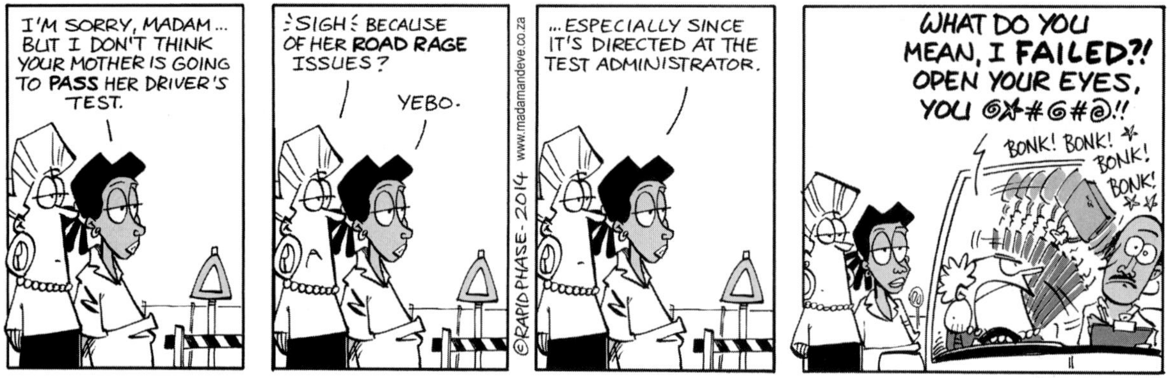
I'M SORRY, MADAM... BUT I DON'T THINK YOUR MOTHER IS GOING TO PASS HER DRIVER'S TEST.
:SIGH: BECAUSE OF HER ROAD RAGE ISSUES?
YEBO.
...ESPECIALLY SINCE IT'S DIRECTED AT THE TEST ADMINISTRATOR.
WHAT DO YOU MEAN, I FAILED?! OPEN YOUR EYES, YOU @✲#@#@!!
BONK! BONK! BONK! BONK!
©RAPID PHASE - 2014 www.madamandeve.co.za

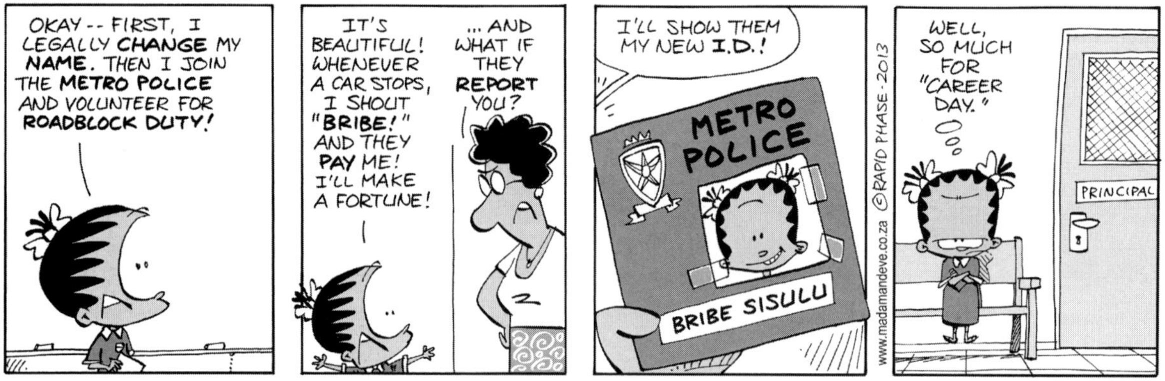
OKAY -- FIRST, I LEGALLY CHANGE MY NAME. THEN I JOIN THE METRO POLICE AND VOLUNTEER FOR ROADBLOCK DUTY!
IT'S BEAUTIFUL! WHENEVER A CAR STOPS, I SHOUT "BRIBE!" AND THEY PAY ME! I'LL MAKE A FORTUNE!
... AND WHAT IF THEY REPORT YOU?
I'LL SHOW THEM MY NEW I.D.!
METRO POLICE
BRIBE SISULU
WELL, SO MUCH FOR "CAREER DAY."
PRINCIPAL
©RAPID PHASE - 2013 www.madamandeve.co.za

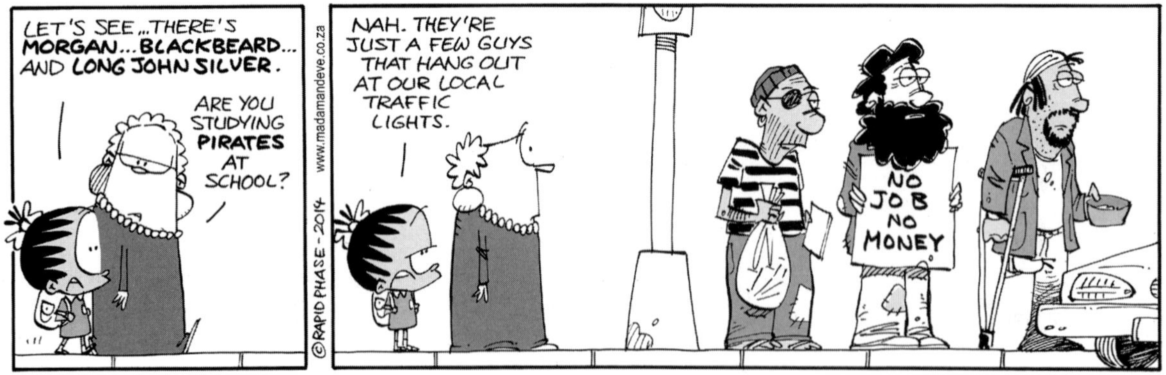
LET'S SEE... THERE'S MORGAN... BLACKBEARD... AND LONG JOHN SILVER.
ARE YOU STUDYING PIRATES AT SCHOOL?
NAH. THEY'RE JUST A FEW GUYS THAT HANG OUT AT OUR LOCAL TRAFFIC LIGHTS.
NO JOB NO MONEY
©RAPID PHASE - 2014 www.madamandeve.co.za

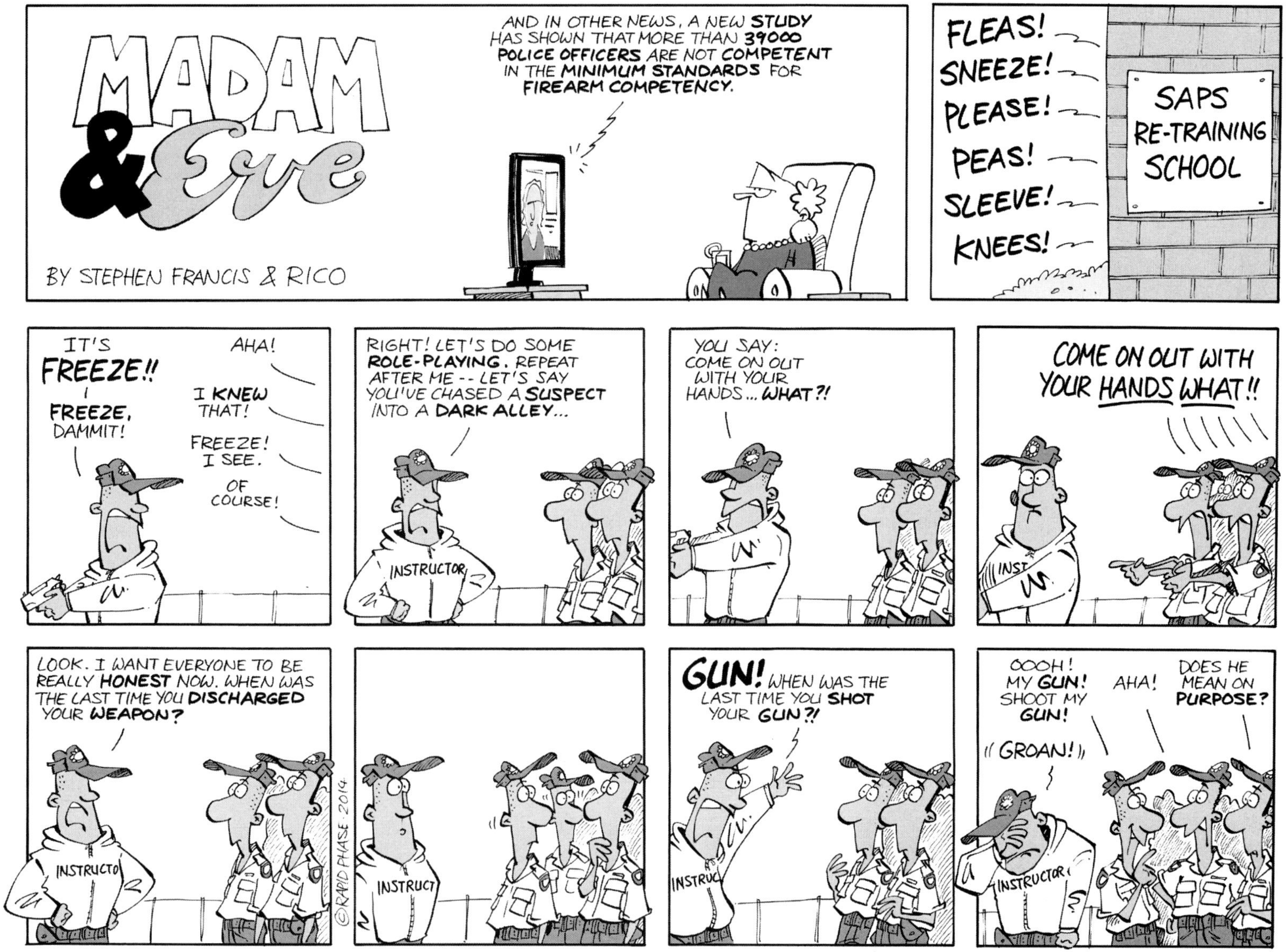
MADAM & Eve
BY STEPHEN FRANCIS & RICO
AND IN OTHER NEWS, A NEW STUDY HAS SHOWN THAT MORE THAN 39000 POLICE OFFICERS ARE NOT COMPETENT IN THE MINIMUM STANDARDS FOR FIREARM COMPETENCY.
FLEAS!
SNEEZE!
PLEASE!
PEAS!
SLEEVE!
KNEES!
SAPS RE-TRAINING SCHOOL
IT'S FREEZE!!
FREEZE, DAMMIT!
AHA!
I KNEW THAT!
FREEZE! I SEE.
OF COURSE!
RIGHT! LET'S DO SOME ROLE-PLAYING. REPEAT AFTER ME -- LET'S SAY YOU'VE CHASED A SUSPECT INTO A DARK ALLEY...
INSTRUCTOR
YOU SAY: COME ON OUT WITH YOUR HANDS... WHAT?!
COME ON OUT WITH YOUR HANDS WHAT!!
LOOK. I WANT EVERYONE TO BE REALLY HONEST NOW. WHEN WAS THE LAST TIME YOU DISCHARGED YOUR WEAPON?
©RAPID PHASE 2014
GUN! WHEN WAS THE LAST TIME YOU SHOT YOUR GUN?!
OOOH! MY GUN! SHOOT MY GUN!
AHA!
DOES HE MEAN ON PURPOSE?
((GROAN!))

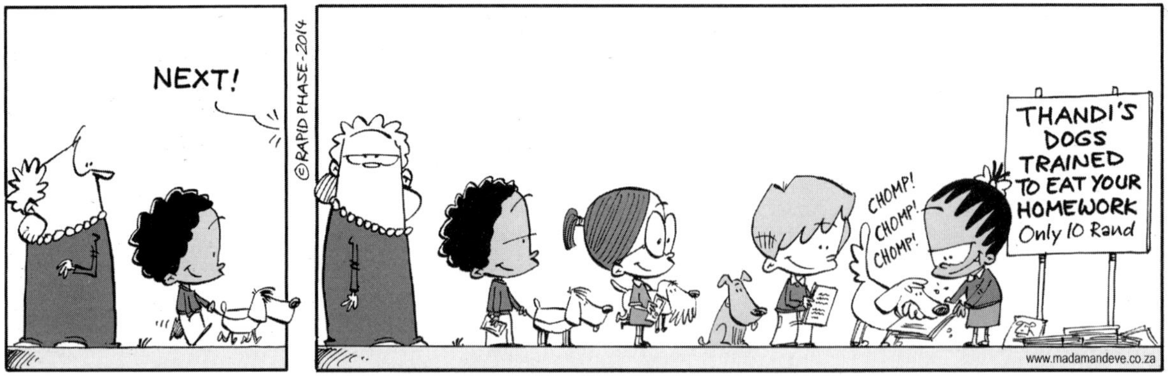
NEXT!
©RAPID PHASE-2014
THANDI'S DOGS TRAINED TO EAT YOUR HOMEWORK Only 10 Rand
CHOMP! CHOMP! CHOMP!
www.madamandeve.co.za

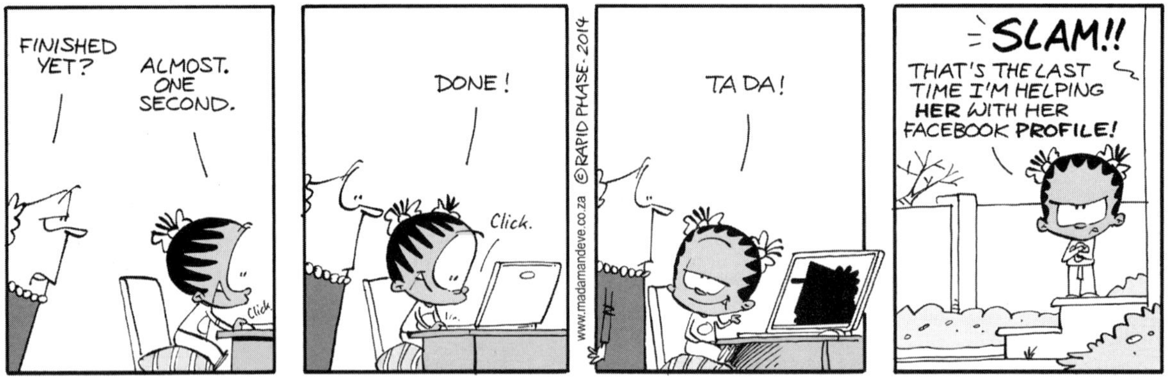
FINISHED YET?
ALMOST. ONE SECOND.
Click
DONE!
Click.
©RAPID PHASE-2014
www.madamandeve.co.za
TA DA!
SLAM!!
THAT'S THE LAST TIME I'M HELPING HER WITH HER FACEBOOK PROFILE!

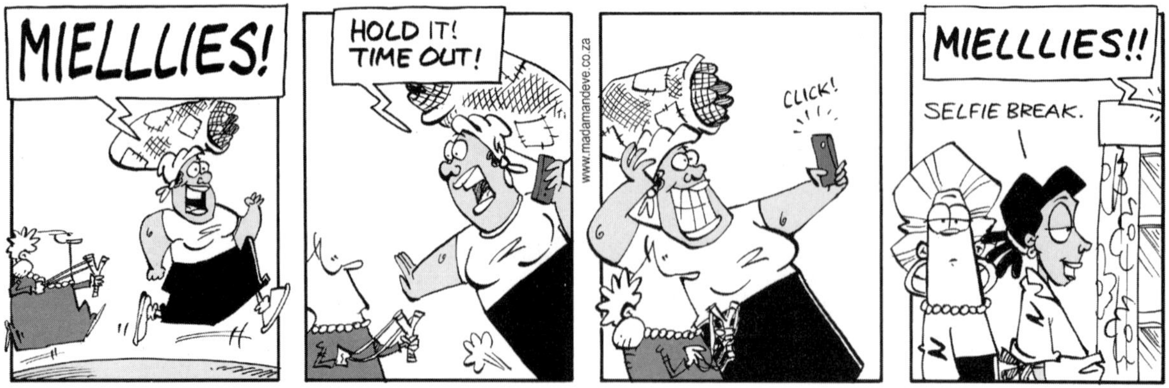
MIELLLIES!
HOLD IT! TIME OUT!
www.madamandeve.co.za
CLICK!
MIELLLIES!!
SELFIE BREAK.

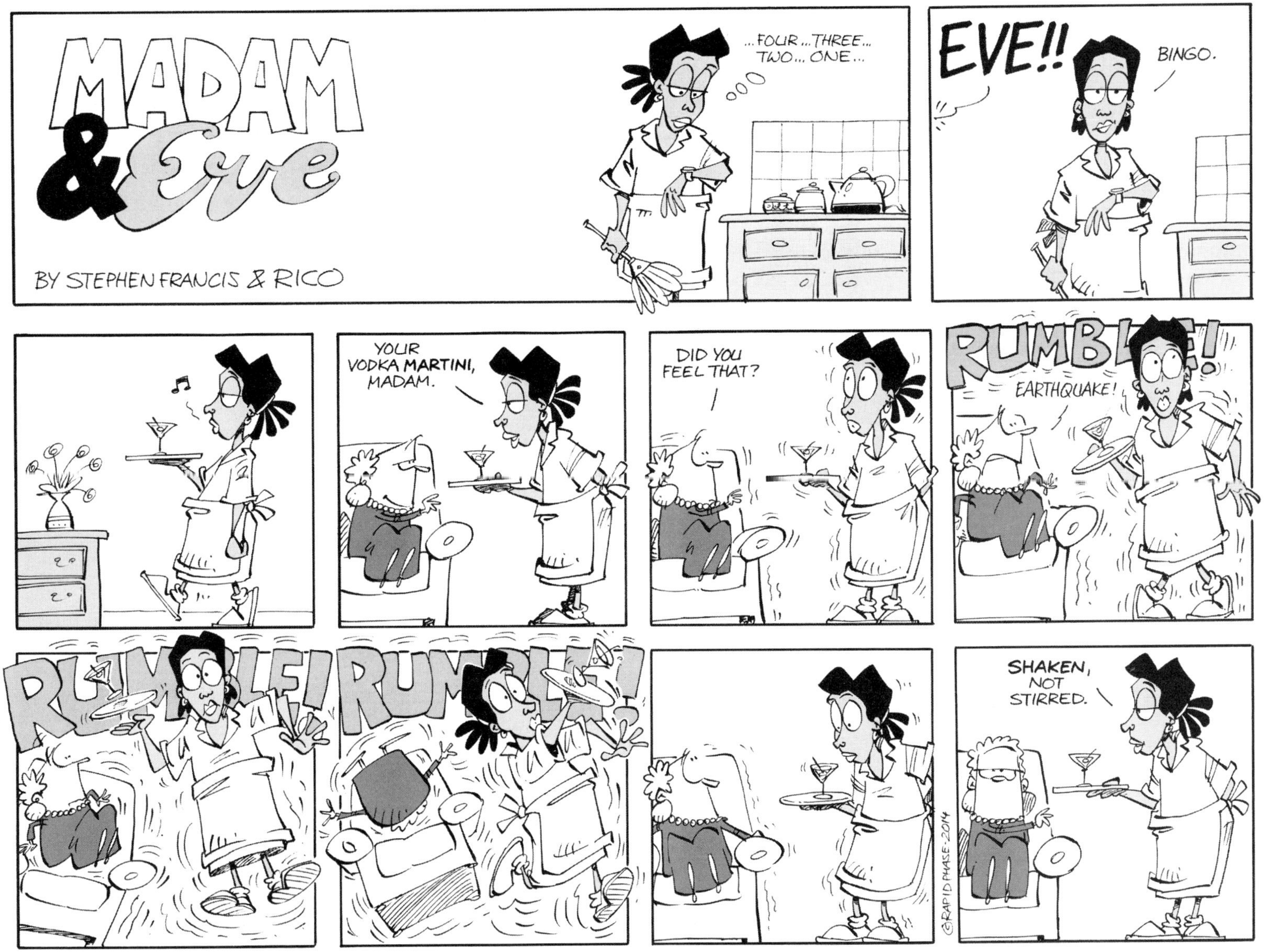
MADAM & Eve
BY STEPHEN FRANCIS & RICO
...FOUR...THREE...
TWO...ONE...
EVE!!
BINGO.
YOUR
VODKA **MARTINI**,
MADAM.
DID YOU
FEEL THAT?
RUMBLE!
EARTHQUAKE!
RUMBLE!
RUMBLE!
SHAKEN,
NOT
STIRRED.
©RAPID PHASE · 2014

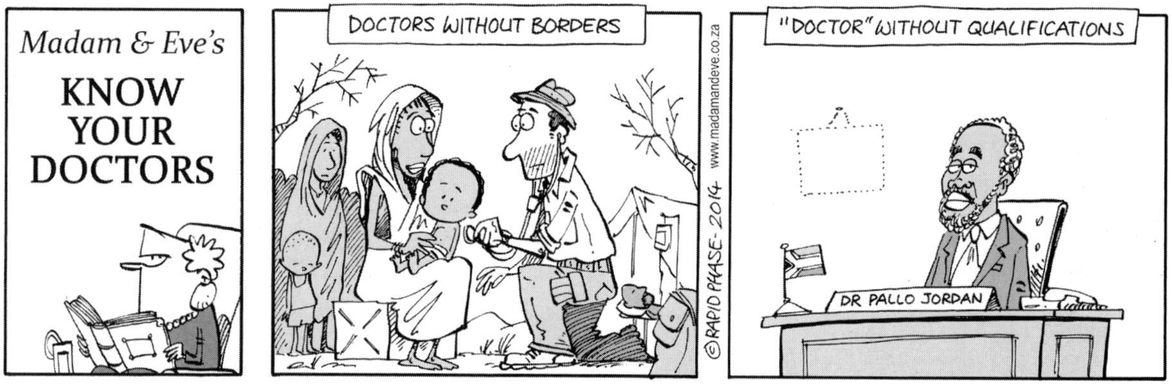
Madam & Eve's
KNOW YOUR DOCTORS
DOCTORS WITHOUT BORDERS
©RAPID PHASE-2014 www.madamandeve.co.za
"DOCTOR" WITHOUT QUALIFICATIONS
DR PALLO JORDAN

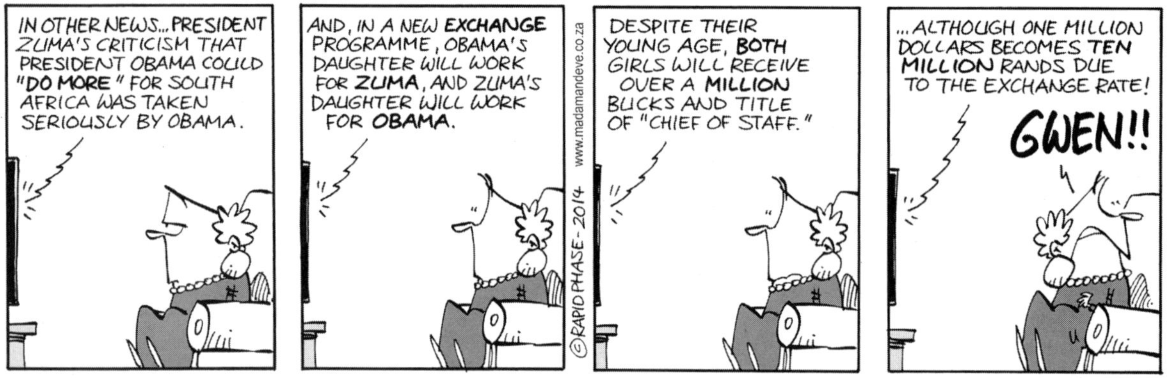
IN OTHER NEWS... PRESIDENT ZUMA'S CRITICISM THAT PRESIDENT OBAMA COULD "DO MORE" FOR SOUTH AFRICA WAS TAKEN SERIOUSLY BY OBAMA.
AND, IN A NEW EXCHANGE PROGRAMME, OBAMA'S DAUGHTER WILL WORK FOR ZUMA, AND ZUMA'S DAUGHTER WILL WORK FOR OBAMA.
©RAPID PHASE-2014 www.madamandeve.co.za
DESPITE THEIR YOUNG AGE, BOTH GIRLS WILL RECEIVE OVER A MILLION BUCKS AND TITLE OF "CHIEF OF STAFF."
...ALTHOUGH ONE MILLION DOLLARS BECOMES TEN MILLION RANDS DUE TO THE EXCHANGE RATE!
GWEN!!

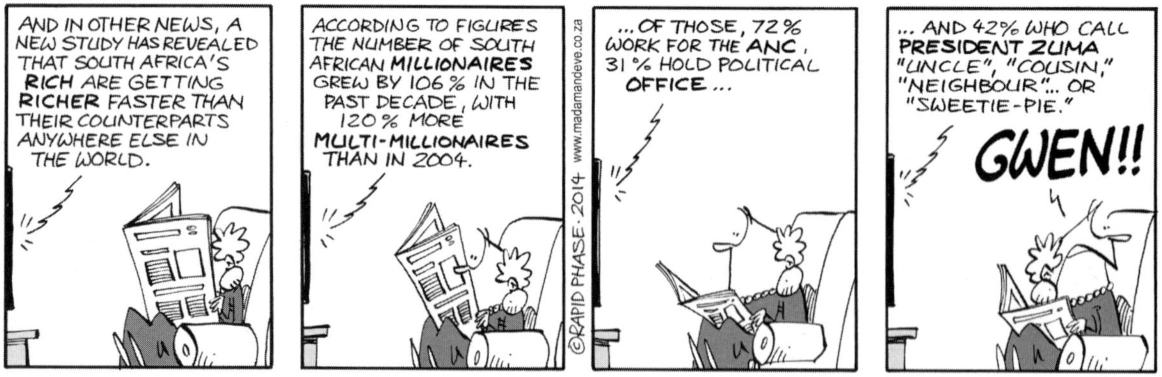
AND IN OTHER NEWS, A NEW STUDY HAS REVEALED THAT SOUTH AFRICA'S RICH ARE GETTING RICHER FASTER THAN THEIR COUNTERPARTS ANYWHERE ELSE IN THE WORLD.
ACCORDING TO FIGURES THE NUMBER OF SOUTH AFRICAN MILLIONAIRES GREW BY 106% IN THE PAST DECADE, WITH 120% MORE MULTI-MILLIONAIRES THAN IN 2004.
©RAPID PHASE-2014 www.madamandeve.co.za
...OF THOSE, 72% WORK FOR THE ANC, 31% HOLD POLITICAL OFFICE...
...AND 42% WHO CALL PRESIDENT ZUMA "UNCLE", "COUSIN," "NEIGHBOUR"... OR "SWEETIE-PIE."
GWEN!!

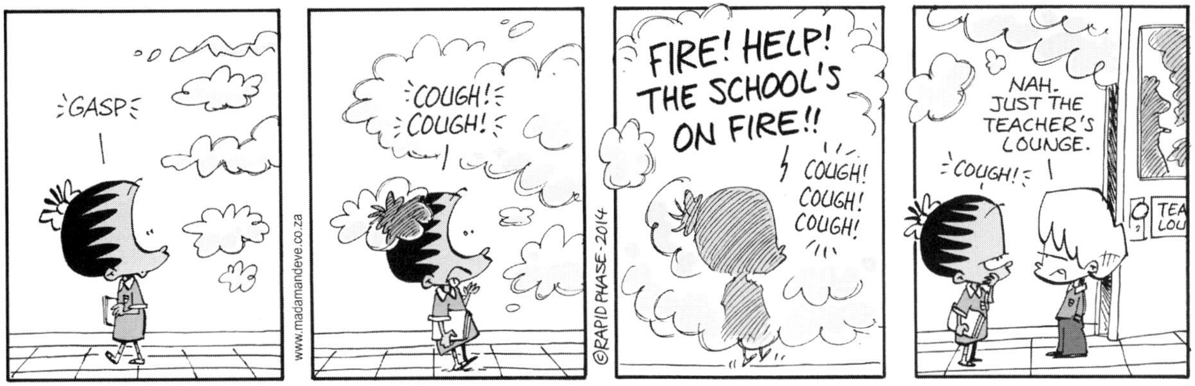
GASP
COUGH! COUGH!
www.madamandeve.co.za
FIRE! HELP! THE SCHOOL'S ON FIRE!!
COUGH! COUGH! COUGH!
©RAPID PHASE-2014
COUGH!
NAH. JUST THE TEACHER'S LOUNGE.

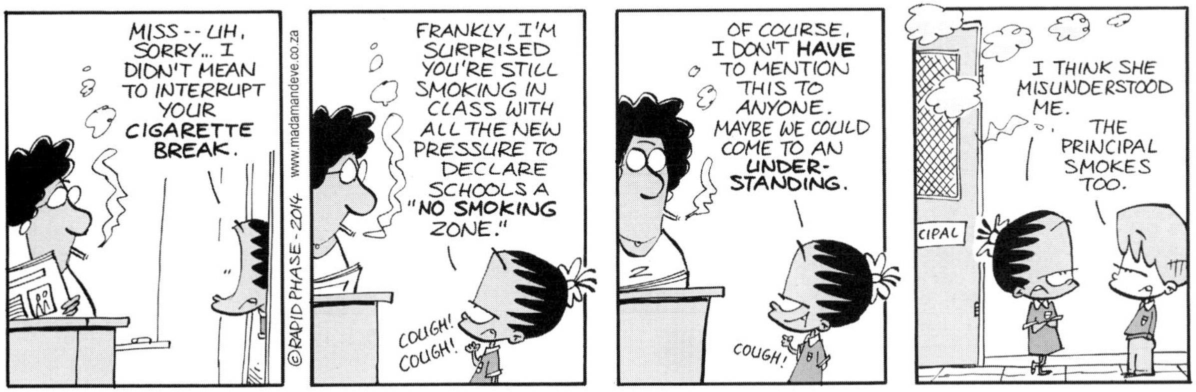
MISS -- UH, SORRY... I DIDN'T MEAN TO INTERRUPT YOUR **CIGARETTE BREAK**.
www.madamandeve.co.za
©RAPID PHASE - 2014
FRANKLY, I'M SURPRISED YOU'RE STILL SMOKING IN CLASS WITH ALL THE NEW PRESSURE TO DECLARE SCHOOLS A "**NO SMOKING ZONE**."
COUGH! COUGH!
OF COURSE, I DON'T **HAVE** TO MENTION THIS TO ANYONE. MAYBE WE COULD COME TO AN **UNDER-STANDING**.
COUGH!
I THINK SHE MISUNDERSTOOD ME.
THE PRINCIPAL SMOKES TOO.

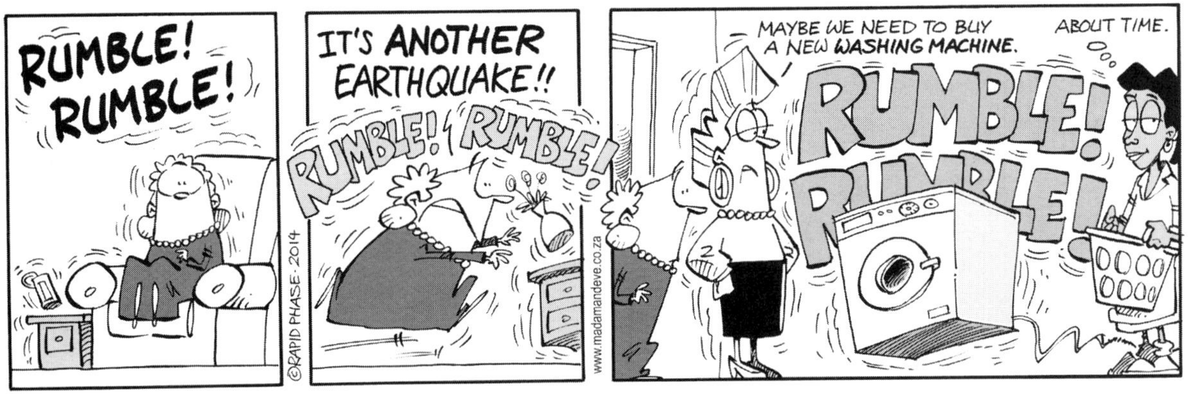
RUMBLE! RUMBLE!
IT'S **ANOTHER** EARTHQUAKE!!
RUMBLE! RUMBLE!
©RAPID PHASE-2014
www.madamandeve.co.za
MAYBE WE NEED TO BUY A NEW **WASHING MACHINE**.
ABOUT TIME.
RUMBLE! RUMBLE!

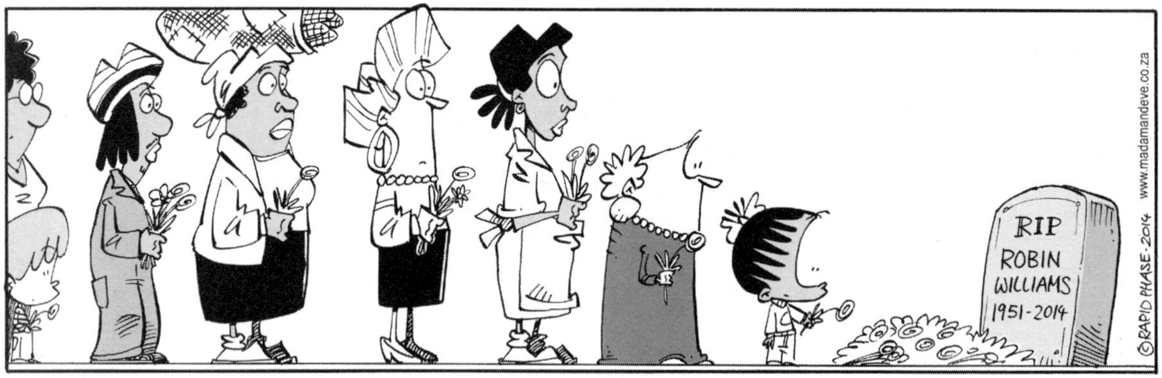
RIP
ROBIN WILLIAMS
1951-2014
© RAPID PHASE - 2014
www.madamandeve.co.za

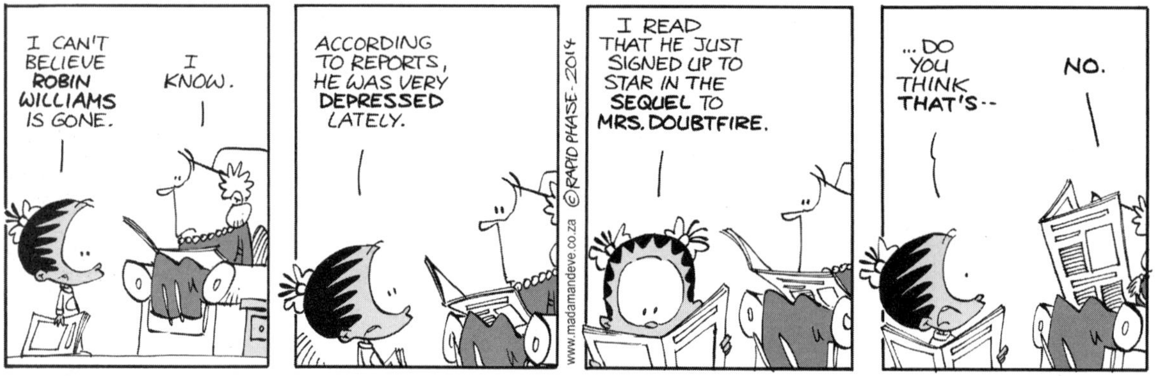
I CAN'T BELIEVE **ROBIN WILLIAMS** IS GONE.
I KNOW.
ACCORDING TO REPORTS, HE WAS VERY **DEPRESSED** LATELY.
© RAPID PHASE - 2014
www.madamandeve.co.za
I READ THAT HE JUST SIGNED UP TO STAR IN THE **SEQUEL** TO **MRS. DOUBTFIRE.**
...DO YOU THINK **THAT'S**--
NO.

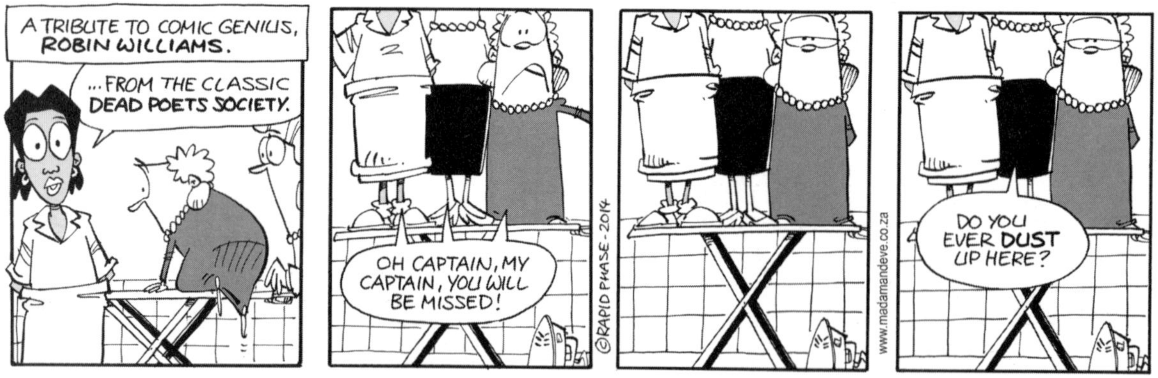
A TRIBUTE TO COMIC GENIUS, **ROBIN WILLIAMS.**
...FROM THE CLASSIC **DEAD POETS SOCIETY.**
OH CAPTAIN, MY CAPTAIN, YOU WILL BE MISSED!
© RAPID PHASE - 2014
www.madamandeve.co.za
DO YOU EVER **DUST** UP HERE?

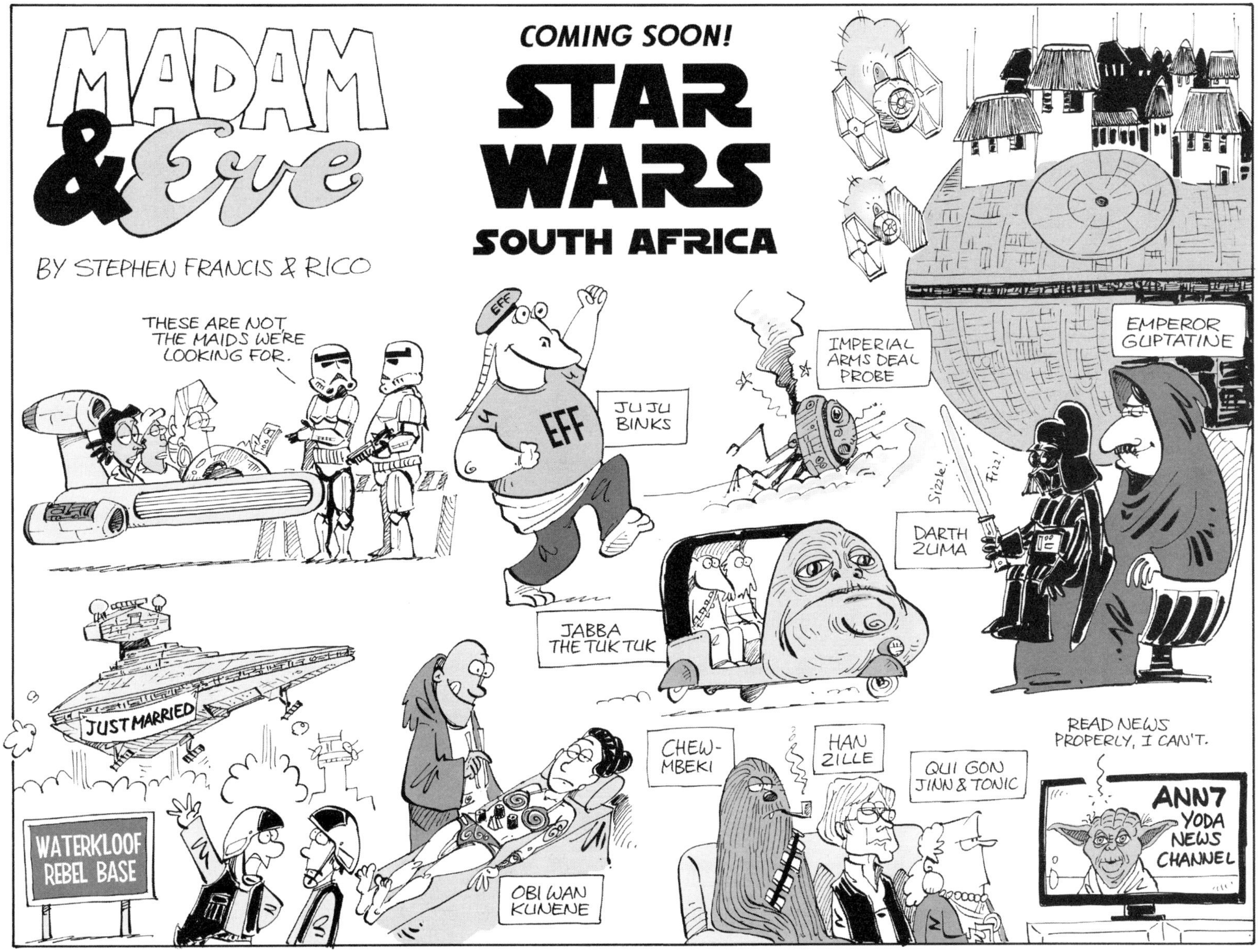

MADAM & Eve
BY STEPHEN FRANCIS & RICO
COMING SOON!
STAR WARS
SOUTH AFRICA
THESE ARE NOT THE MAIDS WE'RE LOOKING FOR.
EFF
EFF
JU JU BINKS
IMPERIAL ARMS DEAL PROBE
EMPEROR GUPTATINE
Sizzle!
Frizz!
DARTH ZUMA
JABBA THE TUK TUK
JUST MARRIED
WATERKLOOF REBEL BASE
OBI WAN KUNENE
CHEW-MBEKI
HAN ZILLE
QUI GON JINN & TONIC
READ NEWS PROPERLY, I CAN'T.
ANN7
YODA NEWS CHANNEL

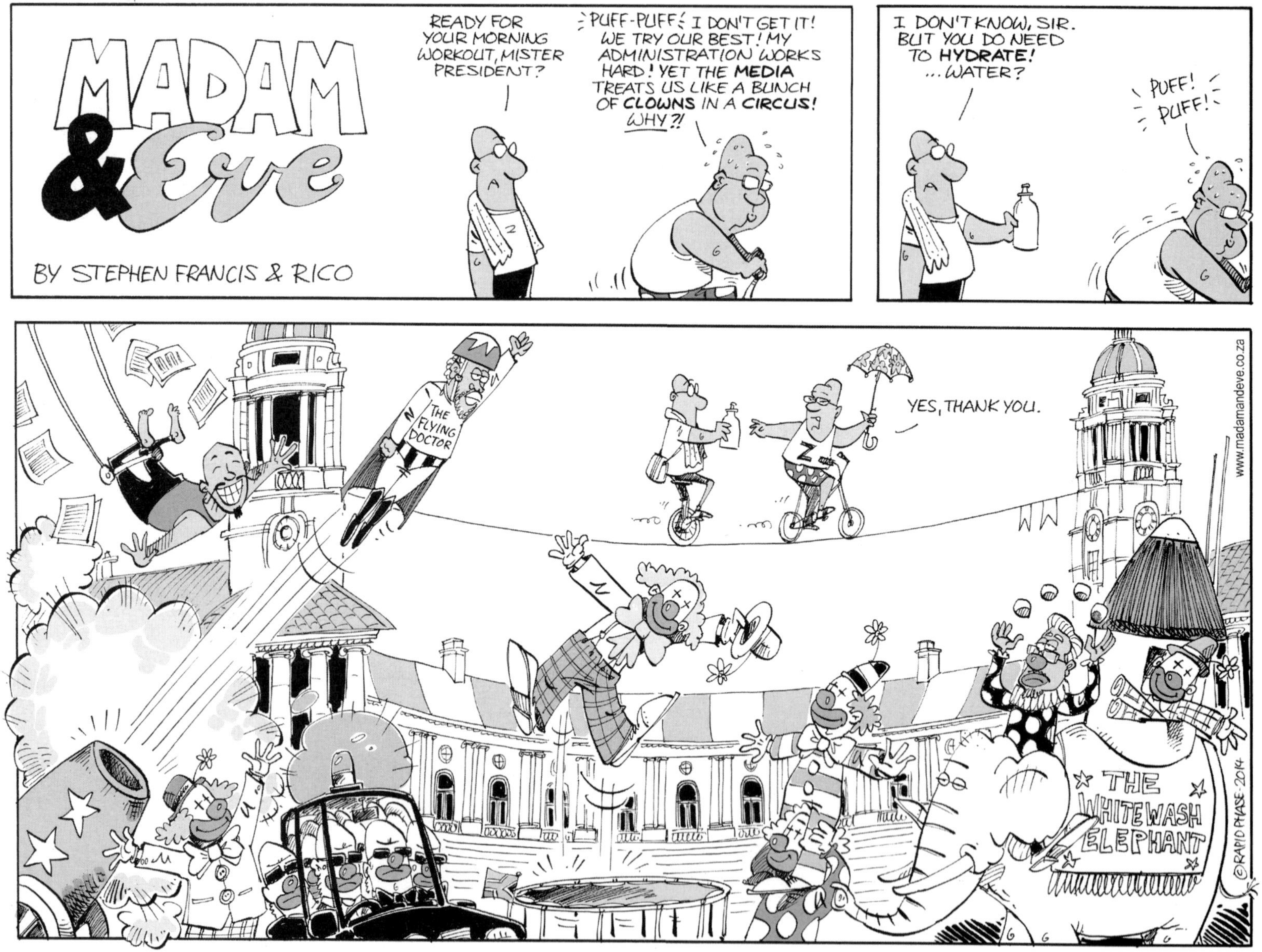
MADAM & Eve
BY STEPHEN FRANCIS & RICO
READY FOR YOUR MORNING WORKOUT, MISTER PRESIDENT?
PUFF-PUFF! I DON'T GET IT! WE TRY OUR BEST! MY ADMINISTRATION WORKS HARD! YET THE MEDIA TREATS US LIKE A BUNCH OF CLOWNS IN A CIRCUS! WHY?!
I DON'T KNOW, SIR. BUT YOU DO NEED TO HYDRATE! ...WATER?
PUFF! PUFF!
THE FLYING DOCTOR
YES, THANK YOU.
THE WHITEWASH ELEPHANT
www.madamandeve.co.za
© RAPID PHASE · 2014